Penguin Education

Law and Society

General Editors: O. Kahn-Freund and K. W. Wedderburn

Race and Law

Anthony Lester and Geoffrey Bindman

Race and Law

Anthony Lester and Geoffrey Bindman

Penguin Books

For Katya and Lynn

Penguin Books Ltd, Harmondsworth,
Middlesex, England
Penguin Books Australia Ltd,
Ringwood, Victoria, Australia

First published 1972
Copyright © Anthony Lester and Geoffrey Bindman, 1972

Made and printed in Great Britain by
Richard Clay (The Chaucer Press) Ltd, Bungay, Suffolk
Set in Monotype Times

Contents

Editorial Foreword

This book by Anthony Lester and Geoffrey Bindman is the most systematic and comprehensive work on the law of race relations so far to have been published in this country. It is therefore a most vital contribution to the evolving discussion on the meaning of equality in our society. Nothing in our present world equals in social and in political as well as in human significance the problem of the relation between the races, and that part of it which Lester and Bindman are here analysing is the touchstone of 'equality before the law' in British society.

It is, however, as the authors emphasize in their Introduction, only one aspect of a much larger problem, and the social as well as the psychological implications of the Race Relations Acts remain incomprehensible unless one takes into account what is happening at the frontier. The reader will be constantly assailed by the question (of which the authors show themselves fully aware): what good can all this produce if the nation proclaims by its immigration legislation that equality does not only begin but also ends at home? However, as the authors rightly say, a second treatise would have been needed to go into the problems of immigration and aliens law. We can only hope that one day we may be able to publish on the 'external' side of race relations a work as comprehensive, penetrating and perceptive as this book on race relations inside Britain.

This is the second work in our series to deal with aspects of race relations. The perspective of the first, Hepple's detailed treatment of employment, *Race, Jobs and the Law in Britain*, differs from that of Lester and Bindman. Hepple sees the principles of equality of access to jobs, equality of terms of employment, and equality of access to union membership far more as part of a system of industrial relations. It is fascinating to see how the difference in focus also produces shades of difference in attitudes, for example, towards the pros and cons of the role assigned by the Act of 1968 to the two sides of industry and their voluntary committees in the enforcement of the principles of the statute.

One of the benefits of the present volume is a long historical perspective, and no one who reads Appendix One is likely to forget its 'Cautionary Tale', which the authors could with great advantage to themselves and to the public have used as a film script. Like so much else in this, as well as Hepple's book, it teaches us not to be too sanguine about the civilizing influence of the law. Racial prejudice sits deep. In our time we can at least claim that those responsible for the statute of 1968 made a start by setting aside political expediency in the cause of justice.

One way of helping that cause is to make it understood by explaining the meaning of equality fully, lucidly and seriously. That is the measure of the authors' achievement beyond their explanation of the social implications of the law, vital though that role also is. We are convinced that their work will meet with a wide response.

O.K.-F.
K.W.W.

Preface

The contents and structure of this book are described in the introduction. We have tried to state the legal position as accurately as possible as it was on 1 October 1971.

In writing the book we have received assistance from a large number of sources. The editors of Penguin Education's Law and Society series, Otto Kahn-Freund and Bill Wedderburn, have shown us the greatest possible kindness. Professor Kahn-Freund made many detailed and important suggestions which we have followed. We are also especially thankful to Charles Clark of Penguin Education for his constant interest and help throughout the long gestation period.

The Institute of Race Relations were good enough to make us a research grant with which we were able to obtain the invaluable services of Laurence Sorkin as research assistant. We also wish to acknowledge the assistance given to us by the staff of the Institute of Advanced Legal Studies and of the India Office Library, and to thank Mrs Mary Remedios for her tireless secretarial help.

Without the encouragement and advice of a large number of friends and colleagues, and the patient tolerance of our families, this book could not have been written. We wish to express our thanks for their advice upon particular sections of the book to the following:

Charles Black,   Alan Haworth,
Haywood Burns,   Harry Lester,
Tom Connelly,   John Lyttle,
Nicholas Deakin,   Julia McNeal,
Vasudha Dhagamwar,   Dipak Nandy,
Norman Dorsen,   Laurence Sorkin,
William B. Gould,   Roger Warren Evans.

Finally, we are indebted to the Race Relations Board, both members and staff, for their cooperation. Our association with them has helped us to see the law from the point of view of those who labour to make it effective. However, we alone are responsible for our opinions, criticisms, recommendations and mistakes.

Introduction

This book deals with a complicated and controversial subject: the use of law to combat racial discrimination and prejudice, or, expressing the same idea positively, the use of law to promote equality of opportunity and treatment regardless of race. It is not a legal text-book in the standard sense of a neutrally descriptive commentary about the law as it stands. Much of what follows will be critical of the existing law and will recommend extensive reforms. It is also unlike a standard legal textbook because it is written as much for the general reader and the social scientist as for the law student or the legal practitioner. The practising lawyer must therefore cite its more speculative passages with caution. And it is hoped that it will provide a much-needed practical handbook for the growing number of public officials, voluntary bodies and private citizens who sometimes refer to themselves ironically as the race relations industry.

Before describing the architecture of the book, it is necessary to locate it within its general landscape. We shall attempt, in discussing the Race Relations Acts, to place them within their wider political, economic and social context, but we remain conscious of some inevitable loss of perspective in scrutinizing the legislation from our particular vantage point.

The most serious loss is that the book will not attempt to relate race relations to immigration and nationality law. To do so would require another volume of at least equivalent length. The omission is unfortunate because it is impossible to understand race relations in Britain adequately without taking account of the history and the legal status of racial and national minorities in this country.

For example, the Jewish refugees who came to Britain in the nineteenth century to escape persecution in Eastern Europe were aliens as well as a distinct ethnic and religious group. The roots of the public opposition to their immigration and settlement here went deeper than simple racial prejudice, drawing strength from the xenophobia and insularity which have been part of our island story for centuries. In the words of one historian

The English view never regarded the mother country as a land of open spaces and unlimited opportunity, but rather as a place of restricted possibilities and fairly fixed social position, with emigration the alternative for the restless and ambitious. . . . The some 120,000 Jewish immigrants who settled in England [between 1870 and 1914] provoked such public attention that they became a leading English political question (Gartner, 1960, p. 274).

The self-conscious homogeneity and insularity of Victorian society, brilliantly portrayed in George Eliot's *Daniel Deronda*, overshadowed its professed ideals of tolerance and fair play. Indeed the homogeneity of English society was at least as much an idealization as a reality. There was an 'English dilemma' to correspond to the American Dilemma – a conflict between the publicly embraced notions of toleration and fair play and the segregated, almost segmental, character of English society. And the insularity of English society was not an isolated feature of English history, but fundamentally linked with the social segregation which characterized English life. As another historian puts it

Empire widened the real gulf between the classes at home, but also provided them with a spurious fraternity. . . . [But] as time went on . . . official nationalism fostered the myth of all Britons, or all Germans, being brothers; class superiority was then transformed into patriotic, or still better into racial superiority, that all could share in. The more democratic Europe became or pretended to become at home the more supercilious it was abroad (Kiernan, 1969, pp. 316–17).

Not surprisingly, the arrival of a relatively small number of Jewish immigrants provoked a profoundly hostile response and led to a blatantly antisemitic campaign to end any further immigration. The campaign largely succeeded with the passage of the Aliens Act, in 1905. Its echoes were heard in the 1930s when the government of the day was driven to appease antisemitism by denying asylum to Jewish refugees from Nazi Germany (although it should be added that the British record in this respect was less discreditable than that of the United States) (Morse, 1968).

The opposition to Jewish immigrants – European in physical appearance and culture – might have led us to expect that the more recent and substantial immigration from Asia and the Caribbean of people with an unfamiliar culture and a different skin colour would meet a strong tide of racial feeling. Still more predictable is this reaction when one recalls the salient chapters of British imperial history: the vast and lucrative trade in African slaves in the seventeenth and eighteenth centuries and the encouragement of a brutal system of servitude in the colonies; the replacement of that system by Asian indentured labour in the nineteenth century; and the creation of rigidly segregated societies, dominated by white settler minorities, in British Africa in this century. In several senses, post-war immigration from the new Commonwealth has transplanted to the old mother country prejudices and patterns of behaviour which could conveniently be ignored or righteously condemned so long as they flourished only within an Empire beyond our shores.

The growth of racial feeling in Britain was both ignored and condemned during the first decade of immigration from the Commonwealth. In the next decade, the existence of a problem was reluctantly recognized; and, once more echoing earlier history, the initial governmental response was entirely defensive and negative. In 1962, after another ugly racist campaign, legislation was passed with the aim of limiting further coloured immigration. Since that date, public attitudes have become increasingly ambivalent. It is now conventional wisdom that Britain is too small and overcrowded to absorb fresh newcomers – unless they are white. At the same time, it is also widely accepted that racial discrimination is economically wasteful, socially divisive, harmful to international relations or morally wrong (according to one's particular standpoint). The approach of successive governments has therefore been that Commonwealth citizens should be excluded from this country because they are coloured, but that Commonwealth citizens who are already here should be treated equally, regardless of their colour. Understandably, few people have grasped the distinction. The more obvious conclusion that has generally been drawn is that if coloured immigration poses a threat to Britain's well-being so does the coloured minority living in Britain.

The law therefore has two faces. One face confronts the stranger at the gate; the other is turned towards the stranger within. They express the ambivalence of public policies. The hostile expression of our immigration law casts doubt upon the friendly expression of our race relations law. However much our legislators might wish it were otherwise, the hostility is taken more seriously than the friendliness – on both sides of the colour line.

The point may be worth underlining if only because it has become unfashionable. If our immigration laws are racially discriminatory in their aims and effect, it becomes difficult to persuade employers, workers, property developers and house-owners to treat people on their merits, regardless of race. If our nationality laws create a pseudo-citizenship, imposing the obligations of allegiance and loyalty to the British Crown upon a group of citizens, while denying to them, as 'non-patrials' or 'non-belongers', the same rights as their fellow citizens, even the wisest and most vigorous policies for racial equality are likely to lack credibility both with majority and minority.

Yet that is precisely the present position. Our immigration laws discriminate racially, in practice if not literally, between people seeking to enter or to remain in Britain. Our nationality law is so lacking in any sense of the positive content and value of United Kingdom citizenship that in 1968, shortly before the passage of the main Race Relations Act, Parliament deprived the East-African Asians, solely on grounds of colour, of the rights enjoyed by their fellow United Kingdom citizens to freedom of movement, employment, residence and family life within their country of citizenship. Because they are brown, they have become second-class citizens.

With one face, the law embodies and reinforces racial inequality; with the other, it expresses and urges racial equality. Our present concern is only with the latter, but it must be stated at the outset that, in our view, the effectiveness of the Race Relations Acts has been impaired by the tensions and contradictions between them and the immigration and nationality laws.

At the time of writing, the racially discriminatory character of Britain's immigration policies is being considered by the European Human Rights Commission, in the *East African Asians*' case. The outcome of that case may eventually prompt our legislators to bring the whole of the law into harmony not only with the spirit of the Race Relations Acts but also with the growing body of International Conventions and Covenants on human rights, which also lie beyond the scope of this book.

However, it would be wrong to see only the shadows cast upon the landscape of race relations by increasingly racial immigration controls. The Race Relations Acts were passed despite powerful opposition and with little public support. They carry the marks of political compromise, but they were also acts of statesmanship. Many of their provisions will have to be criticized in later chapters, but we shall attempt to place them into their proper political perspective, recognizing the courage and skill which were required for their enactment.

The adoption of a law actively to promote equality represented a radical departure from the traditional neutrality and passivity of our legal system. Britain stands almost alone among advanced societies – whether in the Commonwealth, Europe or the United States – in having no written constitution or Bill of Rights to guarantee the equal protection of the law. The Race Relations Acts were a significant step in that direction: an attempt to influence social behaviour and attitudes by a statutory declaration that everyone in Britain was henceforth to be treated on the basis of individual merit, irrespective of colour or race, and to provide an effective legal remedy for the most unfair and degrading type of discrimination.

There is nothing novel about the use of law to protect the community at large against wrongdoing. The criminal law exists largely for that purpose. Nor is it unusual to provide redress for the injury or damage done by one person to another. That is the function of the civil law. In Lord Atkin's celebrated words, defining civil liability for negligence.[1]

You must take reasonable care to avoid acts or omissions which you can reasonably foresee would be likely to injure your neighbour. Who, then, in law, is my neighbour? The answer seems to be – persons who are so closely and directly affected by my act that I ought reasonably to have them in contemplation as being so affected when I am directing my mind to the acts or omissions which are called in question.

The Race Relations Acts simply affirm that people are our neighbours regardless of their racial origins, and that we ought reasonably to

1. *Donoghue* v. *Stevenson* [1932] A.C. 562 (H.L.) at p. 580. Unfortunately, Lord Atkin did not see the relevance of the principle when upholding racial discrimination in the sale of urban housing by a public official in Kenya (see p. 45).

have them in our contemplation as being closely and directly affected by our discriminatory actions – and hence to refrain from discriminating arbitrarily or unfairly against them.

The radical nature of the race relations legislation lies in the practical application of the law to a wide range of situations in which discrimination has hitherto been regarded as unavoidable. We have never taken for granted a duty to observe rational and objective standards of behaviour in the recruitment, training, or promotion of workers, or in the resort to industrial action by trade unions and employers' associations, or in the sale and letting of residential accommodation, or even in the provision of goods, facilities and services to the public. The Race Relations Acts require rational and objective standards in all these situations only to the extent of treating *racial* motives as inherently irrational and unfair. But significantly, since that unfamiliar step was taken, there has been growing recognition in subsequent legislation that other forms of unfair discrimination were not inevitable (e.g. unequal pay for women, other unfair industrial practices by employers and trade unions, and religious discrimination in local authority housing and public employment in Northern Ireland). It may no longer be utopian to hope that the Race Relations Acts, suitably amended, will eventually become a model for more systematic and effective redress in these and other fields.

Before the passage of the Race Relations Acts it was widely supposed that Britain was confronted not with a race problem but with an immigration problem. According to this view, it was the foreignness of Commonwealth immigrants, rather than their colour, which aroused antagonism and resulted in unequal treatment – their poor command of English, their inadequate education and training, their late-night parties, their peculiar cooking and exotic clothes. It was a comforting belief, in some ways as comforting for immigrant as for native. It suggested that there could often be an objective and reasonable justification for apparently discriminatory treatment, and also that the 'immigration problem' would be solved by the mere passage of time. In practice, of course, it eventually became apparent that the very reverse was happening. The children of Commonwealth immigrants – the so-called 'second generation' – born and educated in this country, were not foreigners, despite Enoch Powell's narrow definition of the true-born Englishman. When it became clear that they too were being denied equal access to employment and other opportunities, neither they nor those who discriminated against them could doubt that the real cause of their exclusion was racial. Left to themselves, race relations did not seem to be automatically improving; in default of any governmental policy or action, they appeared to be growing worse. It was the sudden awareness of the danger that the Second Generation might become a coloured underclass, given heightened consciousness by the racial crisis in the northern cities of the United States, which strengthened the case for the new legislation, modelled, not surprisingly, upon American statutes.

The advocates of the legislation have continually emphasized the interests of the new coloured generation, British by birth and upbringing, and have referred to American experience, in order to dramatize the causes and the cost of racial discrimination. Although we share this approach, we recognize that it necessarily distorts the true picture of race relations today. Britain's coloured communities are still more immigrant than indigenous in their composition and character. And the differences between Indians, Pakistanis, Barbadians and Jamaicans are sometimes as significant as the more obvious contrasts between immigrant and native, or between black and white.

Britain is a plural society culturally as well as racially, and the tensions created by cultural diversity may be as onerous for the immigrant generation as the tensions arising from racial differences.

Such questions are outside the scope of a book whose focus is directed to the problems of racial inequality rather than to those created by cultural diversity. But they are important questions which deserve to be answered. It is the proper function of government and law to guarantee individual rights and freedoms, regardless of colour or race, but not to impose what Roy Jenkins has aptly termed 'a flattening process of assimilation' upon Britain's new minorities. Cultural differences will admittedly become blurred with each succeeding generation, whereas racial differences are likely to be aggravated if an indigenous coloured population, entitled to be treated as equal men and women by virtue of their birthright and their citizenship, are treated as inferior.

Some of the problems of cultural diversity can be safely left to solve themselves; some, but not all. It would, for example, be entirely misguided for public authorities to tolerate the exploitation of children or the maltreatment of wives and daughters because such practices were condoned by a particular national, religious or cultural group. Prejudice and discrimination ought to be opposed with equal force, whether among white or black people, natives or immigrants; and cultural tolerance must not become a cloak for oppression and injustice within the immigrant communities themselves.

So much for the general landscape of race relations, which has been carefully explored by Rose, Deakin and their associates in their admirable study (1969). The subject-matter of the present work is specialized and has received far less attention. Hepple has provided an invaluable guide to the employment aspects of race relations law (1970); and MacDonald has produced a useful brief introduction to the legislation on both race relations and immigration (1969). But there has not before been a comprehensive discussion of the legal and political background to the legislation and of the practical operation of the present law.

Because the material is so complex and diffuse, we have tried to make the structure and content of the book as simple as possible. As already indicated, it is designed for several different types of reader and some chapters will be of greater relevance to one than to another. Each section is therefore written so as to be able to be consulted separately, with appropriate cross-references to the rest of the book, and the full text of the Race Relations Acts is set out in Appendices 2 and 3.

Part One contains the background to the present law. Chapter 1 examines the response of the English judiciary to cases involving racial discrimination which have arisen since the days of slavery. Chapter 2 analyses the role of legislation in combating racial discrimination: the idea of equality and the legal philosophy which have inspired the supporters of such legislation. It also discusses the nature of the problems which legislation is intended to tackle: the causes and the consequences of discrimination in employment, housing and elsewhere. Chapter 3 tells the remarkable story of how the legislation was won against formidable political odds, revealing weaknesses both in the legislative process and the present law.

Part Two describes the scope of the legislation. A large number of hypothetical cases are included in this part of the book, so as to bring the law to life and to make it more intelligible to the general reader. Chapter 4 explains the statutory meaning of unlawful discrimination in general terms – the standard of conduct which the law requires, the situations to which it applies, and the exceptions to its coverage. Chapters 5, 6 and 7 examine the detailed provisions on employment, housing, and the provision of goods, facilities and services.

The crucial subject of the enforcement of the law is examined in Part Three. Chapter 8 describes the statutory machinery and the process of conciliation, drawing attention to some weaknesses in the legislation which may impair the work of the Race Relations Board and its conciliation committees. Chapter 9 is concerned with legal proceedings – the ultimate deterrent, intended by Parliament to be invoked only when it is impossible to secure a settlement by conciliation. Here also there are defects which weaken the credibility of the deterrent, and prevent the victim from obtaining adequate redress from the discriminator.

The legal prohibition of racial incitement is discussed in Part Four. It is largely a separate subject, even though it is frequently confused with the anti-discrimination provisions. Because it has provoked deeper controversy and misunderstanding than any other section of the Race Relations Acts, it has to be scrutinized with particular care.

The main part of the book concludes with a summary of recommendations for the reform of the law and improvements in its application. The government responsible for the passage of the Race Relations Acts is no longer in office, but its successors are committed to support the legislation and its objectives. It may therefore be hoped that the statutes will be regarded by Parliament as the beginning rather than the end of wisdom, and that their most glaring deficiencies will soon be remedied.

There is always a danger that such a law may become a ritual totem, worshipped in the name of liberal morality, without any marked effect on the conduct of the governors or the governed. The danger is recalled in a cautionary tale, set out in Appendix 1, about the fate of a little-known provision, passed by Parliament long ago to prohibit racial and religious discrimination in the Indian civil service. The story is reserved for an appendix so as not to interrupt the main themes of the book; but it is more than an interesting historical episode. It is meant to have a moral for those who believe that the law can help to improve race relations in contemporary Britain.

Part One

Part One

Chapter 1
Inequality before the Law

The English law of race relations is the handiwork of Parliament rather than the courts, but long before the enactment of legislation on the subject, English judges had to decide cases which differed widely in character, but had as their common element the unfair treatment of people because of their race or colour. Some of these cases are relevant because in spite of the new legislation, they are still part of the law; others are significant because they may be considered relevant by the judges when they interpret the new legislation; others still are not strictly part of English law, but illustrate the traditional English judicial response to problems of race relations which have arisen in British Dominions and Colonies. Above all, these different decisions of the courts illustrate why the Common Law, made by the judges, could not deal adequately with problems of the unfair treatment of people on racial grounds, and why Parliament alone could provide an effective legal remedy for the victims of such treatment.

The illusion of legal equality

The concept of equality is, of course, a hallowed virtue of the English legal system. Dicey, who delighted in so many aspects of that system, saw it as a characteristic of the rule of law that

here every man, whatever be his rank or condition, is subject to the ordinary law of the realm and amenable to the jurisdiction of the ordinary tribunals (1961, p. 193).

Now it is true that everyone, whether British or foreign, does have equal access to the courts, and the same remedies, under the same legal system.[1] This is not medieval Britain, where Jews paid special

1. In *Donald Campbell & Co.* v. *Pollak* [1927] A.C. 732 (H.L.), Viscount Cave L.C. said, in the course of considering the basis on which the Courts should

taxes, were tried in a special court, and were obliged to wear yellow badges. This is not seventeenth-century Britain, where African slaves could be lawfully bought, sold and mortgaged as mere chattels in the market-place. Nor is it the Britain of the eighteenth and early nineteenth centuries, where Jews, Catholics and Dissenters were subjected to legal disabilities. These inequalities in the legal status of racial and religious minorities, which were created by Parliament, had, by Dicey's day, been removed by Parliament; and today everyone is equal before the law, whatever his race, colour or creed.

The principle of equality before the law is rightly cherished; it had to be fought for, and in many parts of the world it has still to be won. But it is important to understand the narrow limits of this principle. First, however much the legal system may treat individuals and institutions as equals, it cannot by itself alter the profound inequalities within their actual relationships; law is at best a limited instrument with which to seek greater social justice.

Secondly, English judges tend to treat equality before the law, as Dicey did, as a formal concept concerning equal access to the courts, legal procedures and remedies, not as a principle which entitles them, within the narrow compass of the legal system, to restrain a stronger party from oppressing a weaker one. It is true that the courts have been willing to ignore the results of a discriminatory status existing under *foreign* law (Dicey, 1967, p. 75). For example, they would probably not now recognize the state of slavery,[2] nor disabilities imposed by foreign laws upon Jews living in this country;[3] and they have indicated[4] that they would consider whether a foreign divorce

exercise their discretion to award costs 'if – to put a hypothesis which in our Courts would never in fact be realized – a judge were to refuse to give a party his costs on the ground of . . . some prejudice due to his race or religion or (to quote a familiar illustration) to the colour of his hair, then a Court of Appeal might well feel itself compelled to intervene'.

2. See *Regazzoni* v. *K. C. Sethia (1944) Ltd* [1956] 2 Q.B. 490 (C.A.) at p. 524 *per* Parker L.J.

3. *Frankfurther* v. *W. L. Exner Ltd* [1947] 1 Ch. 629; *Novello & Co.* v. *Hinrichsen Edition Ltd* [1951] Ch. 595; [1951] Ch. 1026. See also *Re Friedrich Krupps A.G.* [1917] 2 Ch. 188; *Oppenheimer* v. *Louis Rosenthal & Co.* [1937] 1 All E.R. 23 (C.A.); *Ellinger* v. *Guinness, Mahon & Co.* [1939] 4 All E.R. 16.

4. *Igra* v. *Igra* [1951] p. 404.

decree granted on predominantly racial grounds was invalid as being contrary to natural justice.

In all these instances, the courts have invoked the notion of 'public policy' – the ethical sense or conscience of the community as reflected in the Common Law – against an offending foreign law. Similarly, the courts have been prepared to refuse to give effect to English contracts which offend against public policy, whether because the objects of the contract are plainly illegal, or because they are harmful to good government, or because they are improper interferences with the working of the machinery of justice, or because they are injurious to family life. But, apart from their disapproval of slavery, English judges have never declared that acts of racial discrimination committed *in this country* are against public policy.

Judicial reluctance to take this step will be apparent again and again in this chapter. It is partly inspired by a desire to avoid making law as opposed to interpreting law. This reluctance is expressed in many metaphors: public policy is said to be 'a very unruly horse, and once you get astride it you never know where it will carry you';[5] it is 'a very treacherous ground for legal decision', 'a very unstable and dangerous foundation on which to build until made safe by decision.'[6] Yet, despite these protestations, judges are often motivated by considerations of policy, even though they do not openly express them in the reasons for their decisions. More commonly, although they see themselves merely as considering technical questions of law, their decisions have important implications in terms of public policy, so that they do make law. And, paradoxically, as will be clear later in this chapter, judicial failure to develop an explicit sense of public policy, instead of preserving certainty and predictability in the law, sometimes has the opposite effect.

The concept of equality before the law is also limited by the inevitably passive nature of the Common Law. For example, although the courts could refuse to enforce a racially discriminatory contract because it was against public policy, they could not, in the absence of legislation, normally interpret the law positively so as to require one person to accord equal treatment to another. They could not

5. *Richardson* v. *Mellish* (1824) 2 Bing. 229 at p. 252 *per* Burrough J.

6. *Janson* v. *Driefontein Consolidated Mines Ltd* [1952] A.C. 484, at p. 500 *per* Lord Davey and at p. 507 *per* Lord Lindley.

compel an employer to recruit workers, or a property owner to sell houses, without taking into account the colour or race of would-be workers or buyers. The courts are bound by the Common Law, and, with rare exceptions, the Common Law does not frown upon racial discrimination.

Lastly, English courts, unlike those of the United States or other countries with written constitutions, are restricted by the lack of any power to guarantee equality if the legislature decides that there shall be inequality; the courts cannot invalidate an Act of Parliament, because they have no power to review the constitutionality of legislative action. Accordingly, if Parliament passes a statute which discriminates against a group of people on racial grounds, the courts must carry out its provisions. As an English judge observed[7] long ago: 'An Act of Parliament can do no wrong, though it may do several things that look pretty odd.'

The limits of the Common Law must be remembered because the judges are imprisoned within them, but a survey of the decided cases suggests that the judges have made their prison more confining than it need have been; they have grown to love their chains.

Cases of racial injustice have come before the courts in three different situations, each involving conflicts because of the movement of members of an ethnic or national group from one country to another. The earliest and most dramatic legal problems resulted from the traffic in African slaves, either because merchants sought to enforce agreements for the sale of slaves in the English courts, or because masters tried forcibly to remove unwilling slaves from England to the colonies. A second series of legal issues were decided by the Privy Council, as the appellate tribunal for the British Empire and Commonwealth, involving discrimination against Chinese and Japanese migrants to Canada, or the descendants of Asian indentured labourers in Africa. And, finally, problems of discrimination have arisen as a result of the immigration to Britain of Jewish refugees and coloured Commonwealth citizens.

The judicial response to these situations is not only of interest to legal historians. It illustrates why the traditional concept of legal equality proved less and less sufficient in the face of social and

7. *City of London* v. *Wood* (1701) 12 Mod. 669 at pp. 687–8 *per* Holt C.J.

economic problems in this country; and in so doing, it throws light upon the English legal system itself.

Slavery

Slavery was an established institution in English society long before the Norman Conquest. In Domesday Book, about 10 per cent of the recorded population were classified as slaves.

Legally no more than chattel goods, these people could apparently be killed by their owners without penalty; if a freeman killed someone else's slave, he was liable only for the man's market value. And yet the slaves of Domesday were entitled by Anglo-Saxon law to specified annual rations and by custom were apparently accorded certain rights to property and free time (Davis, 1966, p. 38).

True slavery in this form did not completely disappear until the thirteenth century, at the very time when villeins were losing what remained of their liberties, and becoming mere serfs. Because there was no Common Law principle which could readily be adapted to medieval serfdom, Glanvill, Bracton, and various minor jurists of the late Middle Ages, all tried to apply the Roman law of slavery for this purpose. And the legal principles developed by these writers

survived as a weapon of social control. In 1547, for example, it was possible to enact a temporary law stating that vagabonds who attempted to escape from enforced service were to be branded on the forehead with the letter 'S' which signified that they would be slaves for the rest of their lives (Davis, 1966, p. 40).

Black slaves first appeared in Britain at the end of the sixteenth century, as an aftermath of the Spanish wars, (Fiddes, 1934, p. 500) and, although in 1596 the Privy Council ordered some of them to be removed from the country in case they deprived Englishmen of employment, they reappeared in increasing numbers, throughout the seventeenth century, as a by-product of the booming slave-trading carried out on the African coast by Britain and the other major European powers. By the second half of the eighteenth century, about

one third of the British merchant fleet was engaged in transporting fifty thousand Negroes a year to the New World. . . . In the England of George

II . . . the slave trader was not only socially respectable, but his business was a recognized route to gentility and was officially approved by the Board of Trade, the navy, and the nobility (Davis, 1966, p. 154).

In view of the lucrative benefits which Britain derived from the slave trade, and the social respectability of slavery, it is not surprising that the English courts were ready to recognize the legality of the institution. Their task was made easier because the appalling traffic and its consequences were kept at a convenient distance in remote colonies. The legal aspects of slavery came before the English courts only where a master sought to enforce his right of ownership in his slave either against some merchant, or against the slave himself in this country.

Since there was no intellectual basis for chattel slavery in existing law, the seventeenth-century English courts upheld the rights of owners to claim Negroes as property by relying upon the fact that they were not Christians, and by appealing to the common practice of merchants, whose trade in slaves was presumed to be sanctioned by the *jus gentium* (Davis, 1966, p. 208).[8] For example, in 1677, an action was brought to recover possession of a hundred slaves, and the court decided[9] that slavery was legal in England because Negroes were infidels and the subjects of an infidel prince, and so without the rights enjoyed by Christian men. And, in a case decided in 1693,[10] Negroes were described as merchandise and compared with musk cats and monkeys. But this approach had the disadvantage that it could not be applied to a slave who was baptized and so could not readily be regarded as an inanimate object, without legal rights.

8. Davis states that 'Both French and English colonial law assumed that the slave had essentially the attributes of personal property, and like a horse or cow could be moved, sold or rented at the will of his owner' (p. 248). This view, which is supported by his examination of slavery throughout North and South America, is contrary to the theory which has been advanced elsewhere (e.g. Griswold, 1964, pp. 105–6) that slavery was more humane in those colonies whose legal systems derived from Roman Law, because Roman Law, unlike the Common Law, had extensive provisions relating to slavery. The truth seems rather to be that both legal systems were equally capable of being used to justify slavery, and that both 'embodied ambiguities and compromises that arose from the impossibility of acting consistently on the premise that men were things' (Davis, 1966, p. 248).

9. *Butts* v. *Penny* (1677) 2 Lev. 201.

10. *Chambers* v. *Warkhouse* (1693) 3 Salk. 140.

The courts resolved the difficulty by treating slavery as a relationship created under local colonial law, and enforcing that relationship as a matter of colonial rather than domestic English law. In this way the judges could uphold the condition of servitude overseas without violating British ideals of personal liberty. For example, in 1701, a merchant claimed £20 in the English courts as the price of a Negro slave sold by him in London to another. Chief Justice Holt began by proclaiming[11] the principle of individual liberty that 'as soon as a Negro comes into England he becomes free; and one may be a villein in England, but not a slave'. But he went on in a more practical vein to suggest that the plaintiff should have alleged that 'the sale of the Negro was in Virginia, and by the laws of that country Negroes are saleable; for the laws of England do not extend to Virginia, and we cannot take notice of their law but as set forth'. And he allowed the merchant to amend his claim so as to state that the law of Virginia applied and that, under that law, Negroes could be 'sold as chattels'.

Chief Justice Holt was at least willing to deny effect to slavery as a matter of English domestic law. For example in 1706, he decided[12] that an action would not lie to recover possession of a slave, after hearing arguments that at Common Law no man could have property in another except in the special circumstances of villeinage and that the law did not recognize that Negroes were different from other men. But during the next decades a conflict developed between those who were willing to give full effect to slavery in England, under English law, and those who accepted Holt's distinction between English and colonial law.

In 1729, a deputation of West-Indian slave owners approached the Attorney-General, Philip Yorke, and the Solicitor-General, Charles Talbot, seeking an assurance that slavery was legal in England. The Law Officers gave full satisfaction to the deputation (Fiddes, 1934, pp. 501–2). A slave, they declared, did not become free on coming to England, nor did he become free by being baptized, and any master might lawfully force his slave to return with him from England to the plantations. In 1749, Yorke, now Lord Hardwicke, reaffirmed his opinion from the Bench.[13] On the other

11. *Smith* v. *Browne and Cooper* (1701) Holt K.B. 495.
12. *Smith* v. *Gould* [1706] 2 Salk. 666.
13. *Pearne* v. *Lisle* (1749) Amb. 75.

hand, in 1762, the Lord Chancellor in *Shanley* v. *Harvey*[14] repeated Holt's maxim that a man became free as soon as he set foot in England, and stated that a Negro could both maintain an action against his master for ill-usage, and have a writ of habeas corpus if restrained of his liberty.

These conflicting judicial attitudes reflected the 'growing contradiction between colonial slavery and British ideals of liberty' which were felt at the time, and were

exposed with unconscious irony by the Englishmen of the 1760s who complained that Negroes in the London area 'cease to consider themselves as slaves in this free country . . . nor more willingly perform the laborious offices of servitude than our own people, and if put to do it, are generally sullen, spiteful, treacherous and revengeful' (Davis, 1966, p. 211, citing *Gentleman's Magazine*, 1764).

It was now, however, that Granville Sharp, the determined and eccentric philanthropist took action to resolve the contradiction in favour of emancipation. Between 1767 and 1772, he devoted himself to rescuing slaves from being transported from England to the colonial plantations, and he supported two attempts to decide the matter in the English courts.

The first effort was made in 1771, in *Thomas Lewis's* case (Fiddes, 1934, pp. 503–4). It concerned the seizure by one, Stapylton, of his runaway slave, Lewis. The slave had been forcibly carried on board ship, and his cries had aroused the attention of a woman who lived near by. She informed Sharp, who rescued Lewis after the ship had left harbour. An action was then brought against Stapylton and the two watermen who had helped him to take the slave.

Lord Mansfield was the judge and he was extremely reluctant to face the question whether a slave master had the legal right forcibly to transport the slave from England. Mansfield said that it had never been decided whether a master had such a right of property in a slave in this country. He tried to leave the matter to the jury, directing them that if there was evidence of such property, they should acquit the master. After the jury had considered their verdict, the foreman said, 'We don't find that he was the defendant's property', and 'there arose at the same instant a general voice of "No property, no property"'. When Mansfield asked if this was a verdict of guilty,

14. (1762) 2 Eden 126.

there was a general voice of 'Guilty'. The Judge then turned to Lewis's counsel and said

You will see more in the question than you see at present . . . there are a great many opinions given upon it. Perhaps it is much better that it should never be finally discussed or settled. I don't know what the consequences may be if the masters were to lose their property by bringing slaves to England. I hope it never will be finally discussed for I would have all masters think them free and all Negroes think them not because they would both behave better.

Despite this pathetic plea, counsel asked for judgment against Stapylton, but Mansfield was not willing to proceed. He threw doubt on the evidence, ignored the jury's verdict and advised that future proceedings should be dropped.

Granville Sharp was understandably furious. In vain he drew up a protest against Mansfield's decision as an open defiance of the laws of England. Then, a year later, he supported another case which came before Mansfield. James Sommersett, an escaped slave had been re-captured and put on board a ship in the Thames bound for Jamaica. Sommersett applied to the court to be set free, whereupon Mansfield advised the merchants to refer the problem to Parliament. He twice suggested an informal compromise by which the slave might be set free. Finally he was driven to pronounce judgment. He declared that

The state of slavery is of such a nature that it is incapable of being intro-duced on any reason, moral or political, but only by positive law. . . . It is so odious that nothing can be suffered to support it except positive law. Whatever inconveniences, therefore, may follow from the decision I can-not say this case is allowed or approved by the law of England; and there-fore the black must be discharged.[15]

Sommersett's case has come to be celebrated as a great constitu-tional landmark, and an example of the judicial protection of per-sonal liberty. The most lavish praise of the decision came from a later judge who proudly recalled that

whilst economists and politicians were recommending to the legislature the protection of . . . [the slave trade] and senators were framing statutes for its promotion, and declaring it a benefit to the country, the Judges . . . dis-daining to bend to expediency, declared that slavery was inconsistent with

15. *The Case of James Sommersett* (1772) 20 St. Tr. 1, at p. 82.

the genius of the English Constitution, and that human beings could not be the subject matter of property.[16]

Now it is true that *Sommersett's* case was decided thirty-six years before Parliament prohibited the slave trade, and sixty-two years before it abolished slavery in the colonies, in 1834. In that sense it was an important decision. But its consequences have been vastly exaggerated. All that the case in fact settled was that the state of slavery could not be enforced in the English courts while the slave was in England. Mansfield himself was later to decide[17] that a slave who continued to work for her old master after being brought to this country had no right to receive wages, while her master could obtain a legal remedy if she were taken away from him. And it seems that since slavery was not proscribed, it 'continued to exist in an attenuated form. Even its worse abuse – the forcible removal of Negroes back to the colonies – continued, though now undoubtedly illegal.'[18]

In 1827, in the case of the *Slave Grace*, Lord Stowell, who described himself as 'rather a stern abolitionist' so far as the slave trade was concerned, held that *Sommersett's* case did not affect the legality of slavery in the colonies.[19] Stowell's wit and erudition were used to masterly effect against Mansfield and those who had exaggerated the importance of the earlier decision. He observed that the arguments of counsel in *Sommersett's* case

16. *Forbes* v. *Cochrane* (1824) 2 B. & Co. 448 at 470 *per* Best J. More recently Diplock L.J. stated in *Chic Fashions* (*West Wales*) *Ltd* v. *Jones* [1968] 2 Q.B. 299 (C.A.) at p. 315 that *Sommersett's* case had decided that the balance between the inviolability of private property and the pursuit of the public weal no longer lay in favour of private property in slaves.

17. See *The Inhabitants of Thames Ditton* (1785) 4 Dougl. 229. In *Gregson* v. *Gilbert* (1783) the owners of the slave-ship *Zong* sued underwriters to recover the value of 132 slaves lost in the passage from West Africa to Jamaica. The captain of the ship had thrown those sickly slaves who were barely alive overboard, and the underwriters argued that there had been no need for conduct so shocking to humanity. In the trial at the Guildhall, the jury found in favour of the owners. On appeal to Lord Mansfield and two other judges, Mansfield observed that 'Though it shocks one very much, the case of slaves was much the same as if horses had been thrown overboard.' However, he did order a new trial on the dual grounds that the jettison had been unnecessary and that the loss was not covered by the insurance policy. The retrial was never reported (Weisbord, 1969).

18. See *The Slave Grace* (1827) 2 St.Tr.(N.S.) 273.

19. At p. 286.

do not go further than to the extinction of slavery in England as unsuitable to the genius of the country, and to the modes of enforcement: they look no further than to the peculiar nature, as it were, of our own soil; the air of our island is too pure for slavery to breathe in. How far this air was useful for the purpose of respiration during the many centuries in which two systems of villeinage maintained their sway in this country, history has not recorded. The arguments . . . do not go further than to establish that the methods of force and violence which are necessary to maintain slavery are not practicable upon this spot.

He referred to Mansfield as having struggled 'hard to decline the office of determining the question', and thought it 'a most remarkable circumstance' that though the case of *Shanley* v. *Harvey* 'had been pressed upon the attention of Lord Mansfield . . . he himself never took any notice of it, although evidently at that time anxious to support his new doctrine, and struggling hard to call in aid every authority that could establish it'.

In the case of the *Slave Grace* itself, the point at issue was whether slaves who had returned to the West Indies after living in Britain could claim freedom before the colonial courts. Stowell rejected the argument that colonial slavery was against public policy, recalling that it had been 'favoured and supported by our own courts which have liberally imported to it their protection and encouragement', and had been continually sanctioned by Acts of Parliament. He held that temporary residence in England did not destroy the status of slavery, which revived on the slave's return to the colonies. As he put it

the law uses a very different language and exerts a very different force when it looks to her Colonies, for to this trade in those Colonies it gives an almost unbounded protection, and it is in the habit of doing so at the present time in many exercises of public authority.

What appears to have especially concerned Stowell was that the refusal by the English courts to recognize colonial slavery would have been hypocritical and unfair; the abolition of slavery and the slave trade was a matter for Parliament rather than for the courts. He explained that

it is in a peculiar manner the crime of this country, and I feel it to be an objection to this species of emancipation that it is intended to be a very cheap measure here by throwing the whole expense upon the Colony.

And, again, if the slave trade 'be a sin, it is a sin in which this country has had its full share of guilt, and ought to bear its full proportion of the redemption'. Six years later, in 1833, Parliament at last passed an Act to abolish slavery in the colonies.

The judgments given by Mansfield and Stowell in these slavery cases reveal a readiness, unusual among English judges, to make explicit the wider matters of policy raised by the immediate legal issues before them. Mansfield admitted that he was anxious to avoid reaching a decision which might threaten the slave trade or colonial slavery; Stowell, though an abolitionist, was troubled by the inherent disadvantages of taking judicial rather than legislative action against slavery in the colonies. Both could claim that the weight of public opinion had supported slavery as long as it was not manifested in England itself. Mansfield was not the courageous emancipator of later legend,[20] but he was at least explicit in his motives,[21] and, like Stowell, he regretted that Parliament had not resolved the dilemma which slavery had created for the Common Law. The same could not be said for the English court which, as late as 1860, refused[22] to invalidate a contract made by a British subject for the sale of slaves in Brazil, because the possession of slaves was lawful in that country. Despite the enactment of anti-slavery legislation, the judges still would not accept that slavery was against public policy.[23]

20. '[At the time of *Sommersett's* case] the tide of public opinion had begun to run strongly against the very idea of slavery, and . . . the righteous indignation against its abominations was fanned by a group of highly skilled propagandists who made great play with a not too accurate account of Lord Mansfield's judgment' (Fiddes, 1934, p. 511).

21. Compare *Dred Scott* v. *Sandford* 19 How. 394 (1854), where the U S Supreme Court held that a free Negro of African ancestry, whose forebears were brought to the States and sold as slaves, was not a 'citizen' within the meaning of the U S Constitution, and could not therefore claim the rights or immunities of a citizen in the Courts. Mr Chief Justice Taney stated (at p. 426) that any other interpretation of the Constitution 'would abrogate the judicial character of this Court, and make it a mere reflex of the popular opinion or passion of the day. This Court was not created . . . for such purposes. Higher and graver trusts have been confided to it, and it must not falter in the path of duty.'

22. *Santos* v. *Illidge* (1859) 6 C.B.(N.S.) 841; (1860) 8 C.B.(N.S.) 861.

23. Happily, it is now clear that the English courts will not give effect to foreign laws concerning slavery, because they are against public policy: *Regazzoni* v. *K. C. Sethia* (*1944*) *Ltd* [1956] 2 Q.B. 490 (C.A.) p. 524, *per* Parker L.J.

Discrimination against Chinese and Japanese Canadians

Ever since 1833, the Judicial Committee of the Privy Council has been the Supreme Court of Appeal for British colonies, and for those independent Commonwealth countries which have preserved its jurisdiction over them. Their members include the Lord Chancellor and Lords of Appeal in Ordinary. Privy Council cases do not bind the English courts, for they are not strictly decisions under English law, but they are treated as being of great weight, and are commonly followed in similar English cases. Since it has been their unusual task to sit as a supreme appellate body in judgment upon the legality of the actions of Commonwealth and colonial governments in distant lands, it is not surprising that the Privy Council have traditionally shown greater sympathy for the needs of the Executive than for those of the individual.

On four different occasions, the Privy Council have had to decide whether it was lawful for the Provincial Government of British Columbia to practise racial discrimination against Chinese and Japanese Canadians. The cases came to the Privy Council because they raised questions about the proper allocation of power between the Federal and Provincial Governments under the Canadian Constitution (the British North America Act 1867). The issue in each case was whether racially discriminatory legislation passed by the British Columbia legislature encroached unlawfully upon the exclusive power of the Dominion legislature over aliens and naturalized persons. If the Provincial and Dominion statutes covered the same ground, it was clear that the Dominion legislation had to prevail.[24] Even though the Privy Council was dealing here with legal questions of an unusual and often highly technical nature, the underlying value judgments are apparent in these decisions.

In the first case, decided in 1899,[25] a shareholder in the Union Colliery Company of British Columbia wanted to prevent the Company from employing Chinese in responsible positions in the mines, because, in his view, they were a source of danger to others. He relied upon a Provincial Act which barred 'Chinamen' from employment

24. *Attorney-General for Canada* v. *Attorney-General for British Columbia* [1930] A.C. 111 at p. 118 *per* Lord Tomlin.
25. *Union Colliery Co. of British Columbia* v. *Bryden* [1899] A.C. 580.

in underground coal workings. The statute disabled Chinese from this work solely because of their racial origins. The Provincial legislature had been trying for years to restrict the settlement of Chinese in the Province and to prevent them from competing with white Canadians. But the British North America Act gave exclusive authority over aliens and naturalized subjects to the Dominion Parliament. It also empowered the Dominion Parliament to carry out Canada's treaty obligations to foreign countries, and two treaties had been made with the Emperor of China guaranteeing the right of Chinese to obtain employment in Canada.

The Privy Council decided that the Provincial statute was unlawful, because it applied to aliens or naturalized subjects, who were under the exclusive authority of the Dominion Parliament. But they took care to confine their decision to a narrow interpretation of the constitutional question, refusing to comment on the merits of the discriminatory statute, since, as they put it, once the Courts have decided the proper limits of the jurisdiction of the legislature, they have 'no right whatever to inquire whether their jurisdiction has been exercised wisely or not'. And they did not consider the possible relevance of the two treaties with the Chinese Emperor. Had the Privy Council observed in the course of their decision that the Canadian Constitution should be interpreted, in the absence of Dominion legislation to the contrary, so as to apply equally to all citizens living in Canada, without unfair discrimination, the subsequent unhappy history might have been avoided. Instead, they chose to remain silent on the issue of principle.

Shortly afterwards, Tommey Homma, a naturalized British subject of Japanese origin, was excluded from the electoral voting register in Vancouver City, under another British Columbia statute which provided that 'any native of the Japanese empire . . . not born of British parents' and 'any person of Japanese race, naturalized or not' was to be denied the right to vote. The Supreme Court of British Columbia held that this provision was invalid, because it related to 'naturalization' within the exclusive competence of the Dominion Parliament. But the Privy Council reversed the decision, and found[26] that Tommey Homma had properly been denied the franchise.

The composition of the Privy Council had become more conserva-

26. *Cunningham* v. *Tommey Homma* [1903] A.C. 151.

tive in the three years since the *Union Colliery* case.[27] And their reasoning in *Tommey Homma's* case was bizarre. They held that the Provincial statute did not encroach upon naturalization, because it applied as much to the child of Japanese parents, born in Vancouver City, as to a naturalized Japanese Canadian. This was to ignore the fact that the statute applied at least in part to naturalized Canadians of Japanese origin. And the Privy Council interpreted the expression 'political rights' in the Canadian Naturalization Act, as not including the right to vote in Provincial elections. As for the *Union Colliery* case, it 'depended on totally different grounds', because the Coal Mines Regulations had been 'devised to deprive the Chinese, naturalized or not, of the ordinary rights of the inhabitants of British Columbia and, in effect, to prohibit their continued residence in that Province, since it prohibited their earning their living in that Province'. It was 'obvious' that 'such a decision can have no relation to the question whether any naturalized person has an inherent right to the suffrage within the Province in which he resides'.

It could only have been obvious to the Privy Council because they had no clear concept of the nature of citizenship. The right to take part in Provincial elections of a naturalized Canadian of Japanese origin, like Tommey Homma, who lived in British Columbia, and who presumably paid Provincial taxes, was as much an essential element of citizenship as the right to live and work there. The Privy Council's decision meant that the right to work was within, and the right to elect a Government was outside, those rights of Canadian citizenship which were reserved in the case of aliens and naturalized subjects, to the Dominion Parliament.

The Privy Council were by no means bound to reach this conclusion. In doing so, they had to distinguish the *Union Colliery* case, over-rule the Supreme Court of British Columbia, and give a narrow

27. In the *Union Colliery* case, the Privy Council were composed of Lords Watson, Hobhouse and MacNaghten, Sir Richard Couch and Sir Edward Fry; in *Tommey Homma's* case, they consisted of Lords Halsbury L.C., MacNaghten, Davey, Robertson and Lindley. Compare the altered composition of the House of Lords during the same years, and a similar shift in judicial attitude with respect to the law of conspiracy in trade disputes: see *Allen* v. *Flood* [1898] A.C. 1 (H.L.) and *Quinn* v. *Leathem* [1901] A.C. 495 (H.L.). Four of the Judges in the latter case (i.e. Lords Halsbury L.C., MacNaghten, Robertson and Lindley) were also members of the Privy Council in *Tommey Homma's* case.

meaning to an important provision of the British North American Act. The result was to give judicial blessing to the complete exclusion of Japanese Canadians from Provincial elections, even though the Privy Council were careful to avoid expressing any view in their judgment about the merits of such a policy.

The matter did not end there. In 1912, the Minister of Lands for British Columbia granted licences to Brooks-Bidlake & Whittal Ltd to cut timber on Crown property. The licences were granted on condition that 'no Chinese or Japanese shall be employed in connection therewith'. This restriction was declared to be invalid by the Provincial Court of Appeal in 1920, but, in 1921, the Provincial legislature passed a statute providing that the restriction had the force of law, and that a violation of it should be a sufficient ground for cancelling a licence. Brooks-Bidlake employed both Chinese and Japanese workers, and sought a ruling from the courts that they were entitled to do so. They claimed that, as in the *Union Colliery* case, the statute was outside the powers of the Provincial legislature, because its 'pith and substance' concerned aliens and naturalization, which were matters exclusively for the Dominion Parliament. They also relied upon the Japanese Treaty Act 1913, which had been passed by the Dominion Parliament to give effect to a treaty under which Japanese subjects were guaranteed the right to equal opportunities in employment in Canada.

On this occasion, the Privy Council consisted of five members of the House of Lords.[28] They decided[29] that the Provincial legislature had acted within their constitutional powers, because the pith and substance of the statute concerned the management and licensing of public property in British Columbia rather than the employment of aliens and naturalized persons. They followed *Tommey Homma's* rather than the *Union Colliery* case. The Privy Council avoided the argument based on the Japanese Treaty Act, by pointing to the fact that Brooks-Bidlake employed Chinese as well as Japanese labour, and that since Chinese workers were not protected by the Japanese Treaty Act, the argument would not dispose of the case against Brooks-Bidlake.

28. Viscounts Cave L.C. and Haldane, and Lords Dunedin, Shaw and Carson.
29. *Brooks-Bidlake & Whittal Ltd* v. *Attorney-General for British Columbia* [1923] A.C. 450.

However, eight months later, the Privy Council were again faced by the question which they had previously avoided. The Attorney-General of British Columbia appealed[30] against another decision of the Canadian Supreme Court, given on the same day as their decision in the *Brooks-Bidlake* case, in which the Supreme Court had ruled that the British Columbia legislature had no power to pass the statute purporting to validate the exclusion of Japanese from employment on Crown property. Two of the five judges in the Privy Council were the same in both cases.[31] But on this second occasion the Privy Council held that the discriminatory statute was invalid because it violated the principle laid down in the Japanese Treaty Act. Viscount Haldane, one of those who had taken part in the *Brooks-Bidlake* case, stoutly insisted that in the second case 'a wholly different question' presented itself, because the employment of Chinese labour was not in issue. Perhaps wisely, he refrained from commenting on the *Union Colliery Company* or *Tommey Homma* cases, though he hinted (contrary to the latter) that the Provincial statute might well have conflicted not only with the Japanese Treaty Act, but also with the British North America Act. Yet Viscount Haldane made it clear that the new decision did not affect the previous appeal, since it was 'concerned with the principle of the statute of 1921 and not with that of merely individual instances in which particular kinds of property are being administered'. In the result Brooks-Bidlake could not have their licence, because they employed Chinese labour, which was not protected by the Japanese Treaty Act, and the Provincial Government could continue to insist on the exclusion of Chinese and Japanese from employment on Crown property, provided that they avoided enacting legislation, or, at any rate, legislation which was unskilfully drafted!

These four cases illustrate some of the worst defects of the traditional English judicial approach, by which legal issues affecting the rights and liberties of individuals and minorities are treated as

30. *Attorney-General of British Columbia* v. *Attorney-General of Canada* [1924] A.C. 203.

31. i.e. Viscount Haldane and Lord Shaw, both Liberals who were probably in the minority in the *Brooks-Bidlake* case among the Conservative Viscount Cave L.C., and Lords Dunedin and Carson. Once more the altered composition of the Privy Council appears to have produced a marked shift of judicial attitude in this series of cases.

linguistic problems to be solved within a moral vacuum, regardless of the social consequences which might be expected to follow. Even though public bodies and interests were directly involved in each case – the Provincial legislature, the franchise and the management and licensing of Crown property – in none of them did the Privy Council recognize that there was any principle of public trust or public policy which required equality of treatment. Even though the cases affected the rights of Canadian-born citizens of Chinese and Japanese descent, as well as aliens and naturalized British subjects, the Privy Council took it for granted that they could be lawfully discriminated against by public authorities solely on racial grounds, and considered only the narrow constitutional question of the respective competences of the Dominion and Provincial legislatures. And, despite the fact that, under the Canadian Constitution (unlike those of the United States or Australia) residuary power is vested in the central rather than the local government, in two of the cases the Privy Council interpreted a provision of the British North America Act which was at least ambiguous, so as to vest greater power in the Provincial legislature. As one Canadian writer has fairly complained,

judicial misconstruction . . . [of the British North America Act] has nullified, with only a few exceptions, the residuary power of the Dominion, and has transferred this power to provincial domain under the guise of property and civil rights (Schmeiser, 1964, p. 9).

Even in the two cases in which the Privy Council invalidated the discriminatory statutes, they did so upon such technical grounds that their decisions had little effect upon the discrimination itself. Taken together, the four cases cannot be rationally reconciled; they contain none of those qualities of certainty, predictability and consistency which are so prized in the Common Law; and they are blind to considerations of equality or individual justice.

After the Second World War, one further case was decided by the Privy Council,[32] which affected the rights of Japanese Canadians not only to employment and the franchise, but to live with their families in Canada. The case challenged the validity of three Orders-in-Council, made in December 1945 by the Governor-General, under the War

32. *Cooperative Committee on Japanese Canadians* v. *Attorney-General for Canada* [1947] A.C. 87.

Measures Act 1914, after the War had ended. These Orders authorized the Minister of Labour to deport to Japan not only Japanese nationals resident in Canada, but also naturalized and natural-born British subjects 'of the Japanese race', together with their wives and children under sixteen years of age. One Order also provided for the appointment of a Commission to investigate the activities, loyalties and extent of cooperation of such persons with the Canadian Government during the War, with a view to making recommendations for deportation.

One of the many arguments put forward on behalf of the Japanese Canadians was that the expression 'of the Japanese race' was too vague to be capable of being applied to ascertained persons, especially since as a result they would lose their status as British subjects. As will be apparent later (p. 66), this is an approach which English courts have adopted in another context. Here, however, the argument was rejected. Lord Wright expressed the matter tersely:

All that can be said is that questions may arise as to the true construction of the phrase and as to its applicability to any particular persons, but difficulties of construction do not affect the validity of the Order.

The Privy Council also rejected the submission that, at the time when the Orders-in-Council came into force, no emergency existed which would justify such action being taken under the War Measures Act. As in the earlier cases, the Privy Council nowhere recognized that what were in issue were the fundamental rights of citizenship of British subjects, born and resident in Canada.

In 1949, the Canadian Parliament abolished the right of appeal to the Privy Council: that tribunal will therefore never again have to decide questions affecting the rights of Chinese and Japanese Canadians. And in 1960 the Canadian Bill of Rights Act was passed with the object of guaranteeing the right of the individual, without discrimination by reason of race, national origin or colour, to life, liberty, security of the person and enjoyment of property, and to equality before the law. The Bill of Rights Act also amends the War Measures Act so as to ensure that its provisions will come into force only when the Governor in Council has proclaimed that a state of war, invasion, or insurrection exists or is likely. Although there are weaknesses in its enforcement provisions, the Bill of Rights has turned the Canadian Courts unequivocally in the direction of equality. It has filled the moral vacuum in which the Privy Council for so long vacillated.

In many respects these decisions of the Privy Council merely reflected the social values of their time, and probably, even if there had been a Bill of Rights to guide the judges, they would not have reached different conclusions. For example, the United States Constitution contains a Bill of Rights, but, until the 1930s the Supreme Court did not interpret the Constitution with due regard for the rights of black Americans.[33] On the other hand, it is ironical that, at the same time as the Supreme Court were failing to uphold the constitutional rights of Negroes, they, unlike the Privy Council, did exercise their judicial powers to protect the rights of oriental Americans and aliens.[34] Even their notorious decision in the *Korematsu* case,[35] which upheld the Government's right to exclude citizens of Japanese ancestry from a part of California, concerned a period of critical emergency during the Second World War, and was based on the Court's express finding that there was such an emergency. On balance, the existence of a Bill of Rights at least encouraged the American judiciary to reflect upon the ethical values and social implications of their jurisprudence and to make them explicit in their judgments.

Racial discrimination in Africa

The worst instance in which racial discrimination was upheld by the Privy Council occurred in 1931 in *Kaderbhai's* case[36] – worst because of the historical background to the case, the relatively recent date of the decision, and the consequences for the future development of race relations in Kenya.

33. See e.g. *Ex parte Commonwealth of Virginia* 100 US 339 (1880); *Pace* v. *Alabama* 106 US 583 (1883); *Civil Rights Cases* 109 US 3 (1883); *Ex parte Yarborough* 110 US 651 (1884); *Plessey* v. *Ferguson* 136 US 537 (1896). See generally Griswold (1964, pp. 109–17).

34. See *United States* v. *Wong Kim Ark* 169 US 649 (1898); *Yick Wo* v. *Hopkins* 118 US 356 (1886).

35. *Korematsu* v. *United States* 323 US 214 (1944).

36. *Commissioner for Local Government Lands and Settlement* v. *Kaderbhai* [1931] A.C. 652.

The issues which arose in *Kaderbhai's* case can be traced to the origins of European settlement in Kenya at the beginning of this century (Sorrenson, 1968). Indians had been introduced into the East Africa Protectorate, with the British government's official encouragement, at the end of the nineteenth century, as troops, as labour for the railway, as subordinate clerical staff, as farmers and as traders. And from the first, pressure had mounted from the European settlers for the British government to exclude them from the highlands and urban areas. In 1903, Sir Charles Eliot, Commissioner of the Protectorate had recommended that Indian settlement should be confined to the lowlands, and that the highlands should be reserved for Europeans. His successors accepted this policy without question and extended segregation to urban land.

The segregation was bitterly, if unsuccessfully, opposed by the Indians. Their main complaints arose from restrictions imposed by the local administration on the acquisition of urban and suburban land, and, particularly in Nairobi, restrictions designed to reserve the most desirable commercial and residential sites for Europeans. Their demands were largely ignored.

In East Africa, as in South Africa, the British government paid lip service to the ideal of equal rights for all British subjects, irrespective of creed and colour, while continuing to accept the practice of discrimination (Sorrenson, 1968, pp. 161–2).

In 1906, this policy was officially endorsed by Lord Elgin, Secretary of State in Campbell-Bannerman's Liberal Government. In 1907, the local Lands Board urged the Government to pass a new Crown Land Bill to make white occupation of the highlands exclusive. Elgin replied:

With regard to the question of granting land to Indians, it is not consonant with the views of His Majesty's Government to impose *legal* restriction on any particular section of the community, but as a matter of administrative convenience grants in the upland area should not be made to Indians.

In 1909, there was a further attempt by the white settlers to write discrimination into the law. The Legislative Council passed a Crown Lands Bill permitting notices of auctions of town land to specify 'whether the plots or any of them may not be acquired by the Asiatic or native'. Covenants were to be able to be inserted in the leases of these plots preventing the lessees from transferring possession to an Asiatic or native, and similar restrictions were to be placed on agricultural land. However, the Bill required the assent of the Colonial Office, and, in 1911, this was specifically refused. It did not prevent the settlers and local officials from achieving their ends by administrative means, with the knowledge and consent of the Colonial Office.

In 1915, after several further drafts had been rejected, a new Crown Ordinance Bill was passed and approved by the Colonial Office. Several of its provisions allowed discrimination against non-Europeans to be practised by rules under the Ordinance and by administrative means. As far as town lots were concerned, the Commissioner of Lands could, before an auction, determine 'the special covenants, if any, which shall be inserted in the lease'. Notices for an auction of agricultural lands were to state 'whether persons other than Europeans will be permitted to bid for the lease of farms'. There was to be an implied covenant in each lease granted to a European that he would not, without the consent of the Governor in Council, appoint or allow a non-European to manage or otherwise to occupy or control the land leased. Finally, all transfers of property which concerned persons of different races had to be notified to the Commissioner of Lands and could be vetoed by the Governor in Council.

The Ordinance was 'an ingenious compromise between the demands of European settlers for total exclusion of Indians from holding land, particularly in the highlands, and the concern of the Colonial Office to prevent discrimination from being written into the law' (Sorrenson, 1968, p. 175). However, although the Ordinance authorized the Commissioner to determine whether 'special covenants' should be inserted in the lease of town plots, it did not provide that such covenants should be racially restrictive; nor, in the case of town plots, as opposed to agricultural lands, did it authorize him to state whether non-Europeans should be permitted to bid at auctions. And it was because the Ordinance was silent on these two matters that *Kaderbhai's* case arose.

The Commissioner gave notice of sale by auction of town plots in

Mombasa and stipulated that only Europeans were to be allowed to bid. The notice also contained a special condition that houses built on the land should not be permitted to be used as places of residence for any Asiatic or African other than a domestic servant. In other words, the Commissioner had acted exactly as though the abortive 1909 Crown Lands Bill had become law, and what he had done was not expressly authorized by the 1915 Ordinance which contained the actual source of his powers.

Kaderbhai, a British Indian subject asked the Courts to permit him to bid at the auction and also to cancel the racial restriction on the use of houses built on the land. The East African Court of Appeals unanimously held that he should be allowed to bid at the auction, but refused to cancel the condition restricting the use of houses. The Privy Council overruled the East African Court, deciding that Kaderbhai could not even bid, and that the Commissioner was fully entitled to impose racially restrictive conditions on the property sold. As in the past, the Judges avoided the ethical and social implications of their decision by retreating within the pale of 'strict' legal reasoning. In Lord Atkin's words

the Courts are concerned only with the bare question of law – namely, the powers of the Commissioner under the Ordinance. Questions of policy, or, in other words, how the legal powers should be exercised, are not matters for the legal tribunal, but have to be determined by the appropriate constitutional authority.

There was nothing in the Ordinance which required the Privy Council to reach this conclusion, even as a matter of strict legal reasoning. The Ordinance treated notices of the auction of town plots differently from notices of the auction of farm leases. Only in the latter case was the Commissioner expressly authorized to state whether non-Europeans would be permitted to bid; so, it would have been a perfectly rational interpretation of the Ordinance that he could not give notice excluding non-Europeans from bidding at an auction for the sale of *urban* land.

Nor was there anything in the Ordinance to suggest that the special covenants which the Commissioner could admittedly insert in the leases of town plots could be racially restrictive. His case was simply that the terms of the Ordinance did not prevent him from imposing racial restrictions. A bold Privy Council could therefore have referred to the fact that the Commissioner was a public official, and have decided that, in the absence of clear language to the contrary, he ought not to discriminate arbitrarily or capriciously between different sections of the community in exercising his legal powers.[37]

Instead, the Privy Council argued that, just as the Commissioner could restrict the sale and use of town plots for particular commercial purposes (e.g. for wharfs, warehouses or factories) by particular people (i.e. wharfingers, warehousemen and factory owners) so he could lawfully restrict their sale and use to particular racial groups. Despite their professed concern with the 'bare question of law', the judges were, perhaps only half consciously, making a value judgment that racial restrictions had as rational and legitimate a basis as commercial restrictions. Indeed, Lord Atkin accepted that racial restrictions were justifiable, because property values might decline if town plots were sold to coloured purchasers.[38]

Perhaps this was the real premise upon which the decision was based, partially concealed by the logical style of the Privy Council's reasoning. In any event, there was no ambiguity about the effect of *Kaderbhai's* case. It gave legitimacy to the practice of racial discrimination by a public official, without a hint of judicial disapproval. And, in the result, it gave the white settlers what they had tried to obtain in their 1909 Bill but had been refused by the Colonial Office in 1911. Henceforth, British subjects of Asian descent could be freely excluded from urban as well as agricultural land.

In another case[39] involving residential segregation in Africa, the Privy Council were driven to uphold a discriminatory law, although on this occasion the result was less open to criticism because the words of the statute were less ambiguous. The Municipal Council of

37. c.f. *Cumings* v. *Birkenhead Corporation* [1971] 2 All E.R. 881 (C.A.) at p. 885 *per* Lord Denning, M.R.

38. Lord Atkin was the most distinguished member of the Privy Council (the other two being Lord Blanesburgh and Sir Lancelot Sanderson), and it was Lord Atkin who gave the reasons for the decision. The case was argued by two outstanding leaders of the English Bar, Sir Stafford Cripps, K.C., the Solicitor-General, for the Commissioner, and Sir Thomas Inskip, K.C. for Kaderbhai.

39. *Madrassa Anjuman Islamia of Kholwad* v. *Municipal Council of Johannesburg* [1922] 1 A.C. 500.

Johannesburg sought to punish the officers of a company for contempt of court. The company had been set up for the purpose of educating and maintaining Muslim children born in a certain town in India and living in Johannesburg. A municipal statute forbade the owner of a stand on public property in Johannesburg from per-mitting 'any Asiatic, native or coloured person (other than the bona fide servant of a white person for the time being residing upon the stand) to reside on or occupy the stand', and a Court order had been obtained restraining the company from allowing an Asiatic named Dangor, or any other Asiatic or coloured person, from residing on or occupying a particular stand. Dangor, who had previously been the tenant of the stand, converted his business into a limited company, which he controlled, and to which the Municipal Council then leased the stand. Neither Dangor nor any of his 'Asiatic or coloured' subordinates resided on the stand, but they did carry on business there, and the Municipal Council alleged that in so doing they had 'occupied' the stand in violation of the statute and in contempt of the Court order.

The Privy Council held that the company's officers were indeed in contempt of Court. This is how Viscount Cave summarized the position:

the object of these provisions was to prevent any Asiatic, native or coloured persons, for sanitary and other reasons, from dwelling or being habitually among the indigenous white population to whom the stands were granted. . . . [I]t is plain from the fact that the prohibition is made to depend on race or colour, that it is the physical presence of the persons described, and not their right of possession in a legal or technical sense, which the statute had in view. . . . Dangor Ltd, having no corporeal existence, could not occupy the stand in the above sense. It was occupied as well after as before the injunction by Dangor with his coloured staff.

No doubt this was a faithful interpretation of the intention of those who had framed the statute; any other construction would have been artificial and strained. But it is interesting that in this case the Privy Council were prepared to reject a strictly technical approach which was open to them, and which would have limited the effect of statute and acquitted the unfortunate Dangor of contempt for having made use of property leased by him from the Municipal Council. They could have held that the company rather than its officers occupied the stand. Indeed, such a view would have been more consistent with the traditional reluctance of the English judiciary to pierce the corporate veil. But here the Privy Council seems to have shared the Municipal Council's view that for 'sanitary and other reasons' it was undesirable for coloured people habitually to be among the 'indigenous white population'. At any rate, there was nothing in the Privy Council's decision to suggest a contrary view.

It is interesting to contrast these colonial cases with a much more recent Privy Council decision involving the interpretation of a constitutional Bill of Rights in an independent African State. In *Akar* v. *Attorney General of Sierra Leone*,[40] the Privy Council declared in a majority opinion (Lord Guest dissenting) that Sierra Leone Acts of Parliament purporting to amend the Constitution (which came into force in 1961 when the former Protectorate attained full independence) were unconstitutional. By introducing as a requirement of citizenship a racial description 'Negro African descent' these statutes offended against the letter and flouted the spirit of the Constitution which protected the individual from 'discrimination on the ground of race'.

The appellant was born in the Protectorate in 1927 of an indigenous Sierra Leone mother and a Lebanese father who had been born and bred in Senegal and had never been to Lebanon. The appellant, who lived in Freetown, was the Director of Broadcasting and of the National Dance Troupe and Secretary of the Hotels and Tourist Board. The legislation purported to amend the Constitution by inserting after the words 'Every person' the words 'of Negro African descent'. If this amendment were valid, the appellant would be deprived retroactively of his citizenship, because neither he, nor his father, nor his father's father was a 'Negro'.

Lord Morris, giving the majority opinion, stated that the amendment was 'discriminatory' within the meaning of the Constitution, because some persons and not others would have disabilities and restrictions attributable wholly or mainly to descriptions by race. It had been argued that the general prohibition against discrimination did not apply by reason of an exception in the Constitution which permitted persons to be subjected to 'any disability or restriction . . .

40. [1970] A.C. 853.

which, having regard to its nature and to special circumstances pertaining to those persons . . . is reasonably justified in a democratic society'. Their Lordships could see no 'special circumstances' pertaining to the appellant or people in his position which made the legislation reasonably justifiable in a democratic society.

Lord Guest said that he dissented on one point only, but it was a critical point. Though the courts were the guardians of the Constitution, he believed that in interpreting it they should tread warily. They could not inquire into the motives or policy behind a particular piece of legislation. They could only as a matter of construction decide whether the Act was or was not within the powers of the Constitution. As a matter of construction, Lord Guest had no hesitation in holding that the statute dealing as it did with citizenship was 'reasonably justifiable in a democratic society'. Any democratic society must have control over the qualifications for citizenship and he would hold that the statute was *intra vires*.

The *Akar* case illustrates the value of an unequivocal declaration of public policy in guiding the judges when they interpret the law. Lord Guest's dissent also provides a healthy reminder that few words are so unequivocal that they cannot be construed in different senses by different judges, and also that the traditional subordination of the British judiciary to the sovereignty of Parliament might well survive the abolition of that sovereignty and the creation of a written Constitution with entrenched rights and freedoms.

Racial discrimination in the United Kingdom

Fortunately, English judges have not been called upon in modern times to give effect to racialist legislation within this country. In one case,[41] an attempt was made by a British steamship company to persuade an English court that Lascars employed on their ships were not 'seamen' within the meaning of the Merchant Shipping Act 1894, but were governed by Indian Acts which required far less crew space to be provided for them than for Europeans. The Merchant Shipping Act discriminated in other respects against Lascars (see pp. 223–4), but the court had no difficulty in deciding that, since the particular

41. *Peninsular & Oriental Steam Navigation Co.* v. *The King* [1901] 2 K.B. 686.

provision drew no distinction between Lascar and European seamen, there was no reason why such a distinction should be made. If equality before the law were to have any meaning, the court could hardly have decided otherwise.

The kind of situation which has been before the courts on several occasions has involved racial discrimination, not by statute or public act, but by private persons against others. And, as in the Privy Council case, with few exceptions, the courts have not been prepared to invalidate such discrimination, and so have indirectly given it the force of law.

Employment

A notorious case involving the right to work in one's occupation came before the House of Lords in 1919.[42] Hugo Weinberger had been a naturalized British subject for thirty years; but he was born in Germany. In 1895 he had paid an entrance fee of five hundred guineas to join the London Stock Exchange, and for twenty-one years he had renewed his membership by paying an annual subscription of thirty guineas. He was married to an Englishwoman of German origin; his two sons were members of their School's Officers' Training Corps, and his wife and two daughters had been engaged in patriotic work since the outbreak of the First World War; two of his partners

42. *Weinberger* v. *Inglis* [1919] A.C. 606. The House of Lords might have relied upon s. 3(1) of the British Nationality and Status of Aliens Act 1914 as evidence that public policy favoured equal rights for naturalized British subjects. That section provided that a naturalized British subject was 'entitled to all political and other rights, powers and privileges . . . to which a natural-born British subject is entitled . . . and . . . [has] to all intents and purposes the status of a natural-born British subject'. However, in *London Corporation* v. *Wolff* [1917] 86 L.J.K.B. 534, the Divisional court rejected such an argument. In that case, a person of German origin, who had been naturalized in 1889, had applied to the London Corporation for a licence to carry on an employment agency in the City for naturalized subjects of German, Austrian or Hungarian birth. No suggestion had been made against his personal character or loyalty, but the licensing authority had refused his application solely on the ground that, during the circumstances of the War with Germany, it was not justifiable to give facilities to such persons. The Divisional court decided that the 1914 Act did not preclude the licensing authority from taking into account the applicant's alien origins, and remitted the case to the authority to consider whether the applicant, being of such origins, was in fact not suitable to hold a licence.

were American citizens and the third was British. When he applied as usual for renewal in 1917, some members, who had formed an organization called the Stock Exchange Anti-German Union, objected to his re-election on the sole ground that he had been born in Bavaria. As a result, Weinberger was not re-elected, and could not continue to practise in his profession. He claimed that the decision of the Committee of the Stock Exchange was arbitrary and capricious and based on irrelevant considerations. But the House of Lords decided that, although Weinberger's loyalty and integrity were beyond reproach, the Committee had exercised their discretion in good faith, and the court would not interfere with what they had done.

Understandably, in the recent case of *Nagle* v. *Feilden*,[43] Lord Justice Salmon declared himself to be astonished that the House of Lords had decided, on the facts of *Weinberger's* case, that the Stock Exchange Committee had not acted capriciously in refusing to re-elect him. *Nagle's* case strongly suggests that the unfortunate Weinberger would have received better treatment from the courts today. It also looks an important development in English judicial attitudes towards public policy and unfair discrimination. Miss Nagle was a horse trainer of long-standing, but she was refused a trainer's licence by the Jockey Club because it was the Club's practice not to grant a licence to a woman in any circumstances. She claimed that this practice was invalid because it was against public policy, and, at a preliminary stage, the Court of Appeal decided that her case was at least arguable. Lord Denning M.R. stated it as a general principle of English law that a person

has a right to work at his trade or profession without being unjustly excluded from it at the whim of those having the governance of it. If they make a rule which enables them to reject his application arbitrarily or capriciously, not reasonably, that rule is bad. It is against public policy. The courts will not give effect to it.

Lord Justice Danckwerts declared that

the law relating to public policy cannot remain immutable. It must change with the passage of time. The wind of change blows upon it,

43. [1966] 2 Q.B. 633 (C.A.).

and he referred to the Sex Disqualification (Removal) Act 1919, not as applying to the facts of the case, but as showing 'the position of present day thought'. And Lord Justice Salmon explained that it would be as capricious to refuse Miss Nagle a licence solely on the ground that she was a woman as 'to refuse a man a licence solely because of the colour of his hair', or as he would doubtless have added, the colour of his skin.

Nagle's case is an important exception in this chapter, for it is a rare example of the creative development of the Common Law by the courts in response to changing social values. The Court of Appeal were assisted by the existence of a statute from which to infer public policy, but their decision went well beyond anything required by Parliament. As a result, if someone were in future to be denied employment in his trade or profession, solely because of his race or colour, by a licensing body, or a professional association, or a trade union controlling a closed shop,[44] the courts would probably have granted him a remedy, even if Parliament had not provided a remedy in the Race Relations Act 1968. But *Nagle's* case applies only to monopoly situations, and even the most creative Court of Appeal could not develop the Common Law to provide a remedy for the most common forms of racial discrimination which have arisen in employment. The Common Law could not, for example, compel an

44. In *Edwards* v. *Society of Graphical and Allied Trades* [1971] Ch. 354, the Court of Appeal applied the *Nagle* principle in this situation. After noting that the power to withdraw a member's union card could deprive him of his livelihood, Lord Denning, M.R. stated that 'The courts of this country will not allow so great a power to be exercised arbitrarily or capriciously or with unfair discrimination, neither in the making of rules, nor in the enforcement of them.' Sachs L.J. considered that 'A rule that in these days of closed shops entitles a trade union to withdraw the card of a capable craftsman of good character . . . for any capricious reason such as . . . having incurred the personal enmity, for non-union reasons, of a single fellow member, the colour of his hair, the colour of his skin, the accent of his speech, or the holding of a job desired by someone not yet a member, is plainly in restraint of trade. . . . It cannot be said that a rule that enabled such capricious and despotic action is proper to the 'purposes' of this or indeed any trade union. It is thus not protected by Section 3 [of the Trade Union Act 1871] and is moreover ultra vires.' It is not clear how far this approach will be taken by the courts. Would they, for example, apply the same principle not only to a trade union, or a licensing body, but to a major employer controlling the supply of labour in a particular area in an arbitrary or capricious manner?

ordinary employer to recruit workers, or to train or promote them, or to provide conditions of work for them, without racial discrimination. *Nagle's* case is a great landmark, but it also marks the point at which land ends.

The result of another recent decision[45] of the Court of Appeal was at first sight opposed to racial discrimination in employment, but on closer inspection it reveals the hidden dangers of the Common Law. The Scala Ballroom was opened in Wolverhampton in 1958, and its proprietors decided to deny entry to all coloured people. As soon as the Ballroom was licensed, the Musicians' Union informed the proprietors that none of its members would perform there until the colour bar was lifted. The proprietors asked the court to restrain the Union's officials from persuading members not to perform at the Ballroom. They claimed that the actions of the Union's officials constituted an unlawful conspiracy. Evidence was given on behalf of the Union that it had many coloured members and that it was considered essential to the interests of members that all manifestations of the colour bar should be lawfully opposed. The court held that the officials had not acted unlawfully, because the purpose of their actions had been the lawful one of protecting the interests and livelihood of their members.

However, the court indicated that the Ballroom proprietors were entitled to maintain the colour bar 'in their own business interests'. The decision did not prevent racial discrimination; it merely allowed the Musicians' Union to act on its own initiative to protect its members' interests. The case might therefore have been cited subsequently to justify similar actions taken by a trade union with a mainly white membership against any employer who *refused* to maintain a colour bar; for, if the test of the legality of the Union's actions was whether they were regarded as being in the interests of members, self-interest could, in a different case, lie in the preservation or creation of a colour bar.

The relevant law was uncertain. On the one hand, it was well established that workers who resorted to strike action 'in contemplation or furtherance of a trade dispute' were protected by the Trade Disputes Act 1906, and, after the *Scala Ballroom* decision it was at least arguable that a strike against the employment of workers

45. *Scala Ballroom* (*Wolverhampton*) *Ltd* v. *Ratcliffe* [1958] 3 All E.R. 220.

of a particular race or colour was such a trade dispute.[46] On the other hand, it had been suggested in an earlier case[47] that, if the object of the collective action of the workers was 'a dislike of the religious views or the politics or the race or colour' of the person affected, it would not be a 'legitimate purpose' so as to be a defence to an action for conspiracy. Nor was the legal position entirely clarified as a result of *Rookes* v. *Barnard*[48] and its subsequent reversal by the Trade Disputes Act 1965 (Wedderburn, 1971, pp. 371–3). However, the matter has fortunately been put beyond doubt by the Race Relations Act 1968 (section 12, see p. 169), which makes it unlawful for any person to induce or incite others to commit acts of racial discrimination, for this would include strike action as well as any other form of inducement or incitement.

Insurance

The limits of the traditional Common Law approach were harshly revealed in the field of insurance, in the little-known case of *Horne* v. *Poland*.[49] Harry Horne was born in 1887 in Rumania, where his father was a Hebrew teacher. Horne came to England when he was twelve years old, but, although he lived with his parents in London, went to school there, adopted an English name, and married an Englishwoman, he never became naturalized. Twenty-two years after arriving in this country, he took out an insurance policy, under which he later claimed £500 from the underwriters for a loss resulting from a burglary.

It is a rule of insurance law that a person has a duty to disclose all material facts about himself at the time when he enters into the contract of insurance. If he fails to do so, he cannot enforce the insurance policy in the courts because he has no right to claim under it. The

46. See generally, Kahn-Freund (1959, at pp. 69–71), where regret is expressed that the effect of section 1 of the Trade Disputes Act 1906 remained undetermined by the *Scala Ballroom* decision. This section is now replaced by section 132 of the Industrial Relations Act 1971.

47. *Crofter Harris Tweed Co.* v. *Veitch* [1942] A.C. 435 (H.L.) at p. 451 *per* Viscount Maugham; see also Clerk and Lindsell on Torts (12th edn, 1961) p. 336; Winfield on Tort (7th edn, 1963) p. 671.

48. [1964] A.C. 1129 (H.L.).

49. [1922] 2 K.B. 364.

underwriters disputed their liability to indemnify Horne on this ground, contending that he had failed to disclose a material fact about himself – his alien origin. The court decided that the underwriters were right: Horne's alien origin was material, and, by failing to disclose it to them he had lost the right to be indemnified under a policy for which he had paid. Mr Justice Lush conceded that the mere fact that a person was a foreigner was not inevitably a material fact, but he went on:

The insurance included, among other risks, loss by burglary or theft, and the risk would vary according to the honesty and good faith of the insured, the methods which he follows and the care he took, in his views of duty, the way in which he would regard his social and legal obligations, and other matters. It is impossible to say that matters such as nationality, caste and early domicil cannot be of importance in judging as to the risk that underwriters run in entering into such a contract. To say that is to say that there are no racial differences as regards training and education and the other matters which I have mentioned. I say nothing, of course, against the national characteristics of the race to which the plaintiff belongs; that is not the question.

But that *was* the question, despite the judge's final disclaimer. What the underwriters had sought to do was to escape from their contractual obligations solely on the assumption that Horne's racial and national origins increased the risk of dishonesty or bad faith on his part. Horne had received his secondary education in England, had lived here for the whole of his adult life, and had made his home here. The underwriters produced no evidence to suggest that he was untrustworthy or careless, or that people with his background were higher risks than others. They had not asked him about his origins when the contract was made. Horne was denied his indemnity because the judge accepted a prejudiced, unsupported assumption by the underwriters that there were relevant racial or national differences, which persisted in spite of his long residence in and close identity with this country.

In this case the court did not maintain a neutral attitude; it decided positively that race was material and it sanctioned overt discrimination. The effect of the court's discrimination was almost the same as if Parliament had passed a statute requiring the disclosure of a person's racial or national origins before he could enter into a valid contract of insurance. Indeed, Mr Justice Lush specifically suggested, with no sense of irony, that it 'would be more just that underwriters should inquire as to the nationality of proposed insurers if they attach importance to it'. And the editors of the standard collection of drafting precedents for lawyers conscientiously followed his recommendations, and included a question about nationality of origin in their model proposal form for burglary insurance policies.[50]

Horne's case has fairly been described (Hasson, 1969, p. 630) as representing 'the high-water mark in terms of injustice and absurdity that a doctrine purporting to apply conduct in conformity with "absolute good faith" has yet achieved', and as a 'gross essay in xenophobia'. Yet no subsequent decision has challenged the premise of the case. The correctness of the decision seems to have been taken for granted, even if its effect has been somewhat limited. For example, in *Becker* v. *Marshall*,[51] Lord Justice Scrutton remarked, *obiter*, that the presence of a foreign name might put 'the underwriter on inquiry as to foreign nationality, if he thought it important'. And, in another case,[52] it was held that the duty to disclose foreign birth did not arise in the case of the insured who had been born in Russia but had come to England at the age of five where he had spent the next sixty years of his life.

Unfortunately, these cases made it possible that an English court would 'follow "industry practice", and hold that a failure on the part of the insured to reveal his nationality (and possibly also his race) voids the policy' (Hasson, 1969, p. 631). The Courts could easily, of course, have reached the opposite conclusion by refusing to recognize that national or racial differences were material, or by treating the matter as one of public policy. But there was nothing about their earlier decisions to suggest that they would have been likely to do so.

However, although these insurance cases deserve to be strongly criticized, it has once more to be recognized that there are limits to

50. *Encyclopedia of Forms and Precedents* (3rd edn, 1944), vol. 7, p. 491.

51. [1922] 12 Ll.L.Rep. 413 (C.A.). The cases are discussed by Hasson (1969, at pp. 629–31).

52. *Lyons* v. *J. W. Bentley Ltd* (1943) 77 Ll.L.Rep. 335. See also *Carlton* v. *Park* (1922) 10 Ll.L.Rep. 818.

what can be accomplished by the Common Law, which the most enlightened judge could not have exceeded. Even if, in *Horne's* case, the court had decided that Horne was entitled to be indemnified under the insurance policy, it could not have given a remedy to anyone if the underwriters had subsequently refused to insure Jews or people of alien origin altogether. The court could not have required them to do business without discrimination, for at Common Law, except in monopoly situations, everyone is free to contract or not to contract as he pleases. Parliament alone could effectively prevent racial discrimination in the provision of insurance facilities; and it has now done so (see pp. 263–5).[53]

Housing

The same limitations of the Common Law – its deference to private contractual law-making, judicial reluctance to adapt concepts of public policy, and the essentially passive character of the Common Law – also made it incapable of combating racial discrimination in the field of housing. In one area the Common Law probably would provide a remedy. If two or more people agreed to act together to prevent someone of a particular race or colour from obtaining a house or flat, it is at least arguable that they would be liable for damages for conspiracy, provided that it could be established that their main object was to harm the victim rather than to protect their own legitimate interests.[54] Otherwise, however, in the absence of legislation, the courts would be unable to help someone who was refused housing accommodation, or even the services of an estate agent, solely on racial grounds, for there is no Common Law duty to do business with anyone. But if the owner in fact lets or sells his property, there are some circumstances in which he would not be permitted, even in the absence of legislation, to prevent it from being sub-let or re-sold by the tenant or new owner to people of a particular race or colour.

The position is better established in the case of lettings and assign-

53. By Race Relations Act 1968, section 2.
54. cf. *Quinn* v. *Leathem* [1901] A.C. 495 (H.L.); *Crofter Harris Tweed Co.* v. *Veitch* [1942] A.C. 435 (H.L.); *Mogul Steamship Co.* v. *McGregor Gow & Co.* [1892] A.C. 25; *Huntley* v. *Thornton* [1957] 1 All E.R. 234.

ments of leases than of outright sales of freeholds. If the lease contains a restriction on the transfer of the property without the landlord's consent and goes on to provide that such consent shall not be withheld arbitrarily, then, at Common Law, the courts would regard it as arbitrary to withhold consent on grounds of race or colour, and, they would not recognize the landlord's racial veto. In one such case,[55] it was decided that the landlords of a public house could not withhold consent to the transfer of the lease on the ground that the purchaser's name (Appenrodt) and nationality of origin would tend to depreciate the trade of the public house. The court was able to reach this conclusion because the lease expressly stated that the landlords' consent should not be arbitrarily withheld; but, if the lease had given an unqualified power of veto to the landlords, the court would probably not have intervened to permit the transfer to be made to Appenrodt. However, the Landlord and Tenant Act 1927 now provides[56] that, whatever the lease might contain, where the landlord's consent to the transfer of a tenancy is required, such consent must not be unreasonably withheld. Probably the Courts would regard it as unreasonable to withhold consent on grounds of race or colour. This was certainly the view expressed by the Home Secretary during the Second Reading debate on the Race Relations Bill 1965, but he explained[57] the reason for including a provision[58] on this subject as being that 'in the absence of any clear judicial authority, the Government have thought it right to include this provision in the Bill so as to put the matter beyond all doubt'.

The Home Secretary's doubt was largely created by the extraordinary case of *Schlegel* v. *Corcoran*,[59] decided not in this country but in Eire, during the Second World War. It was there held that the landlord had not acted unreasonably, under the Irish equivalent of the Landlord and Tenant Act, in withholding consent to the transfer of rooms for a dental practice to one Nathaniel Gross, because he was Jewish. The judgment contained classic expressions of racial

55. *Mills* v. *Cannon Brewery Co. Ltd* [1920] 2 Ch. 38.
56. Section 19(1).
57. Sir Frank Soskice Q.C., M.P., *Hansard* (H.C.) (Fifth Series), vol. 711, col. 934, 3 May 1965.
58. Race Relations Act 1965, section 5.
59. [1942] I.R. 19.

prejudice. For example Mr Justice Gavan Duffy confidently asserted that:

no one, I suppose will deny that the landlady might safely refuse a Hottentot for the sake of her domestic amenities though he happened to be a civilized specimen, but I want to put the case of some not obviously repulsive assignee.

And again:

the Plaintiff may well think that [the dental practice] . . . may, under Mr Gross, develop a Jewish complexion, and such an anticipation is not groundless in a locality with a number of Jewish residents.

And:

the Plaintiff's objection has been characterized as a caprice and as mere prejudice; but caprice is not the right word for an anti-Semitism, which far from being a peculiar crotchet, is notoriously shared by a number of other citizens, and, if prejudice be the right word, the antagonism between Christian and Jew has its roots in nearly 2000 years of history and is too prevalent as a habit of mind to be dismissed off-hand.

So Gross was not allowed to have the tenancy which he had bought, and a clear statutory requirement that the landlady's consent should not be unreasonably withheld was interpreted to sanction racial discrimination.

Apart from the unlikely possibility that an English Court might follow *Schlegel's* case, it would still be open to a landlord, despite the 1927 Act, to impose racial restrictions either by prohibiting the transfer of the property altogether, or by making it a condition precedent to the transfer that the tenant should first offer to surrender the lease to the landlord,[60] who could then accept the surrender and discriminate in re-letting the property. Certainly, no case has ever been decided by the English courts which would justify the optimistic view once expressed by the Attorney-General, Sir Hartley Shawcross, that

a clause in a lease or other agreement discriminating between different classes of His Majesty's subjects on the ground of colour may well be void under the existing law as being contrary to the rules of public policy upheld by the English Courts.[61]

60. See *Adler* v. *Upper Grosvenor Street Investment Ltd* [1957] 1 W.L.R. 227.
61. *Hansard* (H.C.) (Fifth Series), vol. 470, cols. 2–3, 21 November 1949.

And the Common Law is at least as unclear about the effect of racial restrictions on the sale and resale of property. (Yet, oddly enough, although Parliament legislated to remove the doubt about lettings, in the Race Relations Act 1965, it did not include outright sales in that Act) (see pp. 241). The vendor of property is legally entitled to impose, as part of the terms of sale, restrictions on the land sold, which benefit land still retained by him. These restrictive covenants will 'run with the land'; that is, they will bind not only the person who buys from him, but also anyone who subsequently buys the land. And the benefit of these restrictive covenants may be transferred to anyone who later buys the land which is benefited by them. Restrictive covenants are therefore powerful instruments of private law-making, and, if *racially* restrictive covenants are legally enforceable, they may be used, as effectively as any racial legislation, to exclude members of a particular racial group from entire neighbourhoods. This is exactly what happened in countless North American suburbs and seaside resorts, until, first, the courts refused to recognize these racial covenants, and, later, the legislature provided a statutory remedy to those excluded by them.

The validity of racially restrictive covenants has never been determined in English law. It has never been decided, for example, that they are too vague to be given legal meaning, or that they do not confer sufficient benefit on the property retained by the vendor, or that they are against public policy. Probably, the English courts would, in the absence of legislation, have followed the example of the Canadian courts in this respect. The Ontario Court of Appeal there first upheld a covenant which provided that property in a summer resort should never be transferred to, or occupied by, 'any person of the Jewish, Hebrew, Semitic, Negro, or coloured race or blood', but the Canadian Supreme Court decided[62] that the covenant was void both because it was too vague and uncertain, and on the more doubtful ground that it was 'directed not to the land or to some mode of its use, but to transfer by act of the purchaser'. The Court confined its decision to these technical grounds, and did not follow the example set in an earlier case[63] in which the Ontario High

62. *Re Noble & Wolf* [1949] 4 D.L.R. 375 (Ontario Court of Appeal); [1951] 1 D.L.R. 321 (Supreme Court of Canada).
63. *Re Drummond Wren* [1945] 4 D.L.R. 674.

Court had based the same conclusion squarely on public policy.

In the United States, the Supreme Court eventually held[64] that, although private agreements to exclude persons of a particular race or colour from residential property did not in themselves violate the Constitution, it constituted 'State action' for state courts to enforce such agreements, and, since such agreements discriminated on racial grounds between different classes of citizens, it was unconstitutional for them to be enforced; for the courts, as an arm of government, to act in this way would be to deny the equal protection of the law to some citizens.

More recently, the Supreme Court has gone much further in a case[65] in which the main issue was whether purely private discrimination, unaided by any action on the part of government, violated a federal statute, passed during the post Civil War period of reconstruction. The Act provided that 'All citizens of the United States shall have the same right, in every State ... as is enjoyed by white citizens ... to inherit, purchase, lease, sell, hold and convey ... property.' The Supreme Court decided that the Act was constitutional and not an unlawful usurpation by Congress of the power

64. *Shelley* v. *Kraemer* 334 US 1 (1948). See also *Evans* v. *Newton* 382 US 296 (1966), where a tract of land had been bequeathed to the city of Macon, Georgia, to be used as a park for whites only. Although the city resigned as trustee and private trustees were appointed in an attempt to avoid any finding of 'State action', the Supreme Court held that the park was subject to the Fourteenth Amendment. The court observed that 'If a testator wanted to leave a school or center for the use of one race only and in no way implicated the State in the supervision, control or management of that facility, we assume *arguendo* that no constitutional difficulty would be encountered. This park, however, is in a different position. For years it was an integral part of the City of Macon's activities. . . . [I]t was swept, manicured, watered, patrolled and maintained by the City as a public facility for whites only, as well as granted tax exemption. . . . [T]he public character of this park requires that it be treated as a public institution subject to the command of the Fourteenth Amendment, regardless of who has title under State law.' And see *Evans* v. *Abney* (1969) 396 US 435, 90 Sup. Ct 628, where on a motion by the trustees, the Supreme Court held that the testator's property should revert to the heirs, and rejected arguments by the Negro intervenors that the trust should be saved by applying the *cy-près* doctrine to amend the terms of the will by striking out the racial restrictions and permitting integration (Douglas and Brennan JJ dissenting).

65. *Jones* v. *Alfred H. Mayer Co.* 392 US 409 (1968), followed in *Sullivan* v. *Little Hunting Park Inc.* 396 US 229, 90 Sup. Ct. 400 (1969).

of the States, and that the Act was violated if the effect of such discrimination was to deny a citizen the right to rent or buy property solely because of his race or colour. The decision has far-reaching implications in American constitutional law, and it is a measure of the distance which the Supreme Court has been prepared to travel during the past two decades to achieve genuine equality before the law. In this country, that distance has now been covered by Parliament which has made it unlawful to discriminate on racial grounds in disposing of most housing accommodation and property (see ch. 6).

Local authority services

Although there is no constitutional doctrine in English law comparable to that of 'State action' under the 'equal protection' clause of the Fourteenth Amendment to the US Constitution, it is well established that a local authority must not exercise its powers arbitrarily or capriciously. For example, it would clearly be unlawful for a local authority to discriminate on the basis of race or colour in allocating public housing. Similarly, it would be unlawful, in the absence of statutory authority, to make a financial gift to a particular section of the community at the expense of the general body of ratepayers,[66] or to place children in schools on the basis of racial criteria.[67] These examples present no difficulty, but there are other situations in which the extent of local authority discretion is less clear. For example, would it be lawful for a local authority to provide special assistance to schools containing a high proportion of children of immigrants, or to disperse such children from local schools, regardless of their parents' wishes, so that they did not constitute more than a third of the children in any one school, or to exclude people of Commonwealth or foreign origins from the allocation of public housing? In 1966, Parliament empowered the Secretary of State[68] to

66. *Prescott* v. *Birmingham Corporation* [1955] Ch. 210 (C.A.); *Roberts* v. *Hopwood* [1925] A.C. 578 (H.L.), cf. *Hawkins* v. *Town of Shaw* 437 F 21 1286 (1971) where the US Fifth Circuit Court of Appeals held that the unequal treatment of the different racial neighbourhoods in Shaw, Mississippi, with respect to the installation of various municipal services, constituted a violation of the 'equal protection' clause of the Fourteenth Amendment.

67. See *Cumings* v. *Birkenhead Corporation* [1971] 2 All E.R. 881 (C.A.) at p. 885 *per* Lord Denning M.R.

68. Local Government Act 1966, section 11(1).

make grants to those local authorities which were required to make special provision in the exercise of their functions because of 'the presence within their areas of substantial numbers of immigrants from the Commonwealth whose language or customs differ from those of the community'. Such grants were to be used for the employment of staff. And under the Race Relations Act 1968,[69] it is now unlawful for any local authority to discriminate on racial grounds in providing services or facilities, including housing accommodation. However, these provisions have not entirely removed ambiguity from this area of the law (see pp. 266–71).

Innkeepers and common carriers

The one area of the Common Law in which the English courts long ago developed a duty not to discriminate unfairly between members of the public concerned innkeepers and common carriers. In the seventeenth century, when speed and safety were becoming increasingly essential to industrial advance, a traveller in a remote part of the country who was denied lodgings for the night in the local inn, or transport for himself or his possessions, might well have no available alternative. It was during this period that the courts declared that an innkeeper must receive and lodge in his inn all travellers, unless he had some reasonable ground for refusal, and, similarly, that a common carrier was bound to accept goods or passengers for carriage, unless he had some lawful excuse. People in both occupations must provide their services to all comers without discrimination.

In 1944, Learie Constantine succeeded in a claim for damages for breach of the innkeeper's duty when he and his family were refused lodgings at the Imperial Hotel solely because of colour.[70] However, although Mr Justice Birkett found that Constantine had suffered 'much unjustifiable humiliation and distress', he felt himself prevented by previous cases from awarding him more than nominal damages of five guineas.

In *Rothfield* v. *Northern British Railway Company*,[71] the Scottish Court of Session also decided that a person who had been refused lodgings by an innkeeper on racial grounds could obtain a remedy,

69. Sections 2(2) and 5.
70. *Constantine* v. *Imperial Hotels Ltd* [1944] 1 K.B. 693.
71. [1920] S.C. 805.

but the court's application of the principle was disquieting. Henry Rothfield, a financial agent, had for several years been in the habit of living in the hotel in question for two, three or more nights each week, but in 1918 he was suddenly informed by the manager that he would have to give up his room and discontinue his visits there. In their defence, the hotel proprietors stated that Rothfield

is a German Jew, or a Jew of other foreign nationality or extraction, and that he has always been regarded by those in the hotel as a Jew of German nationality or German extraction. His business is that of a money-lender, and he is advertised as such in the Scottish newspapers. . . . His business and methods of doing business have been adversely commented on in the public press.

The Court of Session found that, on the facts of the case, there had been no breach of the hotel proprietors' duty. This is how Lord Salvesen summarized the relevant evidence:

(Rothfield) who is a Jew by religion and of alien extraction, bearing a thinly disguised Teutonic name, and practising the unpopular profession of a money-lender, had made himself somewhat conspicuous at the hotel by his swaggering conduct and had been the subject of remark by other guests; at the time when the country was still at war, and the hotel was largely frequented by young naval and military officers, he associated a good deal with such officers and entertained several of them on occasion; . . . the directors came to the bona fide conclusion that he was using the hotel and associating with these young men for business purposes, and that his presence at the hotel was objected to by other guests.

Lord Salvesen also referred to the fact that Rothfield had associated with a convicted Jewish money-lender, and that his business methods had been criticized in the Press. But what he failed to mention was that Rothfield had denied that he was of German nationality or extraction – in fact, he was born in Britain and had lived here throughout his life; that, in the course of the legal proceedings, he had called on the hotel proprietors to state the names of any guests who had objected to his presence in the hotel, and they had not done so; and that it had never been suggested that he himself had acted unlawfully. The case against Rothfield, put by Lord Salvesen, seems too thin to justify his exclusion from the hotel.

Although the innkeeper's duty is of theoretical interest as a rare example of a Common Law obligation to give equal treatment, its practical value is limited. The courts have consistently refused to extend the duty to other establishments offering services to the public. They have held that the following did not come within the definition of an inn; lodging houses,[72] boarding houses,[73] private residential hotels,[74] alehouses (i.e. public houses where there is no obligation to receive and entertain guests),[75] houses of entertainment,[76] and restaurants.[77] The Common Law therefore could not provide a remedy for someone who was excluded on racial grounds from a public place, unless it happened to come within a category which had been defined before the Industrial Revolution. The Hotel Proprietors Act 1956 incorporated the narrow Common Law definition of an inn in statutory form.[78] And it was only the Race Relations Act 1965 which extended the category to include the main places of public resort.[79]

Wills and trusts

There is one other field in which the English courts have considered the effect of racial restrictions. It illustrates yet again a strong judicial reluctance to develop the concept of public policy, and a rather old-fashioned view of the nature of racial differences. Characteristically, the issue has again arisen because restrictions were sought to be imposed on the transfer of property, this time not by the vendor of land, but by a testator in his will. English law looks with disfavour upon any hindrance to the free transfer of property. Several cases have come to court to test the validity of a condition in a will that a person will inherit a gift only if he marries a Jew, or that he will no longer enjoy the gift, if, after he has inherited it, he marries someone

72. *Parker* v. *Flint* (1699) 12 Mod.Rep. 254; *Thompson* v. *Lacy* [1820] 3 B. & Ald. 283.

73. *Dansey* v. *Richardson* (1854) 3 E. & B. 144.

74. *Duke of Devonshire* v. *Simmons* (1894) 11 T.L.R. 52.

75. *Pidgeon* v. *Legge* (1857) 21 J.P. 743; *Sealey* v. *Tandy* [1902] 1 K.B. 296.

76. *Webb* v. *Fagotti Bros.* (1898) 79 L.T. 683.

77. *Ultzen* v. *Nicols* [1894] 1 Q.B. 92; *Orchard* v. *Bush & Co.* [1898] 2 Q.B. 284.

78. Section 1(1).

79. Section 1(2).

who is not Jewish; the former is known as a condition precedent; the latter is called a condition subsequent.

The leading case of *Clayton* v. *Ramsden*[80] involved a condition subsequent. The testator left a gift to his unmarried daughter, but provided that if she at any time after his death married someone 'not of Jewish parentage and of the Jewish faith' the gift would cease and determine. The House of Lords held that the condition was void and of no effect, because the expression 'of Jewish parentage' and 'of the Jewish faith' were too uncertain to be given legal meaning. Their Lordships had no doubt that Jews were members of a separate racial group and some of them seemed to think that Jews also had their own nationality and blood group. For example, Lord Russell of Killowen complained that 'The testator has given no information or clue as to what percentage or proportion of Jewish blood in the husband will satisfy the requirement that he should be of Jewish parentage', and Lord Romer said 'one of the meanings of the word "parentage", and I am disposed to think its primary meaning, when coupled with a word indicating nationality such as Jewish, English, French or the like, is race or descent'. He asked rhetorically 'what degree of Hebraic blood would a permissible husband have to possess?'

Again, in an earlier case,[81] in which the House of Lords refused

80. [1943] A.C. 320.

81. *Keren Kayemeth Le Jisroel Ltd* v. *Commissioner of Inland Revenue* [1932] A.C. 650 (H.L.); [1931] 2 K.B. 465 (C.A.). Compare *Re Strakosch* [1949] Ch. 529 (C.A.) where a bequest to be held on trust and applied by the trustees 'for any purpose which in their opinion is designed to strengthen the bonds of unity between the Union of South Africa and the Mother Country and which incidentally will conduce to the appeasement of racial feeling between the Dutch and English-speaking sections of the South African community' was held not to be a good charitable gift because of the unrestricted latitude which it gave the trustees; *semble*, however, that a purely educational trust with such objects would have been charitable. In *De Costa* v. *De Paz* (1754) Amb. 228, a bequest for the propagation of the Jewish faith was held to be void because it was for a superstitious purpose; instead, the legacy was ordered to be held on trust for such charitable use as the Crown directed – apparently for the benefit of the Christian religion! *In Re Masters etc. of the Bedford Charity* (1818) 2 Swanst. 470, Jewish residents in Bedford were held to be disentitled from obtaining any benefits under a charity created by royal letters patent 'for the education . . . and instruction of children and youth in grammar and good manners'. The petitioner had lived in Bedford for twenty-one years and claimed that his daughter was qualified to apply for an apprenticeship fee paid to girls living in the town. Lord

to recognize that a body was charitable, for tax purposes, which had been set up to buy land in Palestine and elsewhere 'for the purpose of settling Jews on such lands', although the judges held that the word 'Jew' in English law had almost always been confined to persons practising the Jewish religion, they also regarded Jews as members of a distinct racial group. These cases may be important when the courts have to consider whether Jews are within the protection of the Race Relations Acts against discrimination on grounds of race, or ethnic or national origins (see pp. 156–8).

The courts have refused to give effect to restrictions imposed by Jewish testators both where they were conditions subsequent[82] and also where they were conditions precedent.[83] But, in other cases, the courts have given effect to such restrictions where they were conditions subsequent, in spite of *Clayton* v. *Ramsden*; they have done so on the ground that in such cases it was possible to ascertain whether the particular claimant had in fact satisfied the condition. As Mr Justice Cross explained in *Re Abrahams*,[84] it would be 'absurd to say that one could not be sure whether the Chief Rabbi was a person professing the Jewish faith'. No doubt his task was there made easier because the test was religious rather than racial. However, if all the cases are considered together, it is plain that the distinctions between them rest on 'somewhat shaky logical ground' (Cretney,

---

Chancellor Eldon upheld the trustees' refusal to permit anyone of the Jewish persuasion to benefit from the charity, on the ground that Jewish children could not conscientiously participate in educational activities supported by the charity. Yet the charity was purely educational, and not religious. The Charitable Donations Registration Act 1812 s. 11 expressly excluded 'any person of the Jewish nation' from its benefits. However, the Religious Disabilities Act 1846, section 2 provided that 'Her Majesty's subjects professing the Jewish religion, in respect of their schools, places for religious worship, education and charitable purposes, and the property held therewith, shall be subject to the same laws as her Majesty's Protestant subjects dissenting from the Church of England are subject to'. As to the present position of charities under the Race Relations Act 1968, see pp. 173–266.

82. *Re Tarnpolsk* [1958] 1 W.L.R. 1157.

83. See also *Re Blaiberg* [1940] 1 Ch. 385; *Re Donn's W.T.* [1943] 2 All E.R. 564.

84. See e.g. *Re Selby's W.T.* [1966] 1 W.L.R. 43; *Re Abrahams W.T.* [1967] 2 All E.R. 1175.

1968, p. 1096), and better ground will be found only if a new case is decided by the House of Lords. The cause of the confusion lies partly in the fact that the courts have consistently based their decisions on the uncertainty of the testator's language, rather than on public policy, even though the concealed basis of their decisions is probably one of policy rather than language. What is really at work in the will cases is the courts' hostility to racial or religious restrictions on gifts, but the judges have refused to say so.[85]

The consequences of their refusal to express the matter in terms of public policy were apparent in the more recent case of *Re Lysaght*.[86] By her will Miss Lysaght made a gift to the Royal College of Surgeons to be used for any student who was 'a British-born subject and not of the Jewish or Roman Catholic faith'. The College Council felt unable to accept the gift on these terms because the condition was 'so invidious and so alien to the spirit of the College's work as to make the gift inoperable in its present form'. They therefore applied to the court for permission to remove the discriminatory condition from the terms of the gift. But Mr Justice Buckley rejected all their legal objections to the condition. In his view, it was not void for uncertainty, because a student claiming to be eligible to benefit from the gift would be able to establish with certainty whether he qualified. He also held that the condition was not against public policy. He accepted that 'racial and religious discrimination is nowadays widely regarded as deplorable in many respects', and he thought that Miss Lysaght's desire to exclude Jews and Roman Catholics from the gift was 'unamiable' and 'undesirable'; but said that it was 'going much too far to say that the endowment of a charity, the beneficiaries of which are to be drawn from a particular faith or are to exclude adherents to a particular faith, is contrary to public policy'. Nor

85. In July 1970, the Chancery Court of the Duchy of Lancaster had to consider the validity of a bequest by a mother to her son on the condition that he adopted a coloured child 'to be brought up as one of the family'. The Vice-Chancellor (Mr Thomas Burgess V-C) did not accept that the condition was contrary to public policy but said he could not be certain how to define 'coloured'. On this ground he declared the condition void. 'The area of choice is so large and the variations so numerous that I fail to see how any trustee or beneficiary could say with certainty that the condition has, or has not, been fulfilled' (*Guardian*, 22 July 1970).

86. [1966] 1 Ch. 191. Contrast *Re Dominion Hall Trust* [1947] Ch. 183.

would he regard the Race Relations Bill 1965, which was then pending before Parliament, as sufficient evidence of public policy. Mr Justice Buckley continued:

Obviously a trustee will not normally be permitted to modify the terms of his trust on the ground that his own opinions or convictions conflicted with them. If his conscience will not allow him to carry out the trust faithfully in accordance with its terms, he must make way for a trustee who can and will do so.

In the end, however, he did allow the offending words to be deleted from the trust deed, because the gift would otherwise fail, and with it Miss Lysaght's intention, as the result of the College Council's non-compliance with the discrimination. It was a decision based not on a *judicial* refusal to carry out the prejudiced intentions of the testatrix, but the *trustees*' refusal to do so.

Towards legal equality

The unfair treatment of people because of their race or colour is only one aspect of inequality and injustice. And the impotence of the English Judiciary in the face of racial discrimination is an extreme illustration of the limitations of the Common Law: its neutrality towards profound differences in power between institutions, groups, and individuals; its deference to private contractual law-making by stronger parties to the detriment of the weak, and its reluctance to expand traditional concepts of public policy in accordance with changing social attitudes.

The Common Law acquired much of its present shape during the heyday of *laissez-faire*, when the protection of property and contract rights were the dominant concern of the courts. Many of the cases referred to in this chapter reflect that concern at the expense of the individual who has suffered from the abuse of those rights. But it would be wrong to conclude that the Common Law was incapable of being adapted to a society which increasingly treats decent work, remuneration, housing, social security and leisure with the same respect which was formerly reserved for property, power and profit. A distinguished former judge has urged that the English Judiciary must see themselves as committed for good to the principle that the purpose of society and all its institutions is to nourish and enrich the growth of each individual human spirit. This is the liberty in the sense in which we have chosen to understand it . . . not just the liberty of contract with which English law has been so much concerned, but the complex of liberties which are needed to preserve the freedom of the human spirit. We all feel that there are relationships arising out of human institutions which deserve special protection from outside invasion or even voluntary relinquishment. It is in these matters, when they are threatened by the bullying of property rights or the aggression of contractual claims or, most menacing of all today, the usurping power of association, that public policy . . . should make its voice heard (Radcliffe, 1960, pp. 65–6).[87]

And the English Judiciary have indeed adapted much of the Common Law of negligence, contract, the family and public administration to the facts and demands of modern industrial life.

But judicial reforms have not been based upon a coherent, egalitarian philosophy, and the effect of their ethical aimlessness is especially striking in the relationship between racial discrimination and the Common Law. At the beginning of this century, judicial values merely reflected those of Parliament and public opinion,[88] but, in recent decades, when racial equality has become embedded in the public philosophy, the English Bench have displayed a marked insensitivity to the manifestations of racial discrimination. Again and again, their decisions have either implicitly or overtly condoned the unfair treatment of racial groups, when they could instead have secured a more genuine equality before the law, performing what have been described (Jaffe, 1969, p. 32) as the two vitally important functions of the judiciary as lawmaker: 'first, the protection of individuals and minorities; second, leadership in the solution of social problems requiring the use of law'.

One may summarize the effect of the case-law in this way. The victim of racial discrimination would have a remedy at Common Law if he were arbitrarily denied work by an employer or trade union which exercised monopoly powers and completely controlled entry

87. Lord Radcliffe was not, however, prepared to apply these principles to the English law of race relations; see pp. 90–95.

88. The history of Parliament's vacillating attitudes towards racial discrimination in the Indian Civil Service is summarized in Appendix 1, illustrating that the public philosophy of the legislature was similar to that of the courts.

into his trade or occupation; but he would have no redress if he were denied most types of employment, or were refused work at the level for which he was qualified, or were paid at sub-standard wages, or were given inferior working conditions, or were denied training or promotion earned by length of service and on merit, or were made redundant, solely because of his race or colour. He could obtain no assistance from the courts if he were refused a house or flat which was available and which he could afford, or if he were denied the services of an estate agent; and he could not prevent the publication or public display of blatantly discriminatory advertisements. He might however have his remedy if he were barred from local authority housing solely on racial grounds; and any racial restriction on the transfer of property to him might well be invalidated in the courts. He would also be entitled to prevent a local education authority from allocating his children to schools on the basis of racial criteria. As for commercial services and facilities, he could claim damages if arbitrarily denied accommodation in a hotel, or transport by a common carrier, but would have no remedy if excluded from other public places, such as theatres, cinemas, shops, restaurants, dance halls, holiday camps or boarding houses, or facilities, such as insurance, mortgages, hire purchase and the hire of goods, or if he were offered these services and facilities only upon discriminatory terms.

Even if the courts had been more responsive to changing social needs, they could not have secured equality of treatment and opportunity in these fields. There are inherent limits to the judicial process; courts function best as the creative interpreters of the legislative intent, rather than as the instrument for radical reforms. A shift in social conduct and attitude of the kind required in race relations in Britain, could be stimulated only by Act of Parliament accompanied by a wide range of administrative measures.

However, although Parliament has now passed the Race Relations Acts 1965 and 1968, the Common Law and the judicial response remain relevant. The courts are responsible for applying the statutes, and will interpret their language against the background of existing precedents. In addition the Race Relations Act 1968, section 19 (10) expressly preserves the right to bring any civil or criminal proceedings which might have been brought if that Act had not been passed, so that it is still open to the victim of racial discrimination to seek whatever remedies are available at Common Law. Although section 19 (10) states that nothing in the 1968 Act 'shall affect' such proceedings, one may hope that the legislation will be regarded by the courts as affecting the Common Law to the extent that public policy is now unequivocally against racial discrimination, and in favour of equality of opportunity.

Chapter 2
The Role of Legislation[1]

Political wisdom, I have always believed, consists in trying to narrow the gap between the value which men and women place on their own personalities, and the value placed on them by the community within which they live; furthermore, no community can afford for long to deny the application of this principle to racial minorities as well.

Lord Boyle of Handsworth (1968).

The purpose of this chapter is to examine the role of anti-discrimination legislation, before proceeding to describe the events which have shaped our present statute law. The separate subject of legislation against racial incitement raises substantially different issues and is discussed in Chapter 10.

The conflicting arguments about the use of law to combat racial discrimination reflect deep moral and intellectual differences: about the idea of racial equality, the nature of human beings and their social behaviour, the implications of these matters for government policies, the proper limits to be placed upon law-making, and the best choice of legislative techniques for dealing effectively with problems of discrimination. The outcome of these different arguments provides the yardstick against which the Race Relations Acts may be evaluated.

The idea of racial equality

Every statement about the nature of racial discrimination is based, more or less explicitly, upon an idea of the equality of human beings, which has advanced to its present form only relatively recently. The origins of this idea of human equality may be traced to the traditional Judaeo-Christian belief in the Fatherhood of God and hence in the

1. We are indebted to Mr Dipak Nandy for his contribution to this chapter.

brotherhood of men, each with equal humanity and significance. Accordingly, although human beings are obviously unequal in their skill, intelligence, strength and virtue, they are equal because of their human spirit: 'it is their common humanity that constitutes their equality' (Williams, 1962, p. 110).[2]

In certain fundamental situations, the manifest inequality in individual capacities is *felt* to be simply irrelevant, however difficult the justification of such a view may be. At the dawn of liberal thought in the West, John Locke wrote:

Though I have said . . . that all men by nature are equal, I cannot be supposed to understand all sorts of equality: age or virtue may give men a just precedency: excellency of parts and merit may place others above the common level: birth may subject some, and alliance or benefits others, to pay an observance to those to whom nature, gratitude or other respects may have made it due; and yet all this consists with the equality which all men are in, in respect of Jurisdiction or Dominion one over another . . . (1965 edn., p. 346).

That is, although men are different in innumerable respects, for the purposes of government and of political representation they must be regarded as equal. Their inequalities are not relevant for these purposes. This perception of the fundamental equality of men as men, despite the manifold differences between individuals, lies at the heart of liberal and democratic thought in the West.

The second source of the idea of racial equality, and conversely of the morally unacceptable nature of racial discrimination, derives from the imperatives of a modern industrial society. In traditional pre-industrial societies, economic and social roles were static and social relationships hierarchical. Roles were allocated and performed on the basis of status and rank, rather than of individual merit or choice; the blacksmith was usually the son of a blacksmith. It was natural in such societies for human capacities to be regarded as innate and fixed, because those capacities were related to fixed and sharply defined roles. However, the rise of industrial, urban society has created ever increasing demands for a skilled and mobile working population with widely differing and changing functions. It has generated the need for careers to be open to all with talent. And so,

2. For a remarkably perceptive and prophetic analysis of race relations from this standpoint, see Oldham (1924).

equality of opportunity, based on individual merit, has been transformed from a moral ideal into an economic and social necessity.

Thirdly, this process of industrialization has been accompanied by a powerful belief in the malleability of man (Passmore, 1965): the unequal characteristics of human beings are seen not as the result of innate inferiority or superiority but of the unequal environments into which they are born and must live. If the inequalities in their environments are removed, people will be able to fulfil their real potential.

This belief has been reinforced by the growing body of evidence of social science about the social conditioning of people by their environment. Human potential may be limited by genetic inheritance, but genetic differences are now seen to be a far less powerful source of inequality than environmental factors. And, so far as *racial* inequality is concerned, biological evidence 'indicates that the socially significant group differences are culturally and not genetically transmitted'. However, one must remember that, although this evidence is relevant and important, 'The validity of the declaration that all men are created equal in dignity and rights does not depend upon a permit from the biologists that has to be renewed at regular intervals' (Banton, 1967, p. 4).

This idea of human equality, evolved in Europe during the past three centuries, drawing on a Judaeo-Christian tradition, responding to the imperatives of a modernizing society, and backed by the evidence of social science on the shaping influence of environment, has placed the onus on those who wish to discriminate, to provide a justification for the proposed differential treatment. It may be expressed in the form of a practical maxim: 'treat all men as equal, unless there are good reasons to the contrary'. Alternatively, it may be expressed in the form of a general criterion: 'for every difference in the way in which men are treated, some general reason or principle of differentiation must be given' (Williams, 1962, p. 111).

But it is not enough to require the giving of reasons, for, if that were enough, it would be in accordance with this principle, for example, 'to treat black men differently from others just because they were black, or poor men differently just because they were poor, and this cannot accord with anyone's idea of equality' (p. 111). The reason given must also be *relevant* to the difference which is sought to be made in the way people are treated.

It is, for example, relevant that a worker seeking employment should have the appropriate skill for the job, or that someone wishing to buy a house should be able to pay the purchase price, or that a customer requiring to be served in a public house should behave in an orderly fashion; and it is not relevant in any of these situations that the person in question is black or white. Race and colour are irrelevant because they tell one nothing about the person's intrinsic qualities and qualifications, and they cannot properly be a ground for rejecting or excluding him.

To say of an individual that he belongs to a certain racial group has no uniquely predictive value: we cannot determine whether that person is taller or shorter, darker or lighter, more or less intelligent, than an individual belonging to some other 'race' (Rose *et al.*, 1969, p. 36).

Nor would it be consistent with the idea of equality to accept the prejudices of others as a relevant reason for according differential treatment to members of a particular racial group. If Jones, a black worker, is otherwise qualified for a job, it is as irrelevant a reason for rejecting him that his colour is objected to by other workers as that it offends the employer himself. In both cases, the alleged 'reason' for his exclusion is his colour; in both cases, it is not a relevant reason for exclusion consistent with the idea of equality.

These examples are straight-forward because few could be found, at any rate in Britain, who would explicitly seek to justify the exclusion of people from opportunities for employment, housing or public services, solely on grounds of colour or race. However, the idea of equality makes it similarly impermissible to reject people solely because they were born abroad, or are descended from foreign parents, or belong to a particular cultural group. These are more common grounds upon which members of racial and ethnic minorities are excluded from opportunities in this country, and they suffer from the same vice as racial exclusions. They exclude people not because of individual characteristics, but because of a collective identity which is presumed to provide an accurate assessment of the characteristics of everyone who shares that identity. Yet, it would be almost as irrational to require that a worker or house buyer be born in Britain or that he abandon all 'non-British' characteristics, as it would be to demand that a person change his colour or a woman alter her sex before being allowed the right to vote.

National and cultural categories, like racial categories, have no uniquely predictive value in relation to the individuals concerned. There is no more valid or scientific basis for this kind of categorization than there is for racial categories. What is more, such a categorization can be seen increasingly to run counter to a further and relatively more recent implication of the notion of equality sketched here. The notion of cultural superiority is no more defensible than the idea of racial superiority. The work of anthropologists in the last century brings out the fact that cultures are simply different. To speak of them as being superior or inferior is meaningless.

What this has come to imply is not merely that judgments of superiority or inferiority are inappropriate when dealing with cultural differences, but more positively that, in a plural society, cultural differences (unless they are seriously dysfunctional) have to be accorded equality of respect. An international context, in which societies with cultures very different from those of Western Europe and North America have acquired political power, makes such respect an essential requirement of modern life. Given that context, in a culturally plural society equality of opportunity is too narrow an objective unless it is accompanied by equality of respect for the different cultures of which that society consists.

It was this complex of ideas which lay behind Roy Jenkins's observation that he did not regard racial 'integration' as meaning

the loss by immigrants of their own national characteristics and culture. I do not think that we need in this country a 'melting-pot', which will turn everybody out in a common mould, as one of a series of carbon copies of someone's misplaced vision of the stereo-typed Englishman. . . . I define integration, therefore, not as a flattening process of assimilation but as equal opportunity accompanied by cultural diversity, in an atmosphere of mutual tolerance (1967, p. 267).

A similar notion is contained in the United Nations' definition of 'discrimination', which includes

any conduct based on a distinction made on grounds of national or social categories, which have no relation either to individual capacities or merits, or to the concrete behaviour of the individual person (1949, p. 9).

Sometimes of course, people of a particular national origin or members of a particular cultural group may be excluded from opportunities as an indirect result of their origins or cultural characteristics, without being the victims of any deliberately unfair discrimination. For example, proficiency in the English language or knowledge of local geography may be a relevant qualification for certain types of employment, or length of residence in a borough for obtaining local authority housing, or experience of British driving conditions for obtaining motor insurance at a standard premium, or being six feet tall in order to become a policeman, or being eighteen years old to enter a particular occupation. In each of these cases, a recent immigrant to this country would be more likely to be at a disadvantage than someone who was born here (in the case of recruitment to the police force, if he came from a country whose population had a much lower average height than ours).

Some of these qualifications are open to objection on grounds other than racial discrimination. An 'aptitude' test might be an unnecessarily restrictive obstacle in the sense that it did not measure the objective requirements for a particular job. It might be, as the Department of Housing and Local Government has urged[3] that the local authority should give greater weight to housing need than to length of residence in the locality. The minimum height requirements for policemen may not be an indispensable condition for effective law enforcement. The age qualification may be excessively rigid.

Some qualifications may also be objectionable in their particular application to immigrants. Obviously, they cannot be permitted to be used as a mere pretext for excluding all immigrants;[4] nor can they be applied indiscriminately to exclude all immigrants automatically from opportunities on the assumption that they will be less likely than other people to satisfy the test.[5] And, if it becomes apparent, on closer

3. *The Housing Programme 1965–70* (Cmnd 2828) (1965). See generally, the Cullingworth Report (1969).

4. A minimum age qualification was insisted upon for decades by successive British Governments as a pretext for excluding Indians from senior positions in the Indian civil service (see Appendix 1). Similarly, literacy tests were until recently used in the American South as a device for excluding Negroes from the franchise.

5. For example, the exclusion of Indians from senior positions in the Indian civil service was claimed to be justified on the ground that, although they would

scrutiny, that certain qualifications in practice operate more harshly against immigrants than against the indigenous population (even though those who devised the qualifications do not deliberately intend to exclude immigrants as such) it will be unfair to insist on such qualifications in their existing form, unless they can be independently justified (Cooper and Sobol, 1969; see pp. 190–94).

There is one further and more radical element in the idea of equality. The notion of equality of opportunity 'requires not merely that there should be no exclusion from access [to goods] on grounds other than those which are appropriate or rational for the good in question, but that the grounds considered appropriate for the good should themselves be such that people from all sections of society have an equal chance of satisfying them' (Williams, 1962, pp. 125–6). For example, if, as the result of decades of racial discrimination in education, housing and employment, members of a racial minority are poorly trained, housed and paid, it is not sufficient to remove the existing racially discriminatory barriers and to proclaim that henceforth opportunities will be available to all on the basis of open competition. Equality of opportunity will not then have been achieved because, although no one will be excluded merely for belonging to a racial minority, a causal connection will remain between belonging to that minority and being impoverished and uneducated. Members of the minority will lack the economic, educational and psychological resources needed to participate on equal terms in the competition for the opportunities in question. If they are treated unequally on the ground that they are poor and uneducated, the justification for unequal treatment turns out to depend on contingent (that is, remediable) social inequalities.

In such circumstances, 'there is a necessary pressure to equal up the conditions' (Williams, 1962, p. 127) by more far-reaching reforms so that members of the racial minority will more genuinely enjoy equality of opportunity. This is the intellectual justification, if any is needed, for providing special resources for those in special need, since their unequal environment contributes to inequality. Because of past

pass the 'intellectual test' and 'come in by shoals', they would be 'pretty sure' to fail the 'moral test', because 'we, as a race, are far superior to them in force of character'. George Otto Trevelyan, 5 May 1868, *Hansard*, vol. 191, cols. 1845–6 (see further, Appendix 1).

failure to ensure equality of opportunity, regardless of race, society can move towards genuine equality only by abstracting the racial minority from their unequal environment, that is, by discriminating positively in their favour. The extent to which it becomes necessary to do so is the measure of the extent to which the idea of equality has been previously ignored.[6]

Racial discrimination in Britain

The arguments about the role of legislation in combating racial discrimination originate with the idea of racial equality. But the practical problems of racial discrimination in Britain are obviously of more immediate importance to these arguments. The actual extent of discrimination was systematically investigated for the first time in this country by an independent research organization, Political and Economic Planning (PEP) and their findings were published in April 1967.[7] The PEP report was based on interviews with both white and coloured people, and also on a series of 'situation tests', carried out in six towns. In these tests, first a coloured West Indian immigrant, then a white immigrant of Hungarian origin, and finally a white Englishman applied for various opportunities available in the fields of employment, housing and commercial services. In each test the three applicants claimed equivalent occupational qualifications or housing requirements.

The results of the tests speak for themselves. In the field of housing, out of a total of sixty personal applications to landlords, the West Indian was refused accommodation or asked for a higher rent than the white Englishman on forty-five occasions, and the Hungarian was treated similarly on three occasions. The West Indian was discriminated against in twenty out of thirty inquiries about accommodation at estate agents, while the Hungarian and the Englishman were

6. Compare the recommendations of the Plowden report (1966), that special assistance should be given to educational priority areas where there is the greatest social deprivation and need. For a relevant critique of the methodology of the Plowden Report by one of the authors of the US (Coleman) report (1966), see Cohen (1968). For the use of special measures to overcome the effects of past racial discrimination see pp. 174–9.

7. The main contents of the report are published, with a commentary in Daniel (1968), cf. Jowell and Prescott-Clarke (1970).

treated alike. In employment, in only one of the forty firms tested was the coloured immigrant tester told that a vacancy existed or offered a job; the English tester had fifteen offers, and the Hungarian had ten. And, in six out of twenty applications for motor insurance, the West Indian unlike the others was refused insurance cover altogether, while on eleven occasions he was quoted a higher premium than either of the other two applicants.

These tests were originally designed to provide an objective measurement of discrimination, as a check on the interviews, which, it was thought, would reveal a tendency among immigrants to exaggerate and among those in a position to discriminate to under-estimate the extent of the problem. In the result the tests revealed that immigrants' views about the existence of racial discrimination were not exaggerated, but were closely related to their direct experience or to their knowledge of the experience of others. The following conclusions could be drawn in the field of employment:

In terms of formal qualifications, experience of discrimination was highest among people with the highest qualifications, including those with English trade, professional and school-leaving qualifications.

In terms of English-speaking ability, experience of discrimination was highest among people who had spoken only English as a child and lowest among those who had spoken no English.

In terms of job done before coming to Britain, experience of discrimination was highest among those who had been in full employment and lowest among people who had been unemployed.

In terms of length of time in Britain, the longer people had been here the more discrimination they had faced.

In terms of union membership, which provided some idea of the extent to which they wanted to or were prepared to join English organizations, the proportion of union members experiencing discrimination was higher than the proportion of non-members (Daniel, 1968 p. 81).

As has been observed (Rose *et al.* 1969, p. 414), the finding of the PEP report that racial discrimination varied in extent 'from the massive to the substantial' would, at the time when the report was published

have been anticipated only by very few people. The findings show that the groups who were most physically distinct in colour and racial features from English experienced the greatest discrimination, and that the group who were culturally most like the English, and who sought integration, were the most likely to experience rejection. . . . The Report illustrated how the process of racial discrimination tended to push or keep immigrants in poorer housing and lower status jobs, reinforcing the stereotype and preventing integration.

What the PEP report established above all was that racial discrimination was a serious and growing problem in Britain, that since it was related more to colour than to foreign origin, the problem would not solve itself with the mere passage of time during which the coloured community became increasingly indigenous to Britain, and, indeed, that, if left to themselves, race relations would grow worse.

The PEP report also threw some light upon the causes of the problem. It indicated that people practise discrimination less because they are bigots, than because they fear the prejudices, real or presumed, which are ascribed by them to others – whether customers, managers, workers, tenants or neighbours. The PEP interviews revealed that:

Sometimes the expected hostility or resistance of other white people is imagined; discriminators genuinely feel that there will be resistance when in fact there will not, or at least they have no real evidence that there will be. Sometimes it is an excuse; discriminators are oblivious of the feelings of other people but are content to use them, real or not, as a cloak for their own wishes. Sometimes it is justified; discriminators are justified in believing that other white people would resist, and moreover they practise discrimination because of this, against their own judgment or wishes (Daniel, 1968, p. 211).

Faced with a choice between two applicants, one white and the other coloured, the employer or property owner therefore, reluctantly or readily, takes the line of least resistance: he rejects the coloured applicant even if he is better qualified than the white applicant. Racial discrimination in Britain is as yet more typically the product of social conformity – prejudice by proxy – rather than of personal bigotry.

It is still too early in the history of British race relations to assess whether the findings of the PEP report accurately measured the dimensions of the domestic problem of discrimination. However, few could ignore the warning about the consequences of complacency provided by the tragically familiar sequence of events in the Northern cities of the United States (Clark, 1965). There, countless individual rejections of black people by a conforming white majority have hardened after a generation or so into discriminatory patterns which are as rigid, respectable and comprehensive as if they were imposed by the law, until it is customary to practise racial discrimination throughout an entire neighbourhood or industry. Discrimination in housing, education and employment reinforce each other. So, unable to escape from the poor, overcrowded and decaying urban ghettos, black parents are forced to send their children to local schools, which suffer from all the disadvantages of slum schools, with the added stigma of being racially separate through no choice of their own. Black children, having received an unequal education, are unqualified for the better-paid skilled jobs, from which they would probably be excluded on grounds of colour even if they were adequately trained. Deprived of a living wage, they find it even more difficult than it was for their parents to obtain decent housing. Black neighbourhoods become festering sores, infecting those who are trapped within them with bitterness and despair. The discriminatory spiral descends from exclusion in one field to deprivation in another, until the black minority ironically come to resemble the prejudiced stereotypes held about them by the very people whose actions have resulted in their inequality.

It is not inevitable that an identical development will take place in Britain, where there are as many differences from as there are similarities to the United States. But the appalling cost to British society of permitting such a process to develop is too great to allow the risk of prolonged inaction. It is at least possible that here, as in the United States, discrimination might offer a tempting line of least resistance, at any rate in the short run. The exclusion of first-generation coloured immigrants might be perpetuated against the next generation, who were born and educated in Britain. Indeed the PEP report indicated that the danger is far from being hypothetical; and it was central to Roy Jenkins's notable speech, on 23 May 1966 in which he said:

we are beginning to move from the era of the first-generation immigrant to that of the second-generation immigrant. Many were born in this country, many more wholly educated here. They are not so much Asians or West Indians as coloured Britons, dressing and speaking much as we do, and looking for the same opportunities as the rest of us. . . . The more talented ones will have full normal expectations for professional, for white collar, for scientific and technological jobs. And if we allow their expectations to be disappointed we shall both be wasting scarce skills and talents, and building up vast trouble for ourselves in the future. In the next decade this, to my mind, will become the real core of the problem (1967, p. 271).

This emphasis on safeguarding the future of the second generation did not, of course, imply that racial discrimination against their parents was any the less reprehensible. Indeed, since the immigrant community is on average much younger than the rest of the population, it will be likely to meet the problem for many years, and their parents' experience of discrimination will inevitably influence the attitudes and aspirations of the second generation. But, in focusing attention on coloured Britons, born and educated in this country, Roy Jenkins was underlining the permanent character of the challenge now facing Britain and the urgency of the need for speedy and effective action.

If further evidence were needed to support this view, it has been provided by recent studies of the older settlements of coloured communities in the ports of Cardiff and Liverpool (Rose *et al.*, 1969, pp. 487–90). The general picture in Cardiff is of 'a second and third generation which lives in a quasi-ghetto, is denied the opportunities available to white English-speaking immigrants, is less ambitious, and achieves less than they do. . . . They choose to stay in the coloured quarter because it is safer to trust their own kind.' And a report of a Working Party of the Liverpool Youth Organizations Committee, published in October 1968 found that the *second* and *third* generation of coloured youth in Liverpool suffered the same psychological handicaps, met discrimination in employment, and felt very insecure when they moved outside the coloured quarter. The inquiry gave the Working Party 'a deep sense of unease'. They referred to 'the long-standing myth in Liverpool of non-discrimination between people of different racial characteristics', which was a cloak for indifference and lack of understanding. They found evidence of hostility to colour in white downtown areas of a city which has had a coloured population for at least forty years.

The objectives of legislation

The practical effect of racial discrimination, and its disastrous cost to the economic, social and moral well-being of British society, are an essential element in the arguments of those who have advocated the use of legislation. In the words of Lord Boyle:

the purpose of legislation on race relations is not to try to enforce moral attitudes by law. I think that I am more opposed than most people to using the criminal law in order to enforce morality as such. But race relations is not just a matter of private morality – it is a major issue affecting what John Stuart Mill would have called the 'public domain'. Racial discrimination as a practice is both wasteful and divisive, in a manner that quite transcends tastes and prejudices. It is also extremely insidious (1968).

But what could legislation hope to accomplish in dealing with such a complex social problem? In their first annual report, published in April 1967, the Race Relations Board summarized the role of legislation as follows:

1. A law is an unequivocal declaration of public policy.
2. A law gives support to those who do not wish to discriminate, but who feel compelled to do so by social pressure.
3. A law gives protection and redress to minority groups.
4. A law thus provides for the peaceful and orderly adjustment of grievances and the release of tensions.
5. A law reduces prejudice by discouraging the behaviour in which prejudice finds expression (para. 65).

These principles are not vague abstractions; they are directly related to the character of the problem of racial discrimination revealed by the PEP report. The first two and the last of the principles are mainly concerned with the effect of legislation upon people in a position to discriminate. If law can play a repressive role by sanctioning racial segregation and discrimination, as it had done in Nazi Germany, the American South, Rhodesia and South Africa, it can operate with equal force in the opposite direction by declaring that equality of opportunity, regardless of race or colour, is to be pursued as a major social objective. It is a statement of public policy, by Parliament, intended to influence public opinion. Contrary to the belief of some critics, legislation and education are not incompatible; legislation is a powerful form of education, and legislation and education depend upon each other.

In more concrete terms, by condemning racial discrimination, a law makes it easier for people to resist social pressures and to afford equal treatment to racial minorities. Instead of conforming to prejudices ascribed to others, they are able to conform to the law of the land. It is no longer the line of least resistance to practise discrimination, but rather to obey the law. Instead of being a non-conformist, the person who refuses to discriminate racially is conforming to standards approved by Parliament, and the discriminator becomes the non-conforming lawbreaker.

This role of law in liberating people from social intolerance was described in practical terms in evidence given by the President of Levitt and Sons Inc., a major American property developer, to a Congressional Committee. It is worth recalling this evidence in some detail since it has had considerable influence on British legislators. In a statement directed to Title IV of the Civil Rights Bill 1966, which outlawed racial discrimination in housing, he narrated his company's experience as follows:

In 1960 for the first time, we were building in an area where there was an anti-discrimination law on the books – the State of New Jersey. . . . Since that time we have branched out. We are now building at more than a dozen locations in four eastern States, in Puerto Rico and in France. In every area except one we sell on an open occupancy [i.e. non-discriminatory] basis. We do in New York and New Jersey, for instance; the law requires it. We do in Puerto Rico; custom demands it. The one area where we don't is Maryland. That State has no anti-discrimination housing law, so we conform to prevailing practice there. . . . To this date I don't know of a single racial disturbance in any open occupancy community we have ever built. There have been no outbreaks, no violence, no picketing, no commotion of any kind. . . . The really amazing thing, after all the years of fear and hesitation about integrating housing, is that when integration does take place, nothing bad happens – absolutely nothing. . . . It would seem that the evils of picketing, violence, racial tension, stem from non-integration, not from integration. I suggest that removing the cause may eliminate the problems. . . . The human race may be perfectible but it is certainly not perfect yet, and prejudice exists. Because of this, any home-builder who chooses to operate on an open occupancy basis, where it is not customary or required by law, runs the grave risk of losing business to his competitor who chooses to discriminate. That, in a nutshell, is why we follow our present policy in Maryland. We have no choice. The barriers to equal opportunity which have denied to Negroes a fair share of their birth-right as Americans are crumbling everywhere. . . . It is high time we recognized what is already taking place, and write a new set of ground rules in respect to housing which reflects these altered circumstances. It is not only compassion for the Negro and our sense of justice that must guide us; it is common sense as well. . . . The enactment of Title IV as part of the 1966 Civil Rights Act is one of the most important steps the government can take to restore civil peace into the United States.[8]

The fifth principle enunciated by the Race Relations Board is that law reduces prejudice by discouraging the behaviour in which prejudice finds expression (Allport, 1958, pp. 437–40; Berger, 1968, ch. 5). Although the legislation does not deal directly with racial prejudice, it has an obvious indirect effect, not only through public education, and the restraint of prejudiced behaviour, but in enabling racial minorities to obtain opportunities on more equal terms.

The connections between discrimination and prejudice are not at all straightforward. But some propositions can be advanced which are corroborated by common observation. If members of a minority group are actually treated as unequal, then they will come to be seen as unequal. If there is a prevalent prejudice that members of a certain group are incapable of occupying positions of responsibility and authority, and they are prevented by discrimination from occupying such positions, the prejudgment can never be refuted. It is only when they are seen to discharge such responsibility effectively that the belief in their alleged incapacity will disappear. Thus, dismantling discriminatory practices has a significant, if long-term, contribution to make to the reduction of irrational prejudices.

The third and fourth principles advanced by the Race Relations Board are concerned with redressing the grievances of minority groups rather than with curbing discrimination and prejudice among the majority. The unjust exclusion of people, solely on racial grounds, from the opportunities, facilities and services of modern life is at

8. Statement by William J. Levitt before Sub-committee No. 5. Committee on the Judiciary, House of Representative (H.R. 14765) 19 May 1966, published as an appendix in Bonham Carter (1967, at pp. 25–6). Since this statement was made, Maryland has enacted a law against housing discrimination.

least as substantial an injustice as the breach of a contract, the defamation of someone's reputation, or a damaging act of negligence. The law provides the individual injured by these wrongs with a remedy, and it ought similarly to redress the wrong of racial discrimination. Effective legal remedies are required not only to ensure individual justice, but also to avoid social conflict by enabling grievances to be adjusted in a peaceful and orderly manner. In the absence of legal redress, the victim is forced to choose between acquiescing in the discrimination and resorting to self-help. The former is likely to result in greater injustice, and the latter in self-destructive disorder.

These are the objectives which anti-discrimination legislation is intended to achieve. But it is also important to recognize the limitations of such legislation so that it may be seen in its proper perspective. Firstly, no law can restrain the determined law-breaker. It is aimed at the majority of the community who are ordinarily law-abiding. It 'will not deter the compulsive bigot or demagogue. But neither do laws against arson deter the pyromaniac. Laws . . . restrain the middle range of mortals as a mentor in moulding their habits' (Allport, 1958, p. 439).

A second obvious limitation is that legislation will be relevant only if the economic and social environment enables people to develop their individual potential and compete for opportunities on more or less equal terms. The truism is forcefully illustrated by experience in the United States. Legislation against racial discrimination has there been irrelevant to the immediate needs of many members of the black community, who are denied employment not directly because of their colour, but because after decades of racial discrimination, in education and housing as well as employment, they are often not qualified to compete on the basis of merit. Similarly, anti-discrimination legislation cannot provide a remedy for those who are denied work because their lack of qualifications or seniority make them the first candidates for unemployment and technological redundancy, or because of inadequate industrial training programmes. It cannot help them to obtain better housing if high mortgage rates put the price beyond their reach, or if urban renewal means only 'Negro removal' from decayed neighbourhoods without proper re-housing. Anti-discrimination legislation cannot by itself ensure that schools in poor neighbourhoods have good teachers and modern amenities or that the schools overcome the inequalities of class. Nor can it guarantee a sufficiently high standard of social security to alleviate the plight of those in greatest need. Only if such general sources of inequality are removed can legislation be really effective in dealing with the specific inequality of racial discrimination. However, even the mere existence of a formal declaration of equality, such as is implicit in any anti-discrimination law, draws attention forcibly to *de facto* inequalities, which the law itself may not be competent to deal with, but which in the long term may be remedied by fundamental social and economic reforms.

Lastly, it is also obvious that it is not sufficient to enact a well-framed statute; the law must also be effectively implemented. Its contents must be made known to all sections of the community. The procedure for making complaints of violations of the law must be simple, and complaints must be investigated with speed and vigour. The ultimate remedy must as far as possible redress the wrong. The enforcement of the law must not depend solely upon the haphazard process of individual complaints, but should also be concerned to eliminate *patterns* of racial discrimination. And, if the legislation is to succeed in promoting racial equality, it must be reinforced by deliberate programmes of voluntary action carried out by government, industry and voluntary bodies. Legislation and voluntary action are strengthened by each other; the legislative intent has to be translated into practice.

Some objections to legislation

Before considering how the objectives of anti-discrimination legislation can best be realized, we should examine the views of those who oppose the use of law altogether. Even the staunchest opponents of race relations legislation in this country generally accept that people ought to be treated on their own merits, without regard to their race or colour. For example, although Enoch Powell M.P. has asserted that 'The West Indian or Asian does not, by being born in England become an Englishman',[9] and has described some repellent practices

9. Speech at Eastbourne 16 November 1968 in Smithies and Fiddick (1969, p. 67).

as 'typical' of immigrants in Britain,[10] he replied, in answer to the question whether he considered himself to be a racialist:

if, by being a racialist, you mean a man who despises a human being because he belongs to another race, or a man who believes that one race is inherently superior to another in civilization or capability of civilization, then the answer is emphatically no (Smithies and Fiddick, 1969, p. 119).[11]

The use of legislation is therefore not usually challenged by the argument of the fanatic that it is right to deny opportunities to black people just because they are black. The arguments against legislation are more subtle. Many of them were deployed by Lord Radcliffe, a former Lord of Appeal in Ordinary, in a widely publicized lecture (1969), which requires careful scrutiny because of the judicial eminence of its author.

A theme which echoed through Lord Radcliffe's lecture was the foreign character of Britain's coloured communities. As he put it, we are the hosts and they are the guests; they are a 'large alien wedge'; they carry with their colour 'a flag of strangeness and all that strangeness implies'; they are 'rather colonies of immigrant workers than immigrant settlers in the full sense'; many of them will one day return to their homelands; and so on.

This is the crucial starting-point for many opponents of anti-discrimination legislation. It implies that it is understandable, if perhaps regrettable, that coloured people are discriminated against, because of their 'strangeness'; and that the problem of discrimination is a temporary phenomenon, because of the supposedly transitory nature of their residence in Britain. Yet such an analysis ignores the findings of the PEP report that discrimination is likely to become more widespread against the children of Commonwealth immigrants, who are not a 'large alien wedge', but born and educated in this country; and what is conspicuously absent is the simple but vital statement that they are entitled to equal rights on their merits, regardless of colour, origins or descent.

10. Television interview with David Frost 3 January 1969, in Smithies and Fiddick (1967, pp. 99–102).
11. But Mr Powell refused (pp. 120–22) to state his opinion as to whether there was any difference between the intellectual potential of a black man and a white man, because this was a scientific question, and he had not studied the evidence.

Lord Radcliffe's most fundamental objection to legal intervention was apparently philosophical. He doubted whether racial discrimination was sufficiently condemned in society to justify its condemnation by the law. In his view, 'the two key words . . . prejudice and discrimination, do not carry any association of moral ill-doing'; and he went on to observe, in criticism of the Race Relations Acts, that law should only be used in 'situations in which the moral issue is generally regarded as being beyond debate'.

No evidence was given by Lord Radcliffe to support his assertion that public opinion is seriously divided about the moral issue. But even if it were true that a majority of the community believed that it was not wrong to discriminate against other people on racial grounds, it would by no means follow that the law should reflect their views.

Such a conclusion would entail acceptance of what Professor H. L. A. Hart has termed the fallacy of 'moral populism':

the view that the majority have a moral right to dictate how all should live. . . . The central mistake is a failure to distinguish the acceptable principle that political power is best entrusted to the majority from the unacceptable claim that what the majority do with that power is beyond criticism and must never be resisted (1968, p. 79).

It is surely one of the most important functions of the law to protect people against persecution; and that function is certainly no less important when the persecution is carried on against a minority in the name of the majority. What is incidentally striking about the use of the moral populist argument is that, while it is raised as an objection to social legislation, such as the Race Relations Acts, it does not generally inhibit the English judiciary from seeking to enforce personal sexual morality.[12]

12. See e.g. *Shaw* v. *DPP* [1962] A.C. 223 (H.L.). Lord Devlin (1968) seems largely to have accepted Professor Hart's strictures against moral populism. Thus he states (at p. 95) that 'The law-maker's task, even in a democracy, is not the drab one of counting heads or of synthesizing answers to moral questions given in a Gallup poll'. And he observes (at p. 91) that 'There are societies today whose moral standards permit them to discriminate against men because of their colour.' And asks 'Have we to accept that? Is reason to play no part in the separation of right from wrong?'. But Lord Devlin's concern is with the legal enforcement of sexual morality. When he discusses the wider social context of the law he becomes a legal abstentionist. For example, he concludes (at p. 39) that 'it is wrong to regard the law of tort as associated with the criminal or quasi-criminal

By arguing that the words 'prejudice' and 'discrimination' do not carry any association of moral ill-doing, Lord Radcliffe was making a linguistic as well as a philosophical objection to the use of law. He was apparently suggesting that these key concepts are commonly used in a neutral or even a favourable sense, and so ought not to be condemned by the law. It is therefore necessary to look more closely at the meaning of both words.

A prejudice is a preconceived opinion either against or in favour of a person or thing. Being preconceived, the opinion or bias is not based on evidence. And usually, prejudice is linked with behaviour; it is not merely an opinion or bias held in the abstract, but a motive for acting in a particular fashion in favour or against someone. In this ordinary sense of the word, it may not always be pejorative to describe someone as being prejudiced, but it would rarely be regarded as complimentary. And when the word 'prejudice' is used in the context of race relations, it has an unmistakably pejorative meaning. It there means 'an avertive or hostile attitude towards a person who belongs to a [racial] group, simply because he belongs to that [racial] group, and is therefore presumed to have the objectionable qualities ascribed to the group' (Allport, 1958, p. 8).

The word 'discrimination' is, admittedly, more ambiguous, because it may be used in more than one sense. To discriminate, in the primary sense of the word, is to observe or make a difference or distinction; and it is complimentary to describe someone as 'discriminating'; it means that he is discerning or acute. However, discrimination is also used in a pejorative sense, and, when used in that sense, it means distinguishing unfavourably. The difference between the two usages can be brought out by saying that in the first (favourable) sense, we talk of people discriminating *between*, whereas

---

law in the work of promoting good standards of behaviour in the community'. Although he accepts that the terms of standard contracts may be oppressive, he doubts (at p. 50) 'whether there is a moral issue involved', apparently because exception clauses are 'a social nuisance rather than a moral evil'. Presumably, since the Race Relations Acts have created a statutory tort rather than a crime, Lord Devlin would not regard them as promoting good standards of behaviour in the community, and would consider that they deal with a 'social nuisance' rather than a 'moral evil'. It is this preoccupation with personal rather than social morality which is so often reflected in the decisions of the English courts.

in the second (pejorative) sense, we talk of people discriminating *against*. What this difference makes clear is that the notion of harm or of unfair deprivation is built into the concept of discrimination in its pejorative sense. If the ground for such unfavourable treatment is a person's race or colour, then the pejorative meaning of the word becomes obvious, and that is its meaning in the context of race relations. Racial discrimination describes one form of 'detrimental distinction which does not take account of the peculiar characteristics of an individual as such' (Allport, 1958, p. 51).

The relationship between racial prejudice and discrimination, and its relevance to legal sanctions, may be briefly stated as follows:

discrimination without prejudice leads to discrimination with prejudice; conversely, prejudice shorn of its capacity to manifest itself in discrimination withers away little by little. Strong and strictly enforced sanctions against any form of discrimination . . . would certainly not succeed overnight in eliminating blind out-group hostility. But they would go some way towards bringing it home to all of us that the life and rights of every human being are a matter to be seriously considered (Tajfel, 1966, p. 84).

However, Lord Radcliffe complained too of the *legal* imprecision of the concept of racial discrimination (a complaint, incidentally, which has not deterred English judges from applying far less precise concepts in other areas of the law). He

wrote down four different descriptions or definitions of it and none of them was the same as another [*sic*].

And he continues:

I cannot for myself, imagine how juridical notions can be founded on such vague conceptions. The conduct of human life consists of choices, and it is a very large undertaking indeed to outlaw some particular grounds of choice, unless you can confine yourself to such blatant combinations of circumstances as are unlikely to have any typical embodiment in this country. I try to distinguish in my mind between an act of discrimination and an act of preference, and each time my attempt breaks down.

The fact that legal definitions of discrimination may differ is to be expected. Indeed, what is surprising is the extent of the similarity between the concepts of discrimination which are contained in the many international conventions, written constitutions and statutes dealing with the subject, where it is always expressed in the second (pejorative) sense. The concept of discrimination is not entirely new even to the Common Law (see pp. 51–2).[13] And it has been defined both generally and in each particular situation covered by the Race Relations Acts (see chapter 4). It broadly means treating some people less favourably than others on racial or similar grounds, but it is also precisely defined in the legislation. And the distinction between an act of discrimination and an act of preference is that an act of discrimination is necessarily detrimental to someone, unlike an act of preference, which does not necessarily involve the notion of harm or unfair deprivation.

Lord Radcliffe also criticized the race relations legislation for providing that 'You must not have bad thoughts'. This reflects a common misconception. Whether one refers to the prohibition against racial discrimination or against incitement to racial hatred in the Race Relations Acts, neither set of provisions forbids 'bad thoughts', but only 'bad conduct'. In both cases, it is normally a necessary element in the unlawful action that it is done intentionally, but, unless the intention is translated into action, there is no violation of the law.

A further criticism made by Lord Radcliffe was that the type of racial discrimination which is made unlawful by the Race Relations Act 1968 is private in character and ought therefore to be beyond the reach of the law. He referred to an

immense difference in principle between imposing conditions on persons whose calling excludes freedom of choice, or preference as between members of the public, such as innkeepers, restaurant keepers and common carriers [as was done by the Race Relations Act 1965] . . . and persons such as employers and landlords, who are bound by the nature of their position to exercise preference and selection [as was done by the Race Relations Act 1968].

Lord Radcliffe therefore approved of the 1965 Act, which extended the innkeeper's Common Law duty to serve all comers without unfair discrimination to other places of public resort; but he disapproved of the 1968 Act, which extended the same duty to the fields of employment, housing and the provisions of commercial services.

13. cf. *London Electricity Board* v. *Springate* [1969] 3 All E.R. 289 (C.A.) (undue preference or discrimination under the Electricity Act 1947).

The answer to this argument is contained in one of Lord Radcliffe's earlier lectures, in which he recognized that:

there are relationships arising out of human institutions which deserve special protection from outside invasion or even voluntary relinquishment. It is in these matters, when they are threatened by the bullying of property rights or the aggression of contractual claims or, most menacing of all today, the usurping power of associations, that public policy . . . should make its voice heard (Radcliffe, 1960, pp. 65–6).

These words might have been specially written to express the philosophy of the Race Relations Acts, which are intended to ensure the 'special protection from outside invasion' of the rights of racial minorities and others to employment, housing and commercial services, when those rights are threatened by the 'bullying of property rights or the aggression of contractual claims or . . . the usurping power of associations'. The employer and the landlord are no doubt, in Lord Radcliffe's words, 'bound by the nature of their position to exercise preference and selection'. But the law requires they must not exercise their freedom of choice on racial grounds, because their contractual claims or property rights will then unfairly limit the rights of others to equal opportunities of obtaining employment and housing.

The denial of work by employers, the barring of membership by trade unions, the exclusion from housing by local authorities or private owners, solely on racial grounds, are not matters of *private* morality. They are as public in their effect as overcrowding, harassment, or extortion in the letting of residential accommodation, or 'sweating' or providing unsafe conditions at work, or enforcing restrictive practices in commerce. Parliament has legislated against each of these abuses of property and contract rights because they affect the public domain. There is therefore no departure from principle in legislating against racially discriminatory restrictions and exclusions based on these same rights of property and contract.[14]

14. This was recognized in a qualified form by Quintin Hogg M.P. (now Viscount Hailsham) during the Third Reading debate on the Race Relations Bill 1968. He said 'I recognize that individual liberty involves the liberty to do what other people regard as wrong. I would fight for that liberty even where it was unpopular to do so . . . I am, however, bound to add this proviso to that doctrine. Where individual acts add up cumulatively to a large-scale social injustice, it is, at least, for consideration whether Parliament ought not to deal

The Race Relations Act 1968 does no more, as a matter of principle, than apply the innkeeper's duty, developed by the courts in a pre-industrial age, to the necessities of modern, urban life.

One further objection is made to the principle of legislating against racial discrimination: it is said that such a law creates an unfair preference in favour of racial minorities, and thereby discriminates unfairly against the majority of the population. For example, Judge Harold Brown commented, in the course of awarding damages for trespass to the Brighton Corporation against a group of squatters in empty corporation property:

It seems curious that if a landlord closes the door on a coloured applicant merely because of his colour he might well get into serious trouble. But if he closes his door on white people with children merely because they have children, he is under no penalty at all (*Guardian*, 2 August 1969).

Similarly, Enoch Powell complained that:

a one-way privilege is to be established by Act of Parliament: a law, which cannot, and is not intended, to operate to protect them [i.e. the majority of the population] or redress their grievances, is to be enacted to give the stranger, the disgruntled and the *agent provocateur* the power to pillory them for their private actions.[15]

If they are understood in their most superficial sense, these criticisms are plainly false, for the Race Relations Acts are drafted in neutral language, which does not favour any racial group. Any victim of racial discrimination, white or black, may claim redress. If the protection of the law is sought more often by members of racial minorities, it is not because they are privileged, but because they are

with them. Where one is dealing with services offered to the public . . . and more particularly where those services are offered to a section of the public by one of the great sources of supply – the great landlords, the great trade unions, the great businesses or the great providers of transport – I begin to think that one is dealing with something where, if the individual right to the service is infringed, a serious source of injury might take place. In at least two of the areas . . . those of housing and employment, there is positive evidence that injustice on a serious scale may be taking place. I cannot therefore, say that it is inherently and necessarily an infringement of the liberty which I respect to attempt to legislate about it.' 9 July 1968, *Hansard* (H.C.), vol. 768, cols. 473–4. See also Quintin Hogg's Carr-Saunders Memorial Lecture (1970).

15. Speech at Birmingham 20 April 1968, in Smithies and Fiddick (1969, p. 40).

more commonly the victims of unfair treatment on grounds of race or colour. And it is no more accurate to describe the legislation as discriminatory in giving redress to the victim of racial discrimination than it would be to regard the Common Law as discriminatory in providing a remedy for the innocent party to a broken agreement, or for the man who is damaged by his neighbour's negligence.

But there is, of course, truth in the observation that the Race Relations Acts deal with only one of many forms of unfair discrimination. The worker who is refused employment, the would-be tenant who is denied accommodation, or the car owner who is charged an exorbitant insurance premium, has a legal remedy under the Acts if he has been discriminated against on racial grounds: but he has no remedy if the discrimination is on any other arbitrary or capricious ground.[16] So Quintin Hogg argued, during the Committee Stage of the 1968 Bill, that

If we are to create a series of acceptable social conditions in which discrimination does not take place, we must not . . . create a privileged class. . . . But [the Bill does create] a privileged class, because if we legislate by relation to race, only, we create a privileged class of victims.[17]

He therefore tabled an amendment which would have added to the Bill the wide definition of discrimination contained in the UN Universal Declaration of Human Rights, so making it unlawful to discriminate on the ground of 'race, colour, sex, language, religion, political or other opinion, national or social origin, property, birth or other status'. However, the amendment was never debated, because it was beyond the scope of the Bill's Long Title and out of order.

No doubt it would be desirable to provide legal redress for the victims of other, equally arbitrary, types of discrimination. Meanwhile, however, the victims of racial discrimination are 'privileged' only in the rather academic sense that they alone may seek a remedy under the Acts. It is because they are a gravely *under*-privileged group suffering from a high incidence of discrimination of a peculiarly

16. But the Court of Appeal in *Edwards* v. *Society of Graphical and Allied Trades* [1971] Ch. 354, has made it clear that the Courts will now intervene to prevent arbitrary or capricious behaviour by a trade union towards its members or would-be members. See further, p. 52.

17. 9 May 1968 Official Report (H.C.) Standing Committee B, col. 58.

insidious kind, that Parliament chose to legislate specifically against racial injustice. The fact that Parliament has not dealt with the many other forms of injustice is scarcely a convincing reason for opposing the Race Relations Acts; for that would be tantamount to saying that no injustice ought to be removed unless all similar forms of injustice are also simultaneously removed.

In practice, the introduction of a statute, admittedly limited in scope, frequently acts as a spur to further legislation covering similarly affected groups. Thus, knowing that the government were committed to legislation against racial discrimination in the field of employment, the Donovan Commission on Trade Unions and Employers' Associations observed that it would be invidious if one group of workers alone had redress against arbitrary dismissals, and recommended machinery to deal with arbitrary dismissals generally in industry.[18] Here a remedy proposed for a limited group of victims acted as a catalyst for wider reforms.[19]

The form of the law

It is obviously as important to frame the legislation in an effective, practicable form as it is to define its objectives. The role of legislation cannot be fully understood without some awareness of the type of law proposed to combat racial discrimination. In October 1967, Professor Harry Street's Committee published their report, which examined the legislative choices available to Parliament.[20] The Street Committee were not asked to consider whether it was desirable to introduce anti-discrimination in Britain, but to assess the effectiveness of such laws in other countries, and to recommend the type of law which would be appropriate if Parliament decided to introduce legislation here.

The Street Report emphasized that the scope of the law had to be

18. Royal Commission on Trades Unions and Employers' Associations (Cmnd 3623) (1968) para. 543.

19. The recommendation has now been enacted in the Industrial Relations Act 1971 (see pp. 201).

20. Report by Professor Harry Street, Sir Geoffrey Howe, Q.C. and Geoffrey Bindman, sponsored by the Race Relations Board and the National Committee for Commonwealth Immigrants, and published by Political and Economic Planning.

wide enough to cover the most damaging forms of racial discrimination: in employment – in recruitment, training, promotion, redundancies, conditions of work and membership of trade unions; in housing – in the sale of or letting of both private and local authority property; and in a great variety of commercial and social facilities and services. It made one exception to this principle: where racial discrimination occurred in relationships which were 'so personal and intimate that legal intervention is either likely to be ineffective or is politically or socially unacceptable, such matters should be outside the scope of the legislation. The Committee considered that the following categories might come within this exception: small lodging houses; employment in small firms and domestic service; and private lettings in which certain facilities were shared by resident landlords and tenants. However, the Committee were divided about whether the sale of houses by individual owner-occupiers ought also to be outside the scope of the law.

The Committee were impressed by the method of enforcement adopted in the United States and Canada, where special administrative agencies use education, persuasion and conciliation, and, only in the last resort, make legally enforceable orders. The Street Report endorsed the philosophy underlying this North American legislation that 'the primary aim is not to seek out and punish discrimination. The law is concerned to create the climate of opinion which will obviate discrimination.' It therefore took the view that similar techniques of law enforcement were appropriate for Britain.

The Street Committee did not discover the extent to which criminal laws against racial discrimination had actually been enforced in those countries which had enacted them.[21] Their preference for administrative rather than criminal enforcement was partly based on their conclusion that criminal proceedings would be much less likely to be brought. They also referred to several other disadvantages of the criminal process.

21. e.g. Brazil (Law No. 1390 of 1951), Ceylon (Prevention of Social Disabilities Act 1957); Costa Rica (Act No. 2694 of 1960); Liberia (Code of Laws, s. 263); and Panama (Act No. 25 of 1956). The constitutions of most East European countries also include criminal sanctions against racial discrimination e.g. Byelorussia, Bulgaria, Czechoslovakia, Hungary, Poland, Rumania, Ukraine, USSR and Yugoslavia, as does the Honduras constitution.

For example, in view of the obvious difficulties of obtaining evidence of racial discrimination, it would often be impossible to satisfy the criminal burden of proof beyond reasonable doubt, whereas it would be practicable to satisfy the civil standard of proof on the balance of probabilities. Criminal proceedings would be brought by the police or a public prosecuting authority, neither of which would be especially skilled in problems of race relations. Cases would be tried summarily by magistrates or on indictment by a jury; the former would often lack the necessary time or expertise, especially when dealing with the complexities of employment and housing; the latter might sympathize more with the accused, than with the victim of his crime. On the other hand, an administrative agency would have specialist skills; proceedings in civil courts would conveniently explore the complex issues involved in allegations of unlawful discrimination; and the courts could be assisted in their adjudication by lay experts in the fields of employment, housing and commerce, and race relations. Criminal proceedings would generate wide publicity in a punitive context, which might cast the discriminator in the role of martyr rather than law-breaker. And perhaps most important of all, the punishment of the wrongdoer, by fine or imprisonment, would not provide any remedy for the wrong suffered by his victim.

The alternative method of enforcement favoured by the Street Committee,[22] was first introduced in New York in 1945 by the Ives–Quinn Act and has since been adopted in many United States Federal and State anti-discrimination statutes, as well as those of most Provinces in Canada. It is a uniquely North American invention. The constitutions of most Western European countries[23] and new Commonwealth countries [24] contain guarantees of equality before the law,

22. The first detailed academic analysis and support for this approach in England was provided by Jowell (1965).

23. e.g. Austria (art. 6), Belgium (art. 6), Federal Republic of Germany (art. 3), France (arts. 2 and 77), Italy (art. 3), Luxembourg (art. 11), Netherlands (arts. 4 and 5) and Switzerland (art. 4). Discrimination based on nationality is prohibited between member countries of European Economic Community under the Treaty of Rome 1957 (arts. 7, 48 and 49), and the European Court of Justice has jurisdiction to determine whether there has been a violation of the Treaty.

24. e.g. Barbados, Botswana, The Gambia, Guyana, India, Jamaica, Kenya, Lesotho, Malawi, Malaysia, Nigeria, Pakistan, Sierra Leone, Trinidad, Uganda and Zambia.

without unfair discrimination, which may be directly invoked in the ordinary courts. However although the United States constitution and the Canadian Bill of Rights Act 1960 may both be enforced in this way in the courts, the anti-discrimination statutes of these countries are enforced by special administrative machinery.

Typically,[25] a commission is created under these statutes to eliminate and prevent racial and certain other forms of discrimination in employment, housing, and the provision of commercial facilities and services. The commission is authorized to receive and investigate complaints of discrimination, and is empowered to eliminate any discrimination discovered after investigation, by a process of private and informal conciliation. If conciliation fails to produce a satisfactory settlement, the commission usually has power to convene a public hearing to determine whether there has been unlawful discrimination and, where appropriate, to order a discriminator to 'cease and desist' from his unlawful conduct, or to pay compensation to the complainant for the loss which he has suffered. The commission may subsequently enforce its orders through the courts, and any person claiming to be aggrieved by the commission's decisions may appeal to the courts on points of law. In addition to these powers of investigation, conciliation and enforcement, the commission is normally responsible for organizing educational programmes aimed at reducing and eliminating discrimination and prejudice.

The anti-discrimination commission is modelled upon a typical American administrative body – the regulatory agency. For example, the Federal Communications Commission, the Federal Trade Commission, the National Labour Relations Board and the Securities and Exchange Commission all conduct investigations, hold hearings, and make enforceable orders, in discharging their functions of regulating the industries within their respective jurisdictions. They are able to compel witnesses to attend before them, bringing relevant documents with them, and to take evidence on oath. They are administrative bodies, but they also exercise judicial powers, subject to the overriding control of the ordinary courts.

There are several advantages in using machinery of this kind to

25. There is considerable variation among the different state commissions; typical powers are summarized in the Street Report, at chapter 4.

secure compliance with anti-discrimination legislation. The commission is able to meet the alleged discriminator on more equal terms than would be the case if the victim were left to seek his own remedy in the courts. It is better for race relations that discrimination should be eliminated by private, informal conciliation than by open litigious conflict. The commission is able to look beyond the facts of a particular complaint to the pattern of discrimination of which it is only one instance and which is revealed by previous complaints and by independent research. In settling the individual complaint, the commission is in a position to seek a strategic solution which will break the entire discriminatory pattern. The commission can provide a specialist investigation and conciliation service. It is well placed to make known the provisions of the law to members of racial minorities, to inform the general public about the purposes of the law, and to help industry and commerce to introduce their own programmes of voluntary action designed to promote equal opportunities.

However, as the Street Committee themselves reported, in practice, the actual achievements of the North American anti-discrimination commissions have been disappointing, and indeed American critics[26] have themselves drawn attention to the relative failure of the commissions to eliminate discriminatory practices, because of two main types of weakness: namely, defective powers and defective administration.

In the first category, the Street Report identified several weaknesses in the powers of enforcement. Some commissions were entirely dependent on receiving individual complaints before they could investigate apparently discriminatory situations; and, since many victims of discrimination felt too embarrassed, humiliated or intimidated to make complaints, or were unaware of their legal rights, or did not realize that they had in fact been discriminated against, the enforcement procedures were often vitiated at the outset. Some commissions lacked the power to require the attendance of witnesses or the pro-

26. See e.g. Sovern (1966); Norgren and Hill (1964a); (1964b); Report of the Sub-Committee on the Continuing Gap, of the Committee on Civil Rights and Responsibilities (1968). These critics suggest that the defects in the commissions are, to some extent, inherent in administrative agencies which have to perform the dual functions of conciliation and judicial enforcement; this duality of functions, inevitably, encourages too much conciliation and too little enforcement.

duction of documents and were therefore unable to obtain vital evidence. In some states it was difficult for the commissions to deal with breaches of conciliation agreements. In many states the remedies which could be obtained were insufficient to redress the wrong done to the complainant.

The Street Report also referred to criticisms of the manner in which the commissions exercised such powers as they possessed. There was often undue delay in dealing with complaints. Some commissions were suspected of bending under political pressures. It had been alleged that commission staff were not qualified or competent to carry out their duties with the requisite skill, energy and persistence. Inadequate or 'soft' settlements were often accepted by commissions which were reluctant to press a complaint, however apparently well-founded, against an intransigent discriminator. It was said that there was over-anxiety to conciliate at the expense of effective enforcement, and that there were unsatisfactory (or non-existent) procedures for checking whether conciliation agreements were being observed. Some commissions failed to ensure that other public agencies and licensed private bodies had carried out the objectives of the legislation. Many of these faults were the result of the failure of state and federal governments to give the commissions adequate support, particularly financial support.

However, the Street Committee did not regard these defects as irremediable; and with a few modifications they recommended that the American model could be transplanted to Britain. While recognizing the weaknesses of the North American commissions, they considered that their defects could be avoided by giving the Race Relations Board the powers which some American commissions lacked. Where the defects had been in the actual administration of the law, the Committee expressed the hope that they would be avoided by a 'governmental determination that it shall succeed'. And they added that 'this whole-hearted support from the government requires financial backing adequate to man the structure with competent and sufficient personnel', since, 'there is no necessary correlation between the quality of the drafting of a code concerning racial discrimination and the effectiveness of that code in operation. The machinery to implement the law is as important as the substantive law itself.'

The Street Report's recommendations were both novel and radical, within the context of existing English law. Although the principle of conciliation by an administrative body – the Race Relations Board – had been introduced in the Race Relations Act 1965,[27] neither the Board nor any other administrative agency in Britain possessed the wide range of new powers which the Street Committee proposed for the Race Relations Board.

The Report recommended that the Board and its local committees should continue to be responsible for securing compliance through conciliation, but suggested that, where conciliation failed, the Board should be empowered to bring enforcement proceedings before an independent tribunal, chosen from a special panel of judges and lay experts. The Board would also have the power to compel witnesses to attend before a local committee and produce relevant documents, during the conciliation process. The parties would be entitled to legal representation at hearings before the tribunal. The tribunal would make findings of fact and law, assess damages (if requested to do so by the Board), and recommend the form of any order which might be made against the respondent. The statute would contain a list of the types of orders the final choice of which would be left to the Board. The list would include orders requiring the respondent to cease and desist from further unlawful practices, or, positively, to sell or lease property, or offer employment, to the complainant, or to report to the Board the steps taken to comply with the law. In cases of emergency, the Board would be able to obtain temporary injunctions to prevent the respondent from disposing of property or filling a job vacancy before it was able to investigate the alleged discrimination. It was also recommended that non-discrimination conditions should be inserted into all government contracts, and that a special

27. See pp. 289–90. An interesting and little-known precedent was provided by the Race Relations Ordinance (No. 32) which was introduced in Northern Rhodesia in 1960. It created a Central Race Relations Advisory Committee and a Race Relations Board. The latter body had power to impose conditions and monetary penalties upon and, in the last resort, to withdraw licences from, proprietors and specified places of refreshment and recreation against whom allegations of racial discrimination were proved. It seems that the Board 'did valuable work in eliminating discrimination against Africans at the unofficial level'. (de Smith, 1964, p. 135). It is not known whether the draftsman of the British race relations statutes was aware of this Ordinance.

division of the Race Relations Board should supervise the proper performance of these conditions.

The aggregate of these proposals would have given the Board as much power as is possessed by any of the North American state commissions. They would not, however, have given the individual victim any right to bring proceedings on his own behalf in the courts. The Street Committee hoped that

speedy determination of complaints, together with interlocutory relief and the power to award damages proposed to be conferred on the Board, should make it unnecessary to create new causes of action for damages. We do not seek a proliferation of proceedings: the enactment in the public interest of laws restraining discrimination does not entail the creation of new remedies in tort.

In this respect the Street report did not go as far as Title VII of the US Civil Rights Act of 1964,[28] which permits the complainants to bring a civil action in the federal courts in cases of employment discrimination where the Equal Employment Opportunity Commission has been unable to secure voluntary compliance with the law by 'conference, conciliation and persuasion'. And the Street Committee were, of course, also unable to recommend that the individual should have equivalent judicial remedies to those available in the United States for violations of the 'equal protection' clause of the Fourteenth Amendment to the US Constitution (see pp. 177–8); for there is no fundamental Bill of Rights guaranteeing equal protection in English law.

The key to the enforcement of the legislation was an effective process of persuasion. To achieve this objective, the Street Committee placed their confidence in the ability of a strongly armed Board to encourage most people to accord equality of opportunity, regardless

28. S. 706 (e). That provision also gives the court discretion to permit the Attorney-General to intervene in the civil action if he certifies that the case is of general public importance. However, the Equal Employment Opportunity Commission, unlike its counterparts under US State laws, is not entitled to issue 'cease and desist' orders to deal with patterns of discrimination. The Chairman of the Commission has commented that 'The only thing we can do if we find discrimination is to sit down with the employer or with the unions and negotiate or conciliate the particular case. . . . It is almost impossible for us to do the job that has to be done unless and until we get cease-and-desist powers.' *New York Times* 21 July 1969, cited by Gould (1969, p. 237).

of race or colour; and, where persuasion failed, to secure an adequate remedy for the victim of discrimination. The absence of any individual right of action in the courts placed a heavy burden on the proposed statutory machinery. Everything depended upon the Board having a precisely defined role, coupled with sufficient legal powers.

The issues were clearly formulated by the Street Report. The objectives and the means of achieving them had been defined. It was now for Parliament to decide whether and to what extent the Street proposals and the ideals of the supporters of legislation should be translated into English law. To understand the shape of the present Race Relations Acts one must trace the history of the making of the Acts.

Chapter 3
The Making of the
Race Relations Acts

The first occasion on which Parliament legislated against racial discrimination was more than a century ago, in the Government of India Act 1833. It may also have been the first statutory provision in any country dealing specifically with the problem. The 1833 Act provided that no one should be denied employment in the Indian civil service solely because of his race or colour. But that provision and its subsequent fate are a forgotten chapter of British Imperial history (see Appendix 1); and the direct origins of the present antidiscrimination legislation in this country are much more recent (Hindell, 1965).

The process by which the Race Relations Acts were fashioned is described in some detail in what follows, to explain why the legislation was enacted in its present form. There are many aspects of the present law which can be understood only against this background. The history of the legislation also illustrates some of the main virtues and defects of the British method of law-making; it is for others to decide whether and in what respects that system could be improved. And this chapter is also a reminder of the obvious fact, too often forgotten by lawyers, that Acts of Parliament are not divine commands inscribed since time immemorial upon tablets of stone. Sometimes, they are spurred by complex social forces which compel the law to recognize new patterns of behaviour. Sometimes they are the product of a conviction that certain kinds of behaviour are morally or socially unacceptable in the current state of civilization. Almost invariably the actual shape taken by legislation is the result of a political process of intricate bargaining and compromise.

In 1950, Reginald Sorensen M.P. introduced a Colour Bar Bill which would have made it a criminal offence to discriminate on racial grounds in providing services and facilities in specified public places, or to publish or display notices or advertisements indicating that racial discrimination would be practised in such places. The maximum penalties were a fine of £5 for a first offence and £25 for a second or subsequent offence. The Bill, like many others which were later to be introduced, was not debated by the Commons.

Two years later, the Commonwealth Sub-Committee of the National Executive Committee of the Labour Party asked two experts to advise whether anti-discrimination legislation should be sponsored by the Labour Party. Professor Kenneth Little, a distinguished social anthropologist, replied that, in his view, there was 'a good case both in principle and in fact for the enactment of colour bar legislation . . . as a means of stirring the national conscience and of creating a new standard of public behaviour in relation to coloured people'. He also recommended that administrative machinery, similar to that which had been created in New York in 1945, should be set up to deal 'both practically and positively with the wider implications of the problem'. The other consultant, Sir Lynn Ungoed-Thomas M.P., a former Solicitor-General who was later to become a High Court Judge, thought that it would be better to confine legislation to specific abuses, such as discriminatory clauses in leases, discrimination in inns, public houses, lodging houses and dance halls, and also in employment, rather than to use it for 'purely propaganda value'. Like Little, he also believed that administrative action could be of value, especially in dealing with landladies who discriminated against coloured students. The National Executive Committee took no action on this advice at that stage.

In 1956, Fenner Brockway, M.P., introduced a Racial Discrimination Bill to prohibit racial and religious discrimination in various public places. The Bill also sought to make it illegal for an employer of more than fifty people to discriminate in recruiting, promoting or dismissing workers or in the terms and conditions of employment, and would have made discriminatory covenants in leases void. As in the Sorensen Bill, anyone found guilty was to be liable to a maximum fine of £25, but the Brockway Bill went on to provide that anyone suffering damage as a result of racial discrimination should be entitled to recover damages in a civil action, and that any person practising racial discrimination in an activity for which a licence was required might be deprived of his licence by the appropriate authority.

During the next eight years, Fenner Brockway introduced eight similar Bills. In those published after 1960, he omitted the provisions against employment discrimination. He has since explained (1967, p. 81) that he did so

because of some trade union opposition. I wanted to get the *principle* of non-discrimination accepted and was prepared not to go the whole way in the first instance. I am not sure that I was right, because employment, with housing, is now proving the severest sphere of discrimination.

Brockway's 1961 Bill also differed from previous versions by including a clause making it an offence to incite to racial hatred,[1] whether by speech or writing, and by increasing the fine for unlawful discrimination to £100. The incitement provision originated not so much in racialist propaganda against coloured people as in a mounting tide of anti-semitic speeches which were being made at well-publicized public meetings in the early 1960s; and it was keenly supported by the Board of Deputies of British Jews which continued to organize a strong campaign for legislation on this subject.

Although Brockway succeeded in obtaining a Second Reading for his 1957 Bill,[2] it was counted out because fewer than forty Members were present for the debate. It is perhaps an ironical commentary on the extent of public indifference to the growing problem of racial discrimination in Britain that the Parliamentary response was so poor only a year before racial violence erupted in Notting Hill. However, in 1958, largely as a result of the Notting Hill disturbances, the Labour Party committed itself to making racial discrimination illegal,[3] and, in 1959, the Labour Opposition's Front Bench spokesman, James Callaghan, urged the Government[4] to introduce legislation prohibiting racial discrimination in any public place. The request went unheeded.

In its manifesto for the 1964 General Election, the Labour Party pledged itself to legislate against racial discrimination and incitement

1. Incitement to racial hatred is discussed in chapter 10.
2. 10 May 1957, *Hansard* (H.C.), vol. 569, cols. 1425–38; 24 May 1957, cols. 1602–08.
3. 'Racial discrimination', statement by the Labour Party, 1958, p. 4.
4. 7 December 1959, *Hansard* (H.C.), vol. 615, cols. 115–16.

in public places. The Liberal Party's manifesto also stated that 'Liberals reject racial discrimination for they believe fundamentally in the brotherhood of man,' but it did not contain any specific commitment to legislation. The Conservative Party's manifesto made no reference to the subject. The Conservatives were reluctant to introduce legislation because they believed that any prohibition of racial discrimination would be ineffectual, and doubted whether it was in any case right to do so.[5]

At the beginning of 1964, the Shadow Labour Cabinet and the Society of Labour Lawyers were both asked to draft proposals which would give effect to the Labour Party's pledge. The Shadow Cabinet's working committee (Sir Frank Soskice, Douglas Houghton and Gilbert Mitchison) were mainly concerned with the problem of racial incitement. The Soskice Committee concluded that the Public Order Act 1936 should be extended so as to make it illegal to defame individuals or groups with the deliberate intention of stirring up racial hatred, and they proposed severe penalties of up to three years' imprisonment or a £10,000 fine.

The Soskice Committee were content to confine the scope of legislation against racial discrimination to public places. They refused to follow the Brockway Bills by banning discriminatory leases, or by providing for the withdrawal of licences from discriminators or the bringing of civil proceedings against them. Racial discrimination was to be a criminal offence, and prosecutions would be brought only with the consent of the Attorney-General.

Meanwhile, the Society of Labour Lawyers had set up a Committee on Racial Discrimination, under the chairmanship of Andrew Martin, Q.C.[6] They too proposed that it should be made unlawful to promote racial hatred or to discriminate on racial grounds in places of public resort. They recognized the importance of racial discrimination in employment and housing, but (with a minority dissenting[7]) made no proposals in these areas. They did, however, observe that

5. See Written Answer by the Home Secretary (Rt Hon. Henry Brooke, M.P.) 6 February 1964, *Hansard* (H.C.), vol. 688, cols. 214–15; Viscount Kilmuir, L.C., 14 May 1962, *Hansard* (H.L.), vol. 240, cols. 507–20.

6. The other members were Cedric Thornberry, Peter Benenson, Anthony Lester, F. Ashe Lincoln, Q.C., Evi Underhill and Michael Zander. E. J. B. Rose and Nicholas Deakin also participated as experts in race relations.

7. i.e. Lester and Zander.

American administrative techniques of conciliation might be more appropriate than criminal penalties if legislation were brought in to deal with discrimination in those areas.

This was the state of opinion on the eve of the General Election in October 1964. The exploitation of racial prejudice as a significant factor in that Election underlined the political importance of the problem (Deakin, 1965; Foot, 1965). In the weeks which followed, a small informal group,[8] which included the dissenting members of the Labour Lawyers' Committee, drafted proposals which were designed to persuade the new Labour Government to tackle racial discrimination in employment, housing and commercial services.

The group were all Labour Party supporters. They were impressed by North American evidence that anti-discrimination laws were more likely to be effectively enforced by administrative machinery than by proceedings in the criminal courts; but they realized that the Government were already committed to introducing criminal sanctions against racial discrimination in public places. Their strategy was therefore to present a scheme which was not inconsistent with the Government's intention, and which could eventually be strengthened and expanded. In late November 1964, they sent their proposals to the Prime Minister, the Home Secretary, the Lord Chancellor and the Law Officers. They suggested that a Citizen's Council should be created modelled partly upon the Press Council. It should be empowered to investigate discrimination on the ground of race, colour, religion, sex and national origin, in the fields of education, employment, housing, insurance, the grant of credit facilities and the administration of justice. The Council would have statutory powers to compel the attendance of witnesses and the production of documents and other information. Its principal weapon would be publicity, and its main task would be the education of public opinion. It would publish findings and make recommendations, and would be empowered to attempt to end discrimination by persuasion and conciliation. It would also be able to conduct general research into problems of discrimination.[9]

8. i.e. Nicholas Deakin, Bernard Donoughue, Jeffrey Jowell, Anthony Lester, Ian MacDonald, Roger Warren Evans and Michael Zander.
9. The Group had been impressed by the arguments set out in Bonfield (1964). Their own views were elaborated by Jowell (1965).

The Group won support for their Citizen's Council from several national newspapers and also from some Members of Parliament. However, they failed to obtain a positive response from the Government. Then, in the following month, a multi-racial Campaign Against Racial Discrimination (CARD) was set up after meetings between representatives of the main immigrant groups. Until the creation of CARD, the voices of members of the coloured communities had been conspicuously silent during public discussion about anti-discrimination legislation. Henceforth, during the next three years, CARD was to play an important role in lobbying for legislation on behalf of the victims of racial discrimination (Rose *et al*, 1969, pp. 507–9, 525–7, 543, 546).

The CARD Legal Committee, which included several of those who had advocated the Citizens' Council,[10] developed the previous proposals in greater detail, and, at a meeting in February 1965 the membership of the organization debated and approved them. It was agreed that the scope of legislation should be wide enough to include the main problems of racial discrimination in employment, housing and the provision of commercial services, and that the law should be enforced by a statutory body empowered to investigate, conciliate, hold hearings and to make legally enforceable orders against those found to have violated the law. The CARD resolution stated that the object of legislation should be to alter conduct and provide individual remedies, rather than to punish. As for incitement to racial hatred, the CARD meeting accepted that legislation was desirable but warned that it should not encroach upon legitimate areas of free speech. After this meeting, lobbying activities were intensified, and, by the end of the following month, those politicians and journalists who favoured anti-discrimination legislation, had broadly accepted CARD's main proposals.

They were also broadly supported by the various immigrant organizations which were either directly affiliated to CARD or involved in similar activities, including the Indian Workers' Association (Southall), the West Indian Standing Conference, and the Federation of Pakistani Associations.

On 9 April 1965, Sir Frank Soskice published his Race Relations Bill. He had not been convinced by the lobbyists. Under the Bill,

10. i.e. Jowell, Lester, MacDonald and Zander.

racial discrimination was to be a criminal offence, punishable by a maximum fine of £100, if practised in hotels, public houses, restaurants, theatres, cinemas, public transport and any place of public resort maintained by a public authority. The Bill did not deal with discrimination in employment, and its only reference to housing was a clause dealing with discriminatory restrictions on the disposal of tenancies. Prosecutions were to be brought only with the authority of the Attorney-General. There was to be no conciliation agency, and no civil remedy for those damaged by racial discrimination. Incitement to racial hatred was to be made illegal and punishable by up to two years' imprisonment or a maximum fine of £1000 and the Public Order Act 1936 was to be extended to cover threatening, abusive or insulting words or behaviour which were likely to cause a breach of the peace.

On the day of the Bill's publication, the Society of Labour Lawyers, on whose reconstituted Race Relations Committee the previous minority were now in the majority, issued a further interim report, recommending the extension of the Bill to discrimination in housing, employment, and certain credit and other service industries, and the establishment of a Conciliation Commission. At the same time, a number of newspapers greeted the Bill critically, and echoed the view of CARD and the Labour Lawyers that it did not deal with the real problems and did not use the right means of enforcement.

Then, shortly before the Second Reading of the Bill, the Conservative Opposition decided their attitude towards the Bill. Their approach may have been influenced by an informal meeting between the Shadow Home Secretary, Peter Thorneycroft, and representatives of CARD, at which the principle of enforcement by conciliation had been urged on CARD's behalf. The Opposition's position was to prove decisive in the subsequent shaping of the Bill. They decided to oppose any use of the criminal law in dealing with racial discrimination, and to emphasize the threat to freedom of speech which they claimed was posed by the incitement provisions. It was a subtle strategy, for it enabled the Opposition to avoid appearing to be wholly negative in rejecting any kind of legislation. Instead they joined the main supporters of anti-discrimination legislation, outside the Government, in advocating the use of conciliation in place of criminal sanctions.

Sir Frank Soskice does not seem to have had much enthusiasm for the race relations legislation to which the Government were committed. And he was faced with the difficult task of steering the Bill through a divided Parliament, with a tiny Government majority, in an atmosphere of growing racial intolerance among the general public. Although it is inevitably a matter for speculation, it seems likely that, because of these difficulties, soon after the Bill was published he decided to seek a wider consensus in support of the Bill. He would do so by making a substantial concession to the lobbyists and to the Opposition by substituting conciliation for criminal sanctions; and at the same time he would try to secure Opposition approval by defending the Bill against the attempts of his own backbenchers to widen its scope or strengthen its enforcement.

In introducing the Bill during the Second Reading debate, Soskice explained[11] that it was

concerned with public order. Overt acts of discrimination in public places, intensely wounding to the feelings of those against whom these acts are practised, perhaps in the presence of many onlookers, breed the ill will which, as the accumulative result of several such actions over a period, may disturb the peace.

This was the classic justification for using the criminal law: not the redress of individual wrongs, but the preservation of the peace. But Soskice expressly recognized that Government policy had to deal with the wider subject of employment, housing, education and the administration of the social services, and that, if the Bill had been intended to deal with these issues, civil sanctions might have been more appropriate. He promised to 'take careful note' of what was proposed in argument in favour of conciliation in the course of the debate.

Thorneycroft then moved an Opposition amendment declining to give a Second Reading 'to a Bill which introduces criminal sanctions into a field more appropriate to conciliation and the encouragement of fair employment practices while also importing a new principle into the law affecting freedom of speech'. He doubted whether discrimination was widespread in the narrow area covered by the Bill, and appeared to criticize the measure for not dealing with the most

11. 3 May 1965. The debate is reported in *Hansard* (H.C.), vol. 711, cols. 926–1060.

important types of discrimination in employment, housing, boarding houses and clubs. He deplored the attempt 'to import the taint of criminality into this aspect of our affairs', and supported the conciliation method; not 'conciliation without teeth', but conciliation followed where necessary by proceedings in the civil courts. And he devoted most of his remaining criticisms to the part of the Bill which dealt with racial incitement.[12] All the Labour Members who spoke during the debate[13] also favoured the principle of enforcement by conciliation and civil proceedings, and several of them referred to the CARD proposals and to North American experience. However, there seems to have been some misunderstanding on the Government Front Bench about what the critics were proposing, for, in his winding-up speech, the Solicitor-General was under the mistaken impression that cases of racial incitement as well as those of racial discrimination might be dealt with by conciliation.[14]

In view of the subsequent religious disturbances in Ulster, it is interesting to recall that two Members, Bernard Floud and Norman St John-Stevas, attempted to persuade the Government, during the Second Reading debate, to include religious discrimination in the Bill, and to apply it to Northern Ireland. The Home Secretary explained that the Northern Ireland Government had opposed the application of the Bill in their part of the United Kingdom. Robert Chichester-Clark, Member for Londonderry, claimed that the safeguards against religious discrimination in the Government of Ireland Act 1920 were 'completely adequate'. Bernard Floud wondered 'how many people living in or with experience of Northern Ireland felt that that Act has been effective in preventing religious discrimination'. But another Ulster M.P. Captain Orr, replied that Parliament had 'set up a subordinate Parliament representing the people of Northern Ireland' and 'that is the place to test the matter'.[15]

12. Racial incitement is considered in detail in Chapter 10.

13. i.e. Sir Barnett Janner, Reginald Freeson, David Ennals, Shirley Williams and Donald Chapman. Jeremy Thorpe expressed similar views on behalf of the Liberals.

14. *Hansard* (H.C.), vol. 711, col. 1041.

15. A similar attempt was made subsequently to apply the Race Relations Act 1968 to Northern Ireland, but it was opposed by the Attorney-General and the Shadow Home Secretary, and so met with the same lack of success.

During the three weeks between the Second Reading and the Committee Stage, the Home Secretary drafted amendments to his own Bill. Criminal sanctions were to be dropped in cases of discrimination and retained only for racial incitement. Instead, a Race Relations Board was to be created to secure compliance with the anti-discrimination clause. The Board would appoint local conciliation committees to investigate complaints of discrimination and settle disputes, and generally to secure compliance with the law. If conciliation failed to achieve these objects, the local committee would report to the Board, which, in cases in which the Board considered it likely that discrimination would continue, would refer the matter to the Attorney-General. If he confirmed the Board's view, the Attorney-General would be empowered to bring proceedings in Court seeking an injunction to restrain further acts of discrimination from being committed. The ultimate sanction against disobedience of such an injunction would be the usual one in such cases: a fine or imprisonment for contempt of court.

These Government amendments represented a real victory for the lobbyists. They had pressed for a conciliation agency and civil enforcement because they wanted the legislation to cover discrimination in the complex fields of employment and housing where, in their view, conciliation and civil proceedings were more likely to be effective than criminal sanctions. Because of the Opposition's support for this approach, they had succeeded in changing the method by which the Bill would be enforced. The most difficult step remained; to extend the scope of the Bill.

However, Soskice refused to widen the Bill's coverage in any way. Although it no longer contained criminal penalties for discrimination, he continued to treat it as though it were penal in its consequences; nor was he willing to give a personal remedy to the individual victim of discrimination. At the first sitting of the Standing Committee, he explained[16] that 'The remedy is still a public remedy. No remedy is given to any individual.' And, at a later sitting, he said that he did not 'think it right that the negation of civilian rights in this case should result in proceedings, many of which may be embittered, as between individuals. This is a question of a general public

16. See generally, *Official Report*, Standing Committee B, 25 May 1965–1 July 1965, cols. 3–412.

relationship which should be asserted in the name of the public at large by the Attorney-General resorting to the county court.'

There was little for the Opposition to criticize in Soskice's position. Thorneycroft was left to 'welcome this change of heart' on behalf of the Opposition, and to complain about the procedural irregularity and resulting inconvenience to members of the Standing Committee in introducing such substantial amendments after the Second Reading of the Bill.

Soskice's strategy had succeeded. He could be certain of carrying his Bill with Conservative support, against all attempts to widen its scope or strengthen its enforcement provisions. But the strategy was bought at some immediate cost to Labour Party unity. Seven[17] of the thirteen Labour M.P.s on the Standing Committee openly expressed their view that the Bill was inadequate; and the Home Secretary's support from the Labour Benches was limited to the three tied Government men, Edward Milne (Soskice's Parliamentary Private Secretary), William Whitlock (a Whip) and George Willis (Minister of State for Scotland). The Labour critics pushed their amendments to a division four times, but on each occasion they were defeated by an alliance between the Front Benches.

The first skirmishes were fought over clause 1 of the Bill, which defined the 'places of public resort' to which the Bill applied. The definition did no more than extend the innkeeper's Common Law duty (see pp. 63–5) to provide refreshments and lodgings to all comers without unfair discrimination, to certain specified places of public resort. Donald Chapman moved an amendment which would have enabled the Courts to apply the Bill to public places which were not specifically mentioned in clause 1. He was supported by a Conservative, Norman St John-Stevas, who warned that, unless the amendment was accepted, hairdressers, beauty parlours, lodging houses and private hotels would be able to practise racial discrimination. David Ennals also criticized the omission of shops, holiday camps and clubs from the Bill. However, Soskice insisted that it was essential that such novel legislation should be precisely worded, and the amendment was defeated. Chapman expressed disappointment that, in the result, clause 1 was 'a sledgehammer to crack a nut'.

17. Donald Chapman, David Ennals, Reginald Freeson, Dr Maurice Miller, Ivor Richard, Paul Rose and Shirley Williams.

Chapman then attempted to meet Soskice's objection to imprecise definitions by moving an amendment which would have applied the Bill to 'any shop, office, agency or similar place where goods or services are customarily available to members of the public'. But Soskice complained that the change 'enormously widens the scope of the clause'. He asked the Standing Committee to 'think of all the shops throughout the United Kingdom; the large shop, the small shop, the big store, the village grocer and the rest of them. They would all be brought in.' The amendment was rejected by ten votes to six.

Chapman also attempted to alter clause 2 of the Bill (which was to become section 5 of the Act). This provision prevented a landlord from restricting the transfer of the tenancy of his property to someone on racial grounds. Chapman sought to apply the clause to similar restrictions on the transfer of *freehold* property. The Common Law position about such restrictions was obscure (see p. 60), and he wanted Parliament to put the matter beyond doubt. However, after an esoteric debate, which did not entirely remove the obscurity, Chapman accepted the Home Secretary's assurance that the amendment was unnecessary because racially restrictive covenants would not, in Soskice's view, be enforceable at Common Law.

Finally, the Labour critics tried, again without success, to strengthen the powers of the Race Relations Board. Chapman sought to give the Board the power to hold hearings, summon witnesses, publish its findings and to bring civil proceedings in the county court itself. Soskice argued that 'The function of the conciliation committees ... is that of conciliation in the real sense, without compulsion', and that it would be 'a mistake to open the door to individual complaints which could be pressed further and further'. When Shirley Williams referred to evidence from the New York Commission on Human Rights that 'it was absolutely essential to have the individual sanction of the right to bring a civil action', Soskice insisted that

The whole point of the Bill is that we are dealing with a public wrong. We are talking of an infringement of rights owed by a section of the community. We are trying to get the battle away from a battle between an aggrieved person and the person who is said to have aggrieved him.

The Home Secretary returned to this theme of keeping the problem away from the courts during the Report Stage of the Bill.[18] After referring to the uncertain position of gypsies under the statutory definition of discrimination, he said, 'Possibly that is one of the puzzles which ultimately will come before the court. I hope that it will never come before the court, because I hope that this Act will not result in proceedings.' At any rate so far as the anti-discrimination provisions of the 1965 Act were concerned, his hope was to be realized.

Soskice finally reflected more generally on the future of the legislation with these words:

We have taken what in a sense is a first step. I hope that events will show that it is not necessary to take any further step and that this may be the last step. If the Bill turns out to be a successful Act of Parliament and to achieve its purpose, it will, by a paradox . . . very rarely need to be called into operation. . . . [T]he Government will watch the situation as it develops. Should it appear that the provisions are inadequate to deal with the mischief against which it is directed, it may well be necessary for the Government later – one hopes never – to expand its scope and to reconsider its effect and operation. I have said and I repeat, that I pray that we shall never be faced with that need. It would be an ugly day in this country if we had to come back to Parliament to extend the scope of this legislation, which is designed to prevent friction from developing between different communities in this country.

For the Home Secretary, it was the end of the chapter of law-making. But for the lobbyists it was only the beginning. They had begun their campaign too late to alter the Government's main policy towards legislation, which had been formulated eight years before, but they had succeeded in substituting conciliation machinery for criminal proceedings. The legislation did not deal with the worst problems of racial discrimination, and the conciliation machinery lacked teeth. But the Home Secretary could not have dreamt, when he made his final speech in the Commons debate in July 1965, that the 'ugly day' would arrive so soon when Parliament would again have to return to the subject.

Meanwhile, if the lobbyists could find some satisfaction in the final shape of the Bill, both Government and Opposition could also claim

18. 16 July 1965, *Hansard* (H.C.), vol. 716, cols. 969–1065.

to have won substantial victories. By introducing conciliation without strengthening the Bill, the Home Secretary had carried the Conservative Front Bench with him. And by successfully urging the conciliation process upon the Government, while opposing the racial incitement provisions, the Opposition could boast its concern both with practical commonsense and with freedom of speech.

During the period from shortly before the 1964 General Election until the Race Relations Bill finally became law, a profound change occurred in the Government's attitude towards coloured immigration from the new Commonwealth (Rose *et al.*, 1969, ch. 16; Foot, 1965, ch. 8). In 1961, the Labour Opposition had fiercely resisted the Commonwealth Immigrants Bill, mainly on the ground that it was blatantly discriminatory to seek to limit the entry into Britain of coloured immigrants; and the Opposition had succeeded in modifying several of the Bill's harshest provisions. However, by 1964, the Labour Party had come to accept, as they expressed the matter in their Election Manifesto, that 'the number of immigrants entering the United Kingdom must be limited', and that 'until a satisfactory agreement covering this can be negotiated with the Commonwealth, a Labour Government will retain immigration control.' By the middle of the following year, the Government had grown acutely sensitive to mounting Conservative pressure for still more stringent controls to be imposed upon coloured immigration to Britain.

This shift in Labour's attitude was exemplified by a speech made by Roy Hattersley in a debate on immigration in March 1965. After recalling that he had passionately opposed the 1962 Act, he said that in retrospect he felt that

the Labour Party of that time should have supported it. . . . I now believe that there are social as well as economic arguments [for limiting Commonwealth immigration], and I believe that unrestricted immigration can only produce additional problems, additional suffering and additional hardship unless some kind of limitation is imposed and continued.[19]

It should perhaps be recalled that the political controversy was not and had not been about whether 'some kind of limitation' should be imposed on immigration. The real dispute was about whether immigration control should be based on colour, and also about whether

19. 23 March 1965, *Hansard* (H.C.), vol. 709, cols. 380–81. See also, Hattersley (1965).

it was right to introduce only negative controls, unaccompanied by positive measures to facilitate the settlement of Commonwealth immigrants in Britain. To those who still believed that the 1962 Act had been rightly opposed, it seemed that the appeasement of racial prejudice through racially discriminatory controls would not improve race relations in Britain, but would only encourage the opponents of coloured immigration to increase their demands. On the other hand, the Government itself came largely to accept the Opposition view that the larger the number of coloured people who were admitted to Britain, the more racial prejudice was likely to increase.

It is not possible to evaluate all the factors which influenced this shift in the Government's attitude, but they probably included the small size of the Government's Parliamentary majority, the prospect of another General Election in the near future, and the electoral unpopularity feared to have been incurred by passing the Race Relations Act. As a result, in August 1965, the Government reacted by introducing a White Paper on Immigration from the Commonwealth.[20] The White Paper fell into two main parts: one section dealt with immigration policy and the other included departmental proposals to tackle the problems of integration. Under the first section, the total number of employment vouchers issued to Commonwealth immigrants was reduced to a maximum of 8500 a year (of which 1000 were to be allotted to Malta); entry of unskilled workers without specific jobs to come to was abolished; 'strict tests of eligibility' were to be applied to the entry of dependants; powers of medical examination extending to dependants were to be sought; and, finally, new powers were to be sought to combat evasion of immigration control, including an extension of the Home Secretary's deportation powers. The introduction of an inflexible limit on the number of Commonwealth immigrant workers who could enter Britain each year was a major innovation; and it did not apply to alien workers.

The White Paper met with a storm of protest against both the immigration provisions and also against the apparent connection made in the second section of the document between housing, education and health problems and the presence of coloured immigrants.

20. Cmd 2739, August 1965.

During the months between the publication of the White Paper and the coming into force of the Race Relations Act (in November 1965) the continuing public debate about race relations was diverted from the subject of anti-discrimination legislation to that of coloured immigration. Few observers would then have predicted that the two issues were again to be thrust together into the cockpit of politics less than three years later.

At the end of December 1965, Sir Frank Soskice retired, owing to ill-health, and was replaced by Roy Jenkins. The change was of decisive importance to the making of the Race Relations Acts (Rose *et al.*, 1969, ch. 26). Jenkins was firmly committed from the outset to the view that legislation had an important role to play in combating racial discrimination. For several reasons, however, remarkable political skill was called for in order to extend the 1965 Act. The Government had only recently tackled the subject, and it had no mandate to legislate in the field of employment or housing. Any extension of the Act might well be electorally unpopular, and would be better made long before a General Election; but there was scant support in the Government, the Labour Party, or the trade union movement for such a bold and rapid action. In retrospect it is striking that Jenkins decided on his objectives and his strategy at such an early stage and that he remained true to both in spite of formidable opposition.

One of Jenkins's first decisions in his new office was to appoint Mark Bonham Carter to the chairmanship of the Race Relations Board, which was fortunately still vacant. Bonham Carter 'made it a condition of appointment that he should be able to put the case, after a year's operation, for the extension of the scope of the Act and a revision of the Board's powers' (Rose *et al.*, 1969, p. 520). In selecting John Lyttle as its Chief Conciliation Officer, the new Board chose someone who had acquired invaluable experience as a senior research officer at the Labour Party's headquarters. In January 1966, Maurice Foley moved from the Department of Economic Affairs, where, somewhat incongruously, he had acted as Minister with special responsibility for immigrants, to continue in that capacity as junior Minister at the Home Office. Foley shared Jenkins's belief in the need for further legislation, and was to prove a valuable ally in subsequent events.

The tactics initially adopted by Jenkins were to make a series of carefully timed speeches committing himself (and, by implication, his Ministerial colleagues) further and further in the direction of legislation. His first speech was not made until after the General Election of March 1966. Then, on 23 May 1966, he said at the National Co-ordinating Conference of Voluntary Liaison Committees

Some of you, I know, will think we have a better Race Relations Board than we have a Race Relations Act. I would say two things on this. First, I think a lot can be done under the present Act and, secondly, as I have told the Board, my mind is far from being closed about future changes to the Act. . . . But that cannot be this session. . . . Many, I know, take the view that discrimination in employment and indeed housing should be covered by legislation. For the moment, I reserve judgment on the legislative point (1967, p. 270).

A month later, two studies were commissioned jointly by the Race Relations Board and the National Committee for Commonwealth Immigrants (NCCI), the voluntary forebear of the present statutory Community Relations Commission, at Jenkins's personal instigation. The first study, financed by the Rowntree Trust, was undertaken by the independent research organization, Political and Economic Planning (PEP) to evaluate the nature and extent of racial discrimination in Britain (see p. 80). The second inquiry was carried out by three lawyers,[21] under the chairmanship of Professor Harry Street, to examine overseas experience regarding anti-discrimination legislation, and to recommend how English law might best be amended in the light of this experience, assuming that Parliament decided that further legislation was desirable.

Meanwhile, the pressure for new legislation continued. Three advisory panels of the NCCI drafted proposals for the amendment of the 1965 Act. In mid-June 1966 a letter was sent to the Home Secretary by eighty-seven clergymen of all denominations from most of the major areas of Commonwealth immigrant settlement in Britain. The letter urged that the 1965 Act be extended to cover racial and religious discrimination in employment, housing, the granting of credit facilities and mortgages, and in insurance. It drew

21. i.e. Professor Harry Street, Sir Geoffrey Howe, Q.C. and Geoffrey Bindman. The cost of the Street Report was met by Marks and Spencer Limited. Its recommendations are summarized on pp. 98–106.

attention to the startling unawareness by many public figures of the extent to which racial discrimination was actually practised in their areas, to the future social dangers of such discrimination, particularly against the second generation, and to the degree of alienation of a great majority of coloured immigrants (Patterson, 1969, pp. 330–31).

During the summer, CARD organized a project using volunteers to test the existence of discrimination and make complaints to the Race Relations Board, whether or not such complaints came within the scope of the 1965 Act. Fifty cases were sent to the Board, of which forty involved young coloured people, born and educated in Britain. Shortly afterwards, the Home Secretary expressed concern at the implications of the growing body of evidence of discrimination against the second generation.

In November 1966, the Society of Labour Lawyers published its third report on race relations. The report recommended that far-reaching changes should be made to the 1965 Act, modelled on North American legislation. The scope of the Act should be extended to all places of public resort, including those maintained by the Crown, and to employment, housing, and the provision of commercial and other services. The Race Relations Board should be enlarged, and it should be empowered to hold hearings and make legally enforceable orders. In the same month, a Fabian Society conference on 'Policies for Racial Equality' reaffirmed these principles.[22]

The centre of activity once more shifted to Parliament. On 8 December 1966, David Winnick introduced an adjournment debate in the Commons on the employment of coloured school leavers.[23] Shirley Williams, now Parliamentary Secretary to the Ministry of Labour, agreed with him that there was a real problem of racial discrimination in employment, especially in retail distribution and some other service industries. Ten days later, Maurice Orbach introduced a Private Member's Bill[24] which contained the provisions which had been recommended by both CARD and the Labour Lawyers. Six

22. The proceedings of the conference were published in Lester and Deakin (1967).

23. *Hansard* (H.C.), vol. 737, cols. 1715–26.

24. 16 December 1966, *Hansard* (H.C.), vol. 738, cols. 897–952. The Bill was drafted by two members of the CARD Legal Committee, Anthony Lester and Roger Warren Evans.

other Labour M.P.s and the Liberal spokesman supported the Orbach Bill, and two Conservatives spoke against it. Charles Fletcher-Cooke, speaking from the Opposition Front Bench, made a strongly encouraging speech, in which he expressed his view that the matter 'should be kept under review constantly', and said that he thought that 'the scope of the conciliation provisions may well have to be extended to jobs and homes'. On behalf of the Government, Maurice Foley set out the arguments for and against amending legislation, and promised, in the light of the findings of the PEP report to give 'serious consideration to the need for and the feasibility of strengthening the existing law and administrative machinery'. Although Orbach tried unsuccessfully to obtain a stronger undertaking from the Government, he withdrew his Bill at the end of the debate without pressing it to a Division.

On 19 December, Lord (Fenner) Brockway introduced an almost identical Bill[25] into the Lords. The Bill was debated at length and was supported by the majority of those who spoke. However, some Peers criticized the Bill in the mistaken belief that it contained criminal sanctions; and others objected to the inclusion of clubs, or doubted whether it was proper to legislate at all against racial discrimination, or whether such legislation could in practice be enforced.

Lord Sorensen was chosen to speak for the Government, and confessed that, as the pioneer of the first anti-discrimination Bill, it was ironical that he was 'a poacher turned gamekeeper'. He repeated the Government's view that it was premature to proceed with the Bill until the extent of the problem had been revealed by the PEP Report, and urged Lord Brockway to withdraw. But Brockway insisted on putting the Bill to a vote, and it was defeated by sixty votes to twenty-three.

The Parliamentary pressure continued. A month after the Lords debate, David Marquand introduced an adjournment debate[26] in the Commons on racial discrimination in the field of insurance. He

25. *Hansard* (H.L.), vol. 378, cols. 1838–50; 1854–1910. The differences between the two Bills were dictated by the limits of the Long Title of the Orbach Bill, which prevented it from dealing with religious discrimination and racial incitement. The Brockway Bill included these additional matters.

26. 17 January 1967, *Hansard* (H.C.), vol. 739, cols. 384–94.

quoted several instances of racial discrimination and stressed the absence of any statistical data which indicated that coloured people represented actuarially higher risks than white people. Marquand also argued that public policy was especially involved in the matter of motor insurance because the insurance companies were acting as agents of the state in administering the compulsory insurance scheme. George Darling's reaction, on behalf the Board of Trade, was more negative than any previous Government statement. He confined himself to expressing the Government's opposition to racial discrimination and colour prejudice, doubting whether the problem was significant in insurance, and promising to investigate any specific complaints. Oddly enough, in the period which followed, the British Insurance Association was to prove less inflexible on the subject of anti-discrimination legislation in the field of insurance than the Board of Trade.

The Board of Trade's tepid reply in the Adjournment Debate indicated that Jenkins's support for legislation had not spread to all Government departments. But the likelihood of further legislation was now sufficiently strong to provoke the joint opposition of the two major bodies on each side of industry: the Confederation of British Industry and the Trades Union Congress. In the negotiations which followed, the CBI was content to leave the brunt of the attack to the TUC (Rose *et al.*, 1969, pp. 529–37), but throughout their manoeuvres the two organizations shared a common hostility to any form of legislative intervention against employment discrimination.

On 25 January 1967, at a meeting of the National Joint Advisory Council of the Ministry of Labour, representatives of the TUC, the CBI and the nationalized industries presented a joint statement[27] opposing the extension of anti-discrimination legislation to employment or the denial of Government contracts to discriminating firms. The statement, which seems to have been intended to state a bargaining position for purposes of negotiation with the Government, declared that 'improper discriminatory practices in employment or engagement will disappear only when integration has been achieved among work-people regardless of colour, race, ethnic or national origin'. The two bodies stressed the need for their members 'to utilize to the full the methods of voluntary settlement which have

27. The text of the statement is printed in Patterson (1969, pp. 102–3).

been successfully developed over many years' and urged them to review 'the employment policies, practices and procedures in their industries and services which bear on the full achievement of integration and to eliminate any which militate against it'.

Several factors influenced this attitude. The TUC was traditionally hostile to legislative intervention in the field of industrial relations and feared that race relations legislation might be the thin end of a very broad wedge. It did not regard the problem of racial discrimination as sufficiently serious to justify a special statutory remedy, when other malpractices were without proper redress. It believed that the problem would gradually diminish, and that it could be effectively tackled by existing voluntary procedures. And, like the CBI, it was sceptical about the real strength or representative character of the various bodies which had lobbied so intensively for legislation, and about the ability of members of the Race Relations Board to administer a law against job discrimination in a field in which they were inexperienced.

It was at this stage, in February 1967, that the NCCI convened a conference on racial equality in employment, which was intended to reduce the opposition of the TUC and the CBI to anti-discrimination legislation. However, although several distinguished experts from both sides of American industry played a prominent part in the conference, the response from British industry was disappointing. The General Secretary of the TUC (George Woodcock) refused to attend, on the ground that he had been invited only in his personal capacity. Sir Kenneth Allen made a negative speech on behalf of the CBI at the start of the conference, in which he argued that

To treat this one problem in a way which is foreign to our normal way of dealing with industrial relations problems would tend to focus attention on discrimination – and possibly exacerbate it – rather than bring it into a proper balanced perspective.

Allen's speech was immediately answered by Roy Jenkins, who promised that if the results of the conference, the PEP survey and the Race Relations Board's report 'show a clear case that legislation is needed and would be helpful – we shall not shirk the issue'. Most of the few representatives of British industry who attended the NCCI conference were already convinced of the need for legislation.

Some others who were undecided seemed to have been persuaded by the proceedings. But the outcome of the conference was inconclusive. It reflected the deep difference which existed between Roy Jenkins and race relations workers, on the one hand, and the official representatives of industry on the other.

One proposal made at the NCCI conference was however to prove significant later. Oscar Hahn, President of the Birmingham Chamber of Commerce and Chairman of the West Midlands Conciliation Committee of the Race Relations Board, suggested that independent committees established by both sides of industry in firms of more than twenty-five employees, might provide a means of voluntary conciliation within a statutory framework that might be acceptable to both sides. Only if no resolution could be found by the voluntary machinery would appeals be made to a statutory body.

Two months later, the PEP survey and the Race Relations Board's first annual report were both published. The PEP report revealed that the extent of racial discrimination in Britain ranged from substantial to massive, and that, if left to itself, the problem was likely to grow worse (see pp. 80–82). The Board's report contained strong arguments for extending the 1965 Act, not the least of which was the fact that 70 per cent of complaints received by the Board during its first year were outside the scope of the Act (RRB, 1967).

The Board concluded by expressing its belief that

the law has an essential part to play in dealing with this difficult and explosive area of human relations. . . . So long as the law is unequivocal and unambiguous it need not be in any way oppressive as we believe our experience shows. There is no reason to suppose that employers of labour or those who sell houses are in any respect less law-abiding than publicans; nor why they should be any less susceptible to the processes of conciliation backed by an ultimate legal sanction.

Jenkins's two requirements had been satisfied. In a major speech delivered during the following month,[28] he again declared that 'if further legislation is necessary to deal with this issue, we should not be frightened of it.' But the fears of the leaders of industry were aggravated by this assurance. At the end of April, the TUC General

28. Speech to the annual conference of the London Labour Party 13 May 1967 in Jenkins (1967, pp. 278–88).

Council had reached the predictable conclusion that 'neither the proceedings at a conference organized by the NCCI nor the PEP report gave grounds for modifying the attitudes of the General Council.'

However, the TUC Council resolved to accept the CBI's proposal for further discussions on the desirability of establishing appropriate voluntary machinery for dealing with the problem. During the consultations which followed with the Ministry of Labour, the two bodies shifted from outright opposition to any form of legislation, and insisted instead that the industry should have sole responsibility for enforcing the employment provisions of the law through its own voluntary procedures. On 19 June 1967, at a formal confrontation between Ministers and both sides of industry, the TUC representatives stated that they 'did not altogether rule out the possibility that legislation might ultimately play some residual part in the process'. The leaders of industry had come grudgingly to accept the inevitability of legislation; what was now at stake was the crucial issue of how effectively the new law would be enforced in practice.

On 26 July 1967, while these discussions were still in progress, Jenkins made a statement in the Commons[29] in which he announced that the Government had decided in principle that the 1965 Act should be extended to deal with racial discrimination in employment, housing, insurance and credit facilities, and that public places would be given a wider definition than under the existing Act. However, he promised the CBI and the TUC that details of the employment provisions would be worked out in consultation with them, and that the new legislation would 'provide the fullest possible opportunity for industry to use its own machinery for conciliation'.

The Government statement coincided with the publication of a report by a Labour Party working party on race relations. Their recommendations followed previous proposals, with one significant difference. Instead of empowering the Race Relations Board to hold hearings, the Labour Party report suggested that the Board should be responsible only for conciliation, and that, where conciliation failed, the Board should refer the case to an independent Race Relations Tribunal, whose members would be appointed from among

29. *Hansard* (H.C.), vol. 751, col. 744.

people with special knowledge of industrial relations, law, housing, local government and race relations. The report emphasized that the new machinery should not undermine the familiar procedures of industrial relations, but it recommended that where existing machinery was unable to settle a complaint satisfactorily, it would have to be dealt with by statutory machinery. It was apparently this insistence on the ultimate sanction of the law that prevented the TUC's representative on the working party from signing the report.

On 6 October 1967, the report was debated at the Annual Conference of the Labour Party, and the Conference unanimously adopted a resolution moved on behalf of the Society of Labour Lawyers[30] calling on the Government to extend the scope of the 1965 Act to the main areas of racial discrimination and 'to make such other amendments to the Act as shall ensure its effective enforcement'. In the same month, the Street Committee on Anti-Discrimination Legislation published their authoritative report (see pp. 98–105), which made detailed proposals for the strengthening of the 1965 Act. The Street report received an extremely favourable response in the national press, and its strong recommendations were carefully studied in Whitehall. The path had been cleared for the introduction of a comprehensive Bill.

A month later, sterling was devalued, and Roy Jenkins was moved to the Treasury. His political skill in securing the Government's agreement to legislate, despite the declared opposition of industry, and the possibility of substantial electoral unpopularity, had won him the admiration of even the most demanding supporters of anti-discrimination legislation. But suddenly those supporters were faced, at the vital drafting stage of the new Bill, with a different Home Secretary, James Callaghan, who had played no part in the events which had committed the Government to the measure. They viewed the Bill's foster parent with a mixture of apprehension and stoicism.

Within a few days of this change of minister, the lobbyists were weakened from within their own ranks. A split opened in the Campaign Against Racial Discrimination, which was to destroy the effectiveness of that organization during the crucial period which followed. At the CARD annual convention, the majority of the

30. Report of the Sixty-sixth Annual Conference of the Labour Party, Scarborough, 1967, at p. 312.

executive committee, who had been mainly responsible for the work on legislation, 'were hustled out of office by what must have been ... one of the most curiously assorted coalitions ever to embark on a major tactical operation, all temporarily united under the all-embracing folds of the Black Power banner' (Rose *et al.*, 1969, p. 546).

The disintegration of the CARD alliance was a severe blow to those who had worked to build a multiracial movement for racial equality, led by coloured people, and reflecting the needs and aspirations of Britain's racial minorities. It also meant that the views of coloured people were less forcefully expressed in the critical months ahead. It did not, however, destroy the lobby. Soon after the break-up of CARD, a new organization, called Equal Rights, was created by an independent group.[31] Neither they nor the sponsors of Equal Rights had been involved in the CARD dispute. The President of Equal Rights was Professor Roy Marshall, Dean of the Law Faculty at Sheffield University, and subsequently Vice-Chancellor of the University of the West Indies. Marshall's leadership was a strong asset for the new body. Although a distinguished jurist of West Indian origin, and chairman of the Yorkshire Conciliation Committee of the Race Relations Board, he had not previously engaged in the campaign for legislation.

Equal Rights had a single ambitious objective: to ensure that the new legislation would be comprehensive in scope and capable of effective enforcement. In the interval before the Bill was published, its organizers lobbied intensively to attain this objective. At the same time the Race Relations Board worked actively behind the scenes trying to persuade the Home Office to draft a measure which was as close as possible to the recommendations of the Street Report. They were able to make these efforts because the Home Office had indicated its initial intentions to them.

In retrospect, it is now apparent that the most significant successes for the Board and also for Equal Rights were achieved during these months before the final draft was published. The Government were persuaded, after some hesitation, that responsibility for enforcing

31. The founders were Nicholas Deakin, John Thirlwell and Roger Warren Evans who were all members of the NCCI Housing Panel. Dipak Nandy later served as Hon. Secretary.

the law should be transferred from the Attorney-General to the Board. They also accepted that the Board should be able to obtain damages as well as injunctions against those who violated the law. And they agreed that the Bill should cover discrimination in the controversial area of the sale and letting of private housing, together with the allocation of local authority housing.

However, several of Equal Rights' main principles were not accepted by the Government during this pre-publication stage, even where they were recommended by the Street report and had the Board's support. For example, the Equal Rights' statement of policy had argued that 'there should be no arbitrary limitations upon the scope of the Act: . . . to admit any substantial exemptions from the operation of the Act, would undermine the moral and educative effect of the legislation as a whole'. This point was largely but not entirely accepted by the Government. More important, the Government refused to give the Board the wide range of enforcement powers which had been recommended by the Street report: the power to subpoena the attendance of witnesses or the production of relevant documents to the Board; and the power to obtain a court order in an emergency to prevent an alleged discriminator from disposing of his property or filling a vacant job before the Board had a chance to investigate a complaint. Nor would the Home Office agree that, once discrimination was established, the Board should be able to seek a court order positively requiring a discriminator in an appropriate case to put right the wrong done to the victim by offering a house or job to him. The only legal remedies which the Home Office would countenance were negative injunctions against further discrimination, and a narrow measure of damages. Nor was the alleged victim to have any right to bring proceedings on his own behalf; the Board was to have the sole right to bring legal proceedings. Finally, the Government would not agree to make their own departments answerable in the courts for acts of unlawful discrimination. These were all to be targets for further lobbying during the coming Parliamentary debates.

Meanwhile, in this lull before the Bill's publication, the immigration issue once more overshadowed race relations and affected the political climate in which the Bill was to be debated. Throughout the winter of 1967, United Kingdom citizens of Asian origin had come to Britain in increasing numbers from Kenya because their position had been made precarious by the Kenyan Government's policy of 'Africanization'. A campaign was mounted by Duncan Sandys and Enoch Powell to deprive them of their right to enter and settle in Britain. Roy Jenkins had taken no action in response to these pressures, probably in the hope that, if no new controls were imposed, the Kenyan Asians would stop rushing to Britain in such large numbers to avoid being kept out, and that the campaign against them would die naturally. However, Callaghan decided, almost immediately after becoming Home Secretary, to accede to the demands of Sandys and Powell. It may be that he was partly influenced by a desire to reaffirm the severity of the Government's policy on coloured immigration before introducing the controversial Race Relations Bill.

On 15 February 1968, Lord Stonham assured the House of Lords, in his capacity as a Home Office Minister, that legislation to control the entry of Kenyan Asians was unlikely as 'it would remove from them their right to UK citizenship and under the UN Convention of 1961 we are pledged to avoid any further statelessness'. But, a week later, the Home Secretary presented a Bill to the Commons which had exactly this effect; it took away the right of entry into this country from those United Kingdom citizens who had not been born in Britain or whose parents and grandparents had not been born here (Steel, 1969; Rose et al., 1969, pp. 610–14; Cable, 1969).

The Commonwealth Immigrants Bill was introduced, with the support of the Opposition Front Bench, as an urgent measure designed to deal with a grave national emergency. It received hostile criticism from almost the entire Press, but it met with surprisingly little opposition in the Commons. The most forceful and eloquent attacks in Parliament came from members of all three parties in the Lords, but the Bill was hurried unaltered through all its Parliamentary stages in three turbulent days.

Here is not the place in which to discuss the implications of this unsightly measure. In the view of the authors of the most authoritative report on race relations in Britain (Rose et al., 1969, p. 614), its passage 'gravely compromised the position' of the Home Secretary and of David Ennals, his junior minister, 'and hence the credibility of the Government's whole integration programme'. Certainly, if one of the main objects of the Bill was to 'take race out of politics', then, like the previous attempt in the White Paper of 1965, it was a notable failure. It may even have had the opposite effect; by conceding once again to the demands of the extremists, it lent respectability to the proposition that numbers were of the essence, because it suggested that it was the very presence of coloured people in Britain which caused problems.

On 9 April 1968, the Race Relations Bill was published. It made it unlawful to discriminate on racial grounds in employment, housing and the provision of commercial and other services. And it gave the Race Relations Board the duty to secure compliance with its provisions by investigation, conciliation and legal proceedings. The Bill also created the Community Relations Commission to promote 'harmonious community relations', and to act in an advisory capacity on behalf of the Home Secretary, performing, as a statutory body, the tasks previously carried out by the NCCI.

On 20 April, three days before the Second Reading debate, Enoch Powell made a notorious speech on race relations (Smithies and Fiddick, 1969, pp. 35–43), in which he saw 'the River Tiber foaming with much blood'. The Bill received short shrift from Powell. It was 'the means of showing that the immigrant communities can organize to consolidate their members, to agitate and campaign against their fellow-citizens, and to overawe and dominate the rest with the legal weapons which the ignorant and the ill-informed have provided'.

As a result of Powell's speech, the Second Reading debate[32] took place in an atmosphere charged with emotion. The Home Secretary described it as 'a time for responsibility, for leadership and, if I may dare to use the word, for nobility'. The purpose of the Bill was 'to protect society as a whole against actions which will lead to social disruption, and to prevent the emergence of second-grade citizens'.

The Opposition had tabled an amendment declining to give a Second Reading to the Bill 'which, on balance, will not in its practical application contribute to the achievement of racial harmony'. Callaghan, using similar tactics to those employed by Soskice during the debates on the 1965 Bill, tried to persuade the Opposition not to divide the House, but to combine with the Government to form a moderate consensus. He stressed that complaints of racial discrimi-

32. 23 April 1968, *Hansard* (H.C.), vol. 763, cols. 53–168.

nation in employment would be best settled by using industry's own voluntary procedures rather than statutory machinery, and that, in the field of housing, the law was unlikely to be an appropriate weapon, except in the 'most blatant and flagrant case'. And he drew attention to the weak powers of enforcement contained in the Bill. The Race Relations Board would not have 'judicial authority or compulsory powers' to summon the attendance of witnesses or the production of relevant documentary evidence; nor would it be able to obtain interim injunctions from the courts.[33] The process of conciliation was 'the key to the success of the legislation'.

However, the Opposition Front Bench were unmoved. Quintin Hogg's speech, while partly devoted to attacking Enoch Powell for his irresponsibility and disloyalty during the previous weekend, criticized the Bill for dealing only with discrimination on racial grounds, and not including all those forms of unfair discrimination which were defined in the Universal Declaration of Human Rights. He accepted that employment and housing should be within its scope, but opposed the inclusion of insurance and credit services. He wanted to exempt from the Bill the small employer, the small landlord, the person letting his own house, and the owner-occupier who sold his house without employing the services of an estate agent. And he inveighed against permitting the Race Relations Board to obtain damages from the court on behalf of the victim of discrimination; that remedy was, in his view 'a terrible weapon of oppression'.

The speeches which followed were reminiscent of the pattern which had developed during the debates on the 1965 Bill. Several Labour backbenchers urged the Government to widen the Bill's scope so as to include religious discrimination, to remove a clause which would permit employers to discriminate against immigrants in order to maintain a 'reasonable balance of persons of different racial groups' employed by them, and, above all, to strengthen the enforcement provisions of the Bill.

33. He seems to have misunderstood the purpose of interim injunctions, which he described as requiring 'the sale of a house to a particular person' (col. 60). In fact the purpose for which they were recommended by the Street report was to *prevent* the sale of a house to anyone, pending the outcome of the Board's investigations.

On the Conservative side, Ronald Bell deplored the fact that the Bill would 'make very deep and damaging encroachments into the proper sphere of personal decision', and complained of 'a skilful and persistent campaign by a resolute minority' which had led to the introduction of the measure. Dudley Smith declared that Parliament could not 'legislate to make people better in their hearts'. On the other hand, several Conservatives strongly supported the Bill in a way which showed considerable courage. For example, Hugh Fraser said that he believed his Party's Amendment to be 'politically and practically inept', and Nigel Fisher was 'frankly surprised and a little shocked by the Conservative Amendment', and 'confused and concerned about the direction in which the Tory party sometimes seems to be moving'. Nevertheless, Reginald Maudling, summing up for the Opposition, attacked the Bill on three grounds.

First, we believe that it definitely encroaches on individual freedom and individual liberty. Secondly, we believe that it will be unworkable in practice; and, if it does not work in practice, it will be very serious indeed, because the immigrants who believe they will get protection from the Bill will feel that they have been deceived and will turn, not only against the local population, but against the law itself.

So the Opposition voted against the Second Reading, but their Amendment was defeated by a majority of 104 votes.

The Committee Stage occupied thirteen sittings, [34] and, since, ten of them were spent in discussing the scope of the Bill, there was much less discussion of the enforcement procedures. In 1965 the only substantial changes made in Committee were introduced by the Government with the support of the Opposition Front Bench. However, on this second occasion the backbench members of Standing Committee B played a much more significant role, and were able to alter the shape of the Bill in several important respects.

From the outset, the Committee were split into four groups. There was the Government and its almost unfailing supporters.[35] In the debates on the employment clauses, they included Eric Heffer who

34. See generally, *Official Report*, Standing Committee B, 7 May 1968–25 June 1968, cols. 3–828.

35. James Callaghan, David Ennals, Roy Hattersley, James MacColl, Donald Anderson, Bessie Braddock, Kenneth Lomas, Gregor MacKenzie, Gordon Oakes and Ernest Perry.

broadly represented the views of the TUC. Their approach was to defend the Bill as it stood, making only such concessions as would be likely to win a wider consensus when the Bill was again debated in the Commons. The second group consisted of the Conservative Front Bench and their supporters,[36] including Eldon Griffiths, who reflected the views of the CBI and the Police Federation. They followed the line which had been defined by Quintin Hogg. Thirdly, a group of Conservative backbenchers[37] opposed the Bill, root and branch, and seized every chance to weaken or destroy it. Finally there was a group of members from all three parties[38] which formed a coalition to widen the scope of the Bill, and to strengthen the Race Relation Board's enforcement powers. Prominent in this all-party group were four Labour lawyers, Alexander Lyon, Ivor Richard, Paul Rose and Ben Whitaker, and two Conservatives, Nicholas Scott and Sir George Sinclair. They were the largest group, though not large enough to prevail over any combination of the other groups, but, at times, they were able to make temporary alliances with members of the other groups and win sufficient support to carry their amendments. Before each sitting, Equal Rights' legal consultants attended briefing sessions separately with the Labour and Conservative members of the all-party group, and helped them to draft amendments to the Bill.

The Committee began by discussing the definition of discrimination. Under the Bill 'discriminate' meant 'discriminate on the ground of colour, race or ethnic or national origins'. The all-party group argued, with Quintin Hogg's support, that a more informative general definition was desirable to make the objectives of the legislation clear to the public. Eventually, the Home Secretary agreed to reconsider the definition in the light of the debate. An attempt by Quintin Hogg to extend the definition to other forms of discrimination (e.g. on the ground of sex, language, religion, etc.) failed

36. Quintin Hogg, Sir David Renton, Anthony Buck, William Deedes, R. W. Elliott, Eldon Griffiths and Captain Orr.

37. Ronald Bell, Sir Frederick Bennett, Percy Grieve, Evelyn King and Dudley Smith.

38. Sydney Bidwell, Dr John Dunwoody, Joan Lestor, Alexander Lyon, Dr Maurice Miller, Maurice Orbach, Ivor Richard, Paul Rose, Nicholas Scott, Sir George Sinclair, Ben Whitaker and Dr Michael Winstanley. They were joined by Eric Heffer on several issues in which the TUC's interests were not in conflict.

because the Bill's Long Title confined the Committee's discussions to discrimination only on racial and similar grounds.

Eldon Griffiths, speaking on behalf of the Police Federation, had the mistaken impression that the Bill contained criminal penalties. He therefore sought and was readily given an assurance that 'the already overworked British police' would not be obliged 'to report every single putative discrimination to their superiors'. Various attempts were then made to alter the scope of clause 2 of the Bill, dealing with the provision of goods, facilities and services to the public. Hogg tried unsuccessfully to exclude single acts of discrimination from its ambit, and also to exempt insurance and credit facilities altogether. Evelyn King proposed, also without success, that educational services should be left out of the Bill. Whitaker obtained Government approval for an Equal Rights amendment, which made it clear that clause 2 covered racial discrimination by a local or other public authority.

The first important success of the all-party group occurred during the fifth sitting. Paul Rose moved an amendment to delete clause 2 (3). This was a rather obscure provision which made lawful those acts of discrimination 'done in good faith for the benefit of a particular section of the public' which had the effect of 'promoting the integration of members of that section of the public into the community'. Rose suggested that it was superfluous, meaningless and also possibly dangerous, since it might be interpreted as justifying the provision of racially segregated facilities. David Ennals, on behalf of the Government, did not believe that it could have this meaning, but the only justification which he advanced for the provision was that it would enable language classes and other educational resources to be made available to members of particular minorities. However, other members argued that such activities would not, in any event, be unlawful, and clause 2 (3) was deleted against the Government's advice, by fifteen votes to eight.

The employment provisions occupied much of the Committee's attention. The Bill contained a so-called 'tapering' exemption: during the first two years after it became law, employers of not more than ten people were to be outside its scope, and, in the next two years, employers of not more than five people were to be similarly exempted. In this way the employment provisions were tapered to come into effect by stages. The Opposition Front Bench attempted to introduce a *permanent* exemption for employers of not more than twenty-five people, which would have excluded one-fifth of the total working population from the Bill's protection. Roy Hattersley, junior minister at the Department of Employment and Productivity, refused to accept this amendment, but he agreed to consider whether the temporary exemptions should be increased from ten to twenty-five employees in the first two years, and from five to ten in the next two years.

Clause 3 (2) contained a blanket exemption for all existing legislation which contained discriminatory employment provisions. Paul Rose asked the Government to translate this wide escape clause into a list of specific statutory exemptions which could be properly considered on their merits by the Committee. David Ennals explained that the measures affected were mainly those which discriminated against aliens. He undertook to reconsider the drafting of the clause before the Report Stage (although the subject was not in fact referred to again during the remaining stages of the Bill).

Joan Lestor raised the problem faced by Sikh workers who were prevented from obtaining employment, especially on public transport, if they insisted on wearing beards and turbans in conformity with their religious beliefs. The Government's reply was enigmatic. Ennals suggested that even if religious discrimination had been prohibited by the Bill it would not have solved the problem because what was involved was discrimination against beards. He recognized that 'it would be unreasonable ... to require a Sikh to shave off his beard, or not to wear his turban, purely for reasons of uniformity; it would be an affront to his religion and to his human dignity'. But he did not make it clear that such an unreasonable requirement would still be perfectly lawful under the Bill.

Clause 6 made it unlawful to publish discriminatory advertisements or notices, but excluded advertisements or notices relating to the employment of Commonwealth citizens overseas or aliens in Britain. Ben Whitaker objected to this exception because, he said, it would 'permit a Rhodesian or South African firm to advertise in this country for white Commonwealth citizens to fill job vacancies in those countries and would permit anti-semitic firms to advertise here for non-Jewish citizens to fill jobs in Arab countries. . . . There is no case for allowing any such racial discrimination to be practised in Britain, whatever may be the practice in countries overseas.' Ennals explained that the main purpose of the provision was to protect the Ministry of Overseas Development in recruiting people for posts with overseas governments, and to make it possible to advertise for au pair girls or aliens of a particular nationality, and Whitaker's amendment was narrowly defeated on a division.

There was a sharp clash between the Government and the all-party group over clause 8 (2), the so-called 'racial balance' clause. This permitted an employer to discriminate on grounds of colour, race or ethnic or national origins in recruiting workers, if the act of discrimination was 'done in good faith for the purpose of securing or preserving a balance of persons of different racial groups' employed in the particular undertaking 'which is reasonable in all the circumstances' (see pp. 208–13). The Opposition Front Bench, like the all-party group, had tabled its own amendment to delete this clause, and it seemed that the Government would be defeated unless it were withdrawn. The racial balance clause was apparently introduced as a result of negotiations with the CBI and the TUC to protect employers who already employed substantial numbers of coloured workers, and who feared that their white workers might object, and perhaps even leave their employment, if the number of coloured workers were further increased. It was seen by the Government as a provision which would promote the dispersal of coloured workers throughout industry, by discouraging their concentration in particular firms. The Government also pointed to the fact that the clause did not apply to indigenous coloured workers, but was limited to those who had not been wholly or mainly educated in Britain.

As a result of forceful representations which had been made against the racial balance clause by Equal Rights and other organizations, the Department of Employment and Productivity had considered various alternative provisions before the debate in Committee, including the possibility of an exemption permitting an employer to discriminate so as to ensure that his work force did not consist wholly or mainly of members of any one racial group. However, the Government seems to have learnt, shortly before the clause was debated, that the Opposition Front Bench was prepared to withdraw its objection to the existing clause. As a result, the Government's position hardened, and it was decided to push the racial balance clause through unamended. The all-party group mounted a strong attack on the Government position, but the clause was defended by Eldon Griffiths and Eric Heffer, speaking respectively on behalf of the CBI and the TUC. On a division, the all-party amendment was defeated by fourteen votes to ten.

The remaining employment provisions considered by the Committee were less important in their effect. Quintin Hogg persuaded the Government to accept the principle that it should be lawful to select a person of a particular nationality or descent for employment requiring attributes possessed by persons of that nationality or descent. He argued that it would apply, for example, to recruitment of foreign waiters for a foreign restaurant (see p. 214).

Eldon Griffiths failed to convince the Committee that employers should not be liable for acts of discrimination committed by their employees. Ben Whitaker also failed to remove a series of sub-clauses permitting racial discrimination on board merchant ships. He referred to the fact that the National Union of Seamen had recently persuaded the Shipping Federation to withdraw a discriminatory collective agreement because the Race Relations Bill was pending. He was supported by Eric Heffer, who pointed out that if the exemptions were not removed, 35,000 Asian seamen would be outside the Bill's protection. However, the Home Secretary, recalling his personal experiences as a Cardiff M.P., told the Committee that there was 'a long tradition in the United Kingdom that seamen of mixed races are segregated according to race', and that Lascars continue to be employed on British ships 'on terms and conditions of service which are dissimilar to those pertaining to British crews'. He wanted to see this discrimination ended, but would not make an amendment which, 'while no doubt making a great advance in race relations in this respect, would upset a great many other things, too'.

The employment provisions were scarcely changed by the Committee, probably because the Government had become so firmly committed to them in the course of its negotiations with the CBI and the TUC. But the situation was more flexible in the field of housing, and James MacColl, the junior minister responsible for this part of the Bill, was willing to accept several amendments tabled by the all-party group to strengthen the housing clauses, while resisting

Opposition attempts to weaken them. For example, MacColl did not agree to Opposition amendments which would have removed from the Bill all sales of houses by owner-occupiers, or sales of multi-occupied accommodation shared by different residents; nor would he increase the exemption for small boarding houses. And, when the all-party group drew attention to the loose drafting of parts of the housing clauses, MacColl undertook to redraft them before the Report Stage.

His one significant concession to those who sought to weaken the housing provisions also had the support of several members of the all-party group. It became known in the Committee as the 'Colorado compromise' because it was modelled on the Colorado Fair Housing Statute, and it was urged on the Government in an attempt to win Opposition support for the Bill. The Colorado amendment meant that the disposal of housing accommodation was covered by the Bill only if the services of an estate agent were employed or the sale was advertised to the public. Hogg supported the amendment. He and others argued that it would emphasise the public nature of the sale of houses by estate agents and advertising. After initial reluctance, MacColl eventually accepted the principle on the ground that it would be unlikely to lead to widespread evasion of the law, and would affect an insignificant number of sales.

The only issue in the debates on the housing clauses which divided the Government from the all-party group resulted once again from demands made by the shipping industry and although it was tabled as an exception to the housing provisions, it was not an issue which concerned housing. During the tenth sitting, David Ennals introduced a Government amendment which made it lawful to discriminate racially in providing sleeping accommodation for passengers on ships where this was done to avoid 'persons of different colour, race or ethnic or national origins being compelled to share such accommodation'. He explained that it was intended to give 'protection to British shipping companies who try to meet the wishes of their passengers', and he hoped that the Committee would agree that it was a 'reasonable amendment'. Eldon Griffiths described it as 'an eminently sensible amendment in every respect', and wanted, at the CBI's suggestion, to extend the principle to sleeping accommodation which was provided on building sites in remote parts of Britain.

However, Ben Whitaker made an impassioned attack on the provision which he described as 'offensive and discreditable', and as writing *apartheid* into a British statute. He suggested that it undermined the Bill's basic philosophy and was inconsistent with the ancient Common Law duty of common carriers to accept passengers for carriage without discrimination. Other members added their criticisms. Nicholas Scott suggested that the amendment would cut down the existing provisions of the Race Relations Act 1965, which expressly prohibited racial discrimination in providing public transport services. Eric Heffer recognized that the Home Secretary had been under 'fairly strong pressure from some of the shipping companies about this matter', but felt that the pressure ought to be resisted, and Sydney Bidwell suggested that, if the principle were right, it ought logically to be applied to other situations, such as the provisions of sleeping accommodation on trains. However, the Home Secretary repeatedly denied that any shipping company wished to maintain racially segregated sleeping facilities on its ships. Callaghan said that if he had thought that shipping companies wanted the exemption for a purpose that 'would not further the cause of race relations', he would not have commended it to the Committee. At the end of an emotionally charged debate, the Government amendment was carried by sixteen votes to seven. But the Home Secretary later agreed to substitute 'sleeping cabins' for 'sleeping accommodation' so as to narrow the effect of this exemption.

After almost eleven sittings, the Committee at last turned to Part II of the Bill, which defined the functions and powers of the Race Relations Board. The Government was markedly more inflexible in its attitude towards these enforcement provisions than it had been towards those dealing with the Bill's scope.

The all-party group fought a two-pronged campaign to strengthen the enforcement clauses. Firstly, they argued that, since the key to the Bill's success was the process of conciliation, the Board had to be given adequate powers to make that process effective. In particular, the all-party group pressed for the Board to be given the power to obtain relevant evidence from an alleged discriminator who refused to cooperate with the Board at the conciliation stage. In its first annual report, the Board had asked the Government to consider whether, with appropriate safeguards, there should be power to compel attendance before a conciliation committee, or the disclosure of information to the committee. The Street report had also recommended such a power. The all-party group's amendment contained a safeguard: the Board would have to apply to the court to compel the attendance of witnesses or the production of documents, and the court would be able to ensure that the power was not used oppressively. The all-party group contended that racially discriminatory practices were public wrongs, and that the Board should be regarded, by analogy with the Registrar of Restrictive Trade Practices, as acting on behalf of the community to eliminate such practices; the Board should therefore have similar powers to those possessed by the Registrar.

This view was hotly contested by Quintin Hogg, who asserted that it raised the 'gravest constitutional issues'. In his opinion, it would be oppressive to permit the Board to compel people to produce evidence before judicial proceedings had begun, and he rejected the suggestion that the Board was acting in a role like that performed by the Registrar. The Home Secretary agreed with him, mainly because he believed it to be wrong to invoke legal procedures in the course of the conciliation process. Once more, the all-party group was defeated by an alliance between both Front Benches.

The second prong of the all-party group's campaign was an attempt to secure an effective individual remedy for the victim of unlawful discrimination. Several Members argued that, if the Board was not to have the functions of a quasi-criminal watchdog, then it should have the same powers as an ordinary plaintiff in civil proceedings: discrimination should be treated as a statutory tort. They therefore pressed for the Board to be able to obtain a wider measure of damages than that contained in the Bill, so as specifically to include compensation for the humiliation and distress suffered by the victim. And they urged that the Board should be able, in appropriate cases, to seek a court order requiring the discriminator positively to put right the wrong done to the victim, by making the job, house, or service which he had been denied, available to him.

The approach was vigorously opposed by Quintin Hogg, who advocated what he called a 'new and promising field of law enforcement which avoided the pitfalls of tort and the pitfalls of criminal law'. (It seemed to some to be law without enforcement.) Hogg went further, and tried to remove even the limited measure of damages contained in the Bill which, he said would encourage 'speculative litigation'. He almost succeeded, for the Committee were evenly divided in their votes; but for the support of one Conservative Member, Nicholas Scott, the Government would have been defeated on this crucial issue. In the event, the Government was able to resist the demands both of the Opposition to weaken and of the all-party group to strengthen the enforcement provisions. One small change proposed by the group was accepted. The Government agreed to make it easier for the Board to commence proceedings in the courts.

However, the Committee stage ended, as it had begun, with a successful alliance between the all-party group and the Opposition Front Bench, which strengthened the Bill. Under clause 25, the Crown was included in the scope of the Bill; but it was also exempted from any proceedings in the courts. Alexander Lyon moved an amendment to delete this exemption. The Home Secretary replied that it was preferable for a government department against which a complaint of discrimination had been made to investigate the complaint itself and discuss it with the Board, rather than be subjected to legal proceedings. He expressed his belief that most complaints would be satisfactorily settled in this way, and said that, if the Board were dissatisfied with the outcome in any particular case, it would 'be free to draw Parliament's attention to the matter in the course of its annual report', when he had no doubt that 'questions would be asked'. It was unnecessary to make the Crown legally liable, in his view, because Ministers were accountable to Parliament. Not surprisingly, Quintin Hogg was 'singularly unconvinced' by these arguments. The Home Secretary tried to reassure him that cases against the Crown would be 'very few', and that, where discrimination was established against a government department, it would offer the victim an *ex gratia* payment to compensate him. And he added that the Minister would not be personally responsible for acts of racial discrimination, and so should not be the defendant in legal proceedings. Hogg gave a short but eloquent rebuff to these contentions, declaring that he was not prepared to trust the Crown, and that it was unfair to treat private employers more strictly than public employers. The amendment was carried by seventeen votes to nine;

the Government had been defeated, and the Crown had been brought fully within the law.

On 9 July 1969, the Commons debated the Report Stage of the Bill.[39] Bowing to all-party pressure, the Home Secretary introduced a new general definition of discrimination under which a person would discriminate unlawfully against another if, on racial grounds, he treated him 'less favourably' than he treated other people. The Home Secretary must soon have wished that he had left the definition as it stood, for his amendment was criticized by eight Members in the speeches which followed. They doubted whether it would convey to the general public that the main object of the Bill was to guarantee equality of opportunity, and they were alarmed that the definition might be interpreted by the courts to justify the provision of apparently equal but racially segregated facilities.

However, the Government's other amendments were accepted without controversy. The housing exemptions were introduced in a more tightly drafted form, together with the 'Colorado compromise' exempting completely private sales of property from the Bill; and wider 'tapering' exemptions were introduced in both the housing and the employment clauses.

The rest of the debate consisted mainly of further unsuccessful attempts by the all-party group and the Bill's Conservative opponents to win the various battles which they had lost in Committee. In his winding-up speech from the Opposition Front Bench, Quintin Hogg admitted that his 'fundamental assessment' of the Bill had changed since the Second Reading, and told the Commons that he did not intend to vote against the Bill. The House voted for the Third Reading by 182 votes to forty-two, with the Opposition Front Bench abstaining. Callaghan had achieved his objective; he had obtained a tacit consensus of support for the Bill from both sides of the Commons.

On 15 July, the House of Lords gave the Bill its Second Reading.[40] Lord Stonham introduced the debate on behalf of the Government. In anticipation of criticism of weaknesses in the enforcement provisions, he stressed that the Board's task was to settle cases of discrimination by conciliation, and that 'it would be inconsistent

39. See *Hansard* (H.C.), vol. 768, cols. 223–482.
40. See *Hansard* (H.L.), vol. 295, cols. 32–159.

with this to give the Board judicial authority or compulsory powers'. He also explained that the Government had considered whether to allow individuals to bring proceedings on their own behalf, where the Board rejected their complaints, but had decided against it because the Board had a 'public duty to perform in preventing baseless or deliberately vexatious complaints from reaching the courts and innocent parties being put to unwarranted expense'. In his view, the right balance had been struck 'between securing the confidence of minority groups and making the enforcement procedures fair and acceptable to the community at large'.

However, during the debate which followed, most Peers, while supporting the Bill, criticized it for not going sufficiently far. The principal targets were the general definition of discrimination, the racial balance clause, the absence of effective legal remedies for the individual victim, the Board's lack of subpoena powers, and the fact that employment complaints were to be referred initially to the Department of Employment and Productivity, rather than to the Board. The Lord Chancellor agreed to reconsider the general definition of discrimination in the light of the debate, and the Bill was given its Second Reading without a Division.

The Lords Committee Stage lasted two days.[41] On the first day, Baroness Gaitskell moved an amendment, with Government support, which clarified the general definition of discrimination by declaring that racial segregation would constitute unlawful discrimination. A series of amendments were then moved by Lords Brockway, Byers and Gifford covering the main points of criticism of the Bill which had been made in the Commons by the all-party group; but none of them was accepted. However, Lord Gifford successfully persuaded the Lord Chancellor to amend the rigid two-month time limit in the Bill within which the Board could receive complaints, so as to permit the Board to extend the time limit in special circumstances.

On 15 October 1968, when the Lords debated the Report Stage, the Government suffered an unexpected defeat. Lord Conesford moved an amendment to eliminate the provision for the appointment by the Lord Chancellor of two assessors with special knowledge and ex-

41. 25 July 1968, *Hansard* (H.L.), vol. 295, cols. 1270–1388; 30 July 1968, *Hansard* (H.L.), vol. 296, cols. 164–263.

perience of 'problems connected with race and community relations' who were to assist the county court judge in considering cases under the Bill. After a somewhat unenthusiastic defence of this provision by the Lord Chancellor, Lord Conesford's amendment was carried by fifty-seven votes to thirty-six. However, the provision was later restored to the Bill at the insistence of the Commons. The only other changes made to the Bill during its passage through the Lords, were introduced by the Lord Chancellor to enable the terms of racially discriminatory contracts to be revised by the Courts.

On 25 October 1968, the Bill received the Royal Assent, and a month later its provisions entered into force. It was eighteen years after the first anti-discrimination Bill had been presented to Parliament, and five years after the campaign for comprehensive legislation had begun in earnest.

The campaigners had lacked several advantages enjoyed by their North American counterparts. Britain's racial minorities did not have significant voting power; the coloured community consisted mainly of recent immigrants, whose claim to equal treatment was inevitably made with less insistence and understood with less sympathy than if they had been indigenous inhabitants of Britain. When the campaign began, there was little public awareness of the nature or extent of racial discrimination. There was no ideal of equality, embodied in a written constitution or elsewhere, to which the lobbyists could turn in support of their case for using law to combat racial discrimination. Their objective was radical and without precedent in this country. The role of legislation was as novel and unfamiliar to racial minorities as it was to the majority of the community. It was significant, for example, that, after the disintegration of the CARD alliance, immigrant leaders no longer formed the vanguard of the lobby for legislation. Wilfred Wood, an Anglican minister from the West Indies tried unsuccessfully to convince the Government that the new Community Relations Commission should be more directly representative of the immigrant community; but apart from his efforts, during the passage of the 1968 Bill, the main work of lobbying for a strong statute was done by Equal Rights, an *ad hoc* body which sought no following among immigrants. And, finally, the political climate of the 1960s, characterized by increasingly frequent, extreme and effective attacks on coloured immigration and immigrants, grew steadily less favourable to those who were working to reduce racial prejudice and discrimination.

The Race Relations Acts were therefore won against formidable odds. Like much legislation, they were the product of skilful lobbying by interested pressure groups. However, there was something unusual in the process by which the race relations legislation came to be enacted: the legislators yielded to a pressure-group which was urging them to give a lead before the problem of racial discrimination grew worse; they did not merely legislate against existing problems or in defence of legitimate existing interests.

In this respect, the brief period in which Roy Jenkins was Home Secretary was of decisive importance. Unlike many of his political contemporaries, he was sensitive to the pressing international imperatives of the second half of this century, which have made equality of opportunity a requirement for a civilised modern society. Jenkins's personal qualities of skilful and determined leadership have often been stressed by commentators on these events; but what mattered more was his awareness of the need to achieve racial equality, for it was in that direction that he chose to lead public opinion. What was crucial was Roy Jenkins's perception, as a liberal, reforming Home Secretary, that in the moral and political climate of the twentieth century, no civilized society could permit the growth of racial injustice.

Part Two

Chapter 4
The Meaning
of Discrimination

The scope of the legislation

The English statutes dealing with racial discrimination are the Race Relations Acts 1965 and 1968.[1] The anti-discrimination provisions of the 1965 Act are now of mainly academic interest, because they have been repealed,[2] except with regard to discrimination in places of public resort occurring before 26 November 1968 (the date on which the 1968 Act came into force), and discriminatory restrictions on the transfer of tenancies.

The 1968 Act covers discrimination on racial and similar grounds in employment (including trade union membership and benefits), housing, advertising, and the provision of goods, facilities and services. Each of these fields is considered in detail in later chapters.[3] The purpose of this chapter is to examine general aspects of the statutory definition of discrimination which are relevant in each of the various fields to which the legislation applies. It is important to understand the general meaning of discrimination before entering these specific fields.

The grounds of unlawful discrimination

The Race Relations Acts apply to discrimination 'on the ground of colour, race or ethnic or national origins'. The basic premise on which the Acts depend is that there is no moral or other justification

1. For the text of the statutory provisions now in force, see Appendices 2 and 3 below. The Race Relations Act 1968 is hereafter referred to as RRA.

2. RRA, section 28 (8). However, the provisions dealing with incitement to racial hatred remain in force; see chapter 10.

3. See chapter 5 (employment); chapter 6 (housing); chapter 7 (the provision of goods, facilities and services).

for treating people differently because of their supposed membership of a racial, ethnic or national group and the attributes which are presumed to result from such membership. Unfortunately, as will become apparent later in this chapter, Parliament has not been entirely consistent in the way in which it has applied this premise in the legislation. The speeches of some Ministers in explaining the legislation, and some of the exceptions in the 1968 Act, indicate a confused and uncertain attitude towards these categories: that they are regarded for some purposes as improper and for others as legitimate methods of human classification.

However, the general scheme of the legislation is clear. Unlawful discrimination is defined in terms of the attitude and intention of the discriminator, and not in terms of the group identity of his victim. It is unlawful to treat a person less favourably than other people on the ground that he belongs to one of the four categories. It is irrelevant whether the victim of discrimination in fact belongs to such a category, so long as he has been treated less favourably on that ground.

The unlawful grounds have deliberately been expressed in imprecise words, because they are meant to refer to unfair and often prejudiced behaviour, rather than to divide people into racial groups. The pigment of people's skins differs but, as the administrators of South Africa's *apartheid* laws have discovered, it is impossible to classify people precisely on the basis of colour.

Similarly, there is no such thing as the kind of 'race' in which the layman believes, namely, that there exists an indissoluble association between mental and physical characteristics which make individual members of certain 'races' either inferior or superior to members of certain other 'races' (Montagu, 1964, p. 24).

It is because the term 'race' is so often used in this sense, as though it were an objective scientific term with a genetic meaning, that Professor Ashley Montagu and other anthropologists have coined the non-committal term 'ethnic group'. It is an intentionally vague and general term.

For all practical purposes, an 'ethnic group' may be defined as one of a number of breeding populations, which populations together comprise the species *homo sapiens*, and which individually maintain their differences.

physical or genetic and cultural, by means of isolating mechanisms such as geographic and social barriers (p. 25).

In other words, 'ethnic' is preferred to 'racial' as a descriptive term (though both are found in the legislation) because it stresses that the groups to which it refers are the product of social organization and behaviour rather than a biological description of innate human differences.

So, too, the expression 'national origins' is not a precise definition of a person's legal status in terms of his nationality and citizenship. It is broader and more vague, and describes the origin of himself or his forebears in a particular country or territory.

But, although most sections of the legislation do not require an objective meaning to be given to 'colour, race or ethnic or national origins' – because what matters is whether people have been treated unfavourably on such grounds, rather than whether they really belong to groups of such descriptions – the practical interpretation of these words still needs to be explained.

The ground of 'colour' is straightforward. It plainly applies to discrimination against someone solely because of his skin colour – whether it is black, brown, yellow or white. But what is the position if someone refuses to offer a job or to sell a house to all Hindus, Muslims and Sikhs? Religious discrimination is not prohibited by the legislation; on the other hand, the vast majority of Hindus, Muslims and Sikhs in Britain are non-white and of Asian origin. Accordingly, it will be a question of fact in each case whether their exclusion is genuinely based on their religion, or whether a religious bar is being used as a mere pretext for excluding either non-whites or immigrants of Asian origin. Only the latter is illegal.

e.g. An employer in an area of Asian settlement advertises for workers and stipulates that 'Christians only should apply'. His recruitment records reveal that he has employed only white workers and rejected all Asian non-white applicants without making any inquiry about their religious beliefs. The employer has acted unlawfully, using religion as a pretext for discriminating on grounds of colour or national origin.

e.g. An employer refuses to accept workers with beards or turbans, but he does employ workers of Asian origin, including some Sikhs who have abandoned these requirements of their religion. The employers' objection is not unlawful, because there is no evidence that it is based on colour, race or ethnic or national origins.[4]

Jews

The omission of religion from the statutory definition also raises the problem of whether it is unlawful to discriminate against Jews. During the Parliamentary debates on the 1965 Bill, the Home Secretary expressed the view that

a person of Jewish faith, if not regarded as caught by the word 'racial would undoubtedly be caught by the word 'ethnic', but if not caught by the word 'ethnic' would certainly be caught by the scope of the word 'national', as certainly having a national origin.[5]

It is unclear whether Sir Frank Soskice was asserting that Jews would be treated by the courts as actually belonging to a racial, ethnic or national group, and for that reason protected by the Race Relation Acts;[6] certainly that seems to have been what he meant. However, although English judges have been uncertain and inconsistent about whether to regard Jews as members of a racial or ethnic group or of a religious group at Common Law,[7] Parliament has long

4. Compare the case of two Chinese students who were dismissed from holiday jobs as storemen at the Plessey Automation factory in Poole, Dorset, for talking to each other in their own language. The employers stated they had no objection to students speaking in Chinese during private conversations, but that it was necessary for them to speak the English language when discussing business activities with fellow workers (see *The Times* and *Guardian*, 20 August 1969). Although the students' language was an incident of their national origin, there could be no violation of the RRA unless it could have been shown that language was a pretext for dismissing them on one of the unlawful statutory grounds.

5. Second Reading, 3 May 1965, *Hansard* (H.C.), vol. 106, cols. 932–3.

6. To add to the confusion, according to Maurice Orbach, M.P., 'the words "ethnic origins" are used by the Home Secretary [James Callaghan], or, at any rate, by the Parliamentary draftsman, on the basis of including religion. This is exactly what the Home Secretary has told the leaders of the Jewish community on repeated occasions.' *Official Report*, Standing Committee B, 9 May 1968, col. 71.

7. See pp. 66–8. Compare *Shalit* v. *The Minister of the Interior* (*The Times*, 24 January 1970) in which the Supreme Court of Israel held by a majority that the children of a Jewish father and a Gentile mother were entitled to be registered under the Law of Return 1950 (which gives all Jews a legal right to enter and settle in Israel) as of 'Jewish nationality' notwithstanding the rabbinical (religious) principle that the child takes the religious status of its mother.

ceased to refer in legislation to 'persons of the Jewish nation'[8] and now habitually refers to them as a religious group.[9] Under present-day English Law, Jews 'are not looked upon as a separate nationality or a distinct caste, but as members of a dissenting religious denomination'.[10]

The correct view, and it may have been the one which the Home Secretary meant to convey, is that Jews, like any other people, are protected under the Acts not as members of a racial, ethnic or national group – a notion which many British citizens who believe in the Jewish religion would strongly resent – but only if they are discriminated against on the assumption that they belong to such a group.

e.g. An insurance company instructs its agents not to give motor insurance cover to 'persons of Jewish persuasion'.[11] In practice Jews are denied insurance by the company, or are charged exorbitant premiums, regardless of whether they are believers in the Jewish religion. The discrimination is unlawful because it treats Jews less favourably than other people, on ethnic or racial grounds.

e.g. A public school refuses to admit orthodox Jews as pupils on the ground that they will impair the Christian character of the school; however, the school accepts pupils of Jewish parentage, provided that they attend school prayers and play games on Saturdays. The discrimination is not unlawful, because it is based on religion rather than race or ethnic origin.

8. The most recent example appears to have been the Charitable Donations Registration Act 1812, section 11, under which nothing in the Act was to be construed to extend to 'any funds applicable to charitable purposes for the benefit of the Jewish nation'. The provision was repealed as obsolete by the Charities Act 1960, section 39 (1), Fifth Schedule.

9. The Religious Disabilities Act 1846 section 2, removed the disabilities of 'Her Majesty's subjects professing the "Jewish religion" in respect to their schools, places for religious worship, education, and charitable purposes and the property held therewith'. See also Liberty of Religious Worship Act 1855; Places of Worship Registration Act 1855; Jews Relief Act 1858; Oaths Act 1909, s. 2; Marriage Act 1949, ss. 26 (1) (d), 35 (4), 50 (1) (e), 53 (c); Representation of the People Act 1949, Second Schedule, Rule 39 (1); Shops Act 1950, s. 62; Slaughter of Animals Act 1958, s. 1 (3); Factories Act 1961, s. 109 (1).

10. *Halsbury's Laws* (3rd edn), vol. 13, p. 536. See further Henriques (1908); Roth (3rd edn) (1964); *Lindo* v. *Belisario* [1795] 1 Hagg. Cons. 216; *Re De Wilton* v. *Montefiore* [1900] 2 Ch. 481.

11. Until relatively recently, these words actually appeared in the confidential instructions of at least one insurance company (see also *Horne* v. *Poland* [1922] 2 K.B. 364, discussed at pp. 54–7).

Other religious groups may also become isolated from the rest of the community by social or geographic barriers and be subjected to unequal treatment as an ethnic rather than as a religious group. For example, it has been suggested that

There are two communities in Northern Ireland, different in their origins nursing different historical myths, possessing distinguishable cultures, having different songs and heroes, and wearing different denominations of the same religion. Religion is the clearest badge of these differences. But the conflict is not *about* religion. It is about the self-assertion of two distinct communities, one of which is dominant in the public affairs of the province (Editorial in *The Times*, 30 August 1969).

If the Race Relations Acts applied to Northern Ireland,[12] and if a Catholic or Protestant were discriminated against in Ulster on such communal 'ethnic' grounds, the discrimination could be unlawful.

Gypsies

The same approach applies to the position of gypsies under the Race Relations Acts. In some contexts, the expression 'gypsy' may be used without any racial or ethnic connotation.[13] And, during the debates on the 1965 Bill, the Home Secretary doubted whether gypsies who had long been settled in Britain could properly be regarded as having a distinct racial or ethnic character or national origin. It was, he said, a puzzle which he hoped 'would never come before the court'.[14] However, once again, the Home Secretary did not seem to appreciate that the puzzle would not normally come before the courts in that form. If a person alleges that he has been discriminated against on the ground that he is a gypsy, the issue will not be whether gypsies are

12. For the unsuccessful attempts to apply the Race Relations Acts to Northern Ireland, see p. 115. The Commissioner for Complaints Act (Northern Ireland) 1969, appoints a Commissioner to investigate complaints of maladministration by public authorities. Less favourable treatment on the ground of race or religion will no doubt constitute maladministration under this Act. The Commissioner must, like the Race Relations Board, first seek to effect a settlement by conciliation, but if he reports that an injustice has been suffered in consequence of maladministration, the victim may himself bring proceedings in a county court and may be awarded damages.

13. See e.g. *Mills* v. *Cooper* [1967] 2 Q.B. 459, where the Divisional Court construed the expression 'gypsy' in the Highways Act 1959, s. 127 to mean a nomadic traveller and not a person of the 'Romany race'.

14. Report Stage, 16 July 1965, *Hansard* (H.C.), vol. 716, cols. 982–3.

in fact an ethnic, racial or national group, but whether the discriminator has treated the complainant unfavourably on that basis. The same would be true of discrimination against people from England, Scotland, Wales,[15] or a particular county or town. If it was on an ethnic basis, it would be unlawful.

National origins

The last of the four unlawful grounds – 'national origins' – clearly includes discrimination against someone because he or his forebears were born in a particular country. It also seems (*contra* Hepple, 1969, 1970; pp. 49–57) to make it unlawful to discriminate against someone because he has a particular nationality or citizenship. This was certainly the Home Secretary's opinion about the meaning of the expression, during the 1965 debates.[16]

The draftsman of the 1968 Act presumably also thought that 'national origins' included nationality and citizenship for it would not otherwise have been necessary for him specifically to exempt discrimination on such grounds in several provisions of the Act.[17] The exceptions suggest that 'national origins' covers discrimination

15. Several statutes recognize that Welsh-speaking people are entitled to special treatment because they speak a separate language. The most interesting of these is the Mines and Quarries Act 1954, s. 171, which provides that where the natural language of the persons employed at a mine or quarry or of a substantial number of those persons is Welsh, then, in considering the qualifications of candidates for appointments to supervisory posts in that mine or quarry, regard must be had to possession of a knowledge of the Welsh language. See also the Welsh Language Act 1967, which provides for the use of the Welsh language in legal proceedings, and for Welsh versions of statutory forms, etc.

16. 'The word "national" would bring to the mind of the ordinary person the idea of a particular country; a person, for example, who is a German is one regarded as having Germany as his nationality and, if he lived here he and his grouping would have the protection of the Bill.' Report Stage, 16 July 1965, *Hansard* (H.C.), vol. 716, col. 972.

17. i.e. RRA section 6 (2) exempts advertisements indicating that Commonwealth citizens or any class of such citizens are required for employment outside Great Britain or that persons other than such citizens are required for employment in Great Britain; section 8 (11) exempts the selection of 'a person of a particular nationality or particular descent for employment requiring attributes especially possessed by persons of that nationality or descent', and section 27 (9) exempts rules restricting employment in the public service 'to persons of particular birth, citizenship, nationality, descent or residence'.

against people because they are Commonwealth citizens (e.g. those whose fathers or grandfathers were born outside Britain) or Indian nationals, or the descendants of Indian nationals. So, too, it is unlawful to discriminate against people because they are 'Europeans', 'aliens' or 'foreigners'.[18]

In *Ealing London Borough Council* v. *Race Relations Board and Zesko*,[19] a local housing authority adopted a rule that a condition of acceptance on their waiting list for council house accommodation was that 'an applicant must be a British subject within the meaning of the British Nationality Act 1948', and so refused to place a Polish national on the list. The council sought declarations in the High Court[20] that the rule was not unlawful in that it discriminated on the ground of *present* nationality rather than national origins. However, Swanwick J. held that inasmuch as a person's national origins dictated his original nationality and the vast majority of people retained their nationality of origin, the practical effect of the council's rule was to contravene sections 1(1) and 5 of the 1968 Act; the rule placed the vast majority of people of other national origins in a less favourable position than almost all people of British or Commonwealth origin, and was discrimination on the ground of national origins although not expressed in those terms. The council has appealed directly to the House of Lords, and it remains to be seen whether this liberal commonsense interpretation of section 1(1) will be upheld.

On the ground of whose colour, race or ethnic or national origins?

The words 'on the ground of' raise a further problem of interpretation. Do they apply only to discrimination on the ground of a

18. This is illustrated by section 6 (2) which exempts advertisements indicating that persons other than Commonwealth citizens are required for employment in Britain; i.e. either a particular nationality (Swiss waiters) or a vague general category ('EEC nationals'). Similarly, section 3 (2) exempts existing discriminatory employment legislation (*inter alia*) against aliens, e.g. Act of Settlement 1700, s. 3. Aliens Employment Act 1955, Army Act 1955, s. 21, Air Force Act 1955, s. 21, see further pp. 220–21.

19. *Ealing London Borough Council* v. *Race Relations Board and Zesko* [1971] 1 Q.B. 309.

20. As to the Board's objection to this procedure and their contention that the High Court had no jurisdiction to grant the declarations sought, see pp. 325–6.

person's own colour, race, or ethnic or national origins, or do they also include discrimination against a person on the ground of some- one else's colour, etc.? Suppose that an Indian and his English girl- friend go together for a drink in a public house, and the publican refuses to serve the Indian because of his colour or national origin; obviously he has acted unlawfully by discriminating against the Indian customer on those grounds. But what is the position if he refuses to serve the English girl on the ground that she is with an Indian? On a narrow interpretation of the statutes, the publican could lawfully do so, because he was not discriminating on the ground of the English girl's colour or national origin. But that inter- pretation would frustrate the objectives of the legislation. It would mean that both would be the victims of an indirect but blatant form of racial discrimination for they would each be deprived of the com- pany of the other in a place of public resort. Conversely, the publican would be able to deter non-white customers from coming to his premises by practising this form of discrimination by proxy.

The better view is that the Acts cover discrimination on the ground of colour etc., whether it is the colour of the particular victim of the discrimination or that of his companions. It is sufficient that the discrimination is because of the colour of any of them for it to be unlawful. This construction is reinforced by section 1 (2) of the 1968 Act which declares that segregating a person from other people on any of the unlawful grounds is to be regarded as treating him less favourably than they are treated. The discriminator cannot provide separate facilities for white and non-whites and claim that in doing so he is treating both groups equally. Parliament has prohibited racial segregation so as to guarantee equal opportunities for people within a multiracial rather than a racially separated context. And this legislative intent would not be realized if discrimination were per- mitted against someone because he associated with people of a different colour or national origin.

There have been no English cases on the point,[21] but the inter-

21. An Indian lawyer who applied unsuccessfully for three hundred posts in Britain claimed that he was rejected by a Jewish firm with many Jewish clients because his wife was a German (*Guardian*, 6 September 1969). Such an act of discrimination on the ground of his wife's national origins would be unlawful under the 1968 Act.

pretation of similar statutory provisions in the United States accords with this view.[22]

e.g. A white lodger in a private hotel was charged an increased rent because she received Negro visitors in her rooms. The rent increases were made 'because of race', and were therefore unlawful.[23]

e.g. A white woman was arrested for vagrancy while sitting in a nightclub. The arrest was made to enforce a custom of the city forbidding or discouraging white women from frequenting places that were predominantly Negro. The police officers had acted unlawfully in depriving the woman of freedom from 'discrimination or segregation of any kind on the ground of race', guaranteed by the Civil Rights Act 1964.[24]

e.g. A white person who joined Negroes to compel a restaurant to desegregate was refused service. The restaurant's denial to him of its services and facilities was unlawful under the Civil Rights Act 1964; it was a form of 'punishment' because of race or colour as a result of his attempt to exercise the rights and privileges secured by the Act.[25]

The test in every case is whether the victim has been discriminated against on the ground either of his own colour or race, or the colour or race of other people. But an act of discrimination will not be unlawful unless it is because of *somebody's* colour or race. It would not, for example, be unlawful to discriminate against an individual solely because of his views about race relations, or because he was a member of the Race Relations Board, or even because he had given evidence in support of a complaint under the Act.[26]

22. Section 602 of the US Model Anti-Discrimination Act makes it an unlawful discriminatory practice for an owner or any other person engaging in a real-estate transaction to discriminate 'because of race, colour, religion or national origin'. Professor Norman Dorsen, who was Reporter-Draftsman of the Model Act, has commented that the Section 'is intended to cover discrimination against an individual because of the race, colour, religion or national origin of another individual, such as his wife' (*Dorsen*, 1967, at p. 243).

23. *McGill* v. *830 S. Michigan Hotel* 215 N.E. 2nd 273 (1966) (Illinois Ct App.).

24. *Robertson* v. *Johnston* 376 F. 2d. 43 (5th Cir., 1967).

25. *Offner* v. *Shell's City Inc.* 376 F. 2d. 574 (5th Cir., 1967).

26. The US Model Anti-Discrimination Act outlaws various practices which may hinder the enforcement of the statute: e.g. to retaliate or discriminate against a person because he has opposed or complained of discrimination; to interfere with a member or representative of the Human Rights Commission in the performance of his duty; to obstruct or prevent a person complying with the provisions of the statute (sections 801 to 804). Such practices have not been made

Inconsistencies

We have already referred to the inconsistent attitude of those responsible for framing the legislation towards the concepts of colour, race and ethnic or national origins. During the debates on the 1965 Bill, the Home Secretary described British Jews as though they were members of a racial or even a national group, and, at another point, he spoke of 'members of an African race'. Quite apart from this inconsistency his reference[27] to 'ethnic origin' as meaning 'an origin which has something to do with one's blood or the origin from which one proceeds' also suggested a belief in the actual existence of different racial groups with innate genetic differences.

In the same way, section 28 (1) of the 1968 Act defines 'community relations' (for the purpose of describing the duties of the Community Relations Commission) as meaning 'relations within the community between people of different colour, race or ethnic or national origins'. It suggests that each of these categories has an objective basis. However, it would be pedantic to object to this definition, for the notion that the human race is divided into many different races is accepted too widely and insistently by the layman (despite the evidence of biologists and social anthropologists) to be disregarded for the sake of academic purity. As one social scientist has observed, it would be

undesirable to banish completely the notion of race from the study of social relations between categories of people who are popularly identified in racial terms. Beliefs about the nature of race – whether true or false – still have considerable social significance, and, when a category is labelled in the popular mind by racial terminology rather than by religious or class criteria, certain predictable consequences ensue. The social significance of the racial label compared with other identifications is a matter that properly forms part of the study of intergroup relations (Banton, 1967).

For this reason, the racial label also properly appears in a statute

---

unlawful in the United Kingdom. If two or more persons agreed together to do any of these things, however, an action for conspiracy might lie: cf. *United States* v. *Johnson* 390 US 563 (1968).

27. Sir Frank Soskice (now Lord Stow Hill), 16 July 1965, *Hansard* (H.C.), vol. 716, col. 971.

concerned with the consequences of such labelling. Moreover, the definition of 'community relations' in the 1968 Act has the merit of implying that different 'racial' groups are entitled to equality of respect within the community.[28]

But some of the exceptions to the 1968 Act are drafted not only on the assumption that there is an objective basis for the existence of different racial groups. They also require the Race Relations Board and the courts to decide whether individuals should be classified within a particular racial group. For example, section 7 (6) makes it not unlawful to discriminate in providing sleeping cabins for passengers on a ship, where 'persons of different colour, race or ethnic or national origins' would otherwise be compelled to share a cabin. Section 8 (10) contains a similar exception permitting discrimination in employment on a ship, where 'persons of different colour, race or ethnic or national origins' would otherwise be compelled to share sleeping rooms, mess rooms or sanitary accommodation.

If a shipping company were to rely on either of these exceptions as a defence to an allegation of unlawful discrimination, the Board would have to decide whether the persons concerned were in fact of different colour, race or ethnic or national origins. It would be an invidious task. These exceptions are inconsistent with the basic philosophy of the legislation. They legitimize racial discrimination, and they might compel the Board to make racial classifications.

Section 8 (11) also makes it lawful to discriminate in selecting a person of a particular nationality or particular descent for employment 'requiring attributes especially possessed by persons of that nationality or descent'. The purpose of this exception was to enable a Chinese restaurant, for example, to confine its recruitment to Chinese waiters. It is doubtful whether such a wide exception was necessary to achieve this object (see p. 215). The result is that the

28. The same cannot be said for the Local Government Act 1966, s. 11 (1) which empowers the Home Secretary to make grants to local authorities who, in his opinion, are required to make special provision because of the presence within their areas of 'substantial numbers of immigrants from the Commonwealth whose language or customs differ from those of the community'. It contains the unfortunate implication that Commonwealth immigrants with their own language or customs are not part of the community. The vice would have been avoided if the section had referred instead to the 'rest of the community'.

Board may have to decide whether people of a particular nationality or descent possess distinctive attributes other than those of physiognomy.

Racial balance

A provision which is flatly irreconcilable with the principle of racial equality is section 8 (2): the 'racial balance' clause (see p. 208). This makes it not unlawful to discriminate on grounds of colour, race or ethnic or national origins in recruiting people for employment or in selecting them for work, if the act of discrimination is done 'in good faith for the purpose of securing or preserving a reasonable balance of persons of different racial groups employed in the undertaking or part of the undertaking.' For this purpose, section 8 (4) defines 'racial group' to mean 'a group of persons defined by reference to colour, race or ethnic or national origins'; but it adds that 'persons wholly or mainly educated in Great Britain' must be treated for this purpose 'as members of the same racial group'. The results of these curious provisions, if rigorously applied, are bizarre. The Board is required to decide whether employees have a particular colour, race or ethnic or national origin. The employer who has a 'reasonable' balance between Pakistani and British workers in his textile mill is apparently permitted to reject new applicants for employment not only because they are Pakistani but also because they are coloured. People educated wholly or mainly in Ireland or Australia would seem to be regarded by the Act as belonging to a different racial or ethnic group from British subjects educated wholly or mainly in this country. On the other hand, Indians, Pakistanis and West Indians are to be treated as belonging to the same 'racial group' as white people if they have been educated wholly or mainly in Britain. The racial balance clause was designed to help employers with significant numbers of immigrant workers. It is unlikely to find favour among Commonwealth immigrants who are proud of the culture of their country of origin.

The practical importance of the racial balance and other exceptions should not be exaggerated. The main objections to them are that they encourage employers to treat people on the very basis which the law was designed to discourage, and that they might require the Board and the courts in exceptional cases to make fine racial distinctions and classifications.

Discriminatory actions

The 1968 Act contains a general definition of discrimination (s. 1) followed by specific definitions in four of the situations to which the Act applies (ss. 2–5). The general definition was added because of Parliamentary pressure for a definition which would free the statute from unnecessary technicality, and provide a concept of racial equality intelligible to members of the public (see p. 137).

But the general definition satisfies neither aim. Instead of removing the specific definitions or their undue complexity from the statute, it has added to them. One has to interpret the Act so as to reconcile both the general and the specific definitions. And, instead of declaring that the legislation is concerned with *equal* treatment, regardless of race or colour, the general definition introduces the more ambiguous concept of *less favourable* treatment. Under section 1, 'a person discriminates against another if, on the ground of colour, race or ethnic or national origins, he treats that other, in any situation to which section 2, 3, 4 or 5 . . . applies, less favourably than he treats or would treat other persons'. These words were scarcely calculated to contribute to public understanding of the objectives of the legislation. The specific definitions in the four following sections will be discussed in subsequent chapters. For all their unnecessary specificity they are fortunately all based on the requirement of equal treatment: that people should be treated in a similar manner, in similar circumstances, regardless of their colour, race, etc.[29]

The language of the general definition did not remove the danger (which was also latent in the 1965 Act) that the courts might sanction racial segregation, whether in employment, housing, education or public places, so long as separate facilities were provided for different racial groups which were equally 'favourable' to them. The risk, although remote, was not completely hypothetical, for the United States Supreme Court held[30] that 'separate but equal' facilities satis-

29. The drafting style of sections 2–5 is modelled on the Race Relations Act 1965, s. 1 (3) (now repealed), under which a person discriminates against another person 'if he refuses or neglects to afford him access to . . . [a place of public resort], or any facilities or services available there, in the like manner and on the like terms in and on which such access, facilities or services are available to other members of the public resorting thereto'.

30. See *Plessy* v. *Ferguson* 163 US 37 (1896).

fied the unequivocal requirement of 'equal protection of the laws' of the US Constitution, and it took more than fifty years to reverse that decision.[31] The government therefore were recommended to add a clause (s. 1 (2)) declaring that, for the purposes of the Act, 'segregating a person from others' on racial grounds is 'treating him less favourably than they are treated'.

The 1965 Act made it unlawful 'to practise' discrimination (s. 1 (1)) in places of public resort. The word 'practise' suggests habitual and recurring behaviour. A single act of discrimination would therefore not have been unlawful under the 1965 Act, unless it indicated that the discriminator made a practice of discriminating on racial grounds. However, most acts of discrimination do reveal a systematic pattern of behaviour adverse to members of a particular group. The 1968 Act omits the word 'practise' altogether; a single act of discrimination is now clearly unlawful.[32]

In each of the situations to which the 1968 Act applies (with the notable exception of advertising) the act of discrimination must have been done intentionally on one of the unlawful grounds, and it must have been done against a particular person. There must be a causal connection between those grounds and the discriminatory action, and there must be an actual victim of that action.

The test of the discriminator's intention is objective rather than subjective. If he has acted in a way which would lead one reasonably to conclude that his conduct was based on racial grounds, the discriminator will not escape liability by protesting that he was not motivated by racial prejudice; his actions speak louder than his thoughts.

e.g. A hotel refused on three separate occasions to provide accommodation for coloured people, even though rooms were available on each occasion. The hotel proprietor gives evidence that neither he nor his reception clerk are racially prejudiced, and that some of their best friends are coloured.

31. *Brown* v. *Board of Education* 347 US 483 (1954) (separate educational facilities are inherently unequal, even if they are equal in all material respects). See also *McLaurin* v. *Oklahoma State Regents* 339 US 637 (1950).

32. In *Race Relations Board* v. *Lenehan* (Westminster County Court) (*The Times*, 23 and 24 June 1971), the licensee of a public house was held to have acted in breach of section 2 of the 1968 Act by a single refusal to serve a group of West Indians on the ground of their colour.

In view of their previous conduct, they will be held to have acted unlawfully, unless they can give some adequate explanation for what has happened.

e.g. Another hotel refuses to provide accommodation for a coloured person. There is no evidence of similar refusals in the past, and the hotel proprietor is able to show that the real ground for the refusal on this occasion was the fact that the person concerned had arrived at the hotel in an intoxicated and violent condition. There has been no unlawful discrimination.

e.g. A third hotel proprietor tells a journalist that he will never have a coloured person in his hotel. However, no coloured people have ever in fact sought accommodation in the hotel. There has been no unlawful discrimination, because the hotel has not discriminated against anyone.

These considerations do not apply to discriminatory advertisements (pp. 194–7). Section 6 (1) of the 1968 Act makes it unlawful for any person 'to publish or display, or cause to be published or displayed, any advertisement or notice which indicates, or which could reasonably be understood as indicating, an intention to do an act of discrimination, *whether or not it would be unlawful by virtue of any other provision of this Act*'. The 'act of discrimination' in the advertisement or notice must be discrimination on one of the unlawful grounds.[33] But the advertiser need not intend to discriminate on those grounds; it is sufficient that he has published or displayed an advertisement or notice which could reasonably be understood to indicate an intention by someone to do an act of discrimination. Similarly, it does not matter whether anyone suffers personally as a result of the discriminatory advertisement or notice. Parliament has prohibited the publication or display itself, presumably because it is a public insult to those affected, and an apparently easy way of discriminating because the discriminator avoids facing his victim.

e.g. A newsagent displays an advertisement by one of his customers, stating 'Flat to let. Sorry, no coloureds or Irish'. The newsagent has acted unlawfully, even though he himself had no intention of discriminating,

33. This follows because, although section 1 (1) defines the situations in which a person discriminates on those grounds by reference only to sections 2–5, it goes on to provide that 'in this Act references to discrimination are references to discrimination on any of those grounds'; i.e. it applies that definition to the entire Act, including section 6.

and even though no individual coloured or Irish people are identified as actual victims.

It also follows from the wording of the advertising provision that it is unlawful to publish or display a discriminatory advertisement or notice, even where the actual act of discrimination expressed in the document would not, if done, be unlawful (e.g. because it involves 'small premises' (s. 7 (1)) or employment in a small firm before November 1972 (s. 8 (1))).[34] Parliament has determined to prevent discrimination through the medium of advertising, whether or not the discrimination is itself unlawful.

The advertising provision does not prohibit the compilation and publication of statistical and other information on a racial basis. Such information may indeed be essential in establishing the existence or extent of racial discrimination (see p. 248). It is only if the information is compiled with the object of discriminating on any of the unlawful grounds that it may result in a violation of the Act. In such circumstances racial statistics will be evidence of an act of discrimination in employment, housing or the provision of services; or, if such statistics are published or displayed in any document which indicates a discriminatory intention, there will be a breach of section 6.

Obviously, a person cannot avoid liability under the legislation by arguing that he has discriminated against someone, not because he himself objects to their colour or race, but because other people do so. Acts of discrimination are commonly done by proxy – because the discriminator defers to the racial prejudices, real or assumed, of other people, whether customers, workers, neighbours or friends (see p. 82). It would therefore defeat the main objectives of the legislation if racial discrimination could be practised on this basis. However, in the same way that discrimination is unlawful against a person on the ground of another person's colour or race (see p. 161) so also it is unlawful if done on the ground of someone else's objection to a person's colour or race.

The 1968 Act goes further (s. 12) and makes it unlawful for a per-

34. However, by section 6 (2) an advertisement or notice may indicate that Commonwealth citizens or a class of them are required for employment outside Britain, or that non-Commonwealth citizens are required for employment in Britain (see generally pp. 225–6).

son deliberately to aid, induce or incite another person to discriminate in breach of the Act. This provision was designed to relieve the pressure otherwise difficult to resist, from those who were in a position to discriminate. The customer, worker or neighbour who urges the publican, the employer or the property owner to discriminate on racial grounds, is himself guilty of unlawful conduct under the Act, whether or not he succeeds in persuading those people to discriminate against anyone. However, sometimes it may be difficult to prove any unlawful conduct, because a person may succeed in inciting someone to discriminate without revealing his racial motives to him.

e.g. A shop steward approaches an employer and informs him that unless he agrees to exclude coloured people from supervisory jobs in his factory, members of the trade union will withdraw their labour. The shop steward is guilty of incitement to discrimination; so too are any other workers who participate in the incitement.

e.g. The same shop steward approaches the employer and informs him that unless he agrees to exclude a particular person (who happens to be coloured) from a supervisory job in his factory, members of the trade union will withdraw their labour. However, this time the shop steward bases his objection on the ground that the man is unpopular with his fellow workers, and the employer excludes the man for that reason. Unless it can be proved that the employer knew or ought reasonably to have known that the real objection was to the man's colour, and that colour was the ground on which he was excluded, he will not have acted unlawfully in succumbing to the shop steward's pressure. Similarly, the shop steward will escape liability, unless it can be proved that he was really objecting to the man because of his colour.

The 1968 Act also makes an employer liable for the discriminatory actions of his employees, whether or not they were done with the employer's knowledge or approval (s. 13 (1)). But if legal proceedings are brought against an employer, it is a defence for him to prove that he took 'such steps as were reasonably practicable' to prevent his employee from discriminating on racial grounds (s. 13 (3)). And anything done by a person as agent for someone else is treated for the purposes of the Act as done by the principal as well as by the agent (s. 13 (2)). These provisions are included to ensure that those responsible for making policy do not escape liability by blaming their subordinates or their agents. On the contrary, they must do their best to see that their employees and agents comply with the law.

e.g. A West Indian is refused admission to a dance hall. The commissionaire tells him that no coloured people are admitted. It is part of the commissionaire's duties to refuse admission to 'undesirable' people; he has never been instructed to turn coloured people away, but nor have the management taken any steps to prevent him from doing so. The management and the commissionaire are both liable under the Act.

e.g. An insurance broker, acting on behalf of underwriters, demands a higher premium from Commonwealth immigrants and aliens than from UK citizens to insure their property against the risk of theft or fire. The underwriters and the broker, who is their agent, are both liable under the Act.

Exceptions

The various exceptions to the 1968 Act are fully discussed in subsequent chapters. However, it is convenient to summarize all these exceptions at this stage to indicate the limits to the types of racial discrimination which are prohibited under the 1968 Act. It is important to bear in mind, in considering these exceptions, that the exclusion of a particular type of discrimination from the legislation does not make such discrimination lawful. Nothing in the 1968 Act affects the right to bring any civil or criminal proceedings which might have been brought if the Act had not been passed (s. 19 (10)). A discriminatory action may therefore be unlawful at Common Law even though it is outside the scope of the Race Relations Acts (see p. 70–71).

Employment exemptions

Small employers. During the first two years in which the 1968 Act was in force (i.e. until 26 November 1970) employers of not more than twenty-five people were outside its scope; in the next two years (i.e. until 26 November 1972) employers of not more than ten people are outside its scope. After 25 November 1972 the Act applies to all employers regardless of the number of people employed (s. 8 (1)).

Racial balance. It is not unlawful to discriminate in recruitment for or the selection of work in an undertaking or part of an undertaking, if the act of discrimination is done in good faith to secure or preserve a reasonable balance of employees of different racial groups (s. 8 (2)). Workers who have been wholly or mainly educated in Britain, whatever their origins, are to be treated for this purpose as belonging to the same racial group (s. 8 (4)).

Special attributes. It is not unlawful to select someone of a particular nationality or descent for employment requiring attributes especially possessed by people of that nationality or descent (s. 8 (11)).

Discriminatory statutes and rules. The Act does not affect the provisions of other statutes relating to employment or qualifications for employment (s. 3 (2)). The exempted measures are mainly concerned with restricting the employment of aliens. Discriminatory rules restricting employment in the civil service and certain public bodies are also outside the scope of the 1968 Act (s. 27 (9)).

Private households. The Act does not apply to the employment of anyone for the purposes of a private household (s. 8 (6)).

Employment abroad. The Act does not apply to employment or applications for employment wholly or mainly outside Great Britain (s. 8 (7) (a)).

Ships and aircraft. The Act does not apply to employment or applications for employment on British or foreign ships or aircraft outside Britain (s. 8 (7) (b) and (c)); nor to employment on any ship or aircraft in any part of the world, if recruitment took place outside Britain (s. 8 (8) and (9)); nor to employment on any ship in any part of the world, if the discrimination is done to avoid people of different colour, race or ethnic or national origins being compelled to share sleeping rooms, mess rooms or sanitary accommodation (s. 8 (10)).

Housing exemptions

Small premises. The Act does not apply to discrimination in the provision or disposal of residential accommodation in 'small premises'. Properties come within this exception if they contain accommodation for not more than two households in addition to the landlord's, or (where this description is inapplicable) where there is not normally accommodation for more than six people in addition to the landlord's household (s. 7 (2) and (3)).

The small premises exemption applies only if the landlord or a member of his family, resides and intends to continue residing at the premises and the landlord or a member of his family shares some part of the accommodation (other than storage or means of access) with other occupiers (s. 7 (1) and (5)).

Private transactions. It is not unlawful for a person to discriminate in selling a property owned and wholly occupied by him if he does not use the services of an estate agent for the purposes of the sale, nor use advertisements or notices in connection with the sale (ss. 7 (7) and (8)).

Miscellaneous exemptions

Advertising. It is not unlawful to publish or display advertisements or notices indicating that Commonwealth citizens, or a particular category of them, are required for employment outside Britain, or that non-Commonwealth citizens are required for employment in Britain (s. 6 (2)); and it is not unlawful to publish or display advertisements stating the gist of rules restricting employment in the public service to people of particular birth, citizenship, nationality, descent or residence (s. 27 (9) (b)).

Passengers on ships. It is not unlawful to discriminate in providing sleeping cabins for passengers on a ship so as to avoid people of different colour, race or ethnic or national origins from being compelled to share the same cabin (s. 7 (6)).

Charities. The Act does not affect future charitable instruments which confer benefits on people of a particular race, descent or ethnic or national origin; nor does it make unlawful any act done to comply with the provisions of any existing charitable instrument (s. 9).

National security. The Act does not apply to anything done for the purpose of safeguarding national security. A certificate signed by or for a Minister certifying that an act was done for such a purpose is conclusive evidence of that fact (s. 10 (1) and (2)).

Conduct relating to acts abroad. It is not unlawful to discriminate by refusing to provide goods, services or facilities (other than travel facilities) outside Britain; or banking, financial or insurance facilities for a purpose to be carried out, or in connection with risks arising, outside Britain; or to dispose of land, outside Britain (s. 11 (1)). It is also not unlawful to discriminate so as to comply with the laws of a foreign country, while within its territory or waters (s. 11 (2)).

Discriminatory contracts. A contract or a term in a contract is not void or unenforceable if it contravenes the Act; but it may be revised by the court if it is feasible to do so without affecting the rights of third parties (s. 23) (pp. 338–9).

Past discrimination

Under two of the exemptions already referred to, the Act expressly permits a person to discriminate *in favour* of members of a racial, ethnic or national group. The 'special attributes' clause enables an employer to select someone of a particular nationality or descent for work requiring special attributes possessed by people of that nationality or descent; and the charities clause permits a charity to confer benefits upon people of a particular race, descent or ethnic or national origins (or, if the charity existed before the 1968 Act came into force, and its deed so provided, to people of a particular colour).

The 'racial balance' clause also allows an employer who satisfies its conditions to select employees or to allocate work to them on a racial basis. It would enable him to select native workers and to reject immigrant workers for jobs which had previously been filled mainly by immigrant workers; conversely, an employer could discriminate in favour of immigrant workers in recruiting employees for work which had previously been filled mainly by native British workers.

Apart from these three exceptions, the 1968 Act does not permit discrimination on racial grounds in favour of an individual or group, if such action involves treating other people less favourably.[35]

The Government did not accept the Street Committee's recom-

35. The Race Relations Board explains this point by drawing a sharp distinction between the problems which affect any immigrant and 'those associated with race and colour'. 'All immigrants may have difficulties owing to an inadequate knowledge of the English language, inappropriate skills and qualifications, ignorance of the way in which our society works and so on. It is in the interests of the immigrants and of the society to which they migrate to overcome these difficulties. This process can be described as that of helping the unequal to become equal. This is not the responsibility of the Board, whose task is to see that those who are equal are equally treated' (RRB, 1970, para. 96).

mendation[36] that the 'racial imbalance' provisions of the US Model Anti-Discrimination Act[37] should be included in any similar legislation in this country. Those provisions permit voluntary plans to be adopted (subject to the approval of the appropriate Human Rights Commission) 'to reduce or eliminate a racial imbalance' in employment, education or housing. It can be, for example, lawful under the Model Act actively to seek members of a racial minority for employment or housing from which they have previously been excluded, or to allocate them to schools which were formerly racially segregated. Classifications which single out particular racial or ethnic groups for such purposes have become known in the United States as 'benign classifications' (*Harvard L. Rev. Note*, 1969, pp. 1104–5).

In Britain, racial classifications must not generally be acted upon, whether they are benign or malignant. It is true that, under the 1968 Act, the 'racial balance' clause could be used to overcome the effects of past discrimination against *immigrant* workers by enabling an employer deliberately to recruit immigrants for a previously non-immigrant work force – although, oddly enough, it was included in the 1968 Act with the opposite object: i.e. so as to enable those who already employed substantial numbers of immigrants to exclude additional immigrants from their employment (see p. 140). However, the racial balance clause could not be used to enable an employer to recruit black workers who had been wholly or mainly educated in Britain, since they are placed in the same category as white British workers for the purposes of that clause. If racial discrimination were to prevent Commonwealth immigrants and their children from being able to compete equally with white people, the absence of a 'racial imbalance' provision could seriously limit the effectiveness of the legislation.

The Government did attempt to include a clause (2 (3)) in the 1968 Bill which would have permitted discrimination in the provision of goods, facilities and services, if it was done 'in good faith for the

36. Street Report, paras. 130.3 and 131.7. The Report noted that racial imbalance plans were unlikely to be in operation in Britain in the near future, but its authors saw 'no valid reason for not recognizing them as a valid exception provided that they have received prior approval from the Race Relations Board' (para. 130.3).

37. Sections 310, 504 and 608.

benefit of a particular section of the public' and if it had 'the effect of promoting the integration of members of that section of the public into the community'. The purpose of this provision was apparently to enable special facilities to be provided for the benefit of minority groups, and to ensure that local education authorities could lawfully 'disperse' the children of Commonwealth immigrants throughout different schools. The clause was deleted during the Committee Stage (p. 138) because it was regarded as dangerously vague, and capable of being used to justify the provision of racially segregated facilities or services.[38] If it had remained in the Bill, it might have enabled some limited types of 'racial imbalance' plans to be implemented in the field of education. But it could not have had that effect in the fields of employment and housing, since it did not apply to the provisions dealing with those subjects.

However, there are several important methods of remedying the effects of past discrimination, which are not only not unlawful under the 1968 Act, but which are also in accordance with the spirit of legislation. For example, central and local government may, of course, provide special facilities to enable immigrants to become proficient in the English language or to overcome the other handicaps involved in being newcomers to Britain.[39] To the extent that immigrants receive unequal treatment for these reasons, the roots of their inequality can be removed without any need to discriminate in their favour on grounds of colour, race or ethnic or national origins. In the same way, where Commonwealth immigrants form part of the under-privileged section of the community (whether as a result of racial discrimination or for any other reason) they will benefit, like their fellow citizens, from government policies to eradicate poverty.[40]

It is more directly relevant to the subject-matter of this book to observe that, if racial discrimination is allowed to become entrenched in Britain, the courts and the Race Relations Board will be called upon to interpret the concept of equality of opportunity in the Race

38. The language of clause 2 (3) also implied that immigrants needed to be integrated into 'the community'. This unattractively ethnocentric notion of the community which excludes immigrants is also contained in the Local Government Act 1966, s. 11 (see p. 164).

39. See Local Government Act 1966, s. 11.

40. e.g. under the Local Government Grants (Social Need) Act 1969, s. 1.

Relations Acts in its strongest and most active sense. This has been the most striking change in recent years in the judicial interpretation of anti-discrimination legislation and the 'equal protection' clause of the Fourteenth Amendment in the United States. There, the courts have increasingly required positive measures to be taken in favour of black Americans in order to overcome the effects of past discrimination and secure compliance with the law.

For example, in the field of education (Kirp, 1968), it has been recognized[41] that race must be consciously taken into account in eliminating racial segregation. A specific ratio of white to black faculty members has been held[42] to be an appropriate remedy in dealing with past discrimination in the public-school system (i.e. schools supported by the taxpayer). One county has been ordered[43] to levy sufficient taxes to enable public schools (closed in order to avoid racial integration) to be re-opened on an integrated basis. The courts have also attacked[44] a public-school system which was *de facto* segregated because of the existence of separate white and black residential neighbourhoods. In another case,[45] the court ordered a school board to take affirmative action to correct a racial imbalance in schools, to institute compensatory programmes for black pupils, and to abolish a system which placed pupils in faster or slower streams on the basis of aptitude tests held by the court to be inaccurate (because they were culturally biased) reflections of ability.

The Supreme Court has held[46] that, where the illiterate condition of black residents was attributable to past inferior educational opportunities, the state's literacy test for would-be voters had to be suspended so as to comply with the Voting Rights Act of 1965. The state could not take the illiterate black as it found him, for the state's educational system had been responsible for his illiterate condition.

Similarly, in the field of employment, recent United States decisions

41. *United States* v. *Jefferson County Board of Education* 372 F. 2d. 836 (5th Cir., 1966).

42. *United States* v. *Montgomery County Board of Education* US (1969).

43. *Griffin* v. *Prince Edward County* 377 US 218 (1964).

44. *Barksdale* v. *Springfield School Committee* 237 F.Supp. 543 (D.Mass.) *vacated on other grounds*, 348 F. 2d. 261 (1st Cir., 1965).

45. *Hobson* v. *Hansen* 269 F.Supp. 401 (D.D.C. 1967) *aff'd sub. nom. Smuck* v. *Hobson* (D.C. Cir., 21 January 1969).

46. *Gaston County* v. *United States* US 395 US 285, 895 Ct 1270 (1969).

have held that apparently neutral employment standards were racially discriminatory in their effects, and therefore unlawful.[47] For example, in one case,[48] the court found a seniority system to be contrary to Title VII of the Civil Rights Act of 1964. The court observed that 'Congress did not intend to freeze an entire generation of Negro employees into discriminatory patterns that existed before the Act'. It held that the existing consequences of past discrimination – the lack of accumulated seniority credits in what had always been a 'white' department – could be remedied by Title VII. In another case involving seniority rights[49] the issue was whether an employer could continue to award formerly 'white jobs' on the basis of seniority attained in other formerly white jobs, or whether the employer had to consider the employee's experience in formerly 'Negro jobs' as an equivalent measure of seniority. The court decided that the latter course had to be adopted. The seniority system was unlawful because 'by carrying forward the effects of former discriminatory practices the system results in present and future discrimination. When a Negro applicant has the qualifications to handle a particular job, the Act requires that Negro seniority be equated with white seniority.'[50]

It is unlikely that the English courts would at present give this

47. See e.g. Gould (1969); Cooper and Sobol (1969); Gould (1967). However, these articles are critical of recent judicial decisions, on the ground that they are unduly conservative in their approach to Title VII and its implications. See generally *Harvard L. Rev.* (1971).

48. *Quarles* v. *Philip Morris* 279 F.Supp. 505 (E.D.Va. 1968).

49. *Local 189, United Papermakers and Paperworkers*, et al. v. *Crown Zellerbach Corporation* (E.D.La 1969) and see also *United States* v. *Hayes International Corporation* 2 FEP cases 67 (5th Cir., 1969) and *Arrington* v. *Massachusetts Bay Transportation Authority* 306 F.Supp. 1355 (1969).

50. In *Griggs* v. *Duke Power Co.* 28 L. Ed. 2d 158 (1971), the Supreme Court unanimously held that a requirement that all applicants for employment and inter-departmental transfer in a power station should have a high-school diploma and satisfactory intelligence test scores was contrary to section 703 of the Civil Rights Act 1964 since the tests bore no significant relation to successful job performance and the practical effect was to exclude Negroes at a much higher rate than whites. There is, however, a statutory limit to the power of the courts in the United States to sanction efforts to correct past discrimination in employment. Section 703 (j) of the Civil Rights Act 1964 forbids preferential treatment of job applicants on account of an imbalance in the total number or percentage of persons of any race or national origin employed by any employer.

strong and active interpretation of the legal concept of racial equality to the Race Relations Acts. In Britain, as in the United States, the extent to which it becomes desirable to interpret anti-discrimination legislation in this way will be a measure of the extent to which racial discrimination is allowed to harden into widespread patterns of behaviour. If the objectives of the legislation are effectively realized, American jurisprudence concerned with removing the effects of past discrimination will, happily, be of only academic interest. If not, the American legal experience will be of greater and greater relevance.

Chapter 5
Employment

Scope

The 1968 Act makes it unlawful to discriminate on grounds of colour, race or ethnic or national origins (see p. 153) in recruitment, training, promotion, dismissals, and the terms and conditions of employment. The Act applies to the employer, his servants and his agents, and also to discrimination by trade unions and employers' associations. But there are several types of employment discrimination which are outside the scope of the legislation (see p. 207).

Persons concerned
Employers

The 1968 Act applies to a wide range of people. It covers *all* employers, although, during the first two years of its operation (i.e until 25 November 1970), the Act exempted employers of not more than twenty-five people,[1] and, in the following two years (i.e. until 25 November 1972) employers of not more than ten people (s. 8 (1)).[2] Thereafter, all employers must comply with the provisions of the Act. In calculating the number of people in a person's employment, those employed for the purposes of his private household are to be excluded.

1. This exemption excluded about 20 per cent of the working population from the protection of the legislation: see *Official Report*, Standing Committee B, 28 May 1968, col. 324. The reason why Parliament excluded small employers from the legislation during the first four years of its operation was to reduce the volume of work of those responsible for administering the Act while they were developing their procedures and training their personnel.

2. This exemption excludes about 14 per cent of the working population from the protection of the legislation.

In one respect, even the small employer is covered from the date when the Act first came into force (i.e. 25 November 1968). He must not publish or display an advertisement or notice which indicates, or which could reasonably be understood as indicating, an intention to discriminate on any of the unlawful grounds (s. 6 (1)); the prohibition of discriminatory advertisements and notices applies regardless of whether it would be unlawful to do the act of discrimination indicated in such advertisement or notice (see p. 168).

Public as well as private employers are subject to the Act, including the Crown, government departments and any police force (s. 27 (1) and (8)). However, there are special provisions enabling aliens to be excluded from some government departments (see p. 220), and permitting restrictions to be imposed on the employment by the Crown or any public body of people of a particular birth, citizenship, nationality, descent or residence (see p. 218). And, there is an exemption for acts of discrimination done for the purpose of safeguarding national security (see p. 217).

Employees

An employer is liable for the acts of his employees, which are done in the course of their employment, whether or not they are done with his knowledge or approval (s. 13 (1)). In this respect, the Act merely restates the usual vicarious liability of a master at Common Law for his servant's torts. The question whether a wrongful act is within the course of a servant's employment is ultimately a question of fact, and no simple test is appropriate to cover all cases.[3] However, an act will be deemed to be done in the course of employment

if it is either (1) a wrongful act authorized by the master, or (2) a wrongful and unauthorized mode of doing some act authorized by the master.[4]

If an employee acts unlawfully, he will, of course, be personally liable (s. 13 (1)), regardless of whether his employer is also liable.

Even an express prohibition of the wrongful act is no defence to

3. *Staton* v. *National Coal Board* [1957] 2 All E.R. 667, at p. 669, *per* Finnemore J. See generally, Salmond on Torts (15th edn) pp. 620–27.
4. *Poland* v. *John Parr & Sons* [1927] 1 K.B. 236 (C.A.), at p. 240; *Warren* v. *Henlys, Ltd* [1948] 2 All E.R. 935, at p. 937; *Ilkiw* v. *Samuels* [1963] 1 W.L.R. 991 (C.A.), at pp. 997, 1002 and 1004.

the master, if the act was merely a way of doing what the servant was employed to do;[5] so that, in one case,[6] where the servant was doing work which he was appointed to do, but he did it in a way which his master had not authorized and would not have authorized, had he known of it, the master was none the less held responsible.

However, if legal proceedings are brought against an employer in respect of the alleged act of his employee, it is a defence for the employer to prove that he took 'such steps as were reasonably practicable' to prevent his employee from doing acts of that kind in the course of his employment (s. 13 (3)). The employer has the burden of proving to the court that he is entitled to take advantage of the defence. And the mere availability of the defence does not make the act of discrimination lawful. If a complaint is made about an employee's discriminatory conduct, it must be investigated, and the process of conciliation must be attempted, in the normal way. If the employee has acted unlawfully, he will remain personally liable; and the employer will also be vicariously liable, unless he can establish that the employee did not act in the course of his employment, or unless the employer can prove that he took such steps as were reasonably practicable to prevent the employee from acting unlawfully.

e.g. A foreman is told by his employer to find suitable workers to fill vacant jobs in his factory. The foreman, without the employer's knowledge or consent, refuses to accept qualified applicants for vacant jobs because they are coloured. Notices have always been prominently displayed throughout the factory forbidding anyone from practising racial discrimination. But the employer has taken no other steps to prevent his employees from doing so; he has never spoken to them on the subject; nor has he ever checked whether vacancies were being filled on merit, regardless of colour or race. The foreman is personally liable. The employer is vicariously liable and cannot avail himself of the statutory defence.[7]

5. See e.g. *Limpus* v. *London General Omnibus Co.* (1862) 1 H. & C. 526; *Canadian Pacific Ry Co.* v. *Lockhart* [1942] A.C. 591 (P.C.). For a case on the other side of the line, see e.g. *Twine* v. *Bean's Express* [1946] 1 All E.R. 202; *aff'd* 175 L.T. 131.
6. *Goh Choon Seng* v. *Lee Kim Soo* [1925] A.C. 550 (P.C.).
7. Compare *LCC* v. *Cattermoles* [1953] 1 W.L.R. 997 (C.A.).

The reason why the foreman would be personally liable in this example is that, although he is not an employer, the Act also applies to 'any person concerned with the employment of others' (s. 3 (1)); a foreman plainly comes within this category.

However, sometimes the position of an employee may not be so straightforward.

e.g. An Indian hears that a factory has vacancies for lathe operators. He visits the factory to apply for a job, but is told by the gateman that jobs are not available for Indians. The employers are plainly liable for the wrongful act of the gateman unless they can prove that they took reasonably practicable steps to prevent him from acting unlawfully. The gateman himself is 'a person concerned with the employment of others', since he has concerned himself with the employment or non-employment of the Indian applicant. But he is not liable for 'refusing or deliberately omitting to employ' the applicant, because he had no authority to enter into contracts of employment on behalf of the employers.

This example suggests that there may be an unintended loophole in the 1968 Act in respect of people like the gateman.[8] He might be liable for aiding his employers to act unlawfully (s. 12) but the employers have only acted unlawfully because his action is attributed to them and makes them vicariously liable. However, in practical terms this legal conundrum is of little importance, for what matters is that the employers are liable and have a duty to prevent their gatemen and other employees from turning people away because of colour, race, etc.

Agents

Anything done by a person as agent for someone else (with his express or implied authority) is treated for the purposes of the Act as

8. During the Parliamentary debate, Roy Hattersley, M.P., the junior minister responsible for the employment provisions of the 1968 Bill stated that 'the employer has a responsibility to make sure that his gatemen do not exercise . . . [an unlawful] policy and that they do not express . . . [an unlawful] opinion. The corollary, in reason and in justice, and certainly in practicability, is that while we hold the employer responsible . . . for what his gateman said, it would be preposterous if . . . only the employer were responsible for it, because the gateman . . . must himself be subject to conciliatory procedure and to what might operate after it.' *Official Report*, Standing Committee B, 23 May 1968, col. 307.

done by the principal as well as by the agent (s. 13 (2)). This provision again merely restates the normal Common Law liability of principals for the tortious acts of their agents, which are done within the scope of their authority.[9] 'An employer cannot therefore escape liability by using someone not directly employed by him to discriminate on his behalf.

e.g. A personnel manager of a large firm instructs an employment agency to find him an electrical maintenance supervisor and to offer him employment in his firm on specified terms. The personnel manager stipulates that only white people should be offered the job. The employment agency carries out these instructions, and refuses to offer the job to a qualified applicant because he is coloured. The employment agency is liable as agent, and the personnel manager is liable as principal.

Employment agencies and exchanges[10]

The preceding example is rather artificial, for, in practice, an employment agency will rarely be authorized to offer employment to applicants on behalf of an employer. Its usual function will be to refer applicants to the employer for his consideration. An employment agency will therefore normally not be liable for discriminating in recruiting personnel. However, the 1968 Act also makes it unlawful for any person concerned with the provision to the public of facilities or services to discriminate in providing those facilities or services (s. 2). So an employment agency or a government employment exchange is covered by the Act in performing its normal functions. In the preceding example, the employment agency would be liable if it had refused to refer the coloured applicant to the potential employer, whether or not he had instructed the agency to exclude coloured applicants.

Employment agencies will incur no liability for keeping records

9. See e.g. Bowstead on Agency (1968) at p. 330.

10. For the Department of Employment and Productivity's instructions to employment exchanges regarding racial discrimination and the 1968 Act, see the DEP's memorandum to the Select Committee on Race Relations and Immigration, Annex 6, Minutes of Evidence (Session 1968–9) 30 January 1969 (HMSO, 1969). See also, Hepple (1970, at pp. 99–103) for an account of changes in the policy of the exchanges towards racial discrimination over the years before the 1968 Act.

indicating the colour or race of applicants for employment, but such records would be strong evidence that unlawful discrimination was being practised. It is unlawful for an employment agency (or any other body or individual) to publish or display discriminatory advertisements or notices (s. 6 (1)).

Trade unions and employers' associations

It is unlawful for any trade union or employers' association to discriminate by excluding anyone from membership of the organization, or by refusing to accord him equal benefits as a member of the organization, or by expelling him from the organization (s. 4). This provision applies not only to any organization of employers or workers, but also to organizations 'concerned with the carrying on of trades, businesses, professions or occupations'. It would, for example, include a professional association, like the Law Society or the British Medical Association, or a trade association, like the Motor Agents' Association. On the other hand, it would not include a social club or a sports club, even though its members all followed the same trade or occupation. Officials of organizations covered by the Act would also be liable in those situations in which they acted as recruiting agents on behalf of an employer, for they would then be 'concerned with the employment of others' (s. 3 (1)). The most common situation in which such liability is likely to arise is where a trade union controls entry into an occupation by maintaining a closed shop.

Apart from the specific employment provisions, the Act also makes it unlawful for anyone to aid, induce or incite another person to do an unlawful act (s. 12). It would therefore be unlawful for trade union officials to exert pressure on an employer to exclude workers from his employment on racial grounds.

e.g. A manufacturer advertises for an assistant works manager. He considers that a Pakistani applicant is best suited for the post, but feels that it would be prudent to consult the shop stewards before appointing a coloured man to a senior position in the company. The shop stewards threaten to call a strike if he appoints the man. The shop stewards are liable because they have deliberately induced or incited the employer to discriminate on racial grounds. If the employer yields to their pressure, he will also be liable. But the shop stewards will be liable whether or not they succeed in inducing the employer to discriminate.[11]

If the shop stewards were acting as agents for other trade union members or the union itself, then the other members or the union would also be liable.

It may be that the trade union officials would be liable under this provision, even if they did not induce or incite the employer to discriminate against a particular person, but tried to persuade him to practise racial discrimination as a matter of general policy, for such a policy would necessarily involve unlawful acts of discrimination. In certain circumstances there might also be liability for the criminal offence of incitement to racial hatred (see chapter 10).

In none of these cases could the trade union officials avoid liability by relying on the protection of section 132 of the Industrial Relations Act 1971 because this section exempts only liability in tort. Breach of the Race Relations Act is not a tort.

Any person

It is unlawful for *any* person to aid, induce or incite another person to do an unlawful act (s. 12). This applies, for example, to a member of an unofficial group of workers or a customer seeking to persuade a firm to discriminate unlawfully.

Types of unlawful discrimination
Recruitment

It is unlawful for an employer or any person concerned with the employment of others to discriminate against another person, if that other person is seeking employment, 'by refusing or deliberately omitting to employ him on work of any description which is available and for which he is qualified (s. 3 (1) (a)). There must be a deliberate intention to discriminate on one of the unlawful grounds (see p. 167), but the ground need not be the applicant's own colour or race; it may be the colour or race of someone else with whom he is associated (see p. 161). There may be an outright refusal, or merely a deliberate omission to employ, for example, by the pretence that a vacant job has already been filled.

11. Compare *R*. v. *Higgins* [1801] East 5.

There will be no liability under this or any other provision if a person is prevented, on racial grounds, from carrying on an occupation in which he will be self-employed. Section 3 of the 1968 Act applies only to relationships between employers and employees. So it would not be unlawful for a builder to refuse to use the services of a 'labour-only' sub-contractor on the ground that his work force was largely Irish or coloured; nor for a firm of anti-Semitic accountants to refuse to accept a Jew as a partner in their firm. In neither situation is there an employer or a person concerned with employment. But the builder would be liable if he discriminated in recruiting his own employees; and the firm of accountants would be liable if they discriminated in selecting their staff.[12] And, as has already been seen, a professional body or a trade union would be liable for discriminating in admitting members or according them the benefits of membership. Such a body would also be liable at Common Law if it controlled entry into a profession and exercised that control in an arbitrary or capricious manner by discriminating on racial grounds.[13]

It is not unlawful to discriminate unless work is actually available and, it must be assumed, unless it is work which the applicant is in fact seeking.

e.g. A black West Indian applies to a builder for a job as a carpenter. He is told that no coloured workers are employed in the firm. However, at the time of his application there are no vacancies for carpenters. The builder has not acted unlawfully; nor would he have acted unlawfully if he failed to offer the man a general labouring job which was then vacant, because the West Indian was not seeking such a job.

An employer is, of course, entitled to reject an applicant who is not properly qualified for the job for which he has applied, so long as he does not regard colour, race or ethnic or national origins as part of the requisite qualifications. It is for the person alleging unlawful discrimination to show that he had the necessary qualifications. If he

12. Hepple (1970, at p. 111) points out that section 3 does not apply either to certain holders of offices under the Crown, who are not in the employment of the Crown, e.g. members of hospital boards and members of public corporations. Police constables are not employees but for the purposes of the Act they are to be treated as employees of the authority by which they are appointed (s. 27 (4)–(8)).

13. *Nagle* v. *Feilden* [1966] 2 Q.B. 633 (C.A.); *Edwards* v. *SOGAT* [1971] Ch. 354 (C.A.); (see further pp. 51–3).

does so, and the job is available, it is for the alleged discriminator to prove that the applicant was not rejected on grounds of colour, race, etc.

e.g. A tobacco company advertises for clerical staff, stating the requisite qualifications. An Indian woman applies for a job, and is told that Asians are not employed in clerical jobs. No inquiry is made about her qualifications. Although it is clear that she has been rejected on unlawful grounds, the company will be liable only if she establishes that she had the necessary qualifications.

However, it is not necessary for the applicant to show that, but for his rejection on racial grounds, he would have been certain to have been offered the job; it is sufficient for him to prove that he was qualified and that he was rejected on unlawful grounds.

e.g. A local education authority advertises for a primary school teacher. There are twenty replies, including one from a Mrs Singh, who completes an application form showing (as is the case) that she has the necessary academic qualifications and length of teaching experience in Britain. Mrs Singh is not given an interview because the education authority considers a coloured teacher unsuitable for a class of white children. The authority is liable despite its insistence that Mrs Singh would not have obtained the job, if she had been interviewed, because there were other candidates with equal academic qualifications and experience, and despite its assertion that the person who got the post was 'more suitable'.

This example also illustrates that a person's qualifications will be evaluated objectively; it will not be enough for an employer to explain his conduct in terms of his personal prejudices. A recently published survey of recruitment policies in Croydon (McPherson and Gaitskell, 1969) indicated the extent to which objective qualifications are sometimes discounted by personnel staff, who prefer to rely on their own prejudiced assumptions about Commonwealth immigrants and coloured people. These are some samples of the comments which were made to the interviewer by personnel officers:

With the coloured candidate, you can't get the contact. Language problems make this harder, but it isn't the real problem.

A Chinese temple is fine, but not suitable to the middle of Croydon. Someone whose experience is exotic is not a good candidate [for an architect].

You have to be electrically minded to get on in the industry. To my daughter a car, a tape recorder, a TV, are normal because she's lived with them. It's not a question of social skills, because those can be learnt – it's more a natural process . . . probably wouldn't be natural to most coloured people who come in.

With a white person one has standards to assess their professional or other background. With a coloured person one has no standards against which to judge. It is more difficult to assess the motives of Indians and Pakistanis [who are] inscrutable.

Some are extremely good. We would hesitate more over the Asiatic than the Negro . . . Indians and Pakistanis have only one pace, which can never be increased, the others improve with experience. Indians and Pakistanis are good workers but terribly slow.

Female coloured applicants are less aggressive than male – and more acceptable. Men seem to be expecting discrimination, especially dark black people, show a certain aggressiveness . . . and Indians and Pakistanis, a certain craftiness.

If any of these prejudiced assumptions were to be expressed in racially discriminatory treatment, the employer and the personnel officer would be liable under the Act. And, if the employer who had displayed such assumptions were challenged with allegations of unlawful discrimination, it would be difficult for him to meet those allegations without providing relevant and convincing lawful reasons for having rejected an applicant. He would also have to prove that they were the genuine reasons for the rejection. It would not be enough for the employer to assert that neither he nor his staff had any intention of discriminating unlawfully; he would be assumed to have intended the natural consequences of his actions.

Except in the most blatant cases (e.g. where any of the statements referred to above were openly made by a personnel officer to the victim or to a conciliation officer) racial discrimination in recruitment, as elsewhere, will be established largely on the basis of inferences about the employer's real intentions as expressed in his actual conduct. It will, for example, be relevant to consider in what numbers and capacity he has employed coloured people, what steps he has taken to ensure that his personnel officers recruit workers on their individual merits, what methods of recruitment have been adopted in the past, and what the experience has been of other people who have applied for work in his firm. It will be easier to prove the existence of racial discrimination in manual or semi-skilled jobs, where qualifications are simple and straightforward, than in supervisory or managerial jobs, where qualifications inevitably depend more upon the employer's assessment of the applicant's personality and his ability to exercise authority over other people.

In general, 'the use of objective tests of ability in recruitment appears to help rather than hinder the opportunity for coloured or immigrant applicants', whereas 'the interview, compared with examinations or aptitude tests, appears as a danger zone, in which ignorance, racial fear and racial prejudice all make themselves felt, and influence the selection of applicants (McPherson and Gaitskell, 1969, pp. 56–7; Cooper and Sobol, 1969). However, an apparently neutral and objective qualification or test may be used as a disguised method of discriminating unlawfully. A qualification or test which seems to be irrelevant to the job concerned, or which has the effect of excluding members of an ethnic or national group in disproportionately large numbers might raise a strong inference of unlawful discrimination.

e.g. An insurance company requires that applicants for clerical posts must have certain academic qualifications and be less than nineteen years old. The effect of this requirement is to exclude the vast majority of Commonwealth immigrants from obtaining such positions, although they are qualified for them in all other respects. If it were shown that the personnel staff were aware of this effect, and that there was no independent commercial justification for the maximum age requirement, there would be a strong inference that the requirement was being used as a pretext for excluding immigrant applicants.[14]

e.g. A manufacturing company requires all would-be employees, including porters, to take a battery of aptitude tests measuring 'verbal', 'numerical' and 'reasoning' ability. Several immigrant applicants are rejected. The company attempt to justify their exclusion on the ground that they have failed the aptitude tests, although it is established that the company ought reasonably to be aware that the tests do not measure the abilities required of a porter, and are likely to be much more difficult for candidates whose national origin is not British. The use of the tests does not afford a defence

14. For an example of the use of a maximum age requirement as a method of excluding Indians from senior positions in the Indian Civil Service, see Appendix 1.

to allegations of unlawful discrimination in the employment of porters.[15]

In view of the complex factors involved in the use of aptitude tests, it may be useful to refer to their legal status in the United States. Title VII of the Civil Rights Act of 1964 (s. 703 (h)) provides that it is not an unlawful employment practice for an employer 'to give and to act upon the results of any professionally developed test provided that such test, its administration or action upon the results is not designed or used to discriminate because of race, colour' etc. The Guidelines on Employment Testing Procedures of the Equal Employment Opportunity Commission interpret 'professionally developed ability test' to mean

a test which fairly measures the knowledge or skills required by the particular job or class of jobs which the applicant seeks, or which fairly affords the employer a chance to measure the applicant's ability to perform a particular job or class of jobs. The fact that a test was prepared by an individual or organization claiming expertise in test preparation does not, without more, justify its use within the meaning of Title VII (Cooper and Sobol, 1969, pp. 1653–4).[16]

15. Compare *Hicks* v. *Crown Zellerbach Corporation* 58 CCH. Lab.Cas. Para. 9145 (E.D.La., 1968) cited in Cooper and Sobol (1969, at p. 1665). There the employers did not attempt to justify the use of the Wonderlick Personnel Test for janitorial positions, but they did defend their use of the test for certain others jobs on the ground that those jobs involved reading, other arithmetical computations and reasoning. However, the evidence of an expert witness called by the employers revealed that he had not observed the jobs at the plant, but had only discussed them with the plant superintendent. Nor had he troubled to evaluate the relative importance of each of the factors tested in relation to particular types of job.

16. In *US* v. *H. K. Porter Co.* 296 F.Supp. 40 (N.N. Ala., 1968) the court accepted in principle that aptitudes which are measured by a test should be relevant to the aptitudes which are involved in the performance of jobs. But the court refused to consider the differential prediction problem involved in using such tests, on the ground that such consideration would lead to the conclusion that the tests for blacks should be evaluated according to a different standard from whites, and that this 'would itself constitute prohibited discrimination' The court held that the right approach was to require that tests should be accurate. In *Dobbins* v. *Electrical Workers Local 212*, 292 F.Supp. 413 (S.D. Ohio, 1968) the court held that a union membership procedure was illegal which, though 'objectively fair and objectively fairly graded' was unnecessarily difficult. The court observed that 'the fair test of an individual's qualifications to work in the electrician trade in this geographical area is the actual ability to work on the

The same approach should be adopted in interpreting the employment provisions of the Race Relations Act 1968.

Recent United States cases in which apparently neutral employment standards have been interpreted as racially discriminatory reflect the determination of courts and anti-discrimination agencies there to use the law effectively to overcome the effects of past discrimination (see p. 177).[17] In 1968, the Kerner Commission observed that 'racial discrimination and unrealistic and unnecessarily high minimum qualifications for employment or promotion often have the same prejudicial effect'.[18] The Commission recommended that:

recruitment procedures should be re-examined. Testing procedures should be revalidated or replaced by work sample or actual job tryouts. Applicants

---

job in the trade for the average contractor operating in the trade'. But the court upheld tests administered by an apprenticeship committee composed of union and employer representatives on the ground that these tests were 'reasonably related to the proper aptitudes' and 'properly selected by an expert consultant' (Cooper and Sobol, 1969, at p. 1635). Cooper and Sobol regard the findings in these two cases as questionable on the facts, but conclude that the decisions adopt a sound legal principle: that tests must be properly selected and reasonably related to job performance. See *Griggs* v. *Duke Power Co.*, p. 178. On the use of aptitude tests in employment and Title VII of the Civil Rights Act 1964 see *Harvard L. Rev.*, 1120–45 (1971).

17. Thus, in *Asbestos Workers Local 53* v. *Vogler* CCH Empl. Prac. Guide (53 Lab.Cas. Para. 9195) (5th Cir., 1969) a union practice restricting new members to close relatives of existing members was held to be invalid under Title VII of the Civil Rights Act of 1964. Although there was a rational non-racial basis for this rule – the desire to provide family security – the union had previously excluded blacks from membership, and the nepotism rule had the effect of continuing the exclusion; it also served no purpose related to ability to perform the work in the asbestos trade. In *Johnson* v. *Ritz Associates Inc.* (N.Y. State Comm. for Human Rights Annual Report 1966, at pp. 43–4) a hotel's refusal to hire desk clerks who had no experience of working in luxury hotels was held unlawful under the State anti-discrimination law on the ground that few if any blacks could meet the requirement, even though the hotel applied the rule even-handedly. Unlike the nepotism rule, the requirement might have served a legitimate business purpose, in that experience in a similar hotel increased the likelihood that an applicant had the skills and knowledge required for the position. But the Commission held that, the same purpose of determining qualifications could be achieved in other ways without automatically excluding virtually all black applicants (Cooper and Sobol 1969, at pp. 1600–1601).

18. National Advisory Commission on Civil Disorders (1968, at pp. 416–17).

who are rejected for immediate training or employment should be evaluated and counseled by company personnel officers and referred to either company or public remedial programs.

In the same year, the New York Governor's Committee to Review New York Laws and Procedures in the Area of Human Rights concluded that a major factor making New York State anti-discrimination laws ineffective was that these laws were not being aggressively applied to invalidate unnecessary employment requirements (Cooper and Sobol, 1969, p. 1599).

Another important report was published in 1969 by the US Commission on Civil Rights, which analysed the effect of traditional selection procedures on the employment opportunities of minority groups. The report observed that

if job requirements are high and unrealistic, if the screenings and selection processes are long and frustrating, and if overt or subtle discrimination occurs along the way, the most successful recruitment program may leave employment patterns relatively unchanged.[19]

It stated that

a culturally biased test can effectively discriminate against minorities if it eliminates from consideration minority group members who can perform the required duties as readily and efficiently as majority group members who pass the test. This situation can be avoided by using for entrance and promotion examinations only tests which have been validated for the positions for which they are being used. A test is valid when there is a definite relationship between how well the individual scores on the test and how well he subsequently performs on the job.

The report contains detailed recommendations to make selection procedures less unfair for the victims of past discrimination.

Although these United States reports must be viewed in the context of the situation in that country, in which efforts are being made to overcome the effect of decades of racial discrimination, they are also relevant in interpreting the recruitment provisions of the Race Relations Act 1968. Above all, they emphasize that it is not sufficient to accept seemingly neutral employment procedures at their face

19. 'For ALL the People. . . . By ALL the People': A Report on Equal Opportunity in State and Local Government Employment by the US Commission on Civil Rights, 1969.

value. What matters is their effect on the employment opportunities of minority groups.[20]

If racial discrimination were allowed to become entrenched in this country, those responsible for administering the 1968 Act would be faced with the same dilemma as their American counterparts. On the one hand, the law requires employers not to discriminate on grounds of colour, race, etc.; on the other hand, it may be impossible to secure equal opportunities for minority groups without permitting, and, indeed, requiring, employers to recruit members of minority groups, previously excluded from opportunities on racial grounds, and so, by implication, to discriminate against other sections of the community.[21] It could be argued that, in such circumstances, 'positive discrimination' would be lawful as the only means of ensuring that people were no longer discriminated against. But it is unlikely that the English courts would follow the direction taken in recent American decisions unless the 1968 Act were amended to give them an explicit power to do so.[22]

Advertising

An employer, or anyone concerned with the employment of others, and an employment agency or exchange, must, like any other person, not publish or display any advertisement or notice which indicates

20. Compare 'How the Race Relations Act affects Personnel', by Members of the Edinburgh Group of the Institute of Personnel Management (Runnymede Trust Publication, 1969), which addresses the following questions on recruitment to personnel staff: 'Have you checked that the job specifications for every position truly outline the real requirements and specifications for the job?' 'Have you considered using selection tests, as being an objective validated method of improving selection standards?' 'How real is the need to write, or even speak, English fluently?'

21. The Select Committee on Race Relations and Immigration has given its approval to positive action to recruit coloured staff. 'Some firms may wish to go further (than the Act requires) and let it be known publicly that they are 'equal opportunity employers'. This has been the policy of one large retail store and mail order business, with head offices in Liverpool. They also deliberately try to recruit coloured staff. We welcome this initiative, and would hope to see other large firms taking the same steps' (1969, para. 242).

22. The problem of applying the law to past discrimination is discussed at pp. 174–9.

or could reasonably be understood as indicating, an intention to do an act of discrimination. It is irrelevant whether or not the act so indicated would be unlawful under any other provision of the 1968 Act (s.6 (1)). Since the discriminatory act indicated in the advertisement or notice need not itself be unlawful, it follows that an employer exempted from liability elsewhere under the Act would still be liable for publishing or displaying a discriminatory advertisement.

e.g. An Indian restaurant advertises for 'Indian only' to apply for a vacancy as waiter. It is not unlawful for the restaurant to discriminate by refusing to select non-Indian applicants for the job, because the 1968 Act permits the selection of a person of a particular nationality or descent for employment requiring attributes especially possessed by people of that nationality or descent.[23] But it is unlawful to publish or display a discriminatory advertisement or notice stating that only Indians should apply, since it is irrelevant under the advertising provision whether the act itself is unlawful, so long as the advertisement or notice indicates an intention to do an act of discrimination.

The Act does not define the meaning of 'advertisement' or 'notice'. The words should be construed according to their ordinary usage. An advertisement includes any public announcement, whether in a newspaper, on a hoarding, or on a cinema or television screen. A notice includes any sign, placard or document exhibited for the purpose of conveying information, whether in a shop window, on a notice board or elsewhere. A circular letter could also be a notice under this provision, and an application form could be a notice, where its purpose was partly to convey information.

e.g. A firm sends a standard form to all applicants for employment requiring them to give details of their colour, race and place of birth. It is obvious from the rest of the form that the answers to the questions are used in deciding which of the applicants will be interviewed, and the general notes on the form state that preference will be given to 'English applicants'. The form is a notice, because it is intended to convey information to would-be applicants; it is unlawful because it indicates an intention to do an act of discrimination.

However, it is not unlawful under this or any other provision for

23. The 'special attributes' exemption is discussed at pp. 214–16.

an employer to keep records indicating the colour, race or origins of his workers. Indeed, it is often desirable for him to do so in order to ensure that there is complete equality of opportunity and treatment in his firm. It is only unlawful if the employer uses racial records as a means of discriminating on the prohibited grounds that he will become liable under the Act.

Although a theatre manager may restrict his choice of actors to those of particular descent where the role so demands, he may not specify this restriction in an advertisement, and this has been thought by some to impose unreasonable hardship. On 11 June 1969 Mr Hugh Jenkins M.P. was given leave to introduce a Private Member's Bill to amend the Act in order to exempt advertisements or notices indicating an intention to select a person of a particular nationality or descent for employment requiring attributes especially possessed by persons of that nationality or descent. The Bill, however, was not debated.[24]

Later the Board received a complaint about an advertisement which appeared in the *Eastbourne Herald*, on 16 August 1969. The advertisement read: 'Scottish daily for Scottish family able to do some plain cooking, conveniently situated near Town Centre – Apply Box EP. 13475'. Having received such a complaint the Board had a duty to investigate it and the South Metropolitan Conciliation Committee inevitably formed the opinion that there had been a breach of section 6. The Committee informed the newspaper and the advertiser of the breach. The editor of the newspaper undertook to avoid similar wording in the future and no further action was taken, but the incident gave rise to widespread publicity on a national scale, and there was criticism (which could hardly be justified in view of the Board's statutory obligation) of the Board's conduct as well as of the provisions of the Act itself. No doubt the fact that the discrimination contained in the advertisement related to Scottish origins rather than colour or race and that it related to employment in a private household, contributed to the widespread feeling that the case was too trivial to be dealt with under the Act.

The breach of the Act involved in the publication of this advertisement was a technical one, and an unnecessary one, because the advertiser could easily have avoided it by phrasing his advertisement in

24. See *Hansard* (H.C.), vol. 784, cols. 1479–80.

a way which expressed his ·precise requirement, namely, a daily experienced in plain Scottish cooking, rather than one of particular national origins.

A further attempt was made to amend the Act by Mr Jo Grimond M.P., who introduced a Private Member's Bill on similar lines to the earlier Bill introduced by Hugh Jenkins, and with similar lack of success, although on this occasion the Bill was debated. The Race Relations Board took the view, accepted by the Home Office, that it was too early to amend the Act in piecemeal fashion, and that more time was needed to see whether there was a problem of sufficient seriousness to justify a change.

A possible solution which apparently had some support from the former Labour Government,[25] is to allow the Board a discretion not to investigate complaints. The Board has itself expressed support for a discretion in investigating complaints under section 6 (RRB, 1970, para. 70). Such a discretion could be limited to cases in which the Board considered the complaint to be malicious, or, where it considered the particular advertisement not likely to be harmful. A serious objection to the proposal is the difficulty in which newspaper editors would find themselves: until the Board had examined the advertisement it would be uncertain whether it could safely be published. In fact, since the 'Scottish Porridge' case, public interest in this problem has not been apparent, and the significance of the case appears slight. Of real importance is the virtual elimination of explicitly offensive racial advertisements which section 6 has achieved (RRB 1970, Appendix IX, p. 53).

Terms of employment and conditions of work

It is unlawful not only to refuse outright to employ someone on racial grounds. It is also unlawful to refuse or deliberately to omit to afford or offer someone who is employed or seeking employment on work of any description 'the like terms of employment' or 'the like conditions of work' as the employer makes available 'for persons of like qualifications employed in like circumstances on work of that

25. In its manifesto for the 1970 General Election, the Labour Party said (at p. 24) 'We now propose . . . to give the Race Relations Board powers of discretion in taking up complaints.'

description' (s. 3 (1) (b)). This provision applies both at the stage of the initial application for employment and after a person has entered into employment.

e.g. A West Indian is told by the employment exchange that there are vacancies for bus drivers in the local corporation, at a basic weekly wage of £22 together with the prospect of overtime. But when he applies for the job, he is told that he is not likely to get overtime, because it is given on the basis of seniority, and there are already sufficient bus drivers with more than five years' service. Accordingly he refuses the offer of a job with the corporation. He later discovers that overtime is given to white drivers in preference to blacks, and that a white recruit who was given a job shortly after his interview was told that he would definitely be able to work overtime, which would enable him to earn a weekly wage of about £28. The corporation has acted unlawfully. Overtime may not be a term of the contract of employment, but it is certainly a condition of work.

e.g. A textile mill employs only English workers on the day shift and only Asian workers on the night shift. It refuses to allow Asians to work on the day shift. The practice is unlawful, because the employers are providing different conditions of work on the basis of the workers' origins. It is unlawful to maintain separate 'ethnic work units' even if their conditions of work are otherwise identical, because segregation is deemed to be less favourable treatment (s. 1 (2)).

e.g. An Indian paint sprayer complains to his foreman that he is being continually insulted and harassed on racial grounds by his fellow workers. The foreman knows that the complaint is justified, but does nothing about it, although when white workers have had similar problems, he has intervened by disciplining the culprits or arranging for transfers to other departments. The employer and the foreman are liable for discriminating in the conditions of work, and possibly also in the terms of employment.[26]

26. If the employer had notice (for example, as a result of previous complaints) that a fellow worker was so racially prejudiced that he was a potential source of danger to coloured workers, and yet he did not dismiss him, the employer would be in breach of his Common Law duty to take reasonable care to ensure that an employee is not a danger to others. The employer would therefore be liable in negligence for any consequential damage or injury: see e.g. *Hudson* v. *Ridge Manufacturing Co. Ltd* [1957] 2 Q.B. 349. But an employer is not in breach of his duty of care if he employs dangerous staff without knowing of the danger: *Smith* v. *Ocean S.S. Co. Ltd* [1954] 2 Ll.L.Rep. 482; nor where a reasonable man would not have anticipated danger from the employment of such staff: *Smith* v. *Crossley Bros. Ltd* (1951) 95 Sol.J. 655.

Training and promotion

It is unlawful to refuse or deliberately not to afford or offer some-one equal opportunities for training or promotion on the ground of colour, race, etc. (s. 3 (1) (b)). Again, this provision applies both to people seeking employment and those already in employment. The Act requires equal treatment, not special treatment. An employer may, of course, provide special training facilities for immigrant workers, not because of their ethnic or national origins, but because they need training in particular skills. He may, for example, refer them for English language courses, under the Industrial Training Act 1964 – indeed, it will often be desirable for him to do so.[27] What he must not do is to deny workers training opportunities on any of the unlawful grounds. The training provision also has an important application to apprenticeship programmes. But it will not affect industries in which apprenticeships have traditionally been reserved for the children of workers already employed there, although the children of immigrants may be completely excluded, unless the nepotism rule is used as a pretext for excluding them because of their colour, race or ethnic or national origin.

The objective of securing equal opportunities for promotion is likely to be frustrated if, as the result of past discrimination, minority groups are unable to compete on equal terms with other workers; whether, for example, because they have been denied the chance of gaining experience in a particular trade, or of obtaining the requisite qualification for promotion, or because they have been deterred, as a result of past discrimination, from seeking skilled employment or promotion to supervisory jobs.[28]

27. The Edinburgh Group of the Institute of Personnel Management recommends employers to take a fresh look at training practices in the light of the 1968 Act, and, in particular, to consider whether immigrant employees, possibly starting with a different educational and cultural background, require a programme specially tailored to their needs: Runnymede Trust Publication, 1969; see also Select Committee on Race Relations and Immigration Report (1969, at p. 31).

28. The Race Relations Board has drawn a tentative inference from the small number of complaints made against firms in which immigrants are not employed, or are only employed in low status jobs, that 'immigrants are continuing to "play safe" by confining themselves to areas in which there is little risk of discrimination, or to areas in which large numbers of immigrants are already employed' (1969, at para. 58; 1970, at para. 68).

In such situations, the 1968 Act is unlikely to be effective in removing the effects of past discrimination. It is true that it could be unlawful for an employer to select workers for promotion by reference to a seniority system which, to his knowledge, carried forward the effects of past discrimination. But the 1968 Act does not permit an employer to devise a seniority system which deliberately benefits minority workers who have been the victims of past discrimination. The problem is similar to that which arises in recruitment (see p. 194). There is no provision for 'racial imbalance' programmes to be operated with the approval of the Race Relations Board, though, in theory, it is arguable that the Act could be construed as permitting such programmes, since it is only by discriminating in favour of the victims of past discrimination that an employer could ensure that they were no longer discriminating against them because of their origins. However, it is unlikely that the English courts would be willing to give such a strong and active interpretation to the statutory requirements.[29] If racial discrimination were to become endemic in British industry, it would be necessary for Parliament to amend the legislation to remedy this omission.

Dismissals

It is unlawful for an employer or any person concerned with the employment of others to discriminate against a worker employed on work of any description, 'by dismissing him in circumstances in which other persons employed on work of that description by the employer are not, or would not be, dismissed' (s. 3 (1) (c)). If the dismissal is on grounds of colour, race, etc., it will be unlawful regardless of the number of other workers dismissed from or continued in employment (*contra* MacDonald, 1969, para. 70).

e.g. A hospital employs four stokers in its boiler-room, three black and one white. Because of a reduction in the need for stokers, the hospital management committee decides to dismiss one stoker. Although the black stokers have all been employed for longer periods than the white stoker, the committee dismisses a black stoker solely because he is coloured. The dismissal is unlawful. The committee will not avoid liability by relying on the fact that the dismissal was caused by redundancy, or that other black stokers

29. For the trend in recent United States' decisions, see pp. 191–2.

have not been dismissed. But for his colour, the black stoker would not have been dismissed, and the 'last in, first out' rule would have resulted instead in the white stoker's dismissal.

In this example, if a black stoker had been dismissed not on racial grounds but because he was the last of the four men to have been employed by the hospital, the dismissal would, of course, have been perfectly proper under the 1968 Act.[30]

Cases may sometimes arise in which the racial basis of a dismissal is less direct yet equally unlawful.

e.g. A factory maintains separate lavatory facilities for its Pakistani and English workers. A Pakistani worker is dismissed because he insisted on using the 'white' lavatory. The employers are liable, even if they establish that an English worker would equally have been dismissed for using a 'coloured' lavatory. It is unlawful, apart from the dismissals provision, to maintain segregated lavatories as part of the men's working conditions (ss. 1 (2) and 3 (1) (b)). The dismissal itself is unlawful because it is made on the ground of colour, race or ethnic or national origins.[31]

In this example, it would be no answer for the employers to prove that other Pakistani or English workers had persuaded them to install separate lavatories, or to dismiss the man for using the 'white' lavatory.

The Industrial Relations Act 1971 (section 22) now provides a remedy for unfair dismissal to most employees who have served in the same employment for two years or more. Complaints of unfair dismissal can be made to an industrial tribunal which may recommend re-instatement and award compensation (Industrial Relations Act, 1971, section 116–19).

Dismissal on the ground of colour, race or ethnic or national

30. If an employer fails to give the period of notice required by the dismissed man's contract of employment, or by the Contracts of Employment Act 1963, or fails to pay wages in lieu of notice, he will be liable for damages at Common Law or under that Act. If the dismissal is by reason of redundancy, the dismissed man will be entitled to receive a redundancy payment under the Redundancy Payments Act 1965.

31. The meaning of these unlawful grounds is discussed at pp. 153–65. For a case where compensation was paid for such a dismissal because of the 1968 Act see *The Times*, 1 October 1969, and RRB (1970, at Appendix IV (g)).

origins is unfair dismissal, but section 149 of the Industrial Relations Act seeks to avoid duplication of proceedings by requiring the Board (or industry machinery) not to investigate matters which have been or could have been presented to an industrial tribunal.

But after a finding by an industrial tribunal of unfair dismissal, a reason for which was the complainant's colour, race or ethnic or national origins, the Board (or industry machinery) may then proceed under the Race Relations Act for the purpose of securing a written assurance against repetition of the unlawful conduct and may bring proceedings if it appears that such an assurance has been broken.

No power is given to the Board to take proceedings if the employer declines to give an assurance against repetition. As there is no sanction at all for his failure to do so, the chance of any employer giving an assurance in these circumstances would seem to be small. Consequently, unless this gap in the law is filled, the role of the Board is likely to be minimal in cases of discriminatory dismissal which come within the jurisdiction of the industrial tribunals.

Trade union membership and benefits

It is unlawful for a trade union to discriminate against anyone by refusing or deliberately omitting to admit him to membership of the union on equal terms with other applicants (s. 4 (1) (a)). It is also unlawful for the union to discriminate against a member by refusing or deliberately omitting to 'accord him the same benefits as are accorded to other members . . . , or to take the like action on his behalf as is taken on behalf of other members, or by expelling him' from the union (s. 4 (1) (b)). These provisions apply not only to trade unions, but to employers' organizations and other organizations concerned with the carrying on of trades, businesses, professions or occupations (s. 4 (2)).

Before the passing of the 1968 Act, the legal position of these various types of racial discrimination was extremely unclear. Recently it has been established that a trade union or any other body controlling entry into a trade or profession cannot unjustly exclude people and so deprive them of their 'right to work', on racial or other arbitrary grounds.[32] Again, a trade-union member might have contended that he was being wrongfully discriminated against on racial grounds in his enjoyment of trade union benefits, but he would only have succeeded in the courts if he could have shown that he was not seeking directly to enforce his contract of membership with the union.[33] Here, too, before the 1968 Act the state of the existing law was tangled and unpredictable (Wedderburn, 1971, pp. 425–9). But the Trade Union Act 1871 has now been repealed by the Industrial Relations Act 1971, and there is now no legal bar to an action to enforce this contract of membership. Again, if a trade union instructed its members to strike in protest against the employment of immigrant workers, it was once more possible, but not beyond doubt, that the courts would decide that the strike was actionable as an unlawful conspiracy and outside the protection of the Trade Disputes Act 1906 (see pp. 53–4).

The 1968 Act has now made it clear that a trade union and its officials are liable if, on racial grounds, they exclude anyone from membership, or do not give him the same benefits as other members, or do not take the same action on his behalf, or if they expel him from membership of the union. And it is not open to a trade union to claim the protection of the Industrial Relations Act 1971 for strike action in support of a colour bar. Under section 132 (3) of the 1971 Act, an act done in combination in contemplation or furtherance of an industrial dispute is not actionable unless the act would be actionable if done without any such combination. Section 132 cannot protect a trade union because the act of inducing or inciting an employer to discriminate on racial grounds is now unlawful under the 1968 Act whether it is done by an individual or by a group of people (s. 12).

Under section 132 (1) of the 1971 Act, an act done by a person in contemplation or furtherance of an industrial dispute is not actionable on the ground only that it induces some other person to break a contract to which that other person is a party or that it is an interference with the trade, business or employment of some other person. However, whether or not a racial strike can ever be an 'industrial dispute', it is obvious that inducing or inciting an employer to

32. See *Edwards* v. *Society of Graphical and Allied Trades* [1971] Ch. 354 (C.A.). The case is discussed at p. 52.
33. See Trade Union Act 1871, s. 4.

discriminate racially is not actionable *only* on the grounds referred to in section 132 of the 1971 Act; it is actionable on the ground that it violates the Race Relations Act 1968, and it is therefore outside the protection of the 1971 Act altogether.[34]

Collective agreements

Before the passing of the 1968 Act, collective agreements were sometimes made between employers and trade unions, which imposed a wide range of restrictions upon the employment of foreign workers. Agreements of this kind were entered into shortly after the Second World War in almost forty industries;[35] and their 'vague and flexible definitions of the affected workers have occasionally led to interpretations that extend the restrictions to Commonwealth immigrants'.

The 1968 Act does not specifically make it unlawful to enter into a discriminatory agreement. But such an agreement will provide irrefutable evidence of the unlawful intentions and actions of both or either of the parties; and the negotiations leading to such an agreement would doubtless include actions by one party amounting to deliberately aiding, inducing or inciting the other to discriminate unlawfully – whether in recruitment, training, promotion, dismissal, the terms of employment or the conditions of work.

It is unlikely that new collective agreements will in future contain blatantly discriminatory terms. In any event, the 1968 Act provides that a contract or a term in a contract which contravenes the Act is

34. Similarly, if a trade union is concerned with the employment of workers, it will be liable if it discriminates on unlawful grounds in recruitment, training, promotion and dismissals (s. 3 (1)). Section 5 of the Industrial Relations Act 1971 confers new rights to membership of a trade union (and to refuse membership of a trade union) and to participation in the activities of a trade union. An industrial tribunal may award compensation against an employer or person acting on behalf of an employer for infringement of these rights. Where infringement is alleged to be on the ground of colour, race or ethnic or national origins, no investigation may take place under the Race Relations Act but similar steps may be taken under the Act after a finding by an industrial tribunal that the infringement (unfair industrial practice) was on grounds prohibited by the Race Relations Act as may be taken in the case of unfair dismissal (see p. 202).

35. Hepple (1968, at p. 50); he summarizes the information supplied on this subject by trade unions at Appendix 2.

not void or unenforceable by reason of the contravention (s. 23 (1)). It may be revised on the application to the court of the defendant to proceedings under the Act, or of the Race Relations Board on behalf of any party to the contract; and, if it is feasible to do so without affecting the rights of third parties, the court may revise the contract or its terms so as to ensure compliance with the provisions of the Act (s. 23 (2) and (3)). Employers and trade unions which failed to remove discriminatory terms from their collective agreements, would run a risk of being found liable under the Act, particularly if they had neglected an opportunity of using the special revising procedure provided by the Act. A collective-bargaining agreement may not be legally binding;[36] it is only a binding agreement which would be affected by section 23.

Government contracts

In the United States, the Federal Government have led the campaign against racial discrimination in employment by making use of their huge purchasing power as customers of industry. The technique is to incorporate in each contract between the Government and a private firm a clause requiring the firm not to discriminate.[37] But the obligation of the firms goes much further than non-discrimination: they undertake to 'take affirmative action to ensure that applicants are employed, and that employees are treated during employment, without regard to their race, creed, colour or national origin'. This includes posting notices in work-places, which set out the provisions of the non-discrimination clause, notifying trade unions of the provisions, and perhaps most important, making regular reports showing compliance with the law to the Government, and permitting access to the employers' books, records and accounts.

The non-discrimination clause can be an extremely powerful weapon against firms which are dependent on government contracts, but experience in the United States has shown that to be effective it must be supported by specialized enforcement machinery with the

36. See *Ford Motor Co. Ltd* v. *AEF* [1969] 2 All E.R. 481, and section 34, Industrial Relations Act 1971.

37. Executive Order 11246, as amended, 3 C.F.R. s. 406 (1970), 42 U.S.C. s. 2000e (supp. V, 1969). Fora full description of the non-discrimination clause in the United States and its enforcement, see Street Report (1967), chapter 6.

power to impose sanctions.[38] A special section of the Department of Labor, the Office of Federal Contract Compliance, supervises the enforcement of the clause. Where breach of the clause is established, the Secretary of Labor, or the contracting agency, may take all or any of the following steps:

1. Publish the names of contractors who have failed to comply.
2. Recommend to the Department of Justice that it take proceedings to prevent breach of the clause by injunction.
3. Recommend proceedings under Title VII of the Civil Rights Act.
4. Recommend criminal proceedings if any false information has been supplied.
5. Cancel, terminate or suspend the contract, or make its continuance conditional on a specific programme for future compliance.
6. Bar all contracting departments of government from entering into new contracts with the non-complying contractor.

The Street Committee recommended[39] that a non-discrimination clause be introduced into contracts between the British government and private firms. By analogy with the Fair Wages Resolution, made by the House of Commons in 1946, under which government contractors are required to provide wages and working conditions no less favourable than those current in the particular industry in which the contractor is engaged, a non-discrimination clause did not need legislation but could be introduced by such a resolution. The clause could evoke affirmative action to stamp out racial inequality, not merely passive abstention from discrimination. A special subdivision of the Race Relations Board should be created to supervise enforcement. The Board would investigate complaints, make findings and attempt conciliation. But, if conciliation failed, the decision whether to suspend or cancel or black-list the contractor would rest with the contracting government department.

Ministerial statements made it clear that such a clause was under active consideration by the Government even before the introduction of the 1968 Race Relations Bill,[40] but no definite action was taken

38. See Street Report (1967), para. 102. 39. See Street Report, ch. 21.
40. e.g. as long ago as in the summer 1966, the then Chancellor of the Exchequer (James Callaghan M.P.) accepted the principle of a non-discrimination clause (Patterson, 1969, at p. 104; Hepple, 1970, at pp. 276–81).

until 22 October 1969, when the Chancellor of the Exchequer (Roy Jenkins) announced:

We have decided that the standard conditions of government contracts should be amended so as to require contractors in the United Kingdom to conform to the provisions of the Race Relations Act 1968 relating to discrimination in employment. Government departments will be prepared to withhold contracts from firms practising racial discrimination in employment. Further legislation is not contemplated (RRB, 1970, at para. 20).

This statement falls short of the recommendations of the Street Report in three important respects. First, it indicates that the obligation of contractors will not exceed their statutory obligation, i.e. no 'affirmative' action is demanded. Secondly, the sanction is the withholding of new contracts, not the cancellation of existing contracts. If breach of the non-discrimination clause cannot result in cancellation, it has in fact no legal effect at all. No provision in an existing contract is necessary to enable a party to refrain from entering into a future contract. Thirdly, there is no enforcement agency other than the contracting department itself. The Race Relations Board is given no role to play at all in relation to the clause. In practice, an informal reporting system may develop, so that a finding of unlawful discrimination by the Board or the industrial machinery against a government contractor will be notified to the contracting department, which may then use its powers under the non-discrimination clause to supplement the remedies provided by the Race Relations Act. It is plainly too early to assess the effect of the non-discrimination clause which has been introduced but there is no reason to expect that it will be of great practical significance.

Exceptions

Where any exception to the scope of the employment provisions applies, it exempts everyone who might otherwise be liable. For example, it has already been noted (p. 180) that there are temporary exemptions for small employers, during the first four years of the operation of the 1968 Act. In such a case, it is not unlawful for the employer himself, or any of his employees, or agents, to discriminate on racial grounds; similarly, it is not unlawful for anyone to aid, induce or incite another person to discriminate on racial grounds, provided that such discrimination is outside the scope of the 1968 Act. In one instance, however, even those who would otherwise be exempted from the employment provisions will be liable if they discriminate: no one may publish or display an advertisement or notice indicating an intention to do an act of discrimination, whether or not that act of discrimination would itself be unlawful.[41]

Racial balance

Discrimination in engaging workers or selecting them for work within a firm or any part of the firm is not unlawful if it is done in good faith for the purpose of securing or preserving a reasonable balance of workers of different racial groups employed in the firm or part of the firm (s. 8 (2)). In determining whether a balance is reasonable regard must be had to all the circumstances, and, in particular, to the proportion of workers employed in the firm or part of the firm, and the extent, if any, to which the employer engages in any unlawful discrimination in his employment policy (s. 8(3)). 'Racial group' here means a group of persons defined by reference to colour, race or ethnic or national origins; but people wholly or mainly educated in Britain are to be treated as members of the same racial group, regardless of their colour, race or ethnic or national origins.

The Act contains no further guidance about the interpretation of this exemption. However, the Race Relations Board, after consulting with the TUC, the CBI, the Department of Employment and Productivity and the Home Office, has issued guidelines on these provisions (RRB, 1969, Appendix VII). The Board has also decided to give advice to employers about their effect, on the understanding that such advice is only tentative and that it does not prejudice the rights of any complainant (RRB, 1969, para. 41). Although the guidelines do not have any legal effect and are not binding on the courts, they provide useful practical information about the

41. Section 6 (1). However, the advertising provision itself contains exceptions with respect to the employment of Commonwealth citizens outside Britain or non-Commonwealth citizens in Britain; there is also exemption for certain advertisements with respect to employment in the public service (s. 27 (9) (b)), see p. 218.

Board's interpretation of the racial balance provisions, and they will be examined in the following paragraphs.

In the guidelines, the Board observes that, although the racial balance provisions deal generally with workers of different racial groups, it seems likely that in practice the provisions will be most frequently invoked in relation to the employment of immigrants. The purpose of the provisions is to promote racial integration and harmony. In some industries particular parts of a factory or particular occupations have become identified with one racial group, to the exclusion of other groups. Such distinctions, in the Board's view (RRB, 1969, Appendix VII, para. 2), clearly work against integration, and are increasing, and these provisions will, it is hoped, arrest this development.

The guidelines state that the exemption cannot be claimed against a worker, whatever his origins, who has been wholly or mainly educated in Britain. Anyone who has received six or more years of full-time education before reaching the age of twenty-one could be regarded as mainly educated in Britain, but there might be circumstances in which a lesser period, or education beyond the age of twenty-one, could be taken into account. However, despite the advice given in the guidelines, there might be cases in which the exemption could be invoked against British-educated workers, in order to prevent a firm from containing an unreasonably large proportion of them.

e.g. A factory employs 150 British-educated workers, and five foreign-educated workers in part of its undertaking. A British-educated worker is refused employment on the ground that the employers wish to recruit a larger proportion of foreign-educated workers, and so to secure a more reasonable balance in the work-force. The discrimination is not unlawful, because the British-educated worker belongs to the same 'racial group' which is already predominantly employed there.

What the employers cannot do is to select or reject British-educated workers on the basis of colour in a situation in which a substantial proportion of British-educated workers, of whatever colour, are already employed. So the employers could not in the previous example reject a British-educated worker solely because of his colour.

The racial balance provisions can be invoked to justify an act of discrimination only in the recruitment of workers or in their selection for work within a firm. They cannot be invoked as a defence against other acts of discrimination in the employment field, e.g. in the training or dismissal of workers.

The guidelines indicate that, in considering the proportions of people in different racial groups in a firm, the Board will not normally take into account the numbers of workers in the employer's other premises. Similarly, in considering what would be a *reasonable* balance between people of different racial groups employed in part of a a firm, no account will normally be taken of workers in other sections or departments in the same premises, or of workers in substantially different types of occupations even in the same section or department. For example, the employment of a high proportion of first-generation immigrants as labourers or semi-skilled operatives would not normally be a good reason for refusing to engage a clerk or technician in the same part of the undertaking.

Although this interpretation of the racial balance provisions admirably fulfils the spirit of the legislation, it must be added that the language of the exemption is ambiguous, and there is a risk that it might be construed by the courts as justifying a refusal to employ an immigrant clerk or technician in a firm which employs large numbers of immigrants in entirely different and less-skilled jobs, and even in a different department.

The main arguments which were advanced during the Parliamentary debates in support of the racial balance exemption were that integration would be 'hindered if certain types of jobs are allowed to become recognized as immigrant jobs';[42] and that, if this happened other people would not be willing to do those jobs. If British workers are indeed deterred from obtaining work with employers of large numbers of immigrants (and no evidence has been produced to show that this is so) then presumably they are deterred by the overall number of immigrants employed. In such a situation an employer might argue that to add any more immigrants to his work force, *in whatever capacity or department*, would cause British workers to leave his employment or to refrain from applying for

42. David Ennals, M.P. 13 June 1968 Standing Committee B *Official Report*, col. 515. See p. 140.

vacancies, and so would disturb the 'reasonable balance' in his firm. Unfortunately, the provisions have been drafted in a way which enables such an argument to be made, for they refer to recruitment for employment in, or the selection of work within, 'an undertaking or part of an undertaking', without specifying that the exemption can only be used with respect to a racial balance in the part of the undertaking, and in the type of work, which is directly relevant to the exempted discrimination. But although there is this ambiguity in the statute, the guidelines seek to ensure that the racial balance clause will not be allowed to undermine the objectives of the legislation.

The exemption also contains the safeguard that it can be invoked only where an employer is acting in 'good faith'. The guidelines indicate that evidence that the employer has taken reasonable and practicable steps to ensure that all employees concerned with the employment of others were acting upon the provisions of the Act would be regarded by the Board as evidence of good faith. So would evidence that an employer had already integrated persons of different racial groups into his work force on the basis of equality of opportunity and treatment. Again, this approach is obviously in accordance with the spirit of the legislation, and should enable the Board and, if necessary, the courts to overcome the problems arising from the ambiguous drafting of the exemption.

The guidelines state that, in general, an employer will need to have a 'substantial proportion' of persons not educated in Britain in his work force or the relevant part of it before these provisions can be invoked. No precise proportions can be given because the combination of factors which might justify the application of these provisions will vary according to the circumstances.[43] The Board will take account of the degree and kind of adjustment required for particular work groups, and it will normally expect an employer wishing to invoke these provisions to show clearly that recruitment of foreign-educated workers would make the integration of different racial groups more difficult at that time. Evidence that applications for employment are received mainly from foreign-educated workers will also be taken into account. And, an employer's motives will be

43. Mr John Lyttle, the Board's Chief Officer, said in an interview that the Board 'would not consider 10 per cent a substantial number' (*Guardian*, 15 September 1969).

questioned if, for example, there is evidence of unlawful refusal to employ workers or particular racial groups in certain jobs or in certain parts of an undertaking; or of unlawful denial of training and promotion opportunities; or of unlawful offering of inferior terms and conditions; or of unlawful publication of discriminatory advertisements or notices.

If these guidelines are followed by employers and upheld by the courts, the racial balance exemption will not become a source of real abuse. Indeed, the Board had found not only that it has rarely been invoked as a defence,[46] but that the Board's role in advising employers about these provisions has produced 'constructive results' (RRB, 1969, paras. 41–3), since it has enabled it to encourage employers to change their recruitment and selection procedures to comply with the spirit as well as with the letter of the 1968 Act. The objections to the racial balance exemption may arise more in theory than in practice; but they are still real objections.

The main criticism of the exemption is that it is an unnecessary concession to racial prejudice which may actually encourage the very practices which the legislation was intended to eliminate. Unlike 'racial imbalance' programmes in the United States (see p. 175), which enable employers and others to discriminate *in favour* of minority groups so as to overcome the effects of past discrimination, the racial balance provisions enable employers to discriminate *against* minority groups, so as to placate majority-group workers who might otherwise look elsewhere for employment. One of the main causes of discrimination is the fear among people in a position to discriminate of the prejudices of others (see p. 82); yet by this exemption a deliberate concession is made to those prejudices. This is a major departure from the ideal on which the law depends: that people should be treated on the basis of their individual merits rather than according to their colour, race or ethnic or national origins. If employers were actually to apply the statutory concept of 'racial balance' in their recruiting and selection policies, they would have to

46. In one case, the Board has upheld an employer's use of the defence because he established that he had taken steps to integrate workers of different origins and the employer's concern over a racial imbalance was related to one department. The complainant was offered employment elsewhere in the firm (RRB, 1971, para. 53).

determine the colour, race or ethnic or national origins of all their employees, department by department, and discover whether each of them had been wholly or mainly educated in Britain. They would be encouraged by the exemption to maintain quotas for immigrant workers, largely because their colour was objectionable to white workers; yet they would be expected to abolish these same quotas when dealing with the children of coloured immigrants.

The racial balance exemption also results in an artificial and grotesque definition of 'racial groups'. A black worker will count the same as a white worker if both were wholly or mainly educated either in Britain or outside this country. A Pakistani, a West Indian and a white Australian could apparently be counted together as members of particular racial groups for the purposes of discriminating against a Chinese applicant. An employer who had a large number of Cypriots in his work force could exclude Asian workers solely because of their colour.

One of the oddest aspects of these provisions is that there is scant evidence that British white workers have in fact shunned employment in firms with a largely immigrant work force. The more typical position seems rather to be that immigrant workers have moved into areas of employment which were already unattractive to British workers, and in which there was therefore a serious labour shortage. As a result immigrants are certainly now concentrated in certain firms and in particular types of work. But the right approach to this problem is not to permit discrimination against immigrant workers, but to secure equality of opportunity and treatment, regardless of colour, race or origins, throughout all sectors of industry; and, where necessary, to authorize employers to implement racial imbalance programmes under which they recruit minority workers whom they have previously excluded.

The Home Secretary may with the approval of both Houses of Parliament repeal the racial balance provisions, if it appears to him to be expedient to do so (s. 8 (5)). In view of these various objections, and the dangerous ambiguity of the drafting of the exemption, it would be desirable for him to take this course. Better methods can be devised to enable the Race Relations Board to influence employment policies than one which is fraught with so many risks and inconsistencies.

Special attributes

It is not unlawful for an employer, or any person concerned with the employment of others, to select a person of a particular nationality or descent for employment 'requiring attributes especially possessed by persons of that nationality or descent' (s. 8 (11)). This exemption applies only to discrimination in selecting people for employment, not, for example, to discrimination in training, dismissals, or the terms and conditions of employment or work. Nor does it enable an employer or an employment agency to *advertise* for people of a particular nationality or descent (see p. 195).

There are not many situations in which an employer can escape liability under this provision. He must establish that attributes are objectively possessed by people of a particular nationality or descent, and also that those attributes are properly required for the particular type of employment. Obviously, an employer can always insist that an individual applicant should be properly qualified for the job. He need rely on this exemption only if he asserts that a job should be reserved for people of a particular nationality or descent.

e.g. A Chinese restaurant maintains a Chinese decor as part of its appeal to customers. It wishes to employ waiters who are Chinese in appearance, and so refuses to give a vacant job to an experienced English waiter. The discrimination is not unlawful, because it is a genuine attribute of people of Chinese nationality or descent that they look Chinese, and that attribute is properly required for the job.

However, in most other instances the defence is inapplicable.

e.g. The same Chinese restaurant needs a chef who is capable of preparing Cantonese dishes. It refuses to employ an English chef who has been fully trained and has considerable experience in preparing such dishes. The restaurant cannot escape liability by asserting that being Chinese is a special attribute required for the job, for there is no reason to suppose that people of Chinese nationality or descent are *automatically* better qualified in Cantonese cooking than anyone else.

e.g. An English restaurant refuses to employ coloured waiters on the ground that it is an essential attribute for the job that they should 'look English' and so be 'acceptable' to patrons of the restaurant. The discrimination is unlawful because there is nothing about the nature of the restaurant which makes a non-white appearance an essential attribute for employment there. It is not an essential attribute that an employee's colour is acceptable to others – if that were so, then the provisions relating to discrimination in recruitment would have no meaning.

The position might be different in this last example if the restaurant were a replica of an Elizabethan inn and wanted its waiters to dress in period costume and look like sixteenth-century Englishmen. It would then be in the same category as the Chinese restaurant seeking Chinese waiters. But no restaurant could use the 'special attributes' exemption as a pretext for practising racial discrimination. It would have to show that those attributes were genuinely necessary for the job.

Sometimes, borderline cases may arise in which it is difficult to decide whether employment requires attributes especially possessed by people of a particular nationality or descent.

e.g. A stage company decides to employ a coloured actor of African descent to play the part of Othello and rejects all applications by white actors. On the other hand, it employs only white actors to play the other parts, and rejects all applications for them from coloured actors. If the company can show that it is a genuine purpose of the production to employ actors of different descent in this way, and that the purpose cannot be achieved as effectively with make-up, it will be within the exemption.

However, it would be unlawful to insist that Shylock should be performed by a Jew, or that Bassanio should be played by a non-Jew. *Othello* is a rare example, because the characterization of the actors might in some productions really need to be reflected in their natural physiognomy.

These examples have all related to a person's physical appearance which he happens to possess because of his parentage. The statute does not express this idea very happily. It refers to attributes especially possessed by people of a particular 'nationality', yet it is difficult to see what those attributes are, unless one adopts a prejudiced attitude towards different national groups. There are no special physical attributes uniquely possessed by Germans or Frenchmen, except their skin colour, and even that characteristic is not shared by all United Kingdom citizens (who include, of course, many people of Asian descent in East Africa). There are intellectual attributes possessed by many people who come from a particular territory, e.g. a knowledge of the culture, language and structure of society in that territory. But the exemption refers to nationality rather than national origin;[45] besides, if the draftsman had in mind knowledge of this kind, the exemption need not have been included in the legislation. Employers are entitled to exclude workers who are not qualified for the job; if a knowledge of Hindi, or the geography of Maharashtra, or the social patterns of the inhabitants of East Pakistan, is required for a certain type of work, no question of unlawful discrimination arises if a person without such knowledge is rejected. The exemption gives the unfortunate impression that people of a particular nationality or descent may inherit characteristics, other than those of physiognomy, which may be relevant to their opportunities of obtaining employment.

Private households

It is not unlawful for an employer, or any person concerned with the employment of others, or an employment agency or exchange, to discriminate in the employment or non-employment of anyone 'for the purposes of a private household' (s. 8 (6)). This exemption was apparently intended to apply only to the employment of people *in* a private household, such as domestic servants and gardeners.[46] It is

45. Compare Title VII of the Civil Rights Act of 1964, s. 703 (e) (1) which refers to certain instances where '. . . national origin is a bona fide occupational qualification reasonably necessary to the normal operation of . . . [a] particular business or enterprise'.

46. Originally, the exemption referred to employment 'in or for purposes of a private household'. David Ennals, M.P. explained that if the word 'in' were omitted, the exemption 'could cover someone who was not actually employed in the household; he might be employed as a farm hand, or somewhere in the establishment, but not in the household. The purpose is to cover close personal relationships, in the sense of nannies, *au pair* girls, and those who both work in and for the purposes of a private household. If we were to take out either of these two phrases it would substantially broaden the subsection' (18 June 1968, *Official Report*, Standing Committee B, col. 558). This view was not altogether accurate, for the weakness in the subsection was that it contained the words 'for the purposes of' as well as the word 'in'. Somewhat inconsistently, Mr Ennals also stated that the words 'for the purposes of' would not include television repairers, window cleaners and caterers, because 'they are not normally employed in the service of the householder. They are . . . employed for the purpose of the employer's business, not for the purposes of the private householder' (col. 557). However, although he recognized the danger of omitting the word 'in' from the

to be regretted that it does not expressly so provide, for in its present form the exemption is ambiguous. It is arguable that maternity nurses, window cleaners and television repairers who are sent to private households to work may also be discriminated against on the ground of colour, race, etc. (though if this were intended it would have been more natural to say 'for the purposes of a private household or households'). Such an interpretation would create a wide loophole in the employment provisions. The better view is surely that these people are employed for the purposes of their employer's business rather than for the purposes of the private household.

National security

Nothing in the employment provisions, or any other part of the 1968 Act, makes unlawful 'an act which is done for the purpose of safeguarding national security' (s. 10 (1)). This exemption applies not only to discrimination by government departments and public bodies, but also to discrimination by private employers, done for the purposes of national security. No doubt, situations may arise in which it is justifiable to exclude people from work involving classified material, because of their nationality or national origin, but discrimination is in any case permitted in those situations under other exemptions (see pp. 218–21), except in the case of private employers, and except for discrimination on the ground of colour or race. It is hard to understand why anyone should be excluded from work involving national security merely because they are coloured or Jewish. It has been explained to one of the authors by a source close to the Ministry of Defence that the type of situation envisaged was one in which British coloured soldiers might otherwise be sent overseas to a country in which there were racial tensions or disturbances. But employment wholly or mainly outside Britain is in any case outside the scope of the 1968 Act (s. 8 (7) (d)).

A certificate signed by or on behalf of any Minister and certifying

---

subsection, the Government subsequently did so, presumably because it was hoped that the courts would share Mr Ennals's view of the meaning of the words 'for the purposes of'.

that an act specified in the certificate was done for the purpose of national security is conclusive evidence that it was done for that purpose (s. 10 (2)). The certificate may cover acts done by private employers as well as by government departments and public bodies. No doubt it is essential that official secrets should not be publicly aired before the Race Relations Board or the courts, but it seems unnecessarily restrictive to prevent even a private inquiry by an appropriate individual or tribunal into the propriety of discriminatory conduct.[47]

Public service

The Act does not invalidate any rules made by the Treasury restricting employment in the service of the Crown or by any prescribed public body[48] to people of particular birth, citizenship, nationality, descent or residence (s. 27 (9) (a)); nor is it unlawful to publish, display or implement such rules, or to publish or display advertisements stating the gist of the rules (s. 27 (9) (b)).

47. The sweeping nature of the national security exemption seems excessive in view of the fact that 'no one, whatever his origin, is allowed access to classified information unless the Head of the Department is satisfied that he can be trusted; and he is of course subject to the necessary security inquiries' (The Prime Minister, Mr Harold Wilson) 18 November 1964, *Hansard* (H.C.), vol. 701, col. 39).

48. ' "Public body" is defined as a body of persons whether corporate or unincorporate, carrying on a service or undertaking of a public nature . . .' (s. 27 (12)). By the Race Relations (Prescribed Public Bodies) Regulations 1968, the following were prescribed for the purpose of section 27 (a): Bank of England, British Council, British Museum, British Museum (Natural History), Council for Technical Education and Training for Overseas Countries, Development Commission, Forestry Commission, Imperial War Museum, London Museum, National Economic Development Office, National Gallery, National Galleries of Scotland, National Library of Scotland, National Maritime Museum, National Museum of Antiquities of Scotland, National Portrait Gallery, National Environment Research Council, Public Works Loan Board, Royal Commission on Ancient Monuments in Wales and Monmouthshire, Royal Commission on the Ancient and Historical Monuments in Scotland, Royal Commission on Historical Manuscripts, Royal Commission on Historical Monuments (England), Royal Fine Art Commission, Royal Fine Art Commission for Scotland, Science Research Council, Social Science Research Council, Standing Commission on Museums and Galleries, Tate Gallery, United Kingdom Atomic Energy Authority, Wallace Collection.

Under the present rules,[49] to be eligible for appointments in the civil service, a candidate must be a British subject, a British protected person or an Irish citizen, and he must also satisfy one of the following conditions:

1. If he was a British subject, a British protected person or an Irish citizen at birth, then one of his parents must have been a British subject etc., or the candidate must have resided in the Commonwealth or the Irish Republic, or have been in the Crown service for at least five out of the eight years before the date of his appointment.

2. If he was not a British subject etc., at birth, he must have satisfied the Commonwealth residence or Crown service requirements.

3. If he does not satisfy (1) or (2), he must satisfy the Civil Service Commissioners that he is so closely connected with a country or territory within the Commonwealth that an exception may properly be made in his favour.

A candidate is not eligible for appointment to a situation in the Ministry of Technology, Cabinet Office, Ministry of Defence (other than the Meteorological Office) or Ministry of Public Building and Works unless

1. At all times since his birth he has been either a British subject or an Irish citizen.

2. He was born within the Commonwealth or in the Irish republic.

3. Both his parents were born in the Commonwealth or the Irish Republic and throughout their lives had been British subjects or Irish citizens.

Similar restrictions are imposed upon entry into the Foreign Service. But the restrictions may be waived, in respect of most departments, by the appropriate Minister.

Although these rules were criticized by the Race Relations Board before the passage of the 1968 Act,[50] they remain in force, unchanged

49. General Regulations made by the Civil Service Commissioners under the Civil Service Order-in-Council 1965 with the approval of the Treasury and the Foreign Secretary. The regulations are reproduced in *Hansard* (H.C.), vol. 71, cols. 40–42.

50. While it may be reasonable to limit strategic departments in general to British subjects, it is difficult to see what justification there can be for rejecting those whose parents happen not to have been British subjects at some period of their lives. It has been argued that a person with foreign relatives behind the Iron Curtain may be specially sensitive to pressure. This may sometimes be true

and are completely outside the scope of the Act. But if a government department were to exclude applicants on grounds not included in the Treasury rules (e.g. because of an applicant's colour or race, or because of his wife's nationality),[51] the discrimination would not of course come within the exemption.

The 1968 Act also does not affect the operation of any existing discriminatory statutes in the field of employment (s. 3 (2)). Several of these statutes relate to employment in the public service. Under the Act of Settlement 1700, section 3, aliens were disabled from enjoying any office or place of trust, civil or military. The Aliens Employment Act 1955 now permits an alien to be employed in the Civil Service: 1. Inside the United Kingdom, where the responsible Minister, with the consent of the Treasury, issues a certificate permitting a particular individual to be employed in his Department.

---

and may justify restricting access to classified information in individual cases but cannot justify an indiscriminate bar. The rule can work serious hardship. In one case the mother of a boy complained to the Board that after passing all the required examinations for entry to the Royal Air Force, he was rejected on the sole ground that his father had been born in Poland. In another case it was reported that the son of a Czech who had served as a major with the British Army throughout the Second World War, passed two selection boards for Cranwell and was then turned down without being told the reason. Later, he tried to gain admission to Sandhurst and only then was he told that he was excluded by the Nationality Rule (RRB 1967, Appendix VI). One bizarre result is that, unless they obtained a special Ministerial exemption, the former Home Secretary, Sir Frank Soskice, Q.C. M.P. (now Lord Stow Hill), and the present Lord Chancellor, Lord Hailsham, would not have been eligible for civil service posts; the former because he was born in Russia, and the latter because one of his parents was an American citizen. The same would have been true of Sir Winston Churchill whose mother was American.

51. In September 1969, the Home Office issued forms to applicants for the post of adjudicator under the Immigration Appeals Act 1969, asking questions (*inter alia*) about the nationality of both parents and also of an applicant's wife. If the Home Office were to exclude applicants because *both* their parents were not British, this would be unlawful, because the Treasury rules require only that *one* parent should be British in the case of Home Office appointments. Similarly, it would be unlawful to reject applicants because they had foreign wives, since the Treasury rules make no requirements about the nationality of an applicant's wife. Incidentally, the application form asked no questions about the nationality of an applicant's husband, presumably because it was assumed that there would be no female adjudicators!

2. Outside the United Kingdom, in types of service for which the employment of aliens is considered appropriate.

The Army Act 1955, section 21 and the Air Force Act 1955, section 21, also limit the number of aliens at any one time serving (whether as officers or ordinary servicemen) to one-fiftieth of the total number in the service.[52] When aliens or non-patrial Commonwealth or United Kingdom citizens seek employment in Britain, the government may refuse them permission to enter this country, or restrict the period within which they may remain here, or the type of work which they may do, whether in the public service or with private employers.[53] In exercising these powers, the immigration authorities are not affected by the provisions of the Race Relations Act 1968.

Employment abroad

It is not unlawful to discriminate on racial grounds in any aspect of employment wholly or mainly in a country outside Britain, whether in recruitment, training, promotion, dismissals, the terms of employment or the conditions of work (s. 8 (7) (a)). This exemption is couched in much wider terms than its equivalent in Title VII of the US Civil Rights Act of 1964 (s. 702) which exempts only 'the employment of aliens outside any State'.

As a result, a British employer may, for example, exclude coloured workers from work outside Britain, or may employ them on discriminatory terms or conditions, even though the employer is based in this country and recruitment takes place here. He may also openly advertise for a particular category of Commonwealth citizens (e.g. UK citizens who were born in Britain, and whose parents and grandparents were born in Britain) to work overseas (s. 6 (2)). The advertising exemption applies equally to a foreign employer, e.g. a

52. The Army Act 1881, s. 95 formerly limited aliens to the proportion of one for every fifty British subjects, but it added the proviso that 'any inhabitant of any British protectorate, or any Negro or person of colour, although an alien, may voluntarily enlist . . ., and when so enlisted shall while serving in the regular forces, be deemed to be entitled to all the privileges of a British subject'. The reason for this strange example of 'positive discrimination' is not known, nor how it was applied to those whom it appeared to favour with unrestricted access into the British army and equality of treatment there.

53. Immigration Act 1971.

South African, who may advertise for a category of Commonwealth citizens, though not one identified by reference to colour.

The contrast between British and United States legislation in this respect is vividly illustrated by a case in New York State in which the Arabian American Oil Company (Aramco) refused to employ Jews, and asked applicants whether they were Jewish. The New York State Commission against Discrimination granted a waiver to Aramco from the statutory prohibition of religious discrimination. There was no exemption under the New York Statute for employment outside the United States, but the Commission decided that not being of the Jewish faith was a bona fide occupational qualification for Aramco's employees, because any employee might ultimately be needed in Saudi Arabia, and Jews could not gain entry to that country even when employed by an American firm. However, the American Jewish Congress successfully challenged this waiver in the New York State courts. The judgment of the the lower court,[54] which was upheld on appeal, contained this robust declaration:

This court does not pretend to assert that Saudi Arabia may not do as it pleases with regard to whom it will employ within the borders of Saudi Arabia. Nor does this court pretend to say that Aramco may not hire whom it pleases to conform to its Arab master's voice. What this court does say is that Aramco can not defy the declared public policy of New York State and violate its statute within New York State, no matter what the King of Saudi Arabia says. New York State is not a province of Saudi Arabia, nor is the constitution and statute of New York State to be cast aside to protect the oil profits of Aramco.

By contrast, under the 1968 Act, a British employer could exclude Jews from employment wholly or mainly in foreign countries, regardless of whether recruitment took place here or overseas, or whether the discrimination was done to conform to its foreign master's voice.

Ships and aircraft

The 1968 Act contains no less than seven separate exemptions for discrimination in employment on ships or aircraft. The British ship-

54. *American Jewish Congress* v. *Carter* 190 N.Y.S. 2d. 219 (1959); 199 N.Y.S. 2d. 157 (1960); 9 N.Y. 2d. 223 (1961). The proceedings before the Commission and the Courts are discussed by Higbee (1966, at pp. 185–95; 297–303).

ping industry has practised racial discrimination against coloured seamen, with some statutory backing, since the early nineteenth century, and probably even earlier (Hepple, 1970, pp. 120–22). It is ironical that legislation which was intended to eliminate discrimination should now have given more extensive Parliamentary approval to these practices than had previously existed, and should have sanctioned discrimination on aircraft.[55]

It is not unlawful to discriminate in any aspect of employment *wholly* on a *British ship or aircraft* in a country outside Britain, or *wholly or mainly* on a foreign ship or aircraft outside Britain, even if the person seeking employment or employed was engaged or applied for it *in* this country (s. 8 (7) (b)) and (c). It is not unlawful to discriminate in any aspect of employment on a *British or foreign ship or aircraft* in *any part of the world*, including Britain, if the person employed or seeking employment was engaged or applied for it *outside* Britain (s. 8 (8)).

e.g. A British shipping company doing business mainly with South Africa employs coloured seamen in inferior, segregated, working conditions, at discriminatory rates of pay, and without any opportunities for promotion. The discrimination is not unlawful. Nor would it be unlawful for the same company to pursue the same policies on British ships in British territorial waters or British ports, provided that the seamen were recruited outside Britain.

If a person is brought to Britain with a view to his entering into an agreement in Britain to be employed on any ship or aircraft, he is to be treated as engaged for or seeking the employment outside Britain (s. 8 (9)), so that he can be freely discriminated against in all aspects of employment as though he had been recruited abroad. This obscure exemption needs some explanation. Under the Merchant Shipping Act 1894, section 125, the master or owner of any ship, or his agent, could make an agreement with 'a Lascar, or any native of India' binding him to come either as a seaman or as a passenger to any United Kingdom port, and there to enter into a further agreement to serve as a seaman in any ship which happened to be there, and to be bound for any port in British India. If the lascar or native of India refused to enter into the second agreement (under which he

55. The relevant Parliamentary debates are referred to at pp. 141–3.

was employed on blatantly discriminatory terms) he was liable to the same consequences, and to be 'dealt with in all respects in the same manner, as if he had voluntarily entered into the same'. In other words, he could be punished under the criminal provisions of the Act for desertion or indiscipline. Much of the 1894 Act was repealed by the Merchant Shipping Act 1970, which did not re-enact the Lascar clauses.[56] However, under the Race Relations Act 1968 (section 8 (9)), this practice of making racially discriminatory agreements with coloured seamen brought to Britain for this purpose, was given fresh statutory blessing. The only difference is that coloured seamen are no longer subject to criminal penalties if they refuse to enter into the second agreement in Britain, under which they may be required to work their passage home to India on discriminatory terms and conditions. One of the oddest features of this unsightly exemption is that it is necessary only so as to permit racial discrimination to be practised in employment on British ships wholly or mainly in British ports or British waters, for the other exemptions amply cover employment elsewhere on British and foreign ships.

Nor is this all. It is not unlawful to discriminate against anyone in respect to employment on a ship (but not an aircraft) in order to avoid people of different colour, race or ethnic or national origins 'being compelled to share sleeping rooms, mess rooms or sanitary accommodation' (s. 8 (10)). Once more, this ugly exemption dupli-

56. The Merchant Shipping Act 1970, s. 1 & sch. 3, also repealed section 185 of the 1894 Act which made the master or owner of a ship liable to a fine if any native of any country in Africa or Asia were brought to Britain in a ship, and, within six months, were awarded the earlier equivalent of social security benefits. And it repealed the Aliens Restriction (Amendment) Act 1919, s. 5, under which it was an offence to employ an alien as master, chief officer or chief engineer of a British merchant ship, or as skipper or second hand of a fishing boat registered in the United Kingdom (other than a ship or boat employed habitually in voyages between ports outside Britain). Section 5 (2) of the 1919 Act provided that where aliens 'of any particular race' were habitually employed afloat 'in any capacity or in any climate for which they were specially fitted', aliens of 'such race' had the right to be employed at the same rates of pay as those fixed for British subjects 'of that race'. This meant that 'a British sailor from Hong Kong will be paid the same as a Chinese sailor from Shanghai working on a British ship but he may earn considerably less than a French sailor on a British ship. The French sailor is entitled to be paid at the same rate as European British subjects' (Hepple, 1968, p. 45).

cates several other exemptions, and applies to all aspects of employment on British or foreign ships in this country and overseas. It would permit any shipping company to refuse to employ a coloured seaman because no racially segregated accommodation was available or to maintain segregated living quarters, mess rooms, wash rooms or lavatories.

Lastly, nothing in the 1968 Act makes unlawful any act done on a British ship while in the waters of a foreign country, or on a British aircraft while in, or in flight over, a foreign country, in compliance with the laws of that country (s. 11 (2)). In view of the battery of other shipping and aircraft exemptions, it is not likely that any British shipping company or airline would ever need to rely upon this provision to escape liability for discriminating in employment on ships or aircraft. Nor is it necessary in order to enable them to segregate passengers.[57]

Advertising

It is not unlawful to publish or display an advertisement or notice which indicates that Commonwealth citizens, or any category of Commonwealth citizens are required for employment *outside* Britain, or that non-Commonwealth citizens are required for employment *in* Britain (s. 6 (2)). The first of these exceptions would apply, for example, to an advertisement for doctors in India restricted to those of Indian citizenship (or, for that matter, of UK citizenship); the second would exempt an advertisement for a French girl[58] to work as a mother's help. But an advertisement for an Australian, Cypriot or Maltese girl to work in Britain is unlawful, because they are Commonwealth citizens. There is a further exemption for advertisements which state the gist of any Treasury rules restricting employment in the public service to people of particular birth, citizenship, descent or residence (see p. 218).

57. A shipping company may also discriminate in providing sleeping cabins for passengers on a ship in order to avoid passengers of different colour, race or ethnic or national origins being compelled to share the same cabin (s. 7 (6) see further pp. 254–5).

58. David Ennals, M.P. said of this exemption: 'It makes it possible to advertise, for instance, for a German *au pair* girl, or a Swedish *au pair* girl . . .' 13 June 1968, *Official Report*, Standing Committee B, col. 449. But it is not clear that an *au pair* girl enters into an employment relationship.

Apart from these exemptions, it is unlawful to publish or display an advertisement or notice indicating an intention to do an act of discrimination, whether or not the act of discrimination would itself be unlawful under the 1968 Act. Accordingly, it would, for example, be unlawful to advertise for Indian waiters for an Indian restaurant (see p. 195), or for white seamen for employment on a segregated ship in British waters, even though the acts of discrimination indicated in these advertisements are outside the scope of the 1968 Act.[59]

59. *Contra* MacDonald (1969, para. 120), where he suggests that 'advertisements indicating an intention to do discriminatory acts in respect of employment, which are permitted by section 3 (2) of the 1968 Act [and] are not affected by the employment provisions of that section' are not unlawful under section 6 'because those discriminatory acts are not "acts of discrimination" within the definition of section 1'. However, section 3 (2) contains an exemption only for the purposes of that section, and does not affect the scope of section 6. Section 1 defines 'discrimination' to include discrimination on grounds of colour, race, etc., but does not limit it to situations in which sections 2–5 apply.

Chapter 6
Housing

General observations

The 1968 Act prohibits racial discrimination in disposing not only of housing accommodation but also of business premises and other land. However, in practical terms, the real problem with which Parliament was concerned is discrimination in the field of housing accommodation, which is the subject-matter of this chapter. The disposal of building premises and other land is only of ancillary importance in the field of race relations.

The housing provisions of the 1968 Act are less complicated and require less explanation than the employment provisions. It is relatively easy to describe them. What is much more difficult is to relate them to the problems which they were designed to tackle and to assess their effectiveness in dealing with those problems. It is beyond the scope of this book to explore all the intricacies of private and local authority housing in the context of race relations in this country.[1] But some general observations must be made at the outset to put the legislation into context.

The causes and consequences of discrimination in housing, employment and education are closely linked (see p. 83). Job discrimination reduces a person's potential income, and makes it more difficult for him to obtain decent housing accommodation for himself and his family. Educational opportunities in a poor, overcrowded urban area are more limited than in more fortunate neighbourhoods. The worker who has been unable to obtain adequate instruction

1. See generally *Council Housing Purposes, Procedures and Priorities*, Ninth Report of the Housing Management sub-committee of the Central Housing Advisory Committee (HMSO, 1969, ch. 9) (Cullingworth Report); Rose *et al.* (1969); Rex and Moore (1967) and Report on Housing by Select Committee on Race Relations and Immigration (HMSO, 1971).

and training is excluded from skilled and well-paid employment. And so on. But, though all three problems are interlinked, discrimination is more widespread and entrenched in housing than in employment or education. Unfortunately, housing is also the field in which anti-discrimination legislation is likely to make the least practical impact.

The problem about enforcing the law is not one of proving allegations of housing discrimination. On the contrary, except in the complex area of local authority housing, it is easier to establish the existence of discrimination in housing than in employment. The qualifications of the would-be house purchaser or tenant are normally straightforward. He must have the financial means of acquiring the accommodation which he seeks; and, in the case of the would-be tenant, he must be able to satisfy the landlord's requirements for the protection of his property or the well-being of other tenants in the property, such as the requirement that he will keep the flat in a reasonable state of repair, or will not use it for business or immoral purposes, or will not make a noise late at night. These are matters which can be evaluated objectively. By contrast, in the field of employment, the qualifications of a would-be employee, especially for skilled or supervisory work, training or promotion, often depend upon the employer's hunches and predilections which are hard to weigh objectively (see p. 190).

Discrimination is easier to *prove* but much more difficult to *remove* in the field of housing than in employment. The source of the difficulty is the difference between the market forces in the two situations. This difference may not always exist, but is certain to face us for many years to come. In the labour market, although the level of unemployment has increased alarmingly in recent years and there is a serious threat of greater technological redundancy in the future, there are chronic shortages of workers for skilled and even unskilled employment in many sectors of industry and commerce. Those shortages were, of course, what brought so many Commonwealth and foreign workers to this country after the Second World War. A situation in which employers are short of labour is the most favourable context in which to apply a law guaranteeing equality of opportunity and treatment in employment. It is favourable because the employer who needs workers has no commercial incentive to practise racial discrimination and also because his existing work-force will not feel threatened by the risk of unemployment and of competition from outside sources of labour.

But the housing market is characterized by serious and persistent shortages of residential accommodation – the equivalent, for the victim of racial discrimination, of high unemployment in the labour market. A situation of chronic and acute shortage does not encourage property owners to offer equal housing opportunities to would-be residents, regardless of their colour or race. On the contrary, housing shortage creates powerful financial incentives for the property owner to practise racial discrimination. Such a situation can be exploited in many ways.

For example, a large property owner or a ring of estate agents may exclude coloured people from obtaining accommodation in a suburban neighbourhood, while encouraging white residents to fear that coloured neighbours will depress the value of their homes. 'Exclusive' prices may be charged to preserve the 'exclusive' character of the neighbourhood. In such an atmosphere, if coloured families move in, existing residents may panic, perhaps with deliberate encouragement from unscrupulous estate agents, and hastily sell their homes. If the panic spreads and leads to a mass exodus, property values will indeed fall. The property company is then able to purchase the homes cheaply, and to sell them at a later date to more coloured families at vastly increased prices.[2]

The same property company may meanwhile be active in another, poorer neighbourhood, where it is taking advantage of the housing shortage and the extent of racial discrimination to sell or let slum properties to coloured families at exorbitant prices.

The opportunities for profiting from the housing shortage are increased by the fact that over a quarter of all households in England and Wales live in local authority properties, and that coloured immigrants are excluded from local authority housing to a disproportionate extent by rigid residence and other requirements (Cullingworth Report, 1969; Burney, 1967).

2. The Street Committee proposed that this practice, known in the United States as 'block-busting', be penalized in the Race Relations Act but this was not done (Street Report, 1967, para. 134.9). See generally, Report of the Committee on Housing in Greater London (Cmd 2605) (HMSO, 1965, ch. 9) (Milner-Holland Report).

As a result of these and other pressures, housing patterns have already developed which are markedly unfavourable to coloured people in Britain. Typically, they do not qualify for local authority housing, and are excluded by a combination of racial discrimination and lack of means from a large section of private housing. Their situation may be measured against the different types of access to housing in a modern city as described by Rex and Moore (1967, p. 274), who distinguished the following types of housing situation:

1. That of the outright owner of a whole house.
2. That of the owner of a mortgaged whole house.
3. That of the council tenant:
   (a) in a house with a long life.
   (b) in a house awaiting demolition.
4. That of the tenant of a whole house owned by a private landlord.
5. That of the owner of a house bought with short-term loans who is compelled to let rooms in order to meet his repayment obligations.
6. That of the tenant of rooms in a lodging-house.

As Rex and Moore comment:

The six housing situations mentioned above take the order 1–6 in a scale of desirability according to the status values of British society, except that lack of capital puts the first two situations beyond the means of many urban residents, who can therefore aspire only to a ceiling of situation 3 (a), and that there will be some overlapping between situations 3 and 4 and particularly between 3 (b) and 4 (i.e. many private tenancies will be more desirable than some council house tenancies) (p. 275).

Coloured immigrants are not often found in situations 1 or 2. They are increasingly qualifying for council housing, but, if they obtain a council house, it tends to be in situation 3 (b) rather than 3 (a). They are unlikely to be in situation 4. Their most common type of residential accommodation is in situations 5 and 6, either as owners of houses bought with short-term loans (often at discriminatory rates) who are compelled to let rooms to other coloured immigrants in order to meet their repayment obligations, or as tenants of rooms in a lodging-house. And situations 5 and 6 occur most frequently not in neighbourhoods which are being redeveloped by the local authority, but in the neglected 'twilight areas' or 'zones of transition'. To add to the problem, within those areas, the amount of available private rented accommodation is rapidly shrinking.[3]

For anti-discrimination legislation to be effective it has to reduce discrimination in the situations in which racial minorities are now typically housed, while at the same time promoting equal opportunities for them to move into better residential accommodation. In other words, the legislation has to apply to situations 1 to 6 and to encourage a shift from situations 4, 5 and 6 into situations 1, 2 and 3. Ultimately, these objectives cannot be achieved unless the general housing shortage is sharply reduced, and unless the law is applied with equal vigour and effect throughout the entire housing market, private and local authority.

Obviously, even the most skilfully drafted race relations statute, with the widest and most flexible powers of enforcement, could not achieve these aims unless it were accompanied by general economic and social measures to eliminate urban poverty. Those measures are beyond the scope of this book (see Rose *et. al.* 1969). But the character of Britain's housing needs also has important implications in assessing anti-discrimination legislation.

First, if it is to be effective, the scope of the law must include all types of residential accommodation. The commercial incentives to discriminate against racial minorities, and the social and financial anxieties on which they play, will only be removed if there is no important sector of the housing market in which discrimination is permitted and no neighbourhood or housing estate which is, or can become, racially segregated.

Secondly, some exceptions have to be made to the scope of the legislation because it is impracticable to enforce the law where accommodation is shared in conditions of close personal proximity. But those exceptions must be narrowly drawn and justified only on strictly practical grounds to avoid defeating the main purpose of the law.

Thirdly, because of the nature of the housing market, special

3. It has been rapidly shrinking throughout the country. In 1947, 61 per cent of dwellings in England and Wales were privately rented; in 1961, the proportion was 31 per cent; and, by 1967, it had fallen to 23 per cent. On the other hand, owner-occupied dwellings increased from 27 per cent in 1947 to 50 per cent in 1967; and local authority accommodation grew from 12 per cent in 1947 to 27 per cent in 1967 (Cullingworth Report, 1969, p. 5).

powers are necessary to ensure that the law is not thwarted before the statutory machinery is able to investigate allegations of discrimination and to secure an adequate remedy for a victim.

Fourthly, in view of the complex nature both of the allocation of local authority housing, and of the functions of local government in controlling or re-developing property in twilight urban areas, special provisions are needed to prevent discrimination in this crucial sector of the housing market.

These four conditions provide a yardstick against which to evaluate the housing provisions of the 1968 Act. Those provisions must now be described.

Scope of the legislation

The 1968 Act makes it unlawful to discriminate on racial grounds (see p. 153) against any person seeking to acquire housing accommodation, business premises or other land, or against the occupier of such accommodation, premises or land (see p. 237). The Act applies to the owner of property and also to anyone authorized by the owner to dispose of his property. Its scope includes the sale and letting of property, whether by private individuals, commercial organizations, government departments or local authorities. But there are important exceptions in the case of residential accommodation (see p. 249). The 1965 Act also contains a provision preventing the enforcement of racial restrictions on the transfer of tenancies (see p. 240).

Persons concerned

The 1968 Act applies to 'any person having power to dispose, or being otherwise concerned with the disposal, of housing accommodation, business premises or other land' (s. 5). It covers not only the owner of a freehold or leasehold interest in property, but also a tenant who sublets his tenancy, or a housing manager who controls the allocation of a block of flats, or an estate agent who helps the owner to dispose of his property. Even if these lack the power to dispose of the accommodation, they are still 'concerned' with its disposal. Similarly, a porter living in a block of flats would come within the scope of these words if, in the course of his work, he provided information to would-be tenants about vacant flats, because he would then be concerned with the disposal of the flats.

The owner of the property is also liable for the acts of his employees, done in the course of their employment, whether or not they are done with his approval (s. 13 (1)) (see p. 181). So he will be held responsible if his housing manager or porter discriminates unlawfully. And, since anything done by a person as agent for someone else (with his express or implied authority) is treated for the purposes of the Act as done by the principal as well as by the agent (s. 13 (2)) (see p. 183), the owner is also liable if an estate agent or solicitor discriminates unlawfully on his behalf with respect to the disposal of his property.

Estate agents and local authorities are liable as persons concerned with the disposal of housing accommodation. But they are also liable under the more general section of the Act (s. 2) dealing with the provision of facilities or services to the public or a section of the public, as is the proprietor of a boarding house or residential hotel (see p. 262).

Anyone who deliberately aids, induces or incites another person to do an act of unlawful discrimination is himself treated as acting unlawfully (s. 12). Accordingly, the Act would apply to an individual or a group of residents who tried to coerce a property owner or an estate agent into discriminating unlawfully. It is also unlawful for any person to publish or display any advertisement or notice indicating an intention to do an act of discrimination (s. 6 (1)).

Types of unlawful discrimination
Disposal of housing accommodation etc

It is unlawful for any person having power to dispose, or being otherwise concerned with the disposal of, housing accommodation, etc., to discriminate against any person seeking to acquire any such accommodation, etc., by refusing or deliberately omitting to dispose of it to him, or to dispose of it to him on the like terms and in the like circumstances as in the case of other persons (s. 5 (a)).

There must be a deliberate intention to discriminate on any of the unlawful grounds, but the ground need not be the would-be purchaser's or tenant's own colour or race; it may be the colour or race of someone else with whom he is associated, such as his wife (see p. 161). And a person will be liable under this provision whether he refuses outright to dispose of the property on racial grounds, or he deliberately omits to do so, for example upon the pretext that the property has already been sold or let to somebody else.

It is not unlawful to discriminate in disposing of accommodation unless the person discriminated against is actually seeking to acquire the accommodation at the time.

e.g. A West Indian, having heard rumours that a property company maintains a colour bar in some of its properties, decides to test the truth of the rumours and applies to the company for a flat in a particular building. He is informed that flats in that building are not let to coloured people. Since he is not seeking to acquire a flat, but only to test the company's policy, there has been no unlawful discrimination. However, the West Indian's experience in conducting the test would be very strong evidence of unlawful discrimination if the company were to refuse, on apparently racial grounds, to let accommodation to someone else who was genuinely seeking such accommodation; it would also entitle the Board to initiate an investigation under section 17 of the Act (see pp. 311–13).

A property owner is, of course, entitled to refuse to dispose of accommodation to someone who cannot pay the purchase price or the rent, or who is regarded as unsuitable for some other non-racial reason, such as the size of his family or his insistence on keeping a pet animal in the premises. But if it is shown that a person was genuinely seeking to acquire the accommodation, and that the reason for his exclusion was racial, he need not establish that he would with certainty subsequently have acquired the accommodation. It is sufficient to prove that the exclusion was on unlawful grounds.

Obviously, a person is not liable for refusing to dispose of accommodation unless it is available. But the accommodation need not be *immediately* available. This is nicely illustrated by *Race Relations Board* v. *Geo. H. Haigh & Co. Ltd*,[4] the first case to have been taken to court under the 1968 Act.

4. Leeds County Court, Judge D. O. McKee and Assessors (Professor P. S. James and Rev. J. M. Furness). The case is reported in *The Times*, 11 September 1969. The action was dismissed because, although the defendants had discriminated unlawfully against the complainant, the court held that the Race Rela-

The defendants were developing a housing estate in Huddersfield. The system they adopted was to enter into agreements with prospective customers to build or complete a house in accordance with agreed plans and to grant to the customer a lease of the selected site for a period of 999 years upon completion. The defendants admitted that they had refused to enter into such an agreement with the complainant on the ground of colour. But they contended that there was no completed house on their estate available for sale and that they were not persons 'having power to dispose of housing accommodation' when the complainant applied to them. The court rejected this argument. It found nothing in the Act to say that accommodation must be immediately available, and observed that there was nothing in law to prevent an owner from letting or selling a house which would not be available for some time. The court also rejected the argument that an incomplete house was not housing accommodation. The judge commented that if that argument were valid it would mean that owners of any housing estate which was being developed could avoid the provisions of section 5 by deliberately leaving the houses incomplete until sold to persons of whom they approved. Using words in their normal meaning one would properly describe a partially built house which is to be completed as 'housing accommodation'.

This decision is clearly in accordance with Parliament's intention. Indeed, the Act refers not only to 'housing accommodation' but also to any 'other land'; so it is broad enough to include a building site, whether or not it has been built upon.

With some important exceptions, which will be discussed below, the Act applies to the sale or letting of part of the owner's property as well as to the whole of the property. It makes no difference whether what is being disposed of is a house or a flat, a freehold, a long lease, a short tenancy or a licence.

It is unlawful not only to refuse outright to dispose of property on racial grounds, but also to refuse on racial grounds to allow someone to acquire it on equal terms or in equal circumstances.

---

tions Board's arrangements for discharging their statutory functions had not been approved by the Home Secretary at the material time, in accordance with section 14 of the Act. However, after the hearing, the company stated that they would 'reluctantly' in future sell their houses to coloured persons (*Guardian*, 11 September 1969). Meanwhile, ironically, the complainant had bought a house built by the defendants from a white person who was its first owner (*The Times*, 11 September 1969).

e.g. A property company grants tenancies to coloured people only if they agree to pay higher rents than white tenants and to undertake more onerous repairing obligations. The company is acting unlawfully because it is refusing to dispose of the tenancies 'on the like terms . . . as in the case of other persons'.

e.g. A house owner tells a coloured would-be purchaser that he will accept the price offered by him for his house, but he refuses to allow him to have the house surveyed. Since the owner would allow a white would-be purchaser to carry out a survey, he is acting unlawfully because he is refusing to dispose of the house 'in the like circumstances as in the case of other persons'.

A property owner cannot escape liability by employing someone else to discriminate on his behalf, for he is liable for the unlawful acts of his servants or agents. And an estate agent or accommodation bureau accepts discriminatory instructions from a property owner at its peril, for it will be liable as agent and also in its own right for discriminating in the running of its business.

e.g. An Indian visits an accommodation bureau and tells the receptionist his requirements for a suitable furnished flat. The receptionist sends him to two flats, which he finds have already been let to other people. But the receptionist fails to give him the addresses of two other flats, because their owners have specified 'no coloured', nor of a third flat, because the receptionist assumes that the owner would not want a coloured tenant. Unless the flats are within the exceptions for residential accommodation, the accommodation bureau is liable for omitting on racial grounds to disclose details about them. It is liable as agent for those owners who specified that they would not take a coloured tenant; and it is liable with respect to all the flats (whether or not their owners made such a stipulation) for discriminating in providing its facilities and services to the public.

The scope of these provisions is wide, and their impact in discouraging discrimination in the disposal of housing is not likely to be undermined by the fact that there are exceptional situations which are beyond the reach of the law. However, there are serious weaknesses, not in the coverage of the law, but in the absence of adequate means of preventing evasion, or remedying the wrong done to the victim of a discriminatory sale or letting. For example, if an owner-occupier refuses to sell his house to a coloured person, the Race Relations Board is powerless to prevent the house from being sold to a third party before it is able to investigate the case. The Board lacks the power, which was recommended by the Street Report, to post a notice on the property warning the public that it is the subject of a complaint or to obtain a temporary injunction preventing its disposal for a limited period. And, if it is later proved that there has been unlawful discrimination, the Board cannot obtain the wide range of remedial orders which again were recommended by the Street Report. The owner cànnot, for example, be required to sell a house to the complainant or to rescind a transaction made in defiance of a posted negative injunction. The only available remedies which can benefit the victim are damages and an injunction. The former is significant only in those rare cases in which the complainant has suffered a quantifiable loss; the latter, which can be granted only when a *second* similar act of discrimination is proved (s. 21 (1) (b)), will assist him only where the owner has some suitable property which is available for disposal to him (see p. 332).

Treatment of existing occupiers

It is unlawful for any person having power to dispose, or being otherwise concerned with the disposal, of housing accommodation, etc., to discriminate against any person occupying such accommodation by deliberately treating him differently from other occupiers in the like circumstances (s. 5 (b)). So, although a landlord may agree to let property to someone without discrimination; he will be still liable if he then proceeds to treat him differently from other tenants on racial grounds.

e.g. A property company lets flats regardless of colour or race. Six of the fifty flats in its building are occupied by coloured families. As a result of complaints made by some white tenants the company requires the coloured tenants to keep their refuse bins in a separate part of the building, and to confine themselves to a separate part of the communal gardens. The requirement is unlawful because the company is treating the coloured families differently from white families, in like circumstances.

Nor would it be a defence in this example for the property company to show that the separate facilities were equally favourable, because the segregation of a person from other people on racial grounds is deemed to be less favourable treatment (s. 1 (2)) (see p. 166).

Lists of persons

It is unlawful for any person having power to dispose, or being otherwise concerned with the disposal, of housing accommodation, etc. to discriminate against any person in need of such accommodation by deliberately treating that other person differently from others in respect of any list of persons in need of it (s. 5 (c)).

The main object of this provision is to prevent local authorities from discriminating in their treatment of people on a waiting list for council housing (see p. 243). Such discrimination would infringe section 2, which applies to the services of local authorities, and it is curious that separate provision was again made in section 5.

But it also applies to any other person concerned with the disposal of housing accommodation. Where, for example, an estate agent, or a university lodgings bureau maintains lists of those in need of accommodation, or where a building developer keeps lists of potential purchasers of completed houses, they must not discriminate in their treatment of people on their lists.

Nor must they discriminate by refusing to supply copies of their lists. For example, in *Race Relations Board* v. *London Accommodation Bureau*, the Board alleged that a large agency had acted unlawfully by refusing to supply a black student from Uganda with a list of accommodation made available generally to white applicants. The case was heard in the Westminster County Court in February 1971. During the hearing, the Bureau admitted that they had unlawfully discriminated against the complainant and Judge Herbert granted a declaration to that effect. The Bureau signed an undertaking not to discriminate in the future, agreed to pay the costs of the action and to pay the complainant £5 damages for loss of opportunity (RRB, 1971, Appendix V).

Advertising

It is unlawful for any person to publish or display, or to cause to be published or displayed, any advertisement or notice[5] indicating an intention to do an act of discrimination (s. 6 (1)). It does not matter

5. The meaning of 'advertisement or notice' is discussed at p. 195.

whether the property to which the advertisement or notice refers is exempted from the scope of the 1968 Act. It is the publication or display which is made unlawful because it is offensive to those whom the advertisement or notice seeks to exclude, and it makes racial discrimination seem to be respectable. So a newspaper may not publish an advertisement for the sale or letting of property stating that 'no coloureds need apply'; nor may a newsagent display a notice to the same effect in his shop window, even though it is not unlawful for the owner of the property to practise discrimination because the property is within the exception for 'small premises' etc.

There is evidence that the Act has already had a substantial effect in removing advertisements of this offensive kind, which, before the Act came into force, were very widespread. The Milner-Holland Committee found that in four areas of London in August 1964 coloured tenants were excluded from one third of all lettings advertised in newspapers. On 2 July 1968, before the Act came into force, eighteen discriminatory advertisements for accommodation appeared in that day's issue of the *Hackney Gazette and North London Advertiser*. In the issue of 4 July 1969 there were none (RRB, 1970, Appendix IX).

In May 1970, the Board commenced legal proceedings in the Southampton County Court against a boarding house in the Isle of Wight which had published a brochure bearing the words 'sorry, no coloured visitors', and which had declined to stop doing so. After the proceedings had been started, the owner of the boarding house issued a new brochure without the offending words and gave a written undertaking not to repeat the offence. The Board accordingly withdrew the proceedings (RRB, 1971, para. 8).

Aiding, inducing or inciting

It is unlawful for any person deliberately to aid, induce or incite another person to violate the housing provisions of the 1968 Act (s. 12). A residents' association or a group of neighbours would therefore be liable for putting pressure upon an estate agent, property company or local authority to refuse to do business with, or to provide services for, members of a particular racial group. If it were shown that their main object was to harm a member of such a group rather than to protect their legitimate interests, they might also be liable at Common Law for having committed the civil wrong of conspiracy.[6]

Restrictive covenants

One of the provisions of the 1965 Act which was not repealed by the 1968 Act relates to racially discriminatory restrictions on the transfer of tenancies. It is a complicated provision which has not been made simpler by the need to reconcile its contents with the housing provisions of the 1968 Act.

The 1965 Act provides that where the licence or consent of the landlord or any other person is required for the disposal[7] to any person of a tenancy, such licence or consent shall be treated as unreasonably withheld if and so far as it is withheld on racial grounds (s. 5 (1)). Leases and tenancy agreements often contain restrictive covenants under which the benefit of the lease or agreement must not be transferred without the landlord's consent. Where they contain such a clause, the landlord is not entitled to withhold his consent unreasonably (Landlord and Tenant Act 1927, section 19 (1) (a)). The 1965 Act makes clear what was in any case probably the position at Common Law (see p. 60), namely that it is unreasonable for a landlord to withhold consent on racial grounds. If a landlord withholds his consent on such grounds, the tenant is free to disregard the covenant and to transfer the tenancy regardless of the landlord's objection. However, this provision is limited to the case where the landlord (or the person whose consent or licence is required) either does not live on the premises, or else lives there but shares only the means of access to the premises with his tenant (s. 5 (1)). It is arguable that a refusal on racial grounds to consent to the transfer of a tenancy would have been unenforceable at Common Law regardless of whether the landlord lived in the premises. If so, the 1965 Act may actually have cut down the Common Law position.

The 1965 Act also provides that any covenant, agreement or stipu-

6. See e.g. *Quinn* v. *Leathem* [1901] A.C. 495 (H.L.); *Crofter Harris Tweed Co.* v. *Veitch* [1942] A.C. 435 (H.L.); *Mogul Steamship Co.* v. *McGregor Gow & Co.* [1892] A.C. 25 (H.L.). The courts would probably not regard the exclusion of coloured people for the protection of property values as a legitimate interest; but the point has not been decided.

7. This includes both assignment and subletting (s. 5 (3)).

lation which purports to prohibit the disposal of a tenancy to any persons on racial grounds is to be construed as prohibiting such disposal except with the consent of the landlord, such consent not to be unreasonably withheld (s. 5 (2)).

These provisions may be criticized on several grounds. Firstly, they deal only with racial restrictions in leases and tenancy agreements; they do not apply to racial covenants contained in agreements for the sale of freehold properties which restrict their re-sale on racial grounds. The validity of such restrictions at Common Law is unclear (see p. 60). By failing to prohibit them, Parliament has increased the uncertainty about their legal effect. This failure to legislate against restrictions on the re-sale of property is curious, for a person who sells his freehold interest in land is less likely to retain any continuing interest in the racial identity of those to whom the purchaser may resell, than the landlord who continues to own the property which he lets to his tenant.

The second objection to these provisions is that, instead of making it unlawful to insert racial restrictions into leases and tenancy agreements, the 1965 Act merely states that if such restrictions are made, they are to be treated as requiring the landlord's consent to the transfer of a tenancy, such consent not to be unreasonably withheld. There is no sanction against the landlord who continues to impose racial restrictions in his leases, knowing that they are unenforceable in the courts but hoping that his tenant will mistakenly believe them to be legally binding.[8] Instead it should have been made unlawful to enter into an agreement containing racial restrictions on the disposal of property and such restrictions should have been made void.[9] It is

8. In the United States, although they were held unenforceable in *Shelley* v. *Kraemer* (334 US 1 (1948)), 'not many states specifically void racially restrictive covenants (only Colorado, Minnesota and New York). Although not judicially enforceable, these covenants still are widely employed, and they are often respected despite their unenforceability. Perhaps in many cases individuals do not realize the covenants will not hold up in Court, and no doubt in other cases individuals feel morally obligated to uphold them as a matter of abiding by an agreement' (Lockard, 1968, p. 120).

9. The Street Committee proposed (p. 89) that 'Covenants in conveyances or leases, imposing discriminatory restrictions would be declared void, and it would be unlawful to rely on such void covenant.' However, this proposal was not implemented in the 1968 Act.

possible, but by no means certain, that a landlord seeking to include a new discriminatory restriction in a lease would incur liability under section 12 of the 1968 Act, for inducing or inciting his tenant to discriminate unlawfully. It is probable that the tenant would not himself escape liability by pleading his reliance on the discriminatory restriction. But the power given to the Board to seek revision of contracts is not likely to have any impact in this situation, for it can only be invoked in proceedings brought by the Board after an investigation into an alleged act of discrimination (s. 23) (see p. 339).

Thirdly, no attempt seems to have been made to reconcile the provisions of the 1965 Act with the housing provisions of the 1968 Act. Where racial restrictions are imposed in any agreement for the disposal of residential accommodation which is subject to the 1968 Act the position is fairly clear. The presence of written restrictions of this kind will be strong evidence that the person concerned with the disposal of the property has discriminated unlawfully or that he will do so at some future date. But even under the 1968 Act it is not unlawful[10] to enter into such contractual restrictions, and the 1968 Act expressly states that any contract or term in a contract which contravenes Part I of the Act shall not be void or unenforceable by reason only of that contravention (s. 23 (1)). A property owner will only act unlawfully if he seeks to rely upon a racial restriction so as to prevent the transfer of his property to a particular person. And no doubt many purchasers and tenants of residential accommodation will mistakenly regard such restrictions as legally enforceable, and will obediently refrain from transferring property to members of racial minorities.

Confusion about the validity of these restrictions is likely to be increased by the different tests used in the two Acts to determine whether a landlord is exempted from their scope. The 1965 Act exempts a landlord living on the premises and sharing accommodation other than means of access with his tenant. The 1968 Act exempts the landlord living on premises in which there is not normally accommodation for more than two households other than his own, and sharing accommodation other than means of access or storage accommodation with his tenants (see pp. 250–51).

10. Unless there is 'aiding, inducing or inciting' (see p. 239).

The effect of these different exemptions is that it is not unlawful to include racial restrictions in agreements for the sale or letting of residential accommodation, but it is unlawful to rely upon racial restrictions so as to discriminate in the subsequent disposal of such accommodation if the disposal is within the scope of the 1968 Act. Where the disposal of property is exempted from the 1965 Act (i.e. because the landlord shares storage accommodation with his tenants, or because the restriction is upon the sale rather than the letting of the property) but not from the 1968 Act, again it will not be unlawful to make racial restrictions but it will be unlawful under the 1968 Act to act upon them. Where the disposal of property is exempted from both Acts (because it satisfies the requirements of the exemptions to the 1968 Act) it will not be unlawful to rely upon such a racial restriction to prevent the property from being transferred to third parties, although it may be that such a restriction would still not be enforceable at Common Law.

The law in this field is therefore a tangled and illogical maze. The confusion which must result encourages the risk that racial restrictions will continue to be included in leases and conveyances and will be acted upon by people who are misled by their legal effect. The Race Relations Board may apply in proceedings brought under the 1968 Act to the county court, on behalf of any party to a contract, to revise any term in the contract which contravenes the Act (s. 23 (2)). But this provision cannot by itself cure the mischief caused by the obscurity of the law.

Local authority housing

The 1968 Act makes no distinction between privately-owned and local authority housing. Whether the person concerned with the provision of housing accommodation is an individual, a property company or a local authority, there must be no racial discrimination against people seeking or occupying such accommodation; and there must be no discrimination with respect to housing lists, or advertising, or the enforcement of racially restrictive covenants. A local authority is treated in the same way as a property company in that both are under a double duty; they must not discriminate in the disposal or management of housing accommodation, under section 5, and they must not discriminate in providing facilities and services to the public, under section 2.

However, although local authorities are not treated differently from anyone else under the 1968 Act, their functions are of such significance in the housing market that they merit special scrutiny. Council housing is far more extensive in this country than in the United States.

More than four million households in England and Wales now live in council houses. This is over a quarter of all households; in some areas the proportion is much higher. Each year local authorities allocate about 350,000 houses: about 145,000 to existing council tenants transferring to different houses and over 200,000 to households living in the private sector or without separate accommodation. Looking at the situation in another way, of the one and a half million households who move each year, about a quarter are housed by local authorities (Cullingworth Report, para. 54).

It is obviously of the greatest importance that racial minorities should be able to obtain council houses on the same basis as other people, because local authority housing represents such a substantial proportion of the available housing stock; because a council house is so highly prized by many people in this country, and because the public sector has a duty to set an especially good example of fair treatment to private bodies controlling the disposal of housing.

The housing provisions of the 1968 Act enable the Race Relations Board to deal as effectively with *clear* acts of discrimination by local authorities as by anyone else. For example, it is unlawful for a local authority to require residents who are not natives of Great Britain to wait longer than other residents before being allocated to a council house. This issue was contested by a local authority which challenged the Board's interpretation of the statutory requirements. It raised clear-cut issues of law rather than of fact. There was no dispute about whether the authority was discriminating for that was admitted. The controversy was only about whether the discrimination was unlawful (RRB, 1971, paras. 35, 37).

However, such cases are not typical. Most instances in which allegations of racial discrimination are made against a local authority are likely instead to raise very complicated questions of fact. It may be contended, for example, that an authority has used the fact that many Commonwealth immigrants were living in multiple-occupied houses, or in furnished tenancies, or in overcrowded conditions as an excuse for discriminating against them in the exercise of its housing functions. The validity of allegations of this kind can only be tested after a full-scale inquiry has been made, perhaps involving thousands of individual decisions based upon a host of racial, political and economic considerations. It is in these more typical and difficult cases that the 1968 Act is least able to provide an effective remedy.

The problems which may be expected to arise in practice were fully discussed by the Street Report (paras. 131–132.1), and it is a matter for criticism that they have not been faced by Parliament. The authors of that Report drew attention to the complex of powers and duties with regard to housing which are exercised by local authorities. They are empowered by various statutes to demolish unfit houses, to clear and redevelop slum areas, and to execute schemes of urban renewal and planning development.

The result of this complex set of provisions is that, in practice, over large areas of their housing activities local authorities have an uncontrolled discretion how they carry out their obligation to rehouse and their powers of providing housing. The Ministry of Housing and Local Government do not record information about how these powers are in fact exercised by the various authorities. If the present system for the control and management of public housing is to continue it does not seem to us possible to eliminate discrimination without making provision for much more detailed control, which would have the specific purpose of requiring local authorities to satisfy the Ministry about the non-discriminatory nature of all their policies (para. 131.4).

The significance of this conclusion is all the greater because the Street Report contemplated that the Race Relations Board would have much wider enforcement powers than have in fact been conferred by Parliament. It proposed that the Board should be able to issue a subpoena for the purpose of obtaining vital evidence, that certain forms of temporary relief by notices and injunctions should be available to protect the successful complainant from being deprived of premises by a transfer of them before his case could be decided, and that a wide range of remedial orders should be available against those found guilty of unlawful discrimination. None of these powers have been included in the 1968 Act. Yet the Street Committee concluded that even if there were these powers, they would not be sufficient to remove discrimination in local authority housing. In the absence of such powers, the ineffectiveness of the legislation in this field seems likely to exceed their worst fears.

The Street Report proposed that the Minister should be empowered to review and amend the allocation codes of local authorities so that the needs of applicants could be fairly weighed. The Board might make representations to the Minister that the code of a particular authority in fact operated unfairly against those protected by the Race Relations Act. It might also be desirable for an applicant to have some means of verifying that he had been allocated the correct number of points under the authority's code. It also recommended that the existing rehousing provisions should be made more uniform. And whenever schemes involved displacing persons, the local authority might be required to report to the Minister which categories of occupants they were rehousing. Sub-tenants, furnished tenants, occupants of houses in multiple occupation and the like could be excluded only with the Minister's approval in respect of the particular scheme. The local authority might also be required to state according to what criteria categories of housing would be allocated to those displaced. And the Race Relations Board might be authorized to make representations to the Minister in respect of any particular scheme. These proposals would have ensured that coloured applicants were not simply allocated housing which was due to be demolished. At the same time, the Street Report observed that an authority ought not to be prevented (as it is by the 1968 Act) from pursuing a fair policy of reducing or eliminating imbalance between different areas by discriminating in favour of members of a particular minority group. It proposed that such a plan should be submitted to the Race Relations Board, and if it were then approved, the execution of the plan would not constitute unlawful discrimination.

The Street Committee recognized that one gap remained in these proposals. Local authorities might omit from clearance schemes those areas with a dense immigrant population so as to be relieved from the burden of rehousing them. Similarly they might not enforce overcrowding provisions in such areas. However, the Street Report did not consider that it was feasible to devise legal controls to prevent these practices; they had to be left to political accountability. The authors of the Report recognized that their recommendations would entail big innovations in local government practice. But they doubted whether effective control of discrimination in this 'large and critical area of municipal housing' could be achieved merely by outlawing racial discrimination.

The main thrust of the Street Committee's approach was to make the basis upon which local authorities exercised their housing functions more uniform and open to public scrutiny, while giving administrative powers to the Minister and the Race Relations Board.

More recently, the Cullingworth Report has also called attention to the need for a policy of housing coloured people 'which goes beyond a simple ethical statement. . . . Local authorities are responsible elected bodies: their policies must be explicit, publicly stated and defensible, and above all demonstrably fair.' It has warned that

At present, the bad housing conditions of so many coloured people helps to reinforce prejudice against them, and put them at a positive disadvantage in matters of health, education and employment. Typically, these bad conditions exist in the twilight areas of multiple occupation in large cities, and the slums of old industrial towns. They are shared by many more white than coloured families; but coloured families as a whole are far worse off than the average (para. 362).

The Cullingworth Report found that some local authority policies and practices have a discriminatory effect. Coloured people, being largely newcomers, are affected by residential qualifications. Again, because newcomers tend to take furnished accommodation they are particularly affected by an interpretation of rehousing obligations which excludes those in furnished tenancies. These, and similar, generally applicable rules 'have the effect (though not the purpose) of discriminating against coloured immigrants'. Coloured immigrants, like any group from cultural backgrounds which are 'strange' to housing visitors, may also tend to be unfavourably treated. 'This stems from the practice of assessing applicants according to their housekeeping standards: a practice of which we are severely critical'. Coloured people 'will also tend to be ignorant of the "council house system". They may find it incomprehensible and shrouded in mystery. . . . To our minds it underlines the need for better publicity, for better public relations and for a housing advice service.'

In all these matters, the Cullingworth Report rightly realized that coloured people would benefit from the reforms and improvements which it recommended on general grounds: for example, the collection and publication of more information on such matters as housing allocations and make-up of housing lists; the imposition of a statutory duty upon local authorities to publish their methods of selection; the Report's 'major pleas' for more weight to be given to social need; the recommendation that no one should be precluded from applying for, or being considered for, a council tenancy on residential or any other grounds whatsoever; and that the rehousing obligations of local authorities should extend to all households and parts of households irrespective of size or tenure, the reasons for the displacement, or the statutory powers used.

To the extent that these reforms and improvements would make the system of housing allocation more objective, more uniform, more open to review and better known, they would also make the race relations legislation a more effective instrument for removing discrimination against racial minorities. The Cullingworth Report also made one recommendation which would have greatly strengthened the strategic position of the Race Relations Board. It proposed that local authorities should maintain records of coloured residents. Such records would enable an authority to satisfy itself that it was not following policies or practices which led to the very discrimination which it wished to avoid. They would ensure that an authority knows:

Whether coloured people are being helped as they should be, that those who should be on the housing list are, that coloured people are not unintentionally being allocated disproportionate numbers of poorer-quality houses, that maximum dispersal which is compatible with the wishes of coloured citizens is taking place (para. 418).

We would only add that properly kept records would also enable the Race Relations Board to perform its task of securing compliance with the 1968 Act in an area in which the Board now labours under formidable disadvantages. They would give the Board knowledge which is the key to enforcement of the law. As the Cullingworth Report emphasized, the keeping of records does not imply special lists or quotas for the housing of ethnic minorities or immigrants.

Obviously, records can be misused, but the risk of abuse must be taken, for this information is vitally necessary if the statutory prohibition of racial discrimination is to be genuinely enforced. This conclusion has been endorsed by the Board itself (RRB, 1971, Appendix VIII).

Unless and until the main recommendations óf the Street and Cullingworth Reports are implemented by central and local government, the 1968 Act will not 'go beyond a simple ethical statement' in relation to the most important aspects of local authority housing. In the words of the Street Report, 'It is true of several aspects of racial discrimination that effective remedies are of a kind that might usefully be applied for more general purposes.' They would discourage not only racial discrimination but other kinds of unfair treatment of those in need of adequate housing.

Mortgages

Local authorities, building societies and insurance companies provide the vast bulk of mortgage finance for house purchase. Racial discrimination by such bodies on a large scale could have a dramatic effect on the opportunities of racial minorities to become owner-occupiers and there is evidence that such discrimination has been widely practised (PEP, 1967, pp. 78–81). The prospective mortgagee is not, however, in a position to *dispose* of accommodation or land. The prohibition in section 5 (a) against discrimination in relation to disposal cannot affect him. As a person 'concerned with the disposal', however, he may be liable for discriminatory treatment of a person in occupation of accommodation, e.g. by discriminatory enforcement against a mortgagor of the obligations imposed on him by the mortgage deed (s. 5 (b)). The application of section 5 to mortgagees is generally of academic interest only, because institutional lenders must comply with section 2, being 'concerned with the provision to the public or a section of the public . . . of . . . facilities or services'.

Exceptions

Just as the housing provisions of the 1968 Act apply alike to local authority and privately-owned housing, so the exceptions have been drafted without regard to the type of ownership involved. But because of the nature of the various exceptions, in practice they affect only the private sector. That is indeed the justification of the main exceptions – that they omit from the scope of the legislation those areas of the housing market which are so 'private' that the law cannot be effectively applied.

Small premises

This limitation upon the reach of the law is expressed above all in the small premises exception. It is not unlawful to discriminate against any person with respect to the provision or disposal of any residential accommodation in any premises if, at the time of the disposal:

1. The premises are 'small premises'.
2. The person having power to provide or dispose of the accommodation (referred to as 'the landlord') resides and intends to reside on the premises.
3. There is on the premises, in addition to the accommodation occupied by the landlord, 'relevant accommodation' shared by him with other people residing on the premises who are not members of his household (s. 7 (1)).

The exception applies only to residential accommodation. But it can apply to residential accommodation which is provided as a service or facility to the public (and which would, but for the exception, fall within the scope of section 2), e.g. by a hotel or boarding house (s. 7 (5)). It does not, however, exempt discrimination in the letting of commercial tenancies, nor does it affect local authority housing, because the landlord of business premises and the local authority do not reside on their premises. And it applies only if all three conditions are satisfied, each of which must be separately considered.

Premises are treated as 'small premises' in two different situations. The first is where one part of the premises is occupied by the landlord or a member of his family (s. 7 (4)), and other parts are separately let to not more than two other households (s. 7 (2) (a)). The second situation arises where the landlord or a member of his family lives in part of the premises, without separately letting other parts, and makes available residential accommodation on the premises for not more than six people in addition to himself and his household (s. 7 (2) (b)); before 26 November 1970, the number of people in addition to the landlord's household was fixed at twelve instead of six (s. 7 (3)).

e.g. A widow lives on the first floor of her house and lets the ground floor to a family and the second floor to a student. These are small premises, because not more than two households occupy the house, apart from the landlady, under separate lettings. They would not be small premises if there were another floor let separately to a second student.
e.g. A retired married couple run a boarding house. They live there themselves, and have sufficient accommodation for eight guests. The boarding house counts as 'small premises' because there is accommodation for less than twelve people other than the proprietor and his wife.

In the last example, the boarding house is within the definition of 'small premises' because the Act expressly provides that 'residential accommodation' includes accommodation in a hotel, boarding house or similar establishment (s. 7 (5)), and the total number of persons is below the limit. However, it would not be within the exception if the eight people occupied the boarding house not as ordinary paying guests but under separate tenancy or service agreements, for it would then fail to satisfy either the separate letting or the boarding-house category of 'small premises'.

In addition to this requirement, the exception only applies if the landlord or any member of his family[11] lives and intends to continue to live there; and if the landlord shares relevant accommodation with other people living on the premises who are not members of his household. 'Relevant accommodation' means any accommodation other than storage accommodation or means of access. It would include a kitchen, bathroom, lavatory or living room, but not an attic used for storing luggage, or a staircase or corridor.

If all three conditions are satisfied, it is not unlawful for *any* person – whether the landlord himself, his employees, an estate agent or an accommodation bureau – to discriminate in disposing of residential accommodation in the premises. But the exemption applies only to the *disposal* of property; it does not excuse the discriminatory treatment of existing occupiers of small premises who share relevant accommodation with their landlord. It would not enable a landlord

11. The members of the family are defined in section 7 (4).

to allow only his white tenants to hang their washing in the garden. And, as has been seen already, it is in any case unlawful to publish or display discriminatory advertisements or notices relating to the disposal of residential accommodation, whether or not the accommodation itself is exempted from the scope of the 1968 Act.

The 'small premises' exemption places a reasonable limit upon the application of the housing provisions. It recognizes the practical difficulty of attempting to enforce the legislation against the landlord, living in his own home or boarding house, and sharing accommodation with his tenants or paying guests. It is carefully drafted to avoid abuse by landlords who dispose of residential accommodation on a substantial scale. And it complies with the principles contained in the Street Report (see pp. 98–9).

Private transactions by owner-occupiers

It is not unlawful for a person who owns and *wholly* occupies property to discriminate in disposing of the property *unless* he uses the services of an estate agent for the purposes of the disposal, or publishes or displays, or causes the publication or display, of an advertisement or notice in connection with the disposal (s. 7 (7)). A person is an owner-occupier for this purpose if the freehold or leasehold interest in the property is vested in him (s. 7 (8)). He must occupy the whole of the property to come within the exemption, and he must also dispose of the property without either using the services of an estate agent for that purpose, or, for example, advertising or displaying a 'for sale' or 'to let' notice. An estate agent is a person who 'in connection with the disposal' in the course of his trade, business or profession, brings together or takes steps to bring together the owner and the prospective purchaser, or who acts as an auctioneer (s. 7 (8)).

e.g. The owner of a house, which he wholly occupies, sells the house without either advertising the sale or displaying a 'for sale' notice outside the house. It is not unlawful for him to discriminate in effecting the sale.
e.g. The owner of a three-storey house wishes to sell his property. But he cannot give vacant possession of the whole house because a sitting tenant occupies the top floor. He must not discriminate on racial grounds in selling the house because he does not occupy the whole of the premises.
e.g. An owner-occupier engages an estate agent to value his house, but he

does not engage the estate agent to dispose of the property for him, nor to find him a prospective purchaser. After obtaining the valuation, he disposes of the house privately, without advertising for a purchaser. It is not unlawful for him to discriminate in effecting the sale.

e.g. An owner-occupier instructs his solicitor to act on his behalf in finding him a purchaser. He is not entitled to discriminate in effecting the sale, because he is using the services of a person in the course of his profession to bring together or to take steps to bring together the owner and a prospective purchaser.

The owner-occupier exemption was introduced by Parliament during the Committee Stage of the Race Relations Bill (see p. 142) to emphasize the public nature of the disposal of residential accommodation through estate agents or advertising. The Street Committee had been divided about whether the legislation should include sales by owner-occupiers (para. 134), and the exemption was a reasonable compromise (known as the 'Colorado compromise' because it was modelled on the Colorado Fair Housing Statute). It is of very limited application, since the vast majority of sales by owner-occupiers are inevitably negotiated either by an estate agent, or as the result of advertising, or by means of a 'for sale' notice. It would be practically impossible to enforce the law in respect of private transactions which are not negotiated by these means.

Charitable housing trusts and associations

Nothing in the 1968 Act is to be construed as affecting a provision in any charitable instrument which comes into existence after 25 November 1968 (the date upon which the 1968 Act became law) and which confers benefits on persons of a particular race, particular descent or particular ethnic or national origins (s. 9 (1) (a)). And nothing in the 1968 Act renders unlawful any action taken in accordance with the provisions of any charitable instrument which came into existence before 26 November 1968 (s. 9 (1) (b)). It is unlikely that there are any charitable housing trusts or associations in this country whose trust deeds or constitutions require the exclusion of racial minorities from residential accommodation;[12] but, if there are,

12. In the experience of the Charity Commissioners, 'it has been very rare for trusts which have been accepted as charitable to provide for discrimination

the trustees may continue to discriminate on racial grounds to comply with charitable instruments in force before the 1968 Act became law. And new charitable housing trusts may now be created which confer benefits on a particular racial, ethnic or national group, such as people of Jewish, Asian or French descent.

Sleeping cabins

It is not unlawful to discriminate against any person in providing sleeping cabins for passengers on a ship to avoid people of different colour, race or ethnic or national origins being compelled to share a cabin (s. 7 (6)). This provision is included in the list of exceptions 'in the case of residential accommodation', although it has nothing to do with the disposal of housing accommodation. It is an exception to section 2 of the 1968 Act, which prohibits discrimination in the provision of goods, facilities and services, including 'facilities for transport or travél' (see p. 277).

It is one of the oddest exceptions to the scope of the 1968 Act. At Common Law, a shipping company which provides regular passenger services is a common carrier; as such, it has a duty to accept passengers for carriage without discrimination (see p. 63). If a common carrier were to refuse to carry a passenger on the ground that he was coloured and would otherwise have to share a sleeping cabin with a white passenger, there would be a clear breach of this Common Law duty. Yet the 1968 Act, which was introduced to remove racial discrimination makes it not unlawful to refuse to carry a passenger on this blatantly discriminatory ground.

The shipping cabin exemption is also extraordinary because it is in clear conflict with the former provisions of the Race Relations Act 1965, which the 1968 Act was intended to extend and strengthen. Under section 1 of the 1965 Act, it was unlawful to practise discrimination on racial grounds against anyone seeking access to or facilities or services at a place of public resort. A 'vessel . . . used for

---

against any group of people, in the sense of disqualifying them from benefits which are available to the rest of the community. . . . [T]he only case . . . which the Commissioners could find related to a religious disqualification' (David Ennals, M.P. 18 June 1968, *Official Report*, Standing Committee B, col. 587). For the position of discriminatory trusts at Common Law, see pp. 66–7.

the purpose of a regular service of public transport' was expressly included in the definition of places of public resort. So it would have been unlawful under the 1965 Act for a shipping company to refuse sleeping accommodation to someone on a ship engaged in a regular service of public transport, on the ground that he would be sharing with people of a different colour, race or origins.

No complaints seem to have been reported from shipping lines or passengers that the 1965 Act worked oppressively against their interests. The shipping cabin exception is therefore contrary to those provisions of Common Law and statute law which imposed a duty not to discriminate; it is inconsistent with the spirit of the 1968 Act; it is objectionable; and it is apparently not even the result of practical problems which have arisen in the shipping industry.[13]

Disposal of land overseas

It is not unlawful to refuse or omit on racial grounds to dispose of land outside Britain, even though the act of refusal or omission occurred within this country (s. 11 (1) (b)). This exception is unlikely to be of much practical importance, unless the habit of owning a villa or holiday bungalow abroad becomes widespread amongst people in this country.

Evaluation

It is too soon to make a confident evaluation of the effectiveness of the housing provisions when the legislation has been in force for such a brief period of time. But some conclusions can be reached even at this stage.

We suggested earlier in this chapter that four conditions had to be satisfied if the law were to succeed in removing discrimination from the field of housing. The first two conditions related to the coverage of the law: its scope must include all types of residential accommodation, and, although some exceptions are inevitable, they must be narrowly drawn and justified only on strictly practical grounds. In general, the 1968 Act meets those conditions. It applies to all types

13. However, it appears to have been included in the 1968 Act as the result of pressure from the British shipping industry (see pp. 141–3).

of housing, public and private, and the exceptions are drafted with sufficient care to make it unlikely that they will undermine the objectives of the law. The only area in which there is a practical need for improvement concerns the provisions dealing with racial restrictions upon the transfer of tenancies. The present law is too narrow, too timid and too confused to discourage property owners from inserting such restrictions into leases and conveyances, or tenants or purchasers from obeying them. It should be made unlawful to include racial restrictions in any documents relating to the ownership or transfer of property, and all such restrictions should be made completely void.

The serious weaknesses may prove to be not in the scope of the housing provisions but in the powers and functions of the Race Relations Board in enforcing them. The third condition which was suggested was that special powers are necessary to ensure that the law is not thwarted before the statutory machinery is able to investigate allegations of discrimination and, where appropriate, to secure an adequate remedy for the victim. That condition has certainly not been met in the 1968 Act. The Board cannot post a notice on premises or obtain an injunction to prevent an alleged discriminator from selling or letting his property before an investigation has been completed or even begun. And, if discrimination is proved, the Board cannot obtain an order from the court requiring the offending owner to take any positive steps to put right the wrong done to his victim, for example, by selling or letting particular premises to him. The only relief which may be obtained from the court is damages in those rare cases where the victim has suffered a quantifiable loss, and a negative injunction restraining the respondent from breaking the law again in future. The absence of such powers seems certain to disable the Board from combating evasion of the law occurring through speedy transfers of property in the private sector of the housing market.

The final condition for an effective housing law is that special powers must be given to the Board to deal with discrimination in local authority housing. Here again the 1968 Act is seriously inadequate. Local authorities exercise many of their complex housing functions with virtually complete autonomy. Their systems of allocation differ widely and are highly subjective. In the absence of any power in the Board to compel authorities to keep records or provide relevant evidence, it is almost impossible to discover whether there is full compliance with the 1968 Act.

The housing provisions are weakest in precisely those areas of the housing market where they are most needed – in owner-occupied private accommodation and in council housing. They are the most desirable areas; and if racial minorities are excluded from them because of these weaknesses, the law will be left to what will be the impossible task of reducing discrimination in the shrinking twilight areas at the other end of the housing market, where coloured immigrants are now typically housed. Unless the law is capable of being effectively enforced in all areas, it will ultimately be rendered ineffectual in all areas. If discrimination is not removed in the most desirable types of residential accommodation, it surely will not be removed in the least desirable. If discrimination is permitted in housing, it will flourish in education and employment. The Achilles heel of the 1968 Act is the inadequacy of the powers of enforcing its wide provisions. The danger is that it may prove fatal to the working of the legislation in many areas of housing – and so indirectly to the other areas covered by the legislation.[14]

14. This danger was not recognized by the Select Committee on Race Relations and Immigration, which concluded that: 'We find no case for any amendment of the Act as it affects housing while its provisions are not fully used. We recommend that immigrant and other organizations should report incidents of racial discrimination to the Race Relations Board, and that the Board should energetically seek to improve and increase its information about what the Act offers.' (Select Committee on Race Relations and Immigration, 1971, para. 212.) This somewhat complacent exhortation ignored the crucial weaknesses in the Board's powers of investigating the housing field and in enforcing the law, especially in relation to the allocation of local authority housing.

Chapter 7
Goods, Facilities and Services

Scope

The 1968 Act makes it unlawful to discriminate on racial grounds (see p. 153) in providing goods, facilities or services to the public or a section of the public (s. 2). Previously, the 1965 Act had made it unlawful to discriminate on those grounds only in certain specified places of public resort. It did little more than codify and slightly extend the ancient Common Law duty of innkeepers and common carriers to serve all comers without unfair discrimination (see p. 63). Unless a particular place of public resort was specifically referred to in the statutory definition, it fell outside the scope of the 1965 Act; and some anomalous situations arose because the statutory definition was narrow and exhaustive (RRB, 1967, para. 38).

The 1968 Act has replaced the 1965 provision with a much broader, inclusive definition, and so has removed the old anomalies.

Persons concerned

The 1968 Act applies to any person concerned with the provision to the public or a section of the public (whether on payment or otherwise) of goods, facilities or services (s. 2 (1)). It covers those responsible for running a commercial undertaking or a financial institution, a government department, a public corporation or a local authority. And, as with the employment and housing provisions, it applies to the employees or agents of the 'person concerned' (s. 13) and also to anyone who deliberately aids, induces or incites him to do any act of unlawful discrimination (s. 12).

Types of unlawful discrimination
Generally

It is unlawful for any person concerned with the provision to the public or a section of the public (whether on payment or otherwise) of any goods, facilities or services to discriminate against any person seeking to obtain those goods, facilities or services (s. 2 (1)). In this field, as in employment and housing, it is unlawful to discriminate by segregating people racially (s. 1 (2)); or by refusing to provide facilities or services to them; or by providing them with facilities or services on discriminatory terms. It does not matter whether the discrimination is on the ground of the colour or race of the person seeking to obtain or use goods, facilities or services, or on the ground of someone else's colour or race (see p. 161). And, again as in employment and housing, a person will not be liable for discriminating on racial grounds unless the act of discrimination was done intentionally on those grounds, and unless (with the exception of 'inducing or inciting') it was done against a particular person. There must be a causal link connecting those grounds with the discriminatory action, and there must be an actual victim of that action.

e.g. A publican compels a coloured customer to leave his premises. He does so not because the customer is coloured but because he has been behaving in a violent and offensive manner. Obviously the publican has not acted unlawfully.[1]

e.g. Another publican tells a customer in the course of conversation that he will not serve coloured people in the saloon bar. In fact no coloured person has ever attempted to be served in the saloon bar. Again, the publican has not acted unlawfully.

Even where someone is discriminated against on racial grounds by a person concerned with the provision of goods, facilities or services to the public, there will be no liability under section 2 unless the

1. In *Race Relations Board* v. *Lenehan*, the licensee of the Painters Arms public house in Luton and his wife attempted to justify their refusal to serve drinks to five West Indians on the ground that they had previously had trouble with West Indians at other public houses under their management and had thought that one of the five had been a troublemaker. However, Judge Ruttle (Westminster County Court) rejected their explanation and awarded each of the complainants £5 damages for loss of opportunity. Costs were also awarded against the defendants (*The Times*, 23 and 24 June 1971).

discrimination occurs in relation to the provision of those goods, facilities or services.

e.g. The members of a set of chambers refuse, on racial grounds, to allow a coloured barrister to join their chambers. The refusal is not unlawful because fellow-barristers cannot be regarded as a section of the public in relation to the members of the chambers, and also because members of the chambers are concerned to provide their facilities and services to solicitors and lay clients rather than to other barristers seeking to become members of their chambers. Nor can the coloured barrister complain that there has been unlawful discrimination under the employment provisions of the 1968 Act, because the relationship between barristers is not that of employer and employee.

The words 'goods, facilities or services' are not defined in the Act. They must be given their ordinary and natural meaning. 'Goods' are any movable property, including merchandise or wares. 'Facilities' include any opportunity for obtaining some benefit or for doing something. 'Services' refer to any conduct tending to the welfare or advantage of other people, especially conduct which supplies their needs. Each of these expressions is deliberately vague and general; taken together, they cover a very wide range of human activity. The Act lists the following examples of facilities and services to which it refers (s. 2 (2)):

Access to and use of any place which members of the public are permitted to enter.

Accommodation in a hotel, boarding house or other similar establishment.

Facilities by way of banking or insurance or for grants, loans, credit or finance.

Facilities for education, instruction or training.

Facilities for entertainment, recreation or refreshment.

Facilities for transport or travel.

The services of any business, profession or trade or local or other public authority.

It must be stressed that they are only examples. Any facilities or services which are provided to the public or a section of the public are covered by section 2, even if they are not specifically referred to in these examples. However, there is no liability unless the person discriminating on racial grounds is someone 'concerned with the provision to the public or a section of the public' of the goods, facilities or services in question. If a particular form of activity is sufficiently domestic or private it will be outside the scope of this provision. For example, 'No one would regard a party to which only the relatives of the giver were invited as a "public" party.'[2] So, even though the giver of such a party provides facilities for entertainment, recreation and refreshment, he provides them to his relatives or friends rather than to a section of the public. Similarly, someone who lends money to a friend, or who allows him to borrow his car, provides facilities for credit, or for transport or travel, but he is not concerned to provide those facilities to a section of the public.

The test of whether someone is providing goods, facilities or services to the public or a section of the public, or to some narrower category of people is one of fact and degree. It is sometimes difficult to apply the test in borderline cases, but it has to be taken into account in considering each of the specific examples set out in section 2, which will now be discussed.

Places open to the public. If members of the public are permitted to enter *any* place, they must be allowed access to and use of that place without racial discrimination. Whereas the 1965 Act covered only 'places of public resort', i.e. places to which members of the public go habitually or regularly, the 1968 Act applies to any place which members of the public are permitted to enter, even upon a single occasion.

This example includes many types of office, shop or other premises which also come within other examples contained in section 2. It does not matter whether the place in question is private property, so long as members of the public are permitted to enter. They might do so, for example, to attend a public auction in a private house and garden.[3]

Nor does it matter that only a particular section of the public is permitted to enter the place and use the facilities there, e.g. only men, or people more than sixteen years old, or wealthy people or research students. For example a male public lavatory, a public house, an expensive restaurant and a library for graduate studies, respectively

2. *Inland Revenue Comrs* v. *Park Investments Ltd* [1966] Ch. 701 (C.A.) at p. 724, *per* Danckwerts L.J. See also *Tatem Steam Navigation Co. Ltd* v. *Inland Revenue Comrs* [1941] 2 K.B. 194, at p. 203, *per* Scott L.J.; *Morrisons Holdings Ltd* v. *Inland Revenue Comrs* [1966] 1 W.L.R. 553 at p. 573, *per* Pennycuick J.

3. cf. *Sewell* v. *Taylor* (1859) C.B.(N.S.) 160, at p. 164 *per* Earle C.J.

restrict access to and use of their premises to those sections of the public but are within the scope of the example.

However, if the category of people permitted to enter were sufficiently narrow, they would cease to be regarded as a section of the public. For example, the Royal Enclosure at Ascot is not open to the public, or even to a section of the public, because anyone wishing to go there has to apply individually for permission to do so, and is only granted permission after his personal credentials have been closely scrutinized; on the other hand, Tattersalls' enclosure is open to a section of the public, namely those who pay the entrance fee, subject to the gatekeeper's right to refuse entry to a particular individual.[4] The question in every case is whether those in control of the means of access to a particular place exercise a sufficient degree of selection, exclusion and limitation (in a non-racial sense) in relation to people whom they allow to enter their premises, to make such people no longer a 'section of the public'. Obviously, the process of selection, exclusion and limitation must be based on some criterion other than colour or race, for, to argue otherwise, would be to destroy the very purpose of the legislation.

Some places are open to members of the public, but are still not covered by the 1968 Act with respect to all their activities. For example, estate agents and employment exchanges have a general duty not to discriminate in providing their facilities and services; but it is not unlawful for them to discriminate against any person in providing or disposing of residential accommodation in premises which are outside the scope of the 1968 Act (see p. 251), or with respect to employment which is outside the scope of the Act (see p. 207). Even in these exempted situations, they must not, however, discriminate in publishing or displaying discriminatory notices or advertisements (see p. 168).

Hotels and boarding houses. The 1968 Act applies not only to hotels and boarding houses, but also to any 'other similar establishment'. This removes the difficulty which previously arose because the 1965

4. cf. *Glynn* v. *Simmonds* [1952] 2 All E.R. 47 at p. 48 *per* Lord Goddard C.J. (general meaning of 'place of public resort' under section 4 of the Vagrancy Act 1824); *Russell* v. *Thompson* [1953] N.I. 51 (C.A.) at p. 56 *per* Lord Mac-Dermott C.J. (general meaning of 'place to which the public have or are permitted to have access' under section 59 of the Summary Jurisdiction and Criminal Justice (Northern Ireland) Act 1935).

Act included only those hotels which came within the definition in the Hotel Proprietors Act 1956. It was often unclear whether an establishment which described itself as a 'private hotel' fell within that definition (RRB, 1967, para. 38, viii).

Under the 1968 Act any hotel, boarding house, hostel, lodging house or private home providing bed and breakfast to travellers, is covered, unless it comes within the 'small premises' exception (see p. 250). The 'private hotel' will usually be liable because, despite its description, it provides facilities and services to a section of the public. And it seems likely that even a private nurses' hostel or a student hostel would be regarded as within section 2, because the nurses or students are a section of the public.

Banking, insurance and credit facilities. It is unlawful to discriminate in providing facilities by way of banking, or insurance or for grants, loans, credit or finance. This includes the provision of private overdraft facilities, commercial financing, mortgages,[5] hire purchase and credit facilities, local authority grants, and life, theft or fire insurance. However, it is not unlawful to refuse or omit on racial grounds to provide any banking, financial or insurance facilities for a purpose to be carried out, or in connection with risks wholly or mainly arising, outside Britain (s. 11 (1) (ii)). So British insurers could, for example refuse to cover property in a black neighbourhood in a North American city against the risk of fire – though, if they granted cover, they could not do so upon discriminatory terms, because the exception refers only to a refusal or omission.

At the time of its enactment, this provision caused widespread protest in the insurance industry on the ground that it would interfere with the exercise of ordinary 'commercial judgment'. To the extent that insurance risks are assessed by reference to race or colour, it must be conceded that commercial judgment is restricted. But commercial judgment may still be exercised in deciding whether and upon what terms to grant insurance or any other facilities. For example, insurers are entitled to demand a higher premium for motor insurance from drivers who do not speak English, or who are unfamiliar with British motoring conditions, just as they are entitled to demand a

5. Discrimination in the grant of mortgages is, of course, in practice more a problem in the field of housing than in that of public facilities and services (see further at p. 249).

higher premium from sports car drivers, or drivers with bad accident records. What they must not do is to assume that drivers of a particular colour, race, or ethnic or national origin are, by virtue of that fact alone, higher risks than other drivers. It was precisely such an assumption which led to the situation in which Commonwealth immigrants had to pay discriminatory rates to insure their private vehicles, while the same Commonwealth immigrants were being employed as bus drivers in public transport.

The premise upon which this provision, like the rest of the legislation depends, is that racial categories have no uniquely predictive character (see p. 76). One could not accurately predict whether an individual would be a good driver by discovering whether he was coloured. At the present stage of race relations in Britain, a 'coloured' category would include many people who spoke poor English and had only recently arrived in this country, but it would also include people who had been born and educated here. It would therefore be no defence for insurers to produce so-called 'evidence' that coloured drivers were worse risks than white drivers.[6] The 1968 Act is based on the assumption that it is unjustifiable to ascribe collective characteristics to members of a racial, ethnic or national group and to treat them less favourably on those grounds. It does not make any difference that those characteristics are ascribed to them as a result of an investigation or a survey. Insurers, like any other commercial under-

6. During the passage of the 1968 Bill, the Lord Chancellor (Lord Gardiner) made a statement which might be taken to suggest that it would be legitimate to discriminate against coloured people if evidence were produced that they were worse risks than white people. He said that 'it was not intended that the Bill should interfere with the exercise of normal commercial judgment. The life offices do discriminate between one person and another, and they would probably have been insolvent a long time ago if they did not. Therefore they are not expected to do other than exercise normal commercial judgment, provided that the discrimination is based on evidence and not on a mere guess. In the case of one insurance company, it was found that they were basing their rates for coloured people in England on statistics which were applicable twenty-six years ago to Negroes in Tennessee. That does not seem to be sound. But in the absence of evidence they should not assume that coloured people are worse risks than white people.' Third Reading, 16 October 1968 Hansard (H.L.), vol. 296, col. 1355. However, the assumption among insurers that there could be evidence of a collective, racial character was part of the mischief which the legislation was intended to remove.

takings, must not regard colour or race as relevant to the facilities or services which they provide for their customers.[7]

Education, instruction and training. Under this example it would be unlawful to discriminate against anyone by refusing on racial grounds to admit him to a school, college or university; or to grant him an apprenticeship; or to refer him for training under the Industrial Training Act 1964; or by placing him in a racially segregated educational institution or classroom; or by treating a child less favourably at school.

A preparatory school or a public school would be liable for discriminating on racial grounds under this provision. Although such a school is privately owned and provides its facilities only for children who pass its entrance examinations and whose parents are able to pay the fees, the category of parents and children for whom the school provides its facilities is a section of the public protected by section 2.[8] So it is no longer lawful for a public school to maintain a 'Jewish quota', placing a ceiling on the total number of Jewish children who may be admitted as pupils, regardless of whether they are religious or non-practising Jews. On the other hand, it would not be unlawful

7. This approach is also in harmony with the recommendations made by McKinsey & Co., a firm of management consultants commissioned in 1965 to investigate the efficiency of the motor insurance industry on behalf of the British Insurance Association. The McKinsey report stated that the assessment of insurance rates by reference to categories unrelated to motoring risks was a major cause of the industry's financial difficulties. It recommended that greater care should be taken to identify relevant factors affecting the individual driver, and that generalized categories should be avoided.

8. cf. *Commonwealth of Pennsylvania* v. *Brown* 260 F.Supp. 323 (1966), where a United States District Court held that Girard College, a charitable school established by a testamentary trust for the training, education and maintenance of poor white orphans was a 'public accommodation' and an 'educational institution' within the meaning of the Pennsylvania Public Accommodations Act, and that the College was not in its nature 'distinctly private' within the meaning of a proviso excluding places of public accommodation which were in their nature distinctly private. Previous efforts to desegregate the College by relying on the Fourteenth Amendment to the US Constitution had failed, because, although it was 'State action' under the Fourteenth Amendment for a Board appointed under a State statute to refuse admission to Negro boys solely because of race (*Pennsylvania* v. *Board of Trusts* 353 US 230 (1956)) private trustees were later appointed and held to be able to discriminate racially in the valid exercise of their discretion (138 A. 2d 844 (1958)); *cert. denied* 357 US 570 (1958).

for a public school of Christian foundation to limit admission to children of the Christian faith, or to children whose parents were willing to have them taught in the Christian faith. It is the exclusion of Jewish children as an ethnic group which is prohibited by the 1968 Act (see p. 156). The Board has decided in two cases that children were refused admission to private schools not because of their Jewish ethnic origin but on bona fide religious grounds (RRB, 1971, para. 19).

It would also be unlawful to refuse on racial grounds to award a scholarship or other educational grant to someone who was otherwise qualified. However, the Act exempts discriminatory acts done in compliance with the provisions of any charitable instrument which existed before the legislation came into force (26 November 1968), even if those provisions expressly discriminate against coloured people. It also exempts acts done in compliance with any charitable instrument coming into existence after that date and conferring benefits on people of a particular race, descent or ethnic or national origins (but not colour) (s. 9 (1)). Many scholarships and educational grants are likely to be within this exemption if they result from a private bequest, or are administered by a charitable body for the benefit of a particular racial, ethnic or national group.

Some interesting problems arise about the legality of government educational policies under section 2. Until recent years tuition fees were charged to full-time and 'sandwich course' students at universities and colleges of further education on the same basis, whether or not they had come from outside the United Kingdom. In 1966 the Government decided, in an attempt to economize, that from the following year overseas students would, with some exceptions, be required to pay a higher level of fees than United Kingdom students.[9] The Departmental Memorandum on the subject[10] defined overseas students as those who had not been resident and whose parents had not been resident here for at least three years before the start of the course. Although this policy treats overseas students less favourably than United Kingdom students, it appears not to be unlawful, because the basis of the discrimination is length of residence in this

9. Department of Education and Science Circular 27/66 (21 December 1966).

10. Department of Education and Science Administrative Memorandum 14–67 (20 April 1967).

country rather than colour, race, or ethnic or national origins.

Nor is it unlawful for a local education authority to provide educational treatment for children born overseas and needing additional instruction in the English language. Such treatment would not be based on the children's ethnic or national origins but on their educational needs. Indeed, it might be unlawful for a local education authority *not* to provide this special treatment. Local education authorities are required, in fulfilling their duties under section 8 of the Education Act 1944, to have regard to the need for securing that 'provision is made for pupils who suffer from any disability of mind or body by providing either in special schools or otherwise, special educational treatment, that is to say, education by special methods appropriate for persons suffering from that disability.'[11] The inability to read or speak English because of recent arrival in this country might well be regarded as a 'disability of mind' requiring special educational treatment under that provision. Whether or not such treatment should be provided in compliance with the Education Act 1944, it seems clear that if special educational treatment were in fact provided to enable pupils to overcome linguistic problems, it would not violate the 1968 Act.

However, the problem does not end there. In a circular issued by the Department of Education and Science in 1965,[12] local authorities were advised to make special arrangements to teach English to 'immigrant children' with language difficulties. But the circular also recommended a 'dispersal policy' whose legality is highly questionable. The circular stated that:

Experience suggests . . . that, apart from unusual difficulties (such as a high proportion of non-English speakers), up to a fifth of immigrant children in any group fit in with reasonable ease, but that, if the proportion goes over about one-third either in the school as a whole, or in any one class, serious strains arise. It is therefore desirable that the catchment areas of schools should, wherever possible, be arranged to avoid undue concentration of immigrant children. Where this proves impracticable simply because the school serves an area which is occupied largely by immigrants, every effort should be made to disperse the immigrant children around a greater number of schools and to meet such problems of transport as may arise.

11. Education Act 1944, section 8 (2)
12. 'The education of immigrants', Department of Education and Science Circular 7/65 (June 1965) to local education authorities and certain other bodies.

The suggestion, in this statement, that immigrant children should be 'dispersed' even if they have no language problems, and indeed even if they were born in this country, was reinforced by the 1965 White Paper on Immigration from the Commonwealth which stated that a proportion of

above one-third of immigrant children is the maximum that is normally acceptable in a school if social strains are to be avoided and educational standards maintained. Local education authorities are advised to arrange for the dispersal of immigrant children over a greater number of schools in order to avoid undue concentration in any particular school.[13]

Only immigrant children were recommended for dispersal under this policy. No definition of the term 'immigrant pupil' was given, but the definition which was subsequently adopted for statistical purposes included both children of immigrant parents born overseas, who had come to Britain, and children born in Britain to immigrant parents who had arrived within the previous ten years (the date being moved up each year).

A local education authority might have applied this recommended dispersal policy in a way which treated 'immigrant pupils' less favourably on the ground of their colour or origins. Such a policy would be unlawful under section 2.[14] Suppose, for example, that children who

13. 'Immigration from the Commonwealth' (Cmd 2739, 1965, at para. 42); see further Rose *et al.* (1969, ch. 18).

14. The Race Relations Board took this view in dealing with a complaint that the Education Committee of the London Borough of Haringey were proposing to allocate children to secondary schools in the Borough on a racial basis. The Board stated that 'the allocation of children on the basis of "banding" by academic ability could not by itself contravene section 2 of the Race Relations Act 1968. But if the Education Committee were to allocate children on the assumption that all "immigrant" children (or, say, all West Indian children) automatically belonged to any particular ability band because of their race, colour or ethnic or national origin, then they would be acting unlawfully'. However, the particular complaint was outside the Board's jurisdiction because no step had been taken to implement the proposals (*Guardian*, 19 April 1969). The Board also investigated a complaint that the number of West Indian children classified by the Haringey education authority as educationally subnormal was disproportionate to the number of such children in the school population, and that the situation had come about because they had been referred and assessed by reason of their colour of origin. Inquiries did not produce evidence of any unlawful act. But the Board noted that this situation

qualified for admission to a good local comprehensive school were allocated to an inferior secondary school some distance away, solely because they were coloured or born overseas and because more than a third of the existing pupils were coloured or foreign-born. Their dispersal would not be based on their individual abilities or aptitudes, and its effect would be to reduce their educational opportunities.

The possibility that the dispersal policy might be unlawful clearly occurred to the Government during the passage of the 1968 Act. The Race Relations Bill originally contained a clause which provided that nothing in section 2 would 'render unlawful anything which is done in good faith for the benefit of a particular section of the public and which has the effect of promoting integration into the community'. One of the main objects of the clause was to exempt the dispersal policy from the Act.[15] The wording of the clause was dangerously vague; it might, for example, have justified the dispersal of *coloured* children for the benefit of *white* children if it were done in good faith to promote integration. However, the clause was removed from the Bill during the Committee Stage (see p. 138), and the Government did not subsequently restore it before the measure became law. Its absence from the legislation strengthens the view that the dispersal of 'immigrant children' on the basis of their colour or origins would violate the 1968 Act.

The Court of Appeal has also recently given a strong indication that a dispersal policy based on colour or origins rather than educational need would contravene the Education Act 1944. In *Cumings* v. *Birkenhead Corporation*,[16] Lord Denning M.R. rejected the argument that a local education authority were in breach of their statutory

---

had come about because the intelligence tests in general use did not effectively distinguish the educationally subnormal from those whose performance is at a similar level as a result of educational or cultural deprivation. The Board raised the matter with the Department of Education and Science which agreed to discuss the problem with the Community Relations Commission (RRB, 1971, para. 18).

15. 'The sub-section covers the sort of system applied by Ealing with the view to having a not-too-high proportion of any particular group within one school' (David Ennals, M.P., *Official Report*, Standing Committee B, 16 May 1968, col. 206).

16. *Cumings* v. *Birkenhead Corporation* [1971] 2 All E.R. 881 (see also at p. 46).

duties in allocating boy pupils from Roman Catholic primary schools to Roman Catholic secondary schools and those from non-Roman Catholic primary schools to non-Roman Catholic secondary schools regardless of the wishes of their parents, because the Court surmised that there were good educational reasons for the policy. But Lord Denning went on:

if this education authority were to allocate boys to particular schools according to the colour of their hair, or, for that matter, the colour of their skin, it would be so unreasonable, so capricious, so irrelevant to any proper system of education that it would be ultra vires altogether, and this court would strike it down at once. But if there were valid educational reasons for such a policy, as, for instance, in an area where immigrant children were backward in the English tongue and needed special training, then it would be perfectly right to allocate those in need to special schools where they would be given extra facilities for learning English. In short, if the policy is one which could reasonably be upheld for good educational reasons, it is valid. But if it is so unreasonable that no reasonable authority could entertain it, it is invalid.

Admittedly, the extent to which the Court of Appeal was willing to give the benefit of the doubt to the education authority in *Cumings'* case, even at the stage of arguments on preliminary issues of law, shows the reluctance of the courts to interfere with the exercise of local authority discretion in this field. But it gives a clear warning that the courts will intervene, quite apart from the Race Relations Act 1968, in a blatant case where children are allocated to schools on a racial basis.

Despite these legal objections to the validity of the dispersal policy – at any rate if pupils are dispersed on a racial basis – the Department of Education and Science have reaffirmed their advice since the passing of the 1968 Act. Their memorandum to the Select Committee on Race Relations and Immigration stated[17] that:

Dispersal has not been universally welcomed and is adopted by only about a quarter of authorities which have more than 2 per cent of immigrants on their school roll. Its opponents regard it as discriminatory, since in practice only immigrant children are dispersed. The children receive their schooling

17. Memorandum by the Department of Education and Science to the Select Committee on Race Relations and Immigration Minutes of Evidence, 11 February 1969 at p. 151.

away from localities where their families live and where they spend their leisure time. The ability to concentrate teachers especially trained in or attuned to the needs of immigrant children is lessened. But equally there are advantages in dispersal, if the alternative would be predominantly immigrant schools in downtown areas, where older overcrowded premises and staffing problems might add to the disadvantages of largely segregated education. In the Department's view, dispersal is not in all cases appropriate, but it can ease the situation in certain circumstances which local authorities are well-placed to judge. A rigid policy applied from the centre would not only be a derogation of authorities' freedom but would be educationally unsound.

In July 1971, however, the Department published a survey on *The Education of Immigrants* (HMSO, 1971) which showed that they had modified their views significantly on dispersal. The theory that there might be an optimum proportion of immigrant children was abandoned and support for dispersal policies is no longer whole-hearted. At least there is clear recognition that any such policy can only be justified on strictly educational criteria and that dispersal on racial grounds would be in breach of the Race Relations Act 1968. More doubtfully, the Department seek to justify the one-sided character of existing dispersal schemes in which only immigrant children have been dispersed . . . with the assertion that 'It does not follow that indigenous children need also be dispersed as a kind of *quid pro quo* to demonstrate racial equality.' Unless dispersal schemes do in fact demonstrate racial equality they are likely to be in breach of the 1968 Act.

Entertainment, recreation and refreshment. Under this example it would be unlawful to discriminate in a place of entertainment, such as a theatre, cinema or sports ground; or in a place of recreation, such as a dance hall, golf course, swimming bath or bowling alley; or in a place of refreshment, such as a restaurant, cafe or public house.

The fact that any of these places described itself as a club would not by itself exempt it from section 2. The test is whether those responsible for running the club were concerned with providing the club's facilities to a section of the public.

There are several different types of club (Josling and Alexander, 1964). In deciding what is its true nature, the courts look at the substance of the club's activities rather than to its legal form. If a club is loosely run, its 'members' will be regarded as members of the public. For example, in *Panama (Piccadilly) Ltd* v. *Newberry*[18] a club was charged with keeping premises 'for public dancing, music or other public entertainment of the like kind' without a licence. The owners contended that 'the public' were not admitted to the premises. The evidence revealed that, on three days a week, music, singing and dancing were performed on the stage in the club's premises. On each day a reception clerk employed by the club said to members of the public, 'You want to see the show? It's worth the money.' On being asked how much it would cost to go in, the reception clerk said, 'It will cost you 25s. which is membership to the club. The first show is free.' Those who were interested were given a blank membership application form, which they filled in and gave to the clerk. On payment of 25s. for which they received a receipt and a voucher stating that the holder was a guest of the committee, they were admitted. The application form provided for a proposer and seconder but none was asked for and there was no further scrutiny of prospective members. When one member stated that he was already a club member, he was given a membership card and told that he must pay 20s. to see the show.

The court held that there was evidence on which the lower court were entitled to decide that candidates for membership were and remained members of the public. Looking at the reality of the situation, the whole purpose of the application for membership and admission as guests of the committee was to get members of the public to see the show. In the absence of evidence of any selective process, there was no sufficient segregation to make a candidate for club membership acquire the status of a club member or to cease to be an ordinary member of the public.

This case shows that the test is one of fact and degree. And the courts would apply the same test in deciding whether a club came

18. [1962] 1 W.L.R. 610. See also, e.g. *I.R.C.* v. *Eccentric Club Ltd* [1924] 1 K.B. 390 (C.C.A.); *National Sporting Club* v. *Cope* [1900] L.T. 352; *Evans* v. *Hemingway* [1888] 52 J.P. 134; [1962] 1 W.L.R. 610. *Casino de Paris Ltd* v. *Newberry* [1960] *Crim. L.R.* 836; *Gardner* v. *Morris* [1961] 59 L.G.R. 187; *R.* v. *Kane* [1965] 1 All E.R. 705; *Carlisle & Silloth Golf Club* v. *Smith* [1913] 3 K.B. 75 (C.A.); *Harms (Incorporated) Ltd & Chappell & Co. Ltd* v. *Mortons Club Ltd* [1927] 1 Ch. 526 (C.A.).

within section 2 of the 1968 Act.[19] They would take into account the name and formal nature of the club, the type of activities in which it was engaged, documents relating to the club's management and control (e.g. its memorandum and articles of association, constitution and bye-laws, membership application forms, notices and circulars), its description to the public in display signs, posters, newspaper advertisements, brochures and directories, its past history, any licences held by the club, and, above all, how the club was managed in practice.

Where a club is run so loosely that its members remain members of the public, the club would be regarded as within the first example in section 2, i.e. it would be a 'place which members of the public are permitted to enter'. And there is little difficulty in applying the test to a club of this nature. It is really a place of public resort. However, section 2 includes places not only which provide facilities or services to the public at large but also places which provide them to *a section of the public*. These additional words must be given meaning. They are wide enough to apply to a club which restricts its membership strictly to a particular category of people.[20] It is therefore necessary to distinguish, as a matter of fact and degree, between those clubs which are sufficiently private and exclusive to be outside the scope of section 2, and those which, while being properly constituted private clubs, are concerned to provide their facilities to a section of the

19. The United States courts have applied this test to determine whether a particular club is within the scope of anti-discrimination legislation. See *Daniel* v. *Paul* 395 US 298 (1969); *US* v. *Richberg* 398 F. 2d. 523 (1968); *US* v. *Jack Sabin's Private Club* 265 F.Supp. 90 (1967); *US* v. *Clarksdale King & Anderson* 260 F.Supp. 323 (1966); *Castle Hill Beach Club* v. *Arbury* 2 N.Y. 2d. 596 (1957); *Fraser* v. *Robin Dee Day Camp* 210 A. 2d. 208 (1965); *Clover Hill Swimming Club* v. *Goldsboro* 219 A. 2d. 161 (1966).

20. cf. section 6 of the 1965 Act, which creates the offence of incitement to racial hatred and defines 'publish' or 'display' to mean 'publish or display to the public at large or to any section of the public not consisting exclusively of members of an association of which the person publishing or distributing is a member'. In *R.* v. *Britton* [1967] 2 Q.B. 51 (C.A.) Lord Parker L.J. observed (at p. 55) that 'a section of the public not consisting exclusively of members of an association of which the person publishing or distributing is a member connotes the idea of an identifiable section of the public who, but for those words, might be said not to be members of the public at large, in other words members of a club or of an association'.

public. The test is the same as before, but it becomes harder to apply to this intermediate range of clubs.

At one extreme there is the type of club which was exemplified in the *Panama* (*Piccadilly*) *Ltd* case. It is so indiscriminate that it is clearly within section 2. At the other extreme, there is the type of exclusive club which exists to foster social intercourse between people with similar interests and a common background. Candidates for membership of such a club are proposed by existing members to whom they are personally well known. They are elected to membership only if they obtain the support of other members, apart from their proposer and seconder. They may be blackballed by existing members. If they are accepted, they may bring guests to the club only at particular times and on limited occasions. Their guests are usually their relatives or friends. They are forbidden to transact business in the club. The entire ambiance of such a club is private and domestic. The criteria for admission are subjective and personal and depend mainly upon the candidate's social acceptability among the circle of existing members. The club's members and their guests cannot be regarded as a 'section of the public' in their relationship with the club. They are not protected by section 2.[21]

Between these two extremes, of clubs run as a business and which are open to the public at large, and clubs which are socially exclusive, and domestic and private in nature, there are many clubs and private bodies which restrict access to and use of their facilities and services strictly to members and their guests and yet should be regarded as providing their facilities and services to a section of the public within the meaning of section 2. The Royal Automobile Club, the Inns of Court, and various professional institutes and societies are examples of such bodies. They are more 'public' in their activities than the night club or gambling club, and they are less 'private' than the exclusive social club.

Even though these bodies are private and strictly run, they possess two characteristics which make it probable, in the unlikely event that they were to discriminate on racial grounds, that they would be regarded by the courts as within section 2. Firstly, although they are

21. A similar domestic test of the meaning of 'the public' has been adopted by the Courts in several tax cases. See e.g. *I.R.C.* v. *Park Investments Ltd* [1966] Ch. 701 (C.A.); *Morrisons Holdings Ltd* v. *I.R.C.* [1966] 1 W.L.R. 553.

social institutions, they also promote wider objects of a public nature. For example, the Inns of Court control admission to the Bar and exercise disciplinary functions with respect to practising barristers.[22] Similarly, the Royal Automobile Club is concerned with improving motoring conditions throughout Britain. Secondly, the qualifications for membership of these bodies are precisely formulated and membership is open to anyone who satisfies them. The conditions of membership are objective rather than subjective; there is no real scrutiny of the social acceptability of individual applicants for membership. They have a large membership and the only common characteristics of their members are that they satisfy the educational, financial or other stated conditions of entry. The relationship between these bodies and their members remains a relationship with a section of the public despite their undoubtedly private character. They must not refuse access to or use of their services or facilities on racial grounds, nor must they discriminate racially in the manner in which they provide facilities and services to existing members.

In *Race Relations Board* v. *Bradmore Working Men's Club and Institute*, the second case brought by the Board under the 1968 Act,[23] the refusal of the defendants to admit a West Indian employee of the Wolverhampton Telephone Exchange, to their premises was held to be in breach of section 2. The defendants were indisputably a private club, but they had hired out their hall for the annual telephone exchange Christmas party. Tickets were sold to employees and they were allowed to bring any friends and relatives they wished. The complainant, having bought a number of tickets, arrived with her friends to attend the party but was denied admission by club officials. They told her that coloured people were not allowed in the club. The defendants made no attempt to deny that an act of discrimination had been done, but they contended that, as a private club, they were not 'concerned with the provision of any goods, facilities or services to the public or a section of the public', and that the complainant was a 'person seeking to obtain or use those goods, facilities or services'. Furthermore, the telephone exchange party was itself a private one,

22. The Inns of Court would probably also be regarded as organizations concerned with the carrying on of a profession and so would be covered by section 4 of the 1968 Act (see further at p. 185).

23. See *The Times*, 10 April 1970 and R R B 1970 (at p. 48).

in that tickets were available only to employees, their relatives and friends. But the Board argued that the private character of the relationship between the club, its members and their guests, was irrelevant; what mattered was the relationship between the club and those invited to the party. The Birmingham County Court (Judge Nicklin) accepted the Board's argument and held that *vis à vis* the club, the guests, or would-be guests, at the party were a section of the public, and that by hiring out the hall for the purpose of the party, the club were 'concerned' with providing facilities or services to them.

Although this case involved a club, the principle is not peculiar to clubs. Indeed the fact that the defendants were a club is strictly irrelevant. As counsel for the Board pointed out, the club were in the same position as a firm of caterers providing a wedding reception. To the caterers, the guests are a section of the public even though from the host's point of view the party is undoubtedly his private one.

In the *East Ham South Conservative Club* case[24] the court was faced with an especially difficult borderline application of the principle. The Board alleged that the club had acted in breach of section 2, by refusing on racial grounds to admit an Indian Conservative applicant to membership. The club's officers denied that they were concerned with providing facilities or services to a section of the public, rather than to their members. The case was argued on preliminary issues of law. It was assumed that the members of the club consisted wholly or mainly of members of the local Conservative Association, and that, in practice, any member of the Conservative Association who applied to join the club and was eligible under the rules was automatically admitted after going through the necessary formal procedures under the club's rules. However, Judge Herbert rejected the Board's argument that the practice of admitting any member of the Conservative Association made the club a 'person concerned' with providing facilities or services to a section of the public.

An appeal is pending against this decision, and two other cases

24. *Race Relations Board* v. *Charter and others*, Westminster County Court (*The Times*, 7 April 1971).

involving working men's clubs have also been commenced. The Board has stated its belief that

discrimination in working men's clubs, usually in the form of a crude colour bar, is increasing and we consider this to be a most dangerous development. . . . [I]n some towns they play a central part in social life. The speed and institutionalization of a segregated pattern of social life in these towns must have effects beyond mere recreation (RRB, 1971, para. 16).

Transport and travel. It is unlawful to discriminate in providing transport facilities, such as the carriage of passengers or goods by air, ship, rail or road, or in providing travel facilities, such as holiday tours or driving licences. The common carrier of passengers or goods is also liable at Common Law if he discriminates on racial or other capricious grounds (see p. 63).

But there are several exceptions. It is not unlawful to refuse or omit on racial grounds to provide goods, services or facilities, other than travel facilities, outside Britain, or a foreign ship or aircraft (s. 11 (1)). It is not unlawful to discriminate on a British ship or aircraft while in or over the territory of a foreign country in order to comply with the laws of that country (s. 11 (2)) (see p. 225). And it is not unlawful to discriminate against anyone in providing sleeping cabins for passengers on a ship, so as to avoid people of different colour, race or ethnic or national origins being compelled to share such a cabin (s. 7 (6)) (see p. 254). These exemptions could lead to some curious results. For example, they would enable a British shipping agent to charge discriminatory rates in carrying cargo belonging to a coloured customer on British or foreign ships outside Britain, or to provide segregated sleeping cabins for coloured passengers on British ships in British waters (so as to prevent their sharing with white passengers), or to maintain segregated dining facilities on a British ship in South African waters (so as to comply with South Africa's *apartheid* laws).

On the other hand, since there is no exemption for discrimination in providing travel facilities outside Britain on a *foreign* ship or aircraft, it would be unlawful for a shipping agent in this country to refuse on racial grounds to carry a coloured passenger on a South

African ship or aircraft to South Africa[25] (though the passenger might be placed in a segregated sleeping cabin), or to allocate a coloured passenger to segregated dining facilities on a South African ship (even when it was in South African waters).

Commercial, professional and public services. The last example in section 2 is the widest of all. It refers to the services of any business, profession or trade or local or other public authority. The words 'business', 'profession' and 'trade' are broad and overlapping. The expression 'business' is capable of including the practice of a profession;[26] it need not be carried on for a profit;[27] it means 'almost anything which is an occupation, as distinguished from a pleasure – anything which is an occupation or duty which requires attention as a business'.[28] 'Profession' is somewhat narrower, for

before one can say that a man is carrying on a profession, one must see that he has some special skill or ability, or some qualifications derived from training or experience. Even then one has to be very careful, because

25. In December 1969, a complaint was made to the New York State Commission by the State Attorney-General alleging a violation of the Law against Discrimination by South African Airways. It was claimed that black Americans seeking to fly to South Africa were advised by the airline that they were required to have a visa issued by the South African Government, and that black Americans had been denied the required visas without explanation by the South African consulate. Since the airline was operated by the Government, the Attorney-General contended that it could not shift its responsibility for discriminatory practices to the consulate which was an arm of the same Government. The airline had 'in effect, carried the apartheid policy of South Africa to the doorsteps of our own State' (*The Times*, 8 December 1969). Since a visa is plainly a travel facility, it is arguable that similar conduct in this country would contravene the 1968 Act. The Board is in the process of investigating a complaint by a Jamaican-born British subject that, although he had been given permission to settle in Australia, the Australian authorities had refused, on unlawful grounds, to grant him an assisted passage. The Assisted Passages Scheme is based on an agreement between the British and Australian governments to 'cooperate to assist suitable persons in the UK to proceed to Australia for permanent settlement'. The Board has been pursuing its inquiries with the Australian authorities through the Foreign and Commonwealth Office (RRB, 1971, pára. 32).

26. *Re Williams Will Trusts* [1953] Ch. 138, at p. 141 *per* Danckwerts J.

27. *South-West Suburban Water Co.* v. *St Marylebone Guardians* [1904] 2 K.B. 174 at p. 180, *per* Buckley J.

28. *Rolls* v. *Miller* [1884] 27 Ch.D. 71 (C.A.) at p. 88 *per* Lindley

there are many people whose work demands great skill and ability and long experience and many qualifications who would not be said by anybody to be carrying on a profession.[29]

Ultimately, a profession must be defined in terms of the current usage of the ordinary reasonable man. 'Trade' is

a term of the widest scope. It . . . indicates a way of life or an occupation. In ordinary usage it may mean the occupation of a small shopkeeper equally with that of a commercial magnate. It may also mean a skilled craft. It is true that it is often used in contrast with a profession. A professional worker would not ordinarily be called a tradesman, but the word 'trade' is used in the widest application in the appellation 'trade unions'. Professions have their trade unions.[30]

Discrimination with respect to membership of organizations 'concerned with the carrying on of trades, businesses, professions or occupations' is dealt with elsewhere under the 1968 Act (section 4; see p. 185).

Section 2 is concerned with discrimination in relation to the public or a section of the public. There may be instances of discrimination which fall between these two types of unlawful conduct and which are outside the scope of the 1968 Act. For example, a firm of insurers who refused to do business with a coloured broker but were willing to grant insurance facilities to coloured customers might succeed in persuading the court that brokers were not a section of the public under section 2; similarly, a builder might refuse to work with a coloured architect and contend that the architect was not a section of the public. However, it is at least arguable that the broker's customer or the architect's client who would plainly be a member of the public, could complain under the 1968 Act if he suffered as a result of racial discrimination against the broker or architect, for he would be the victim of discrimination on the ground of colour or race, though not of his colour or race.

Where a business, profession or trade discriminates in relation to employment or the provision of residential accommodation, it does not act unlawfully (except in advertising) if the situation is one which

29. *Carr* v. *I.R.C.* [1944] 2 All E.R. 163 (C.A.) at p. 166 *per* du Parcq L.J.
30. *National Association of Local Government Officers* v. *Bolton Corporation* [1943] A.C. 166 (H.L.) at p. 184 *per* Lord Wright.

is within the employment and housing exemptions to the 1968 Act. For example, it is not unlawful for an employment agency to discriminate in selecting workers for employment, before 26 November 1972, in a firm employing not more than ten people, or in selecting someone for employment in a private household (see p. 207); and it is not unlawful for an estate agent or a solicitor to discriminate in the course of selling or letting excepted 'small premises' (see p. 250).

Special considerations apply to professional services. Many professions are subject to statutory control, and most or all professions are governed by codes of professional conduct. Although there does not appear to be any professional code which specifically forbids racial discrimination,[31] it would presumably be regarded as unethical and unprofessional these days for anyone to discriminate on racial grounds, and complaints could be made to the appropriate disciplinary body in addition to a complaint to the Race Relations Board.

This example in section 2 also refers to the services of a local or other public authority. The meaning of 'local authority' is obvious, and would include county councils, municipal corporations and other local authorities within the Local Government Act 1933, as well as the Greater London Council set up under the London Government Act 1963. A 'public authority' is a body which has public or statutory duties to perform, and which performs those duties and carries out its transactions for the benefit of the public and not for private benefit.[32] Since the 1968 Act expressly binds the Crown (s. 27 (1)), it is not necessary, as it was under the 1965 Act, to draw the difficult distinction between those public authorities which are servants or agents of the Crown, and those which are sufficiently independent of the

31. The British Medical Association subscribes to the International Code of Medical Ethics, which is embodied in the Declaration of Geneva made by the World Medical Association in 1947. The Declaration contains the statement: 'I will not permit considerations of religion, nationality, race, party politics or social standing to intervene between my duty and my patient.' ('Medical ethics', BMA publication p. 2). In 1966, the Professional Purposes Committee of the Law Society expressed the opinion that it would be improper for a solicitor to refuse instructions from a prospective client merely on the grounds of race, colour or creed (Bindman, *Law Society Gazette*, February 1969, p. 103). Several other professional bodies have stated, in correspondence with one of the authors, that it would be regarded as contrary to professional ethics to discriminate on racial grounds.

32. *Halsbury's Laws* (3rd edn), vol. 30, p. 682.

Crown to be regarded as bound by the 1968 Act.[33] So, the British Transport Commission, the employment exchanges maintained by the Department of Employment and Productivity, National Health Service hospitals, and the many different industrial, commercial and social service corporations are all bound by section 2 in providing their services to the public.

The position of the police under section 2 merits separate discussion. It is obviously especially important for the police to win the confidence of racial minorities, as North American experience all too clearly illustrates. But it seems indisputable that, 'at least in certain areas, an attitude of suspicion and mistrust has grown up between the police and the immigrant community' (Rose, *et al.*, 1969, pp. 349–66, 722–7). The 1968 Act provides a limited form of redress for the citizen who alleges that he has been discriminated against on racial grounds by a police constable, because circumstances may arise in which a complaint may be made against a police constable, or the police authority which has appointed him, of discrimination under section 2.

A constable is a public servant, whose functions of keeping the peace, detecting crimes and apprehending offenders are exercised on behalf of the whole community. But the police sometimes provide services for a particular section of the public or for an individual.[34] For example, they may be asked to help someone to trace a missing relative, or to provide special protection, or to guide a traveller to his destination. There are also situations in which they may provide 'special police services' outside their normal duties, such as controlling a crowd of spectators (or demonstrators) at a football or cricket match, for which they may charge a fee.[35] If a constable were to discriminate on racial grounds in providing these services, a complaint could be made by the victim under section 2.[36]

33. For examples of the anomalies which arose because the 1965 Act did not bind the Crown see RRB (1967, para. 38 (vii)).

34. cf. *Glasbrook* v. *Glamorgan C.C.* [1925] A.C. 270 (H.L.); *Receiver for Metropolitan Police District* v. *Croydon Corporation* [1957] 2 Q.B. 154 (C.A.)

35. Under the Police Act 1964, section 64.

36. Although a police constable is regarded at Common Law as an independent officer, not employed as the servant of the borough, the state or anyone else, the 1968 Act provides that, for the purposes of the Act, the office of constable shall be treated as if it were employment and a constable shall be treated as if he were

However, it would not be unlawful under the 1968 Act for a constable to arrest someone, or to prosecute him, or to assault him, because of his colour, race or origins. Nor is it an offence under the police disciplinary code to display racial prejudice or to act in a discriminatory fashion. The victim of such treatment, like anyone else, may seek an inquiry into his allegations under the Police Act 1964, or may bring Common Law proceedings for false arrest, malicious prosecution, or trespass to the person. The present machinery for dealing with complaints of police misconduct has frequently been criticized. It raises problems far beyond the field of race relations and needs to be tackled outside the framework of the 1968 Act. However, there is no doubt that if better procedures were devised, they would be especially beneficial in improving relations between the police and the coloured community.[37]

Other aspects of the administration of justice might also give rise to complaints under section 2. The courts and the various welfare and other administrative tribunals are undoubtedly public authorities. In much of their work the judges and their officers are concerned to provide a service to a section of the public, namely, the parties to proceedings before them, and so would seem to be within the scope of section 2, if they discriminated on racial grounds.

---

employed by the authority by whom he is appointed (s. 27 (4)). Hence, any unlawful act done by a police constable would be treated as having been done by the relevant police authority, if within the scope of his duties (s. 13 (1)) (see further at p. 181).

37. 'There is no more crucial area for immediate action than to review the mechanism for handling complaints against the police; any lasting improvement through training, recruitment and improved structures for community relations will wait upon action in this field. . . . [A] system of internal review, regardless of its fairness, cannot generate sufficient confidence; and confidence is fundamental to good relations with the coloured communities and with the community at large. . . . We therefore recommend that a select committee of inquiry be appointed to examine procedures for the handling of complaints against the police. . . . We also recommend that the Home Secretary should include in police disciplinary regulations a special category of offence of racial discrimination. This would officially recognize that prejudiced behaviour undermines the basis of trust and integrity upon which good policing depends, and declare within and without the police force that discriminatory behaviours will not be tolerated' (Rose *et al.*, 1969, pp. 725–6).

But it has been clearly established for centuries that persons exercising judicial functions in a court are exempt from all civil liability for anything done or said by them in their judicial capacity.[38] And no action can be brought against the Crown in respect of acts or omissions of persons discharging responsibilities of a judicial nature or in connection with the execution of the judicial process.[39] The ground of this rule is public policy, and the immunity applies to any authorized inquiry, whether before a court of law or before a tribunal which has similar attributes.[40] So no complaint could be made under the 1968 Act alleging that a judge or the members of any judicial tribunal had discriminated on grounds of colour, race, or origins in reaching a decision, although if such an allegation were proved it would no doubt result in a successful appeal to a superior court.

On the other hand, the immunity applies only to judicial proceedings, as contrasted with administrative or ministerial proceedings; and, where a person acts both judicially and also administratively or ministerially, the protection is not afforded to acts done in the latter capacity.[41] For example, the act of hearing and determining a case is a ministerial act, and a refusal, even by a judge of a superior court,[42] to try a case may be actionable, whereas a wrong decision is not actionable.[43] Similarly, where magistrates made an order in their judicial capacity, and later carried it out in their administrative capacity, through their servants, the negligence of their servants was held to be actionable.[44]

To take a far-fetched example, if the officers of a Rent Tribunal were to refuse to provide application forms or to give general information to a landlord or tenant solely on racial grounds, their conduct would be unlawful under section 2; but if the Tribunal were racially biased in its decision, there would be no redress under the

38. *Halsbury's Laws* (3rd edn), vol. 30, para. 1351.
39. Crown Proceedings Act 1947, section 2 (5).
40. *Royal Aquarium & Summer and Winter Garden Society* v. *Parkinson* [1892] 1 Q.B. 431 (C.A.).
41. *Halsbury's Laws* (3rd edn), vol. 30, para. 1354; *Royal Aquarium & Summer and Winter Garden Society* v. *Parkinson*, above at p. 453, *per* Lopes L.J.
42. *Ferguson* v. *Earl of Kinnoull* (1842) 9 Ch. & Fin. 251 (H.L.).
43. *White* v. *Hislop* (1838) 4 M & W 73.
44. *Hardy* v. *North Riding Justices and Yeomen* (1886) 50 J.P. 663.

1968 Act though the victim could, of course, appeal to the High Court under the ordinary law.

Similarly, a coloured person who was otherwise qualified might well be able to complain under the 1968 Act if he were excluded from jury service on racial grounds,[45] but it would not be unlawful under the 1968 Act for a court to take into account a person's origins in sentencing him, although it might be a ground of appeal to a superior court.[46]

There are many other public authorities, such as the various welfare services, and planning and licensing bodies, which exercise purely administrative functions without any judicial element. Where they are concerned, in exercising those functions, with providing facilities or services to a section of the public, they are bound by section 2 not to discriminate on racial grounds. To take a simple example, an exam-

45. In May 1969, a complaint was made to the Race Relations Board regarding the deliberate and systematic exclusion of Asian residents from the jury lists in Bradford. No Asian name had appeared on the Electoral Register marked with the customary 'J' for the preceding ten years. As a result of Home Office intervention the Town Clerk of Bradford announced that the practice would be discontinued. He stated that 'Apparently this has been the practice in Bradford for some time. . . . I think there has been a misguided ruling here which has been going on for many years' (*Race Today*, July 1969). In October 1969, an appeal was dismissed against the refusal of a Sessions Judge to allow counsel to cross-examine jurors to see whether they had any racial prejudices. The defendant, who was born in Jamaica, had been convicted of driving while disqualified. Cantley J. stated, in dismissing the appeal, that in some jurisdictions the practice of cross-examining jurors about their racial prejudices obtained, 'but it has never obtained in this country and there is no foundation in law for introducing it'. The chairman of the Sessions Court had allowed steps to be taken so that the jury included a coloured man. 'He went as far as he was required,' stated Cantley J., and there was no foundation to the complaint that the chairman was hostile to the defendant (*Guardian*, 3 October 1969). In September 1969, it was reported that the Lord Chancellor had informed the chairman of a Leeds bench of magistrates that he had made an 'error of judgment' in excluding a coloured woman magistrate from consideration of whether a white person should be granted bail. The Lord Chancellor's letter stated that it was not uncommon for a magistrate to be asked not to take part in a decision, if there was a risk that the accused might think that the magistrate was in some way prejudiced. But it was absolutely wrong to do so on the grounds of colour, religion or sex (*The Times*, 3 September 1969).

46. See e.g. *R*. v. *Byfield*, *The Times*, 19 April 1967, where the Court of Appeal took an 'exceptional course' in reducing the sentence imposed on a Jamaican for

iner appointed by the Minister of Transport to test the driving competence of an applicant for a driving licence is mainly concerned to protect the public at large from unsafe drivers. But the driving test is also a privilege or benefit enabling someone to obtain the right to drive a motor vehicle on the highway. Just as obtaining a theatre ticket or taking an examination is a 'facility' for entertainment or education, so taking a driving test is a facility for travel; it is a necessary incident of obtaining the benefit of a driving licence. The examiner performs an administrative rather than a judicial function in carrying out the driving test, so it would be unlawful for him to reject candidates on racial grounds. And the existence of a right to apply to a Magistrates' Court for a determination whether a driving test has been properly conducted in accordance with the regulations,[47] would not prevent a candidate from complaining to the Race Relations Board. There are several situations which are covered by the 1968 Act, although the victim of alleged racial discrimination could have resort to another remedy, and nothing in the 1968 Act affects the right to bring civil or criminal proceedings which might have been brought if the Act had not been passed (s. 19 (10)). However, if a candidate were to apply unsuccessfully to a Magistrates' Court, he could not then complain to the Race Relations Board about the Magistrates' decision, because of their judicial immunity.

Finally, there is one blanket exemption which could be relevant to the application of section 2 to public authorities. Nothing in Part I of the 1968 Act (i.e. including section 2) renders unlawful any act of racial discrimination which is done for the purpose of safeguarding

---

having unlawful sexual intercourse with a girl aged fourteen and a half. The appellate court seemed to take account of the origins of the accused. Salmon L.J. stated that 'Whatever the custom in Jamaica, in this country it is a criminal offence to have sexual intercourse with any girl under sixteen, however developed she may be and however eager she may seem. The law of this country must be obeyed.' But he also stated that, in considering the gravity of the offence it was important to bear in mind that the girl came from a place where girls of her age reached maturity, and perhaps greater maturity than English girls of seventeen or eighteen. Although in sentencing the appellant the Recorder was correct in saying that seducing young girls was not the right thing to do, whether it was common in Jamaica was another matter.

47. Road Traffic Act 1960, section 99 (3). See also Motor Vehicle (Driving Licences) Regulations 1963.

national security; and a certificate signed by or for a Minister of the Crown certifying that an act was done for that purpose is conclusive evidence of that fact (s. 10). Although government departments are likely to invoke this exception only rarely, it is couched in such wide terms that, in theory, it could be used to excuse many types of racial discrimination by public bodies.

Part Three

Chapter 8
The Process of Conciliation

Generally

The key to the enforcement of the Race Relations Acts is the process of conciliation. The strategy on which it is based is one of controlled escalation. The Acts provide for administrative machinery to investigate allegations of discrimination; to endeavour to secure compliance with the law; and to resolve disputes between the alleged discriminator and his victim; and, where conciliation fails to achieve a voluntary settlement, to bring civil proceedings in the courts. The process moves stage by stage from the initial investigation to attempted negotiations, and from negotiations to the courts. Judicial proceedings are the ultimate deterrent, intended to carry sufficient credibility so that the need to resort to them should be rare.

The conciliation machinery had dual functions. It has to remove the public wrong of discrimination, which is an offence against the well-being of the community; and it has to remedy the private wrong done to the victim of discrimination. Conciliation, despite the pacific flavour of the word, is not a soft alternative to the enforcement of the law; it is itself a method of law enforcement. But it is an essential element in the rationale of the statutory procedures that they seek to achieve compliance with the law without unnecessary litigation. For this reason, Parliament has adopted a technique which is almost without precedent in our civil law, by entrusting an administrative agency with the sole right to bring proceedings for breaches of the law. But for this, an individual complainant might otherwise resort to litigation without first attempting to settle his differences by private negotiations. As it is, he is compelled to use the statutory machinery which has complete discretion in deciding whether to take his case to court.

This method of enforcement has been incorporated into the

legislation as the result of United States' experience (see p. 99). It was first used in Britain in the Race Relations Act 1965, which created the Race Relations Board and local conciliation committees, but entrusted to the Attorney-General the responsibility for bringing civil proceedings where conciliation failed to secure compliance with the law. The 1968 Act enlarged the functions of the conciliation process from being concerned only with removing a public wrong to the further task of securing redress for the individual victim of the wrong; and the 1968 Act also transferred responsibility for bringing proceedings from the Attorney-General to the Race Relations Board (see chapter 3).

The Board's dual role in securing compliance with the law without unnecessary litigation, and at the same time seeking an adequate remedy for the individual victim is difficult to combine and perform with equal vigour and effect. It means that the Board has to enlist the cooperation of those against whom complaints are made, without losing the confidence of complainants by sacrificing their interests for the sake of easy compromises. The Board's work is made more difficult by the fact that it alone has the right to bring proceedings in the courts. The complainant who is convinced that he is the victim of discriminatory conduct, but who is denied a judicial hearing because the Board refuses to proceed with his case, may all too easily mistrust the Board's actions. He cannot appeal and his resentment may breed cynicism about the Board's work and the value of the law.

In short, the conciliation process can only function properly if the Board can skilfully use the carrot of conciliation and the stick of judicial remedies. Unfortunately, conciliation, which is the essence of effective enforcement of the legislation, is not reinforced by a strong stick. As will be apparent later, the Board has not been given the wide range of powers possessed by the American administrative agencies which originally developed the conciliatory technique, nor can it obtain from the courts the variety of remedies against a wrongdoer which are available in the United States.

The machinery of conciliation

The engine which drives the conciliation machinery is the Race Relations Board created by the 1965 Act, and reconstructed by the 1968 Act. The Board originally consisted of a chairman and two members, and its functions were limited to appointing local conciliation committees, and considering complaints of discrimination which the local committees had been unable to resolve.

Under the 1968 Act, the Board now consists of a full-time chairman (Sir Geoffrey Wilson, K.C.B., C.M.G), ten part-time members appointed by the Home Secretary,[1] and a staff of civil servants appointed by the Board.[2] Its general functions are to secure compliance with the provisions of Part I of the 1968 Act (i.e. those defining unlawful discrimination) and to resolve differences arising out of those provisions (s. 14 (1)).

The Board's functions have been greatly expanded. It retains the duty to appoint conciliation committees to help the Board to discharge its functions locally (s. 14 (5)). But it no longer delegates the investigation and conciliation of all complaints to its local committees. It retains a parallel jurisdiction to deal with complaints itself, and the allocation of complaints as between the Board and its committees is a matter entirely for the Board's discretion.

If the Board suspects that anyone has been discriminated against unlawfully, it may also investigate the matter upon its own initiative, even though there has been no formal complaint (s. 17 (1)). And it is now for the Board rather than the Attorney-General to decide whether to bring proceedings in the courts and to conduct those proceedings (ss. 15 (5) and 19 (1)). The Attorney-General plays no part in enforcing the anti-discrimination provisions; but he does retain the sole right to prosecute cases of incitement to racial hatred under section 6 of the 1965 Act (see chapter 10).

In March 1970, there were sixty-eight members of the Board's Staff. At its London headquarters[3] there were the chief conciliation

1. Section 14 (2). The other members of the Board are Sir Roy Wilson, Q.C., Mr Louis Freedman, Mr Leslie Blakeman, Miss Agnes Patrick, Mr T. S. Roberts, Mr W. Simpson, Mr Mota Singh, Mrs Lena Townsend, Mr M. Rafiq Malik and Miss Elizabeth Steel. Sir Roy Wilson was acting Chairman from 1 January 1971, when the former Chairman Mr Mark Bonham Carter became Chairman of the Community Relations Commission, until Sir Geoffrey Wilson took office on 1 November 1971. A successor has not yet been appointed for the late Lord Constantine, who was a member of the Board from its inception until his death in July 1971.

2. See generally as to the constitution of the Board and Conciliation Committees, RRA, schedule 1.

3. 5 Lower Belgrave Street, London S.W.1.

officer (Mr John Lyttle), the Secretary of the Board, three principal conciliation officers, three conciliation officers, the principal information officer, an information officer and a temporary assistant information officer, a research officer, an assistant research officer, and seventeen executive clerical and typing staff (RRB, 1970, para. 81). Subsequently, Mr Lyttle was given overall responsibility for all the Board's business and his post designated 'Chief Officer and Secretary to the Board'. His deputy, Mr Tom Connelly was appointed Chief Conciliation Officer (RRB, 1971, para. 84). The Board has no legal staff, but a member of a firm of solicitors acts as part-time legal adviser.

The Board has appointed nine conciliation committees (RRB, 1971, para. 4, Appendices II, III). Three cover the Metropolitan area and the others are responsible for Scotland, Wales, the North-West, the West Midlands, Yorkshire,[4] and the East Midlands. Every part of Great Britain comes within the jurisdiction of one of these committees. There is a local office for each committee,[5] manned by at least one conciliation officer employed by the Board, together with secretarial staff. The local conciliation officer acts as secretary of his conciliation committee. The local office is maintained both for the conciliation committee and the Board. By far the largest number of complaints have so far come from London and the South-East; next the West Midlands; fewest of all from Scotland.

The Chairman is the only member who devotes his services full-time to the Board. The other members attend its regular monthly meetings, as well as the meetings of any of the Board's Committees on which they happen to serve. Some months after its appointment, the Board's proposed arrangements for discharging its functions were approved by the Home Secretary as required by the Act (s. 14 (3)). Under these arrangements, an Employment Committee and a General Committee have been set up, each consisting of members of the Board, to whom the Board has delegated some of its duties.[6]

4. In 1969 the North-East committee was merged with the Yorkshire Committee because it appeared that there was insufficient need for two separate committees in that part of the country.

5. The three metropolitan committees all function from the same office which is at the same address as the Board's headquarters. The Welsh committee includes members from South-West England and offices are maintained in Bristol and Cardiff.

6. Such delegation is authorized by section 14 (4). The Committees were

The Board retains the general responsibility for its administrative policy. It appoints members of its own staff and conciliation committees, and organizes information and research services. It considers regular reports about the operation of the conciliation committees, and it receives reports from the Employment and General Committees at its monthly meetings. The Board itself makes an annual report to the Home Secretary (s. 14 (7)). Normally, it is the Board which decides whether to commence proceedings in the courts, but, between Board meetings, a legal committee, consisting of the Chairman of the Board and the Chairmen of the Employment and of the General Committees, may take this decision.

The Employment and General Committees consider complaints which have been allocated to the Board rather than to a conciliation committee for investigation. At present, certain classes of complaint are regularly allocated to the Board, i.e. complaints against the Crown, those concerning insurance, local authorities, housing, children in LEA schools and the police (RRB, 1970, para. 11). The Board sometimes deals with other cases raising especially novel or complex issues, or matters of particular public importance. Its ultimate intention is to deal only with complaints which have some special features about them, and to refer the rest to conciliation committees.

The Board's two main committees also consider whether to initiate investigations under section 17, (p. 311) where unlawful conduct is suspected but no specific complaint has been made. And the Employment Committee has the further function of considering appeals from voluntary industrial machinery in employment cases.

The work of the conciliation committees is similar to their previous

---

appointed at the new Board's first meeting in December 1968, and began to function immediately. However, the Home Secretary did not give his formal approval to these arrangements until 12 March 1969. The hiatus created a legal problem which will not arise again. In *Race Relations Board* v. *Geo. H. Haigh & Co. Ltd* the defendants argued that the General Committee was not validly constituted under the 1968 Act until the Home Secretary's approval had been given, and that as a result the Committee's actions before the date of his approval (which included forming the opinion that the defendants had acted unlawfully in the disposal of housing accommodation) were invalid. This argument was accepted by the Leeds County Court in proceedings brought by the Board (see further, pp. 234–5).

role under the 1965 Act. But their relationship with the Board has changed. Previously, the conciliation committees were exclusively responsible for the process of conciliation, and the Board organized and supervised their work, referring appropriate cases to the Attorney-General. Now, the Board has the main function of securing compliance with the law and the conciliation committees are set up to help the Board to discharge its function. The Board alone may now bring proceedings in the courts where conciliation fails.

The change in the relationship of the Board and the conciliation committees has made little practical difference. Because of the much wider scope of the 1968 Act, new members have been appointed to conciliation committees with knowledge of the fields covered by the legislation. But the actual process of investigation and conciliation has not much altered. The one significant difference between the activities of the old and the new conciliation committees is that, as the Board's staff of conciliation officers has increased in number and expertise, so more of the work of investigation has passed from committee members to the professional staff. The committees are now mainly concerned with considering written statements and documentary evidence rather than with interviewing witnesses. They usually have direct contact with the parties only if the latter accept an invitation to make oral representations to a committee. But despite this change in the nature of their work, the conciliation committees and the Board's Employment and General Committees still carry out the crucial duty of forming an opinion whether or not unlawful discrimination has occurred. The professional staff take statements and assemble the evidence, but it is the committee which ultimately has to form the opinion, not the professional staff.[7]

7. On 1 April 1971 there were eighty-one members of conciliation committees. Hepple (1970, p. 204), has analysed the occupations of those who were conciliation committee members on 1 April 1969. 'Over-all,' he says 'the committees have a very strong professional middle-class bias.' Of the eighty-four members of local conciliation committees at 1 April 1969, the best-represented occupational group was managers and businessmen (eighteen) followed by trade union officers (eleven), practising lawyers (nine), social workers (eight) and school teachers (seven). There were eighteen members in other miscellaneous professional groups (such as medicine and the clergy) and four in miscellaneous jobs. Some fourteen of the eighty-four members appeared to belong to coloured minority groups. The pattern has not significantly changed since 1969.

The Board may appoint as assessors to assist the Board or its committees persons appearing to the Board to have special knowledge and experience of circumstances which are relevant to an investigation (s. 18). The Board has done so on four occasions. In one case the Factory Inspectorate provided a report on the working of a particular type of industrial boiler; in another case a member of the Institute of Photographers provided a report; in the third case a solicitor was nominated by the Law Society to assist in the investigation of a complaint against a solicitor; in the fourth case, the Vice-Chairman of the Hairdressing Council reported on submissions that there were differences in Asian and Negroid hair which justified a differential charge for hair-cutting.[8] Clearly, it would be open to the Board to call an assessor to give expert evidence in any subsequent legal proceedings (see p. 329).

The Board and its conciliation committees deal with all non-employment complaints under the 1968 Act. But where a complaint relates to employment, or to a trade union or an employers' association, and suitable voluntary industrial machinery exists to deal with it, the complaint is investigated in the first instance by the voluntary machinery rather than by the Board's machinery. The Secretary of State for Employment and Productivity decides whether there is suitable voluntary machinery to deal with a particular complaint, and all employment complaints are automatically referred to that Minister as soon as they have been received by the Board or a conciliation committee. If the Secretary of State decides that there is no suitable voluntary machinery to investigate a particular complaint, the complaint is referred to the Board by the Secretary of State to be investigated by the Board or a conciliation committee.[9]

This special procedure for dealing with employment complaints has been grafted on to the normal procedure of investigation and conciliation, to give industry the chance to settle a dispute as quickly as possible. But the combined effect of the normal procedure and the special employment procedure is complicated, and will be described later.

Before turning to the processes of conciliation, one other piece of machinery, created by the 1968 Act, should be briefly referred to. The

8. RRB, 1970, para. 18, RRB, 1971, para. 33 and Appendix V, case 4.
9. See section 16 (1) and schedule 2.

Community Relations Commission has been set up (a) to encourage 'harmonious community relations' and to coordinate on a national basis the measures adopted for that purpose by others; and (b) to advise the Home Secretary on any matter referred to the Commission by him and to make recommendations to him on any matter which the Commission considers should be brought to his attention (s. 25 (1) and (3)). 'Community relations' means 'relations within the community between people of different colour, race or ethnic or national origins' (s. 28 (1)). The Commission controls a network of local community relations committees which work in cooperation with local authorities on various aspects of community relations. However, these local committees must not be confused with the conciliation committees of the Race Relations Board. The Commission's work is intended to complement the Board's functions by improving community relations generally. But the Commission and its local committees do not deal directly with complaints of unlawful discrimination, and so are not part of the machinery of conciliation. They are therefore outside the scope of this book.

Making a complaint

The Board and its conciliation committees have a duty to receive any complaint which is made to them within two months of the act complained of, or, if the Board thinks that 'special circumstances' warrant its late reception, after the two-month period has expired (s. 15 (2)). The Board has complete discretion to decide the special circumstances in which it will receive late complaints. Two months is a very short period in which to require someone to make a complaint.[10] It may only gradually occur to him that he has been treated unlawfully; he may not know his legal rights; he may initially feel too humiliated or embarrassed by his experience to wish to seek the Board's help. So although it is essential for a complainant to act quickly if he believes himself to be the victim of unlawful discrimination, the Board is not

10. US anti-discrimination statutes impose limitation periods varying from sixty days to one year. The Street Report recommended (at para. 147.1) a limitation period of six months 'both because the defence by the alleged discriminator is rendered difficult after such a lapse of time and because it is difficult to imagine circumstances when a period of six months would not afford a victim a reasonable opportunity of making his complaint'.

likely to apply the two-month rule rigorously where it would unjustly exclude any consideration of his case. In any event, it is for the Board alone to decide whether there are special circumstances, so that it would be wrong for a conciliation committee to reject a complaint on the ground that it was out of time before the Board had decided whether to waive the time limit.

A complaint must be accompanied by the name and address of the person by whom it is made, and where an act of discrimination is alleged to have been done against a particular person (i.e. except for complaints about the publication or display of discriminatory advertisements or notices, or the inducement or incitement of discrimination, where there is no need for a particular victim), it must be made by him or with his written authority (s. 15 (2)). Otherwise the complaint need not be in any special form, and it may be made orally provided that the complainant's name and address and any necessary written authority is supplied. As a matter of convenience, the Board publishes and distributes a standard complaint form, and, wherever possible, has complaints reduced to writing and signed by the complainant. Where for some reason the written authority of the alleged victim cannot be obtained, the Board may nevertheless under section 17 of the Act, investigate a suspected instance of unlawful discrimination.

If a complaint alleging a breach of the Act is made within two months, by or with the written authority of the alleged victim, and is accompanied by his name and address, it must be received by the Board or the conciliation committee to whom it has been made. If the complaint is not justified it will subsequently be rejected, but it must initially be received.[11] However, if the complainant fails to make the nature of his complaint sufficiently clear, he will naturally be required to clarify his allegations at the outset, for it may otherwise be impossible to decide whether the complaint should be allocated for investigation to a conciliation committee, or to a Committee of the Board, or referred to the Department of Employment and Productivity. Similarly, if a complaint raises a difficult question of statutory

11. In the unlikely event that the Board or a conciliation committee were to refuse to receive a complaint, they would be in breach of their statutory duty and could be compelled by an order of mandamus made by the Divisional Court to receive the complaint in accordance with that duty.

interpretation, it may be necessary for the Board to take legal advice about it even at this preliminary stage, so as to decide how best to deal with the matter and to avoid wasting time later. Where necessary these steps are taken as soon as a complaint has been received and before it has been formally investigated.

Investigation of complaints

When a complaint has been received it must be investigated. The investigation is done in three stages. First, the Board or conciliation committee dealing with the complaint makes such inquiries as it thinks necessary with regard to the facts alleged in the complaint. Next, it forms an opinion as to whether any person has done an act of unlawful discrimination. Thirdly, if it considers that there has been unlawful discrimination against someone, it must attempt to secure a settlement of any difference between the parties and, where appropriate, a satisfactory written assurance against any further unlawful conduct (s. 15 (3)). Each step must be considered separately.

The inquiry

The Board decides at the outset whether a complaint is to be investigated by a conciliation committee or by the Board itself (s. 15 (2) (a)). Usually, if it is to be dealt with by a conciliation committee, it will be allocated to the committee which has received the complaint.

The form of the investigation is the same in either case. It is conducted by a conciliation officer who acts either in his capacity as an officer of the Board or as an officer of the conciliation committee to which he is attached, as the case may be.

Normally, the conciliation officer's first task is to interview the complainant and to obtain a detailed statement from him. He then informs the person against whom the complaint has been made (the respondent) of the nature of the complaint. If the respondent denies the allegation altogether, the conciliation officer interviews any other witnesses before making his report to the Board or committee for whom he has conducted his inquiry. If the respondent admits the truth of the allegations, or if there are no other witnesses, the conciliation officer makes his report immediately. The respondent is not obliged to make any statement to the conciliation officer.

If at any stage the complainant wishes to withdraw his complaint, he may be allowed to do so.

Forming an opinion

After such inquiries as they consider necessary have been made into the facts alleged by the complainant, the Board or conciliation committee must form their opinion about whether any person has acted unlawfully. Their functions at this stage have been defined with deliberate vagueness by Parliament so as to give them the widest latitude and to make it possible for them to proceed upon a mere suspicion. In the form in which it was originally published the Race Relations Bill required them to 'make a determination' rather than to 'form an opinion'. But the courts might well have interpreted that provision as requiring a full-scale hearing, with legal representation and the cross-examination of witnesses, before any determination could be made. It would also have been easier to challenge the Board's discretion in the courts at a preliminary stage in the process of investigation. And it might have been necessary for there to be a prima facie case (i.e sufficient evidence in support of the complaint so that, if none were given in reply the Board would be justified in finding unlawful conduct) before a 'determination' of unlawful conduct could be made.

The definition was altered by Parliament with the deliberate intention of freeing the Board and its committees from such constraints. The change was made mainly to compensate the Board for the absence of any power to compel the attendance of witnesses or the production of documents by issuing a subpoena. Instead, if the Board or committee is faced with a respondent who refuses to discuss a complaint or to disclose relevant evidence, it may form an opinion that he has acted unlawfully upon a mere suspicion; and, where necessary, the Board may then decide to bring legal proceedings.

Of course, the Board and its committees must still act within the law. They must not exceed their jurisdiction, or adopt an unfair procedure, or form an opinion on the basis of no evidence, or otherwise exercise their functions in a manner which is inconsistent with the intention of Parliament or the policy of the legislation. Were they to do so, their actions could still be challenged in the courts.[12]

In short the Board must act fairly. To this extent the courts will compel the Board to comply with the principles of natural justice explained in a number of recent cases. For example, an immigration officer must give the would-be immigrant, who seeks admission to the United Kingdom, a fair opportunity of satisfying him that he is qualified for entry.[13] The Court of Appeal, in another case,[14] defined the duty of the Gaming Board, which, in deciding whether to give a 'certificate of consent' to the issue of a gaming licence, has to consider whether, in its opinion, the applicant is likely to be capable of, and diligent in, securing that the provisions of the Gaming Act 1968 will be complied with.

'The Gaming Board', said Lord Denning,

can and shall receive information from the police. . . . They can and should receive information from any other reliable source. But that does not mean that the applicants are not to be given a chance of answering it. They must be given the chance subject to this qualification: I do not think they need tell the applicant the source of their information if that would put the informant in peril or otherwise be contrary to the public interest (p. 1017). . . . Likewise with the details of the information. If the Board were bound to disclose every detail, that might itself give the informer away and put him in peril. But without disclosing every detail, I should have thought that the Board ought in every case to be able to give to the applicant sufficient indication of the objections raised against him such as to enable him to answer them. That is only fair. And the Board must at all costs be fair. If they are not, these courts will not hesitate to interfere (p. 1018).

Although the parallel between the function of immigration officers, the Gaming Board and the Race Relations Board is not exact, Lord Denning's words show that the Race Relations Board's duty to be fair requires that both the complainant and the respondent are informed of the substance of the evidence against them and are given an opportunity to meet it. But where evidence has been given to the

12. See e.g. *Padfield* v. *Ministry of Agriculture* [1968] A.C. (H.L.).

13. *Re K(H) an infant* [1967] 2 Q.B. 617 at p. 630 *per* Lord Parker L.C.J.

14. *R.* v. *Gaming Board for Great Britain, ex parte Benaim and Khaida* [1970] 2 W.L.R. 1009 (C.A.).

Board in confidence, only the substance of it need be given; the Board need not disclose the name of the informant nor such detail as will enable him to be identified.

There is good sense in keeping formality to the minimum consistent with fairness. The process of investigation and conciliation is meant to be simple and informal. The Board has not been given the power, recommended by the Street Report (see p. 104), to make enforceable orders against a respondent. It would therefore have been wrong to have required the Board or its committees to preside over a full-scale judicial hearing, with examination and cross-examination and strict rules of evidence, especially since there is provision for such a hearing before a county court, at a later stage, should it prove to be impossible to secure a settlement or assurance (see p. 324). The freedom with which an opinion may be formed does not prejudice the interests of the respondent unfairly. Where an opinion is formed that he has acted unlawfully, the only immediate consequence is that the respondent will be approached by the Board or committee with a view to achieving a settlement or securing an assurance. If he rebuffs this approach, or denies that he has acted unlawfully, he may defend himself in any subsequent proceedings in the county court.

The person who is likely to be prejudiced by the absence of judicial review is not the respondent but the complainant; for he has no legal redress if his complaint is rejected. But the complainant's interests would not be better served by increasing the formality of the investigation process and the possibility of judicial review of the actions of the Board or committee. The real flaw in the present procedure is rather that the complainant cannot take his case to court where the Board refuses to do so on his behalf (see p. 310).

The Board does, of course, follow a procedure which is fair to both parties. What happens in practice is that, after the evidence has been assembled and reported upon by the conciliation officer, whichever party seems likely to receive an adverse opinion is duly informed and given an opportunity to make representations. If the balance shifts as the result of those representations, the other party may make representations in reply. In accordance with this policy, the Board has stressed to its conciliation committees that at every stage of an investigation each party should be made aware of any point or argument which may adversely affect his case and be given the chance to deal with it.[15]

It is not altogether clear whether the Board and its conciliation committees must always form an opinion, or whether they are entitled to conclude that there is insufficient evidence to enable them to do so. Section 15 (3) (a) suggests that they *must* form an opinion, but section 15 (6) provides that, when they have completed their investigation, they are to give a written notification to the parties stating 'whether they have been able to form an opinion with respect to the complaint and, *if they have*, what opinion'. The correct view seems to be that they ought to form an opinion one way or the other unless it is impossible to do so on the available evidence, or the complaint has been withdrawn before the investigation has been completed.

In a large majority of cases, especially in the field of employment, the opinion has been formed that discrimination had not occurred. Only in the case of advertisements and notices has the majority of complaints been upheld. The latest available statistics, covering the period from 1 April 1970 to 31 March 1971, are set out in the following Tables 1 and 2 (RRB, 1971, Appendix IV).

In this period, opinions of unlawful discrimination were formed in nearly 9 per cent of employment cases. In the previous years the figure was 6·4 per cent. The Board has suggested several factors which help to explain why there have been few justified complaints in the field of employment.

We are convinced that the main responsibility for the fact that such a small proportion of employment complaints result in opinions of

15. At first the practice was adopted of forming a 'provisional' opinion which was normally confirmed unless it was altered by evidence or argument put forward by the party to whom it was adverse. However, this practice was criticized on the ground that a view was being taken before representations were considered, and that representations might appear to be pointless. The danger of this practice was illustrated in *The Race Relations Board* v. *Geo. H. Haigh & Co. Ltd* (see pp. 234–5) where the Yorkshire Conciliation Committee had offered to hear representations but, by an oversight, had formed an opinion before the respondents had an opportunity to make their representations. The Board therefore directed the Committee to refer the complaint to the Board which investigated it afresh. The Leeds County Court Judge described the conduct of the Yorkshire Committee as 'contrary to natural justice'. The practice of forming a 'provisional' opinion is no longer followed.

Table 1 Complaints other than Employment:
Complaints by Type and Outcome

Type	Total	Opinion: discrimination	Opinion: no discrimination	Other
Section 2 (Public places)				
Public houses and hotels	51	23	22	6
Clubs	25	11	9	5
Other	86	19	44	23
Section 2 (Goods, facilities and services)				
Motor insurance*	16	9	3	4
Finance and Credit	24	1	18	5
Education	36	1	31	4
Services connected with employment	14	2	8	4
Public services	44		30	14
Professional services	33	1	26	6
Section 5 (Housing)				
Private housing (rent)	65	18	22	25
Private housing (sale)	22	3	18	1
Private housing (other)	30	2	18	10
Local authority housing	34	2	26	6
Section 6 (Advertisements and notices)	50	42	7	1
Total	530	134	282	114

* Includes complaints concerning car hire.

discrimination rests in factors which are largely, although not entirely, outside the control of the Board. It is clear that many complaints originate in the difficulties which arise because the complainant is a comparative newcomer to this country and lacks knowledge of British employment conditions and practices, including industrial relations procedures. In many cases a person may be unsure whether his position is the result of discrimination or of the disadvantage he suffers through being a newcomer. Complaints of this kind are inevitable in the present stage of immigrant development but should diminish as experience and familiarity with British conditions develop.

Table 2 Employment Complaints (Other than those Wholly Handled by Industry Machinery) by Type and Outcome

Subject	Total	Opinion: discrimination	Opinion: no discrimination	Other
Section 3				
Refusal to employ	227	28	143	56
Terms	34		26	8
Conditions	46	1	36	9
Training	5	1	2	2
Promotion	20	1	17	2
Dismissal	222	7	171	44
Other	3			3
Section 4				
Trade Unions	21		17	4
Employers' Organizations	2		2	
Total	580	38	414	128

There were few complaints against firms which discriminate as a matter of deliberate policy. It is not difficult to establish unlawful behaviour when this arises from discriminatory policies, and the resulting gains from doing so in terms of expanding opportunities can be considerable. But we repeat that the reason why few complaints are received against companies with discriminatory policies is probably the 'play safe' attitude of those likely to suffer discrimination and their unwillingness to encounter situations where they risk being humiliated. . . . There have been instances of people contacting the Board to vent their anger over this sort of treatment, yet being unwilling to register a complaint or to provide enough information for the Board to initiate an investigation under section 17. Among reasons advanced for this are the understandable reluctance to re-live a humiliating experience and the fact that the Act does not guarantee a remedy or redress an individual grievance. Whilst some of these reasons are based on misconceptions, this failure to complain represents an adjustment to discrimination which can only maintain and perpetuate existing patterns of discrimination (RRB, 1970, paras. 67, 68; see also RRB, 1969, para. 58 and RRB, 1971, para. 88).

Such problems are inherent in a system of enforcement which depends so heavily upon the making of individual complaints. The Board has no control over the type of complaints which are made.

They may raise important issues about widespread discriminatory practices; or they may be trivial or misconceived. Apart from its limited power to initiate investigations where no complaint has been made (see p. 311), the Board cannot conduct strategic inquiries into policies and practices in employment, housing or the provision of goods, facilities or services. The Board is dependent upon the knowledge, determination and experience of the victim of discriminatory conduct. Often the victim may not know that he has been discriminated against, or may be too frightened or embarrassed either to put himself in the position where he may meet further discrimination or to complain if he does so. In the result the Board has not received sufficient complaints to be able to deal effectively with important areas of discrimination. Indeed, there has been a sharp decrease in the total number of complaints received in 1970–71 as compared with 1969–70 (RRB, 1971, para. 6), and the Board has emphasized that the 1968 Act 'cannot be judged by the outcome of the complaints process' (RRB, 1971, para. 48).

These difficulties are aggravated by the Board's lack of any power to compel the attendance of witnesses or the production of relevant documents. In the absence of such powers the Board and its committees have to rely upon information provided by the complainant or other witnesses, or upon the voluntary cooperation of those against whom complaints are made. And, although they have a wide discretion to form an opinion that there has been unlawful discrimination, they are inevitably reluctant to do so in the absence of convincing evidence, because of the risk that their opinion will subsequently be rejected in the courts.[16] To some extent, therefore, the frequency with which complaints have been rejected may not reflect the incidence of discrimination or the weakness of the complaints, but rather the inability of the conciliation machinery to

16. The former Chairman of the Race Relations Board, Mr Mark Bonham Carter, has suggested that the Board's wide discretion to form an opinion that there has been unlawful conduct 'may be sufficient to prevent people from simply refusing to cooperate with the Board at all. It is a substitute for subpoena powers.' But he added significantly, 'The disadvantage of it is that we might take a case to Court and, when the witnesses appeared and the papers were revealed, we might find ours was a very bad case and would have to withdraw it which would make us look foolish' (H.C. Select Committee on Race Relations and Immigration, Session 1968–9. Minutes of Evidence, 19 December 1968, p. 55).

obtain information on its own initiative and to plan an effective strategy against the most important areas of racial discrimination.

Settlements and assurances

If it forms an opinion that unlawful discrimination has occurred, the Board or committee has a double duty. It must use its best endeavours, by communicating with the parties concerned or otherwise, to secure a settlement of any difference between them. Where appropriate, it must also try to secure a written assurance against any repetition of the act considered to be unlawful or the doing of acts of a similar kind (s. 13 (3) (b)).

Where the act complained of does not involve a particular victim, no question of a settlement between the parties arises, and it is only necessary to seek an assurance against similar wrongdoing in the future (s. 15 (3) (c)). This is so only where a complaint concerns the publication or display of discriminatory advertisements or notices, or the unsuccessful inducement or incitement of an act of discrimination. In all other cases there must be an alleged victim, and the Board or committee must try to secure a settlement. In doing so, it acts as an intermediary between the complainant and the respondent. The 'difference' between the parties refers to whatever the complainant alleges that he has been denied by the respondent's unlawful conduct. For example, if the complaint is about a refusal to employ someone, the difference between the parties which is to be settled is that the complainant has sought employment and the respondent has denied it to him.

No requirements have been laid down about the content of a settlement. In some cases a complainant may be satisfied with a payment of compensation for the loss which he has suffered, or with an apology.[17] In others, it may be impossible to put right the wrong which has been done to him unless he is given the opportunity which he was previously denied — a particular job or house, or services or facilities. But here again the conciliation machinery is not in a strong

17. In *Race Relations Board* v. *Geo. H. Haigh & Co. Ltd* (see pp. 234–5) an apology had been sought as part of the settlement. In his judgment the judge stated that one of the assessors felt that this should not have been done, but the judge himself and the other assessor did not question its propriety.

enough position to be able to protect the interests of the victim adequately in many instances of unlawful discrimination.[18]

It is obviously very difficult for the Board or committee to secure a more favourable settlement voluntarily than could ultimately be obtained through litigation. The courts are not empowered to order a discriminator to put right the wrong done to his victim by making a job, a house or some other benefit available to him; they can only award damages, or make a declaration that an act is unlawful, or award an injunction restraining future unlawful conduct (see chapter 9). These limitations are reflected in the type of settlement which is likely to be made in the course of conciliation. Normally, the only circumstance in which a respondent will be willing to offer a job or a house to the complainant is where he operates on a sufficiently large scale to be affected by the threat of an injunction restraining him from discriminating again in the future. Otherwise the best settlement which can be obtained for the victim is compensation coupled with a written assurance. In practice even this may be hard to achieve. The parties may be unable to agree upon the amount of compensation which ought to be paid; or the respondent may feel that the complainant should be content to accept a written assurance or a bare apology. So far, in the majority of settlements the complainant has received no more than an apology. Occasionally, the respondent has agreed to offer to the complainant the benefit which he has unlawfully denied him. And in a tiny handful of cases, a settlement has included the payment of compensation, ranging from two days' loss of earnings to £150 in respect of the loss of an employment opportunity (see, e.g. R R B, 1971, Appendix III, p. 36).

The Act does not provide a remedy if the respondent fails to implement the terms of the settlement. The complainant could probably enforce the settlement by means of a Common Law action in contract[19] but the Board could not because it is not a party to the settlement.

18. The Board's former Chairman has recognized it as a weakness in the 1968 Act that 'you really offer very little to the complainant; you cannot give him the job back which has probably gone; you cannot give him the house or room back which has gone. What you are really asking him to do is to complain out of a spirit of public duty' (Minutes of Evidence to H.C. Select Committee, at p. 45).

19. *Contra* Hepple (1970, at p. 210). Section 19 (10) does not bar an action in contract because it could have been brought if the Act had not been passed.

In attempting to secure a settlement, the Board or committee attempts to obtain redress for the complainant. In seeking a written assurance, it acts for the community as a whole to prevent further wrongdoing. A written assurance must be sought 'where appropriate'. It is only inappropriate to do where there is no reasonable prospect of any repetition by the respondent of his unlawful actions – for example, because he is retiring from his business – so that an assurance would be superfluous. Apart from such rare cases, an assurance always should be sought.

It is a *written assurance* which must be sought. The Board or committee submits a draft form of assurance to the respondent for his approval. It generally follows a standard formula which is varied to suit particular circumstances. The formula which has so far been used by the Board and its committees records their opinion that the respondent has acted unlawfully, refers to the relevant statutory provisions, and contains an undertaking by the respondent not to act in breach of the provision in the future. In return the Board or committee agrees not to bring proceedings in respect of the complaint which has led to the assurance.

What the standard formula normally does not contain is any admission by the respondent that he has acted unlawfully, and it is possible to argue that this omission falls short of the statutory requirements for a satisfactory assurance. The Act refers to an assurance against 'any repetition of the act considered to be unlawful or the doing of *further acts of a similar kind*' by the respondent. The italicized words suggest that the assurance should contain an admission by the respondent that he has done the act complained of, so as to make it clear that he is undertaking not to repeat an allegedly wrongful act. This view is supported by the fact that the Board has power to seek a declaration from the court that the respondent has committed an unlawful act. Presumably, one reason for including that power in the statute was to enable the Board to deal with the situation in which a respondent was willing to give an assurance that he would comply with the law in the future but not to admit that he had broken the law in the past; the Board could then ask the court to declare that he had done so. The Board and its committees do try, where possible, to obtain an admission of guilt, but their standard form of assurance amounts to little more than a promise to obey the law. And the sanction for breach of that promise is scarcely greater than if the promise had never been made. Where an assurance is broken the Board may determine to bring proceedings without seeking further conciliation (s. 15 (4) and (5)). In that sense the Board is in a stronger position with than without its standard form of assurance. But the absence of any admission of guilt from the assurance prevents the Board when seeking an injunction, from relying upon it, as evidence that the respondent has previously engaged in unlawful conduct. This must be proved before an injunction can be granted (s. 21 (1) (c)). Although the assurance is admissible as evidence in such proceedings (s. 24), the absence of an admission of guilt compels the Board to prove that the respondent had acted unlawfully on the previous occasion as well as on the occasion which gave rise to the proceedings.

Once more the Board and its committees have been led to adopt a weak procedure because of defects in the enforcement provisions of the Act. They are too dependent on winning the cooperation of the person against whom a complaint is made. If they insist upon being given an admission of guilt, they risk that the respondent will refuse to cooperate altogether. Because the Board cannot compel the production of evidence by the respondent or hold a hearing, it may then be faced with an invidious choice between abandoning a complaint and fishing for the evidence in court. If it brings proceedings and its fishing expedition fails, the Board will have no alternative but to withdraw, thereby diminishing its credibility and prestige. In these circumstances, it is understandable if discretion is regarded as the better part of valour. But the Board's support among racial and ethnic minorities is likely to be damaged if it accepts inadequate settlements or ambiguous assurances.

The dilemma which results from the weak enforcement provisions is also illustrated by the Board's early reluctance to publicize details of settlements and assurances or the identity of the parties to them. The legislation leaves the matter entirely to the Board's discretion. Obviously, if it insists on publicity which will identify a particular respondent, it will be much more difficult to achieve a settlement or to obtain an assurance. But if the Board does not publicize its achievements, it reduces its effectiveness in deterring others from breaking the law and in encouraging the victims of racial discrimination to seek its help. Furthermore, an assurance by an employer that he will abandon a discriminatory policy is of little value if those who have been its victims do not know that the policy has changed. The Board has recently begun to publish detailed accounts of cases without names (RRB, 1970, Appendix VI; RRB, 1971, Appendix V), but probably the only wholly satisfactory way of resolving the dilemma is for the powers of the Board and its committees to be strengthened so that the Board is in a sufficiently strong bargaining position to afford to give publicity to its work.

Completion of the investigation

On completing the investigation, the Board or committee must notify both parties in writing:

1. Whether or not they have been able to form an opinion with respect to the complaint and, if they have, what opinion.
2. Whether or not they have secured a settlement or assurance.
3. What action, if any, they propose to take in the matter (s. 15 (6)).

If the Board or committee form an opinion that there has been no unlawful conduct, no further action will be taken. The proceedings are at an end, and the complainant has no right of appeal to the Board. If an opinion has been formed that there has been unlawful conduct, and the Board or committee are unable to secure a settlement or assurance, or it appears to them that there has been a breach of an assurance, then the Board has to decide what further action should be taken. Where the complaint has been investigated by the Board itself, it must determine whether to bring legal proceedings (s. 15 (4)). Where it has been investigated by a committee, the committee reports to the Board, which may either investigate the complaint itself, or, without investigating it, determine whether to bring legal proceedings (s. 15 (5)). Even though the Board or committee may have formed an opinion that there has been unlawful conduct, and have failed to obtain a settlement or assurance, the Board is not bound to bring legal proceedings. And, if it refuses to do so, the matter is at an end. Neither the complainant nor the respondent can take it further unless he can show that the Board or its committees have acted unfairly, or have otherwise failed to comply with the statutory requirements (see p. 299).

Investigation where no complaint made

The Board is not entirely dependent upon receiving complaints. If, either because someone alleges that he has been discriminated against, or 'for any other cause', the Board has reason to suspect that an unlawful act has been done, the Board (but not a conciliation committee) may investigate the matter or refer it for investigation, even though no formal complaint has been received (s. 17 (1)). This power was given to the Board because of the Street Report's recommendation that it should be able to take the initiative in dealing with suspected discriminatory practices.[20] But the power is qualified. The Board must have reason to suspect that there has been unlawful conduct during the two months before the matter first comes to its notice or such longer period as the Board may in special circumstances allow. Except for cases involving the publication or display of discriminatory advertisements or notices, or inciting discrimination, conduct is unlawful only if it affects a particular victim. So although the Board has a wide discretion to investigate suspected unlawful conduct, it can only exercise this power, in most cases, if the act of discrimination involves an identifiable victim. It might not, for example, be sufficient for the Board to act on a suspicion based merely on the fact that a firm operating in a coloured neighbourhood has an all-white labour force, or that it employs coloured workers only in manual jobs, unless it also suspects that someone has been discriminated against.

Here again, the Board's lack of any power to compel the disclosure of relevant evidence from those suspected of unlawful conduct may consciously or unconsciously inhibit its investigations. If the Board takes the initiative where no complaint has been made, it may not have the benefit of a statement from an alleged victim. Without subpoena powers, it must then fish for evidence in the hope of

20. The Report 'attached importance to the Board's moving affirmatively in administering the Act. They should be responsible for uncovering unlawful discriminatory practices and taking action to eliminate them. Unlawful racial discrimination needs to be prevented even though the individual victimized has not initiated proceedings; the Board should be regarded as administratively responsible for carrying out the Act's objectives. We would therefore empower the Board to initiate complaints which would be handled by the local committee in the same way as other complaints' (para. 144.1).

obtaining it from outside sources or from the suspected discriminator. And, since the Board is acting on its own suspicion, it risks receiving a rebuff if no evidence is forthcoming to confirm its suspicion.

Where the Board's suspicion involves a non-employment matter, it may either carry out the investigation itself or refer it to a conciliation committee (s. 17 (1) (a) and sch. 3, pt I). What then happens is similar to the procedure followed where a complaint has been made (sch. 3, pt I). There is an inquiry, and, if an opinion is formed that there has indeed been unlawful conduct, the Board or committee must try to secure a settlement and a satisfactory written assurance. If these efforts fail, the Board decides whether to bring proceedings.

Where the Board's suspicion involves an employment matter, in almost all cases it is not allowed to carry out any initial investigation, but must refer the matter to the Secretary of State for Employment and Productivity (s. 17 (1) (b) and sch. 3, pt II, para. 7). If the Secretary of State is satisfied that suitable voluntary machinery exists to deal with the matter, it is then referred to that body for investigation.[21] If not, the matter is referred back to the Board for investigation by itself or a conciliation committee.

Whatever the arguments may be in favour of entrusting employment cases to voluntary industrial machinery (see p. 314), they are much less convincing where an investigation is begun because of the Board's suspicion rather than as the result of a specific complaint. If the Board has reason to suspect that there has been unlawful conduct in the field of employment, it seems sensible that it should be able to probe the suspected activity itself without having immediately to refer the matter to another body. This procedure is all the more bizarre since the Board is entitled to make an investigation at a later stage, if it is notified by anyone appearing to the Board to be concerned, that he is aggrieved by a decision of the voluntary industrial body (sch. 3, pt II, para. 14).

These provisions shield employers and trade unions from the direct use of even the limited power to initiate investigations. The shield was placed between the Board and industry as a result of a political compromise (chapter 3). Yet there is as great a need for effective inquiry by an independent public body into suspected discriminatory prac-

21. The procedure for investigating employment cases where no complaint has been made is set out in schedule 3, part II to the Act.

tices in employment as there is elsewhere. The shield could be lowered without new legislation, for the Home Secretary is expressly authorized to amend or repeal the provisions for investigating employment matters, where no complaint has been made, by laying regulations before Parliament (s. 17 (2)). By taking this step, he would remove an unjustified fetter upon the Board's freedom of action.

However, the general limitations on the Board's present powers would still remain. The Board cannot move on its own initiative unless there is reason to suspect that an unlawful act has taken place, and it could be inhibited from moving by its inability to compel the disclosure of relevant evidence. It may be for these reasons that the Board has initiated an investigation under section 17 in relatively few cases.[22]

Unless and until the Board's responsibility for uncovering unlawful discriminatory practices is enlarged, its effectiveness will inevitably be determined more by the quality and significance of complaints made to the Board than by an overall national strategy for promoting equal opportunities in areas covered by the Act. The Board has already drawn attention in several annual reports to the misconceived nature and narrow scope of many of the complaints which have so far been received. An expansion of the power to initiate investigations under section 17 could make a major improvement in the Board's ability to enforce the legislation.

Special procedures for employment cases

Where a complaint is made relating to employment, or to membership of, or services or facilities provided by, a trade union or employers' association, although it may be made to the Board or its

22. Between 1 April 1969 and 31 March 1970 there were twenty-nine investigations under section 17. These were generally instituted following a report from a third party who believed he had knowledge that an unlawful act had been done. The Board comments: 'This (i.e. s. 17) is an especially important provision where the victim is not in a position to know that he has suffered unlawful discrimination. But it is no less important where the victim is, for one reason or another, reluctant to come forward with a complaint' (R R B, 1970, para. 13). In the following year, the Board completed thirty investigations into allegations of discriminatory treatment in recruitment, under section 17. Eight of these (26·6 per cent) resulted in opinions of discrimination – a much higher proportion than in cases where specific complaints were investigated (R R B, 1971, para. 47).

committees, it cannot be immediately investigated by them; it must be referred to the Secretary of State for Employment and Productivity (s. 16 (1) and sch. 2). The Secretary of State must then decide whether there is suitable non-statutory machinery for dealing with the complaint. If there is such machinery, it must be given a chance to deal with the complaint before it can be considered by the statutory machinery. If not, the complaint is referred by the DEP for investigation by the Board or its committees in the normal way. However, no reference need be made to the DEP where a complaint relates to a discriminatory act alleged to have been done by an agent (e.g. an employment agency) without the principal's authority, or relates to the breach of an existing assurance.

This special procedure for dealing with employment cases has been grafted on to the statutory procedures so as to give industry an opportunity to resolve differences and eliminate discriminatory practices through its own machinery. Its origins are mainly political (see chapter 3). Both sides of industry originally opposed any form of legislative intervention to deal with complaints of racial discrimination in employment. One of their main objections has been that it was better to use voluntary techniques than legal sanctions. Eventually, the Government won their grudging approval for the 1968 Act by agreeing to refer cases, at least initially, to industry itself.

The reliance on voluntary industrial machinery in the employment provisions of the 1968 Act reflects a tradition which has shaped the present pattern of industrial relations in this country.[23] The unhappy experience of trade unions at the hands of the courts in the nineteenth century created an implacable hostility to the use of law in industrial relations. At its best, the reliance upon voluntary machinery may have some important advantages. Disputes may be settled quickly and informally by representative bodies used to handling industrial grievances. Their authority and expertise can be applied to encourage better employment practices and procedures. Good race relations can be promoted in the context of good industrial relations. It was for these reasons that the Street Report stated that

any existing industrial machinery calculated to remove or control discrimination or to conciliate disputes arising from discrimination should be

23. For a valuable account of the 'tradition of voluntarism', see Hepple (1970, p. 179).

recognized as a highly desirable factor in race relations. No legislation should be enacted which minimized its importance or discouraged its use. When cases were referred to the local conciliation committee the committee would be required to hear any evidence submitted to it of attempts made to settle the dispute through trade channels, and such attempts would have to be taken into account both in the fact-finding processes and in the course of seeking conciliation agreements (para. 149.5).

To that extent, the Street Report recommended that discrimination in employment should be treated separately, but only to that extent, for the authors concluded that in other respects the normal machinery and procedures should be adopted in the field of employment. The Report referred to several disadvantages which would follow if reliance were put upon special employment machinery (paras. 149.1–149.3). Large segments of industry do not have such machinery, and, where they do, it may be ineffective, not fully integrated into the plant and not manned by competent personnel. A very large proportion of labour is not unionized. The task of creating special voluntary machinery throughout industry would be enormous and protracted. It would be difficult to scrutinize the constitution and procedures of such machinery. The mechanism of the Board and its committees would be at a standstill until the industrial machinery decided and reported on a case. The complainant might find the procedure frustrating, if not obstructive, and those with genuine grievances might be discouraged from making complaints, especially since the industrial machinery would often have been set up by the very employer who was alleged to have discriminated against the complainant.

These difficulties have been partially met by empowering the Board to deal with employment cases where no suitable voluntary machinery exists. But it should become clear from the following account of the present system that serious disadvantages remain. The procedures are straightforward and can be described shortly.

Investigation and conciliation

If the Secretary of State is satisfied that a suitable industrial body exists to consider a complaint, it is referred to that body for investigation. If the Secretary of State informs the Board that there is no suitable industrial machinery to consider a complaint, or if it is not appropriate to be dealt with by industrial machinery, it will be investigated by the Board or its committees in the normal way. If the complaint relates to an act done in breach of a relevant assurance, the Board is not compelled to refer it to the Secretary of State; it may choose either to refer it to suitable industrial machinery, if there is any, or to one of its own committees,'or to investigate the matter itself.

Where a complaint is referred to industrial machinery the investigation follows almost the same steps as that of the Board and its committees (sch. 2). The industrial body must make such inquiries as it thinks necessary about the facts alleged in the complaint and then form an opinion whether any person has acted unlawfully. It has the same duty to attempt to secure a settlement of any difference between the parties, and, where appropriate, a satisfactory assurance against any further unlawful conduct. There is one minor difference between the voluntary and the statutory procedures; an assurance given to the industrial machinery may be satisfactory even though it is not put in writing. This departure from the statutory requirement for writing is unexplained, and it might have inconvenient results if a dispute were later to arise about the terms of a particular assurance.

On completing its investigation, the industrial machinery must notify the parties in writing whether or not it has been able to form an opinion about the complaint, and, if so what opinion, and whether or not it has secured a settlement or assurance; and in every case it must inform the parties that it will report to the Secretary of State about its investigation. At the same time it must state the rights of any party aggrieved by its decision to appeal to the Board.

Whatever happens, at the end of four weeks from the reference of a complaint to the industrial machinery, or upon completion of the investigation, whichever occurs first, a report must be made to the D E P. If the Secretary of State receives a report that the industrial body has failed to secure a settlement and assurance, or if he receives no report, he may, after consulting with the Board, request the industrial body to continue to investigate the matter for a specified period, or to cease investigating it.[24] In theory, the Secretary of State could grant one or several extensions of time for much longer than four weeks, but, in practice, it is unlikely that this would happen

24. In 1970–71 the Board disposed of one such case referred by the Secretary of State and formed the opinion that there had been unlawful distinction (R R B, 1971, para. 53).

unless the industrial machinery could show that it was dealing with the matter efficiently and that there were special circumstances which justified a further extension of time.

If the industrial machinery should fail to complete the investigation within the specified time, or having completed it, should fail, where appropriate, to secure a settlement or assurance, the complaint is referred to the Board which must then investigate the matter afresh. In such circumstances the Board cannot refer the complaint to one of its own conciliation committees, apparently because the industrial machinery might be resentful if, after it had failed in its task, the matter were investigated by a subordinate committee rather than by the Board itself.

Appeals

If either party is aggrieved by a decision of the voluntary machinery, he may appeal to the Board (sch. 2, para. 9). He must do so within a week of his being given a written notification of the decision, or within such further period as the Board may in special circumstances allow. The Board then has three possible courses of action: it may reject the appeal without any further investigation; it may refer the complaint again to the voluntary machinery for further investigation; or it may investigate the complaint itself.[25] If the Board decides to investigate the complaint, it must do so itself, following the normal procedures which have already been described. And, in doing so, the Board naturally takes into account the report of the voluntary machinery and any evidence considered by that machinery, as well as new evidence put forward by either party.

Suitable industrial machinery

The 1968 Act does not define the essential ingredients of industrial machinery. It is left to the discretion of the Secretary of State who must be satisfied that there is a body of persons suitable to consider the particular complaint. It is not necessary that the machinery

25. Between 1 April 1970 and 31 March 1971, the Board dealt with twenty-eight appeals from complainants aggrieved by the decisions of voluntary machinery that no unlawful discrimination had occurred. In twenty-two cases it was decided that the complaint should not be further entertained. The Board decided to investigate the other six cases. One case was still under investigation, and in the remaining five cases the Board agreed with the opinion of the voluntary machinery (RRB, 1971, para. 51).

should have existed before the Act came into force. Indeed, all the machinery which has so far been approved has either been specifically created or adapted to fulfil the objects of the legislation.

In December 1968, the Department of Employment and Productivity published guidelines entitled 'Industry machinery dealing with complaints made under the Race Relations Act' which indicated the requirements to be met before machinery was to be approved. Under these guidelines, the DEP requires to be satisfied that the machinery will operate in accordance with the following procedure:

1. Employment complaints will come to the industrial machinery via the Department of Employment and Productivity and will be conveyed in writing.

2. The machinery will first investigate the complaint.

3. It will normally see the complainant and the respondent.

4. It will allow either or both of them, if they so wish, to be accompanied at any hearing by a union representative or where appropriate by a person of their choice.

5. It will attempt to form an opinion whether or not there has been an act on the part of anyone involved which amounts to an act of discrimination as defined in the legislation.

6. It will attempt to dispose of any difference between the parties, whether or not there has been a finding of unlawful discrimination.

7. If in the opinion of the industry machinery there has been an act of unlawful discrimination it will seek an assurance against further acts of a similar kind.

8. It will report on all cases to the Department of Employment and Productivity within four weeks of receiving the complaint, giving such information as is required by the Department.

9. It will give a written report to both the complainant and the respondent recording its opinions and making it clear that if the parties wish to dispute these they must do so in writing within seven days. Notification of disputed opinions received by the machinery should be sent to the Department . . . without delay. Complaints not settled will be referred to the Race Relations Board by the DEP.

10. If more time is required by the industry machinery for investigation and conciliation it will contact the First Secretary before four weeks has passed giving full reasons for the request and an estimate of the further time needed. Such a request may be made by telephone.

11. With appropriate modifications the above procedure will be followed if the DEP, after consultation with the Race Relations Board, extends the time given to the machinery to allow it to complete its conciliation. The extension of time will be for a specific period.

12. If a complaint which has not been disposed of is referred to the Board, the machinery will cease to investigate the complaint if asked to do so by the First Secretary.

The DEP document also gives general guidance on the scope of work to be done by industrial machinery. It is expected to be able to deal with complaints relating to non-engagement, and it should be able to deal with as many as possible other types of complaint in respect of defined grades or classes of employee within an industry, i.e. terms and conditions of employment and training; non-promotion; dismissal; discriminatory notices or advertisements; incitement; and complaints concerning trade unions and organizations of employers. Where the approved machinery states that it is not able to deal with a complaint of a particular type, or a complaint relating to a particular grade or class such as, for instance, a management grade, the complaint will be investigated by the Board. The question of the application of trade union rules, in cases of complaints against trade unions was, according to the document, being considered by the Trades Union Congress in consultation with the DEP.

In some cases, the DEP guidelines recognize that it may be necessary for the two sides of industry to agree to a procedure which deals specifically with complaints under the 1968 Act, and to provide for reference to more than one tier or level of investigation and conciliation.

Where it is practicable to arrange this it will be desirable that the industry's investigators should be independent, in the sense that they do not have responsibilities within an enterprise in connection with the complainant or respondent. Where it is difficult to arrange this, for instance because the approved machinery is self-contained within a large enterprise it may be thought appropriate by the enterprise concerned to invite the aid, for some investigations, of an independent person outside the firm. The machinery should wherever possible be available to any worker and any firm, and should be readily available to any complainant. The First Secretary will keep under review the working of the industry machinery, and it will be open to her to require modifications to it as a condition of her continuing to be satisfied that it is suitable.

The operation of the machinery

The DEP guidelines are flexible, leaving the approved machinery free to regulate its own procedures. By February 1970, the Department had approved machinery in forty-three industries representing about seven million workers (DEP, 1970a, p. 100). It differs widely from industry to industry, where it may be national, regional or local. In some areas, such as the building industry or the health service, a complaint is investigated in the first instance by officials, and only later, where necessary, is there a hearing before a panel. In others, such as British Rail and banking, the panel system is used from the outset.

Procedures also differ within the panel system, but two basic procedures seem to be followed. First, there is a hearing process in which both parties are heard separately and informed later of the panel's opinion; secondly, there is a confrontation process in which the parties meet face-to-face and argue their case.

These procedures have several potential disadvantages. If the parties are heard separately, the complainant, who is usually heard first, may not have an opportunity to rebut the respondent's evidence. This disadvantage is not inherent in the procedure. It is removed if the complainant is given the right to reply, but there have been some cases where this does not seem to have been done. Where there is a confrontation, the complainant may be incapable of presenting his case adequately or of rebutting the arguments against him. It is true that, according to the DEP guidelines, he is entitled to be accompanied by a friend or adviser, but there is no certainty that he will be able to obtain competent assistance. In many cases he is likely to be at a disadvantage in arguing against a respondent with much greater resources. Panels can and do try to help the complainant as much as possible but there has been some criticism of failure in this respect. The difficulty is that the fairness of the proceedings depends entirely upon the individuals in charge.

Again, it seems that panels are often content simply to limit themselves to the assertions made by both parties, without seeking to obtain further documentary or other evidence. This passive approach is likely to work against the complainant's interests where he is unable to gain access to information which will enable him to substantiate his complaint.

The panel system, where it is used exclusively, may sometimes be too elaborate. In some industries the panels consist of senior representatives from both sides of industry who are called upon to deal with a complaint which might have been better considered at a local and more junior level. This has caused frustration and annoyance among some panel members who resent having to spend time on matters which they regard as trivial. There have also been complaints, from those accused of racial discrimination and later exonerated, of the stigma of having been accused before a senior body. On the other hand, the mere fact that a panel is composed of senior representatives does not ensure that it will have the special skills needed to deal with alleged breaches of the 1968 Act. The panel will probably be called upon only sporadically and its members will have little opportunity to acquire the expertise possessed by staff members of the Board.

These disadvantages are related to the very nature of the industrial machinery. The race relations panels are basically an adaptation of normal industrial disputes or grievance committees, and they operate under the 1968 Act on the assumption that racial grievances represent one category of industrial grievance. However, the position of a complainant under the Act is frequently very different from that of the worker whose case is dealt with by grievance machinery.

Under the normal grievance procedure, a worker is represented by a trade union official with experience of handling such cases. Often the individual worker's case raises an issue which affects the interests of many other workers, and the union official has thus a great incentive to win the case. Industrial grievance bodies are composed jointly of trade union and employers' representatives. The worker who complains to them usually enjoys the advantage that the trade union representatives are likely to sympathize with him and use their power and influence to secure some measure of satisfaction for him. In short, the worker can generally expect to be competently represented before a body containing people who may be expected to support his case.

A complainant under the Race Relations Act has none of these advantages. He may or may not be competently represented. He may or may not have the sympathy of panel members. If he is already in employment, he may be regarded with hostility for complaining under the Act instead of using the ordinary grievance machinery.[26] In some cases, the complainant's interests may conflict directly with those of panel members, who will then seem to be judges in their own cause. Where, for example, complaint is made against the exclusion of coloured workers from recruitment or promotion to skilled or supervisory work, remedying the situation may well create problems between management and their existing labour force, or within or between trade unions.

On the other hand, the voluntary machinery has one significant advantage which is not available to the Board and its committees. Cases frequently arise where allegations of racial discrimination prove to be unfounded, but reveal a bad industrial practice which is a justifiable cause for complaint. For example, a worker may believe that he has been dismissed on racial grounds; an investigation may show that he is wrong but that he has nevertheless been unfairly treated. In such cases – and there have been many – the Board cannot take further action, because the matters complained of are not contrary to the 1968 Act. But the voluntary machinery can and often does take steps to remove the real grievance which underlies the complaint.

It is impossible at present to attempt any objective evaluation of how the voluntary machinery is actually operating. Proceedings are held in private, and written records do not have to be kept or published. The DEP may require the voluntary machinery to provide specific information when reports are made to the Department, but

26. Both sides of industry were opposed to the enactment of the 1968 Act, in part on the ground that voluntary machinery would be more appropriate to deal with complaints of racial discrimination. However, despite the introduction of legislation there is still considerable hostility to the use of any special machinery to tackle racial discrimination in employment. For example, the CBI and the TUC both regard race relations as part of industrial relations. They employ no staff to deal exclusively with problems of race relations, and are opposed to special measures designed to tackle them separately from other industrial problems (see generally, Select Committee on Race Relations and Immigration, Session 1968–9, Minutes of Evidence 30 April 1969). Before the 1968 Act was passed, the Engineering Employers' Federation and the Confederation of Shipbuilding and Engineering Unions did agree to establish special machinery to resolve questions involving allegations of racial discrimination outside their normal 'provisions for avoiding disputes'. But in January 1969 the machinery was abolished because the engineering unions regarded it as superfluous in the light of the new legislation. So long as voluntary machinery is used as a shield against statutory intervention rather than as a sword against racial discrimination, its utility will be severely limited.

such information is confidential. Statistics showing the disposal of complaints by voluntary machinery indicate almost nothing about the fairness of the procedure which is followed or of the outcome of the proceedings. All that can be stated with any certainty is that complaints are rejected at about the same rate by both the voluntary and statutory machinery, i.e. in about 95 per cent of all cases.[27]

The only safeguards in the operation of the voluntary machinery are the supervision exercised by the DEP[28] and the right of appeal to the Board. In about one third of the cases where voluntary machinery has formed an opinion that there has been no unlawful conduct, the complainant has appealed to the Board. And, in almost no case has the Board had occasion to uphold an appeal. But the mere fact that appeals rarely succeed does not necessarily mean that the voluntary machinery is operating satisfactorily. Grounds have already been shown for suggesting that many aspects of the system could be improved, but much more needs to be known about its operation. An independent investigation into the working of the voluntary procedures, with the advantage of full access to all relevant information is now due. Such an inquiry would be especially useful because the present system can be amended or abolished without the need for further legislation (s. 16 (2)).

27. 'In the first twelve months (i.e. up to 26 November 1969) 819 employment complaints under sections 3 and 4 of the Act were referred to the DEP. There were suitable bodies in industry to investigate 186 of these complaints; the remainder were passed to the Board . . . of the cases completed by the Board and its conciliation committees during the year, there were findings of discrimination in 5 per cent. The proportion of findings of discrimination by industry machinery was the same' (DEP, 1970a, p. 101).

28. It would be unfair if the reservations here expressed about the effectiveness of voluntary industrial machinery were read as a criticism of the DEP. On the contrary, all the indications are that the DEP are doing everything possible to make the voluntary machinery work. Furthermore, their involvement in race relations as a result of the Act has been a spur to positive effort going beyond the mere enforcement of the statutory provisions. In October 1970, Mr Paul Bryan, Minister of State, DEP, announced the appointment of a further seven race relations advisers. 'There is now an adviser in each of the Department's regions, working in collaboration with its manpower, advisory and employment services and with the Youth Employment Service. They help employers and advisers on request to smooth any difficulties that may result in a multi-racial work force' (*The Times*, 5 October 1970). For a full account of the Department's policy, see DEP (1970b).

Chapter 9
Legal Proceedings

Generally

The procedure for judicial enforcement of the 1968 Act is unique. Generally, proceedings may only be brought by the Race Relations Board; they may bring them only in specially designated courts; and they may claim only specifically defined remedies.

If the Board fails to secure a settlement of any difference between the parties, or, where appropriate, a satisfactory written assurance against any repetition of unlawful discrimination, the Board must determine whether to bring proceedings under the Act. It must also make this determination where there has been a breach of a written assurance. If it decides to bring proceedings, the Board is the plaintiff and the respondent the defendant.

The Board is not obliged to bring proceedings, even if it firmly believes that a complainant has been unlawfully discriminated against, and even if the respondent flatly refuses to offer any redress or to comply with the law. And the complainant has no right of appeal against the Board's refusal to bring proceedings, nor can he bring proceedings on his own behalf.[1] Nothing in the Act affects the right to bring any proceedings, whether civil or criminal, which might have been brought if the Act had not been passed (s. 19 (10)). But there are very few provisions outside the 1968 Act, either at Common Law or under statute law, which could be invoked by the victim of racial discrimination (see chapter 1). Since a refusal to bring proceedings may therefore deprive the victim of a judicial hearing and a legal remedy, the Board will not readily refuse to bring proceedings, if,

1. cf. *Thorne* v. *British Broadcasting Corporation* [1967] 1 W.L.R. 1104 (C.A.) (only the Attorney-General may bring proceedings to enforce section 6 of the Race Relations Act 1965).

having formed an opinion of unlawful conduct, the Board has not been able to deal with it effectively through the process of conciliation.

The nature of the proceedings in England and Wales[2] is civil rather than criminal. The Board may claim (a) an injunction to restrain the defendant from engaging in unlawful conduct in the future, (b) damages to compensate the victim of unlawful conduct, or (c) a declaration that the respondent had acted unlawfully. The Board or the defendant may also apply to the court in the course of proceedings to revise a contract or a term in a contract which contravenes the Act (s. 23 (2)).

Proceedings must be brought only in county courts which have been specially designated for the purpose by the Lord Chancellor (s. 19 (2)). The courts which have been designated[3] are those in Birmingham, Bristol, Cambridge, Canterbury, Cardiff, Carlisle, Exeter, Leeds, Manchester, Newcastle-on-Tyne, Nottingham, Oxford, Plymouth, Southampton, Westminster and Wrexham. Each of the designated courts has jurisdiction over a number of county court districts. The proceedings may be brought either in the court for the district in which the defendant resides, or in which any unlawful conduct is alleged to have occurred, and districts are specially assigned under the Act (s. 19 (3)).[4] A designated court also has jurisdiction to entertain proceedings with respect to things done on ships or aircraft outside its assigned district (s. 19 (6)). None of the usual limits to the jurisdiction of the county court apply to proceedings brought under the Act (s. 19 (2)), so that the Board may, for example, claim damages in excess of the maximum of £750 which can normally be claimed in the county court.

Although only the Board is entitled to bring proceedings in respect of any act alleged to be unlawful by virtue of Part I of the 1968 Act, it seems, as a result of Swanwick J.'s decision in *Ealing London Borough Council* v. *Race Relations Board and Zesko*,[5] that a respondent

2. Similar proceedings in Scotland are provided for in section 20 of the Act.

3. By the County Courts (Race Relations Jurisdiction) Order 1968 (S.I. 1968 No. 1978).

4. See the County Court (Amendment) Rules 1968 (S.I. 1968 No. 2010).

5. [1971] 1 Q.B. 309.

may take the initiative and seek a declaration in the High Court that he has not acted unlawfully contrary to the 1968 Act. In that case, after the Board had formed the opinion that the council had unlawfully discriminated against the complainant on the ground of his 'national origins' (see further, p. 160) but before the Board had determined whether or not to bring legal proceedings, the council sought declarations that they had not acted unlawfully, charming that their conduct was not within the definition of unlawful discrimination in section 1 (1) of the Act. Swanwick J. held that nothing in section 19 or the other provisions of the Act excluded the jurisdiction of the High Court to grant the declarations sought and that the discretion to grant relief by way of declaration would be exercised subject to the contention that the council had acted lawfully.

An appeal against this decision is now pending before the House of Lords. If the decision is upheld it will create an anomalous situation. The respondent unlike the complainant will be entitled to bring legal proceedings. The respondent unlike the Board will be able to launch those proceedings in the High Court. Such proceedings will take place in the absence of the specially qualified assessors. They will entirely bypass the process of conciliation. And the respondent will presumably be able to call for the discovery of documents which would be privileged in county court proceedings by virtue of section 24 of the 1968 Act. There seems little doubt that the 1968 Act was intended to lay down a complete and exclusive code of procedure for legal proceedings. If Swanwick J.'s judgment is affirmed by the Lords, it seems likely that the legislation will have to be amended to remove these anomalies.

Procedure

In general, proceedings under the 1968 Act are conducted like any other actions in the county court. The Board and the defendant serve pleadings on each other, defining the nature of their case. If ordered to do so, they exchange their lists of documents and then inspect each other's documents. Where appropriate, either party may seek the court's permission to interrogate the other in writing before the trial about specified matters. In exceptional circumstances, the Board may apply to the court for an interlocutory injunction restraining the defendant from acting unlawfully before the trial. And either party may apply to the court for a summons to compel the attendance of a witness to give oral evidence or to produce documentary evidence at the trial.

The Board has the burden at the trial of proving, on the balance of probabilities, that the defendant has acted unlawfully. The complainant usually gives evidence about the main facts of the case, and, if possible, his evidence is corroborated by other witnesses. A conciliation officer may describe what has happened since the complaint was made. And, sometimes, the Board may decide to call an independent expert; for example, an assessor, appointed by the Board under section 18, might be able to explain from his special knowledge and experience why a particular practice involves less favourable treatment for the complainant.

However, apart from the contents of a written assurance, evidence cannot be given of anything said or written to the Board or its committees (or, in an employment case, to the DEP or the voluntary machinery) or any of their staff, except with the consent of the person making the communication (s. 24). These communications are privileged from being used in evidence so as to encourage people to co-operate at the conciliation stage. It is similar to the privilege which attaches to 'without prejudice' correspondence between parties, written with a view to compromising proceedings. But it is much wider because it covers communications made at any time, even long before proceedings were contemplated, and the extent of the privilege may sometimes make it difficult for the Board to prove its case. For example, the Board may have brought proceedings in reliance upon an admission by the defendant to their staff that he had acted unlawfully. However, at the trial, the Board will be unable to give evidence of the vital admission. The complete exclusion of such evidence goes well beyond what is necessary to protect the conciliation process.

Each of the Board's witnesses may be cross-examined by the defendant. If the Board's evidence establishes a prima facie case, it is for the defendant to attempt to rebut the case against him. He may be legally represented or he may argue his case by himself.

When the defendant's evidence has been given, and he and his witnesses have been cross-examined, both parties summarize their arguments and the court gives judgment. The legal costs of both parties are normally paid by the unsuccessful party. They may greatly exceed the total damages which may be recovered on behalf of the victim.

As in other county court proceedings, either party may appeal to the Court of Appeal against the judge's decision, whether on issues of fact or of law (s. 19 (9)).

Although the procedure followed in cases under the 1968 Act is generally the same as that in any other county court cases, the composition of the court is different. In the ordinary way, cases in the county court are almost always tried by a judge sitting alone. But proceedings under the 1968 Act have to be heard by a judge assisted by two assessors, appointed from a list prepared and maintained by the Lord Chancellor of people appearing to him to have special knowledge of problems connected with race and community relations (s. 19 (7)).

During the Parliamentary debates, the Lord Chancellor explained the purpose of this provision.[6] He conceded that it was a matter on which there were three perfectly rational views which anyone might take.

The first view, strongly put forward by the Street report, was that there ought to be special race relations tribunals; and many people agreed with that view. The second view taken by the lawyers mainly, was that they did not like the idea of special tribunals; that being lawyers they liked the ordinary courts. . . . The third view is . . . a compromise. . . . That was that there should be selected county courts but that, while the judge should be the only person to decide the case, he should have assessors consisting of people with special experience in race relations to advise him.

The Government had adopted the third view because it was 'most anxious that this Bill . . . should receive the largest measure of support possible.' And although the Lord Chancellor later confessed[7] that it was not his favourite clause in the Bill,' he pointed out[8] that many people 'feel strongly that race relations is such a sensitive subject that it ought to be dealt with by special race relations courts and not left to a judge who may have nothing at all to do with race relations or with coloured people.'

6. Report stage, 15 October 1968 *Hansard* (H.L.), vol. 296, col. 1260.
7. Commons Reasons for Disagreeing with Lords' Amendments considered 24 October 1968 *Hansard* (H.L.), vol. 296, col. 1562.
8. Col. 1572.

The results of the compromise are not altogether happy. The Street Committee had recommended that there should be two distinct types of enforcement machinery: a fact-finding tribunal, selected from a panel of members such as county court judges, recorders and others appointed by the Lord Chancellor, which would determine whether unlawful discrimination had taken place; and the Board itself, which would be empowered to decide what remedies to award against a person found to have discriminated, and to make follow-up checks to ensure that their orders were being complied with. The range of remedies which the Street Committee recommended should be available to the Board, were much wider and more flexible than those which were ultimately included in the 1968 Act. Had they been inserted in the legislation, there would have been a strong case for entrusting the task of awarding and enforcing such remedies to a lay body such as the Board because of the expertise of its members in dealing with the complex problems of housing, industrial relations and race relations.

However, under the 1968 Act, the county court may award only traditional legal remedies; and its trial functions are those performed in everyday litigation. There is therefore not the same need for a special tribunal possessing lay expertise as there would have been under the Street Committee's proposals. In any case, the Board itself has the power to appoint assessors to assist in the investigation of complaints (s. 18), who can be called upon to give expert evidence to the court, and it would always have been possible for the Board, like any other party to county court proceedings, to apply to the judge to appoint assessors to assist him,[9] without the need to make special provision for assessors under the 1968 Act.

Certainly it does seem unnecessarily rigid to require assessors to be appointed in every case, regardless of the issues which have to be determined by the court.[10] Moreover, the qualifications of the assessors who have so far been appointed do not suggest that they always

9. See County Courts Act 1959, section 91 (1). Assessors appointed under this provision as well as under the 1968 Act are merely advisers to the judge, and the judge ought to decide according to his own opinions as to the law and merits of the case: *The Aid* (1881) 6 P.D. 84.

10. For example, it is surely absurd that assessors should have to take part in an interlocutory appeal from the registrar to the judge, or in the trial of a claim for a declaration upon issues of pure law involving the interpretation of the statute.

have special knowledge of problems connected with race and community relations; and it is regrettable that no coloured assessor has yet been appointed. If one of the main objects of this provision was to encourage the largest measure of support possible for the law, it is essential that assessors should include people who enjoy the confidence of the minority as well as of the majority of the community.

Remedies

The forms of relief which may be sought by the Board are defined and limited by the 1968 Act.

Injunctions

The Board may claim an injunction under section 21 of the Act (s. 19 (1) (a)). It may seek either an injunction alone or an injunction and damages (s. 19 (1) (c)). The Board has to satisfy the court of three conditions:

1. That the act complained of was done by the defendant and was unlawful.
2. That the defendant had previously engaged in conduct which was of the same kind as, or a similar kind to, that act and was unlawful.
3. That he is likely, unless restrained by order of the court, to engage in such conduct in the future.

Conditions 1 and 3 are the normal prerequisites in any claim for an injunction. The court has to be persuaded that the defendant has acted unlawfully and that he is likely to do so again before it will make an order restraining him from acting unlawfully. But condition 2 does not have to be satisfied in claims for an injunction outside the 1968 Act. Normally, the fact that a defendant had previously engaged in unlawful conduct might well persuade the court that he was likely to do so again, but it could still infer that there was such a likelihood in cases where no previous unlawful conduct was proved. For example, it is usually sufficient to prove that, although the defendant has committed only one unlawful act, he has expressed his determination to do so again.

That is not enough under the 1968 Act. The Board must prove not only that the defendant has acted unlawfully on one occasion and that he intends to do so again, but also that he has previously engaged in conduct of the same or a similar kind. So, if an employer refuses to give a job to someone on racial grounds and makes it clear that he will continue to discriminate unlawfully with respect to any future vacancies, the Board cannot obtain an injunction unless it is able to establish that he has discriminated unlawfully at least twice in the past; that is, once in respect of the act complained of in the proceedings and once previously. Moreover, the previous conduct must have been the same as or similar to the act complained of in the proceedings. For example, on a narrow view of section 21 (1) the fact that an employer had previously discriminated in a dismissal case might not be sufficiently similar to enable the Board to obtain an injunction against the employer in a recruitment or promotion case.

This obstacle is not removed by the provision which allows the court, in determining whether or not a person has engaged in a course of conduct, to take into account not only the act or acts to which the proceedings relate, but any other act, whether or not it is the subject of an investigation under the Act (s. 21 (3)). That merely means that previous conduct relied upon by the Board need not already have been held unlawful or even officially investigated at all.

This unique restriction upon the power of the Board to claim or of the courts to award an injunction seems to be completely unjustifiable.[11] A single unlawful act coupled with clear evidence that the act is likely to be repeated should entitle the Board to obtain an injunction. Nor is the Board's position improved by its present practice of obtaining written assurances, in the course of the conciliation process, without requiring any admission by the respondent that he has

11. For example, in *Race Relations Board* v. *Geo. H. Haigh & Co. Ltd* (Leeds County Court) (see p. 234) the act of discrimination which was found to be unlawful had occurred only two weeks after the 1968 Act came into force. The defendants' managing director admitted in evidence that it had been their policy for many years to refuse to sell houses to coloured people and that such conduct would in some cases have been unlawful if the 1968 Act had then been in force. However, the Board claimed only a declaration because there was insufficient evidence to satisfy condition (b) of section 21 (1) in a claim for an injunction. Fortunately, although the Board failed on a technical point, the defendants agreed to alter their policy.

acted unlawfully (see p. 308). In the absence of such an admission, the Board has to prove that the original act which resulted in the assurance was itself unlawful; the Board cannot simply tender the assurance as proof of the defendant's previous unlawful conduct.

If the Board is able to satisfy these three conditions, it may apply, in a proper case, for the court to award an interlocutory injunction as soon as proceedings have been commenced, without waiting until the trial. Where the defendant intends to dispose of a property or fill a job vacancy the Board need not therefore watch helplessly while he does so. The court will grant an interlocutory injunction to keep matters as they are until the trial, provided that the Board makes a case on the merits, even though there is a technical defence on which the defendant may succeed at the trial.[12] In deciding whether to do so, the court weighs the balance of convenience to both parties, and the extent to which any damage to the complainant can be cured by the payment of damages rather than by granting the injunction.[13] If a large amount of evidence is disputed, the proper course is for the Board to apply not for an interlocutory injunction, but for a speedy trial.[14]

The court may grant such an injunction as seems to be 'proper in all the circumstances', but the injunction can only be negative in form, restraining the defendant from engaging in conduct of the same kind as his unlawful act or conduct of any similar kind specified in the court's order (s. 21 (1)). The court is not able, under the 1968 Act, to award a mandatory injunction requiring the defendant to do some positive act to put right his wrongdoing, even though it is possible for the court to do so in cases outside the Act. It cannot, for example, order the defendant to offer a house or job to the complainant, or to change his system of recruitment or training.

Where the defendant is a large property owner or employer this may not matter to the victim, because, if suitable accommodation or employment is still available after the court has awarded a negative injunction, the defendant would be in breach of such an injunction were he to refuse on racial grounds to offer it to a prospective pur-

12. See, e.g. *Cory* v. *Reindeer S.S. Co.* (1913) 31 T.L.R. 530.
13. See, e.g. *Denmark Productions Ltd* v. *Boscobel* [1969] 1 Q.B. 699.
14. See, e.g. *Edge & Sons Ltd* v. *Niccolls & Sons Ltd* [1911] 1 Ch. 5 (C.A.).

chaser or employee. But there are bound to be cases in which only a mandatory injunction will provide effective redress. It is regrettable that the court has no power to grant this form of relief.

The court may restrain the defendant from engaging not only in conduct of the same kind as his unlawful act but also in conduct of any similar kind specified in the order. In view of the limited nature of the injunction which can be awarded under the Act, it is important that this provision should be interpreted liberally by the courts. For example, if the defendant is found to have discriminated unlawfully in a promotion case, and it is clear from the evidence that he also discriminates in recruitment or training, the injunction should cover all three aspects of employment, because they are closely related and have a collective effect. On the other hand, there are obvious limits; if the employer also happened to be a landlord, he could obviously not be restrained in an employment case from discriminating against his tenants.

Often it will not be necessary for the Board to seek an injunction on behalf of the particular complainant, for he may no longer want the accommodation, job or other benefit from which he has been excluded by the defendant. In such cases, the only relevant remedy from the complainant's point of view is likely to be the payment of monetary compensation.

But the Board does not act solely on behalf of the individual victim. It is also concerned to protect the community at large against unlawful discrimination, acting in a similar role to that previously performed by the Attorney-General under the Race Relations Act 1965. Therefore, whenever the Board is able to prove that the defendant has acted unlawfully on two or more occasions and that he is likely to do so again unless restrained by the court, the Board ought to seek an injunction.

There is no special sanction in the 1968 Act for breach of an injunction. The normal county court rules apply. A defendant who disobeys an injunction is guilty of contempt and may be committed to prison.[15]

15. See County Courts Act 1959, section 74 and County Court Rules 1936 Order 25 Rule 67. The Queen's Bench Division has jurisdiction to punish a contempt of a county court: see *R.* v. *Staffordshire C.C. Judge* (1888) 57 L. J. (Q. B.) 483.

Damages

The Board may also claim, on behalf of any person alleged to have suffered loss as a result of the defendant's unlawful act, such damages as are mentioned in section 22 of the Act (s. 19 (1) (b)). In seeking this remedy the Board is acting entirely for the victim, and must account to him for any damages which are recovered (s. 22 (3)). In the unlikely event that the Board were to fail to do so, it could be sued by the victim for breach of statutory duty. And, it is at least arguable that if the Board brought proceedings claiming only an injunction, despite the fact that the victim could clearly show that he had suffered loss as the result of the defendant's unlawful act, the victim might be able to obtain an order of mandamus to compel the Board to claim damages in the proceedings on his behalf.

Where damages are claimed, the court, if satisfied that the defendant has acted unlawfully, may award:

1. Special damages.
2. Such damages as the court thinks just in all the circumstances for loss of opportunity, that is to say, loss of any benefit which that person might reasonably be expected to have had but for that act (s. 22 (1)).

However, the Common Law rule concerning the duty of a person to mitigate his loss applies to both types of damages (s. 22 (1)). The maximum amount of damages which may normally be awarded by the county court is £750, but this limit does not apply to proceedings brought under the 1968 Act.[16]

Special damages mean any pecuniary losses which have crystallized in terms of cash value before the trial (Street, 1962, pp. 18–22). They include, for example, expenses which have been rendered futile as the result of the defendant's unlawful act – such as surveyor's fees in a housing case, or travelling expenses in seeking employment; or

16. This appears to follow from the fact that, under section 19 (2) 'Notwithstanding anything to the contrary in any enactment or rule of law relating to the jurisdiction of the county courts, proceedings under this section in England and Wales may be brought in a county court for the time being appointed to have jurisdiction to entertain such proceedings.' Presumably, therefore, an appointed county court is freed from all its normal jurisdictional limits, including the limit upon the maximum amount of damages which it may award.

loss of income resulting from the victim's exclusion from a particular job; or the extra cost of obtaining goods, facilities or services elsewhere, e.g. having to hire a car or to take accommodation in a more expensive hotel.

The concept of damages for loss of opportunity is not entirely novel. At Common Law, compensation can be recovered for any prospective damage which is reasonably anticipated to result from the defendant's wrongdoing, whether in contract or tort. For example, in an action for breach of contract, the innocent party may be awarded damages for loss of profits, or of a bargain, or of the chance of winning a prize;[17] and in a recent case[18] involving the wrongful expulsion of a member of a trade union, the court held that because the plaintiff had been deprived of the opportunity of working in his trade in the printing industry, he could recover the difference between what he could reasonably have expected to earn in that trade and what he would be likely to earn in unskilled work.

A court must not award damages for loss of opportunity unless it is satisfied that, at the time of the unlawful act, the victim was in a position to acquire the goods, services, facilities or land constituting or giving rise to the benefit, or that he had the qualifications necessary for him to obtain or retain the benefit (s. 22 (2)). Under the 1968 Act, as at Common Law, a person obviously cannot recover damages for loss of opportunity unless he can show that, but for the defendant's wrongdoing, he would have been able to enjoy the opportunity.

The court is given a wide discretion in measuring the damages to be awarded for loss of opportunity. It may award such damages as it thinks 'just in all the circumstances'. Sometimes the calculation may be purely actuarial by analogy to the measure of damages for breach of contract. The court will attempt to quantify the financial difference between what the victim would have received or spent if he had obtained the particular benefit and what he will be likely to receive or spend as a result of being deprived of it. This approach may often apply in employment cases, where the main deprivation is a prospective loss of earnings.

But it is important to avoid adopting too materialistic an attitude, instead of having regard to the circumstances of each particular case.

17. *Chaplin* v. *Hicks* [1911] 2 K.B. 786 (C.A.).
18. *Edwards* v. *Society of Graphical and Allied Trades* [1971] Ch. 354 (C.A.).

For example, the victim may have been deprived of the chance to acquire a house in a desirable neighbourhood, yet according to a purely financial calculation he will probably have suffered little if any loss; for it is cheaper to live in squalor than in comfort. Similarly, he may have been barred from a place of public recreation or entertainment in deeply humiliating circumstances, and yet a strictly mathematical calculation would show that he had saved money in not having to pay the entrance fee, and so had suffered no tangible loss.[19] He may have been denied the status and responsibility of a skilled worker and yet suffered no loss of income.

There is no need to measure damages in such cases by analogy to breach of contract. The better analogy is with tort rather than contract. And the language of the statute is broad enough to enable the courts to regard the loss of opportunity as if it resulted from a tort. The courts have to be satisfied that the defendant's wrongful act has deprived the alleged victim of the benefit in question. But, once that is proved, the award should be one which is 'just in all the circumstances'. They are not restricted to tangible, material loss which is largely covered by the separate head of special damage. In an appropriate case they could apply similar criteria to those which are used in personal injury cases. An award could thus include not only a calculation based on the victim's prospective financial loss, but also an element of compensation for his loss of amenity or injured reputation. The overriding principle is that the victim should be compensated for the wrong done to him, so far as the payment of money can do so. This is the only remedy which can be claimed under the 1968 Act specifically on behalf of the victim, and it is important that its effectiveness should not be whittled away by a narrow interpretation of judicial discretion.[20] It remains to be seen how the courts will

19. cf. *Constantine* v. *Imperial Hotels Ltd* [1944] K.B. 693, where the late Lord Constantine was awarded nominal damages of five guineas when he and his family were excluded from a London hotel on racial grounds.

20. American statutes give broad powers to award compensatory damages and there has been a growing inclination to use these powers. 'As a result of increasing positive action taken by the regional offices following decisions of probable cause, compensatory damages were awarded in fifty-five cases totalling approximately $19,000. In several such matters individual awards to complainants exceeded $2,300' (Annual Report of New York State Division of Human Rights for 1968 p. 4). See e.g. *Chance* v. *Frank's Beauty Salon* 316 N.Y.S. 2d 236

in fact exercise their powers.[21]

Declaration

The Board may also claim a declaration that the defendant's act is unlawful (s. 19 (1) (d)). In cases outside the 1968 Act, a declaration may not be claimed at all in the county court unless it is ancillary to a claim for damages.[22] But under the 1968 Act, a declaration may be claimed as the sole form of relief.

Indeed, it might be concluded from the way in which section 19 (1) has been drafted that where a declaration is sought it *must* be sought as the sole form of relief; for the section refers to the possibility of a claim for an injunction and/or damages but does not expressly contemplate the possibility of claiming a declaration in the same proceedings as a claim for the other two forms of relief.

Probably this is an excessively literal interpretation of section (19 (1). But, in any case, it will rarely be necessary for the Board to couple a claim for a declaration with any other relief. The court will only award an injunction or damages if it is satisfied that the defendant has acted unlawfully, so that, where either of those remedies is sought, there is normally no need to claim a declaration.

There are two situations in which a declaration will be particularly useful.[23] First, where the defendant refuses to give a satisfactory written assurance admitting that he has acted unlawfully and promising not to do so again, the Board may want to obtain a declaration

---

(1970) where the New York Supreme Court held that compensatory damages under the Human Rights Law might include damages for mental pain and suffering.

21. In *Race Relations Board* v. *Lenehan*, it was conceded by counsel for the Board that the court was not entitled to award damages for the humiliation and distress suffered by five West Indians refused service in the crowded public bar of the Painters Arms public house on racial grounds. However, he argued that the court had a wide discretion to decide what was 'just in all the circumstances'. Judge Ruttle (Westminster County Court) referred to the fact that none of the complainants appeared to be a 'dedicated drinker' or to have been 'grievously deprived', but he awarded each of them £5 damages (*The Times*, 24 June 1971).

22. See County Courts Act 1959, section 74.

23. For the principles upon which the courts will grant a declaration, see generally Zamir (1962).

that he has acted unlawfully, so as to enable it to obtain an injunction if he repeats the act. Secondly, where the defendant challenges the Board's interpretation of the Act, while indicating that, if the Board were correct, he would reach a settlement and give an appropriate assurance, the Board may seek a declaration to ascertain the proper meaning of the Act.

Revision of discriminatory contracts

Finally, an application may be made, during the proceedings, for the revision of a contract or a contractual term which is alleged to contravene the 1968 Act (s. 19 (1)). The application may be made either by the Board or by any contracting party who is the defendant in the proceedings (s. 23 (2)).

The status of discriminatory contracts under the 1968 Act is unclear and unsatisfactory. The Act provides that a contract or term in a contract which contravenes the Act 'shall not be void or unenforceable by reason only of the contravention but may be revised' (s. 23 (1)). When an application is made for a revision, the court may, if it appears feasible to do so without affecting the rights of persons who are not parties to the contract, revise it so that it no longer contravenes the Act. Thereafter, any party to the contract, whether or not a party to the application, is bound by the order of the court (s. 23 (3)).

Presumably, in certain circumstances it would be unlawful to enter into a discriminatory contract, even though the contract itself would not be void or unenforceable. For example, if A made an agreement with B to assist him in excluding coloured immigrants from his public house, A would be guilty of deliberately aiding B to act unlawfully (s. 12). And, if X agreed to let accommodation to Y upon condition that Y did not sublet to coloured immigrants, X might be liable for deliberately inducing Y to act unlawfully (s. 12). The contract would at least be evidence of the parties' unlawful conduct. It would also be unlawful for either party to a discriminatory agreement to perform the agreement in a manner which contravened the 1968 Act. But if these assumptions are accurate, it is difficult to understand why those terms of a contract which expressly contravene the 1968 Act should ever be capable of enforcement in the courts. If they are not capable of enforcement, then there seems little point in revising them.

The position is made still more obscure by the procedure for revising discriminatory contracts. An application may be made only if proceedings have already been commenced by the Board. It would seem to follow that, unless the Board takes the initiative, one party to such a contract could sometimes be compelled by the other party to perform the contract, unless the courts were willing to treat the contract as illegal or contrary to public policy. And, if the Board does apply to revise a contract, it may do so only on behalf of a party to the contract (s. 23 (2)). Should both contracting parties refuse to authorize the Board to make the application, the contract cannot be revised. Its discriminatory terms will then presumably be in a kind of legal limbo. They are not void or unenforceable under the provisions of the Act, but if either party performs them he will be liable for contravening the Act. Meanwhile, third parties may be expected to assume that the contract is entirely valid and binding, or to be in understandable confusion about the state of the law.

Where the Board is able to apply, the court may not revise a contract unless it is feasible to do so without affecting the rights of persons who are not parties to the contract. This could lead to absurd results. Suppose, for example, that a series of discriminatory agreements are made in similar form in connection with a building scheme, and that the parties to them enter into the agreements in the expectation that they each contain racially restrictive terms which will be performed. The combined effect of these agreements will be to impose a pattern of racial segregation upon the entire estate. And yet it seems that the court could not revise the terms of any one of the agreements, even with the consent of both contracting parties, because to do so would affect the rights of the parties to the other agreements.

These provisions were included in the 1968 Act, with little discussion, at a late stage in its Parliamentary history. They have created several glaring anomalies which could make it easier for some to continue to practise racial discrimination. The proper way of dealing with racially discriminatory provisions in contracts is to make them void for illegality, and to make it an offence to enter into a contract incorporating such provisions.

Part Four

Chapter 10
Incitement to Racial Hatred

Relationship with the anti-discrimination law

Section 6 of the Race Relations Act 1965 created the offence of incitement to racial hatred. A person is guilty of the offence if, with the deliberate intention of stirring up racial hatred, he circulates written matter or uses words in public, which (a) are threatening, abusive or insulting and (b) are likely to stir up such hatred. Section 5 of the Theatres Act 1968 made it an offence for anyone to present or direct a public performance of a play, involving the use of threatening, abusive or insulting words, with the deliberate intention of stirring up racial hatred, if that performance, taken as a whole, is likely to have such an effect.

These offences are entirely separate from the anti-discrimination sections of the Race Relations Acts.[1] They deal with the stirring up of

1. The Genocide Act 1969 has also made it an offence to commit any act falling within the definition of 'genocide' in Article II of the Genocide Convention as set out in the Schedule to the Act. Genocide is there defined to mean 'any of the following acts committed with intent to destroy, in whole or in part, a national, ethnical, racial or religious group, as such:
(a) Killing members of the group.
(b) Causing serious bodily or mental harm to members of the group.
(c) Deliberately inflicting on the group conditions of life calculated to bring about its physical destructions in whole or in part.
(d) Imposing measures intended to prevent births within the group.
(e) Forcibly transferring children of the group to another group.'
If the offence consists of killing any person, there is a mandatory sentence of life imprisonment; in any other case, the maximum sentence is life imprisonment (s. 1 (2)). Since this measure is unlikely to be relevant to any situation which could foreseeably develop in Britain, and which is not already covered by the ordinary criminal laws, it is unnecessary to discuss its contents further. In practice, the most significant provision is probably section 2 (2) under which, for the purposes of extradition, no offence which, if committed in this country would

racial hatred rather than with the acts of racial discrimination; they are criminal rather than civil; and they are enforced by the Attorney-General in the criminal courts, rather than by the Race Relations Board in designated county courts.

To a marginal extent the two types of legislation may occasionally cover similar subject-matter. A person who deliberately incites another to discriminate contrary to the Race Relations Act 1968 is treated as having himself discriminated (s. 12) (see p. 170). If he uses extreme language to incite another to discriminate, with the intention of stirring up racial hatred, he may also be guilty of violating section 6 of the 1965 Act.

The problems which both laws are intended to tackle are also related to each other in a wider sense. Where racial hatred is stirred up, it is obviously much harder to reduce racial discrimination against the victims of such hatred; conversely, where racial discrimination is prevented, the conditions in which racial hatred flourish are likely to be removed.

However, the prohibition of racial incitement raises controversial issues both of principle and practical expediency which do not apply to the law against racial discrimination. It is important that the two subjects should not be confused, and it is for this reason that incitement to racial hatred is separately discussed here.

Legal background[2]

Although section 6 of the 1965 Act created a new offence, it was not unprecedented. It was always possible to use the criminal law against people who incited others to racial hatred if their actions were likely to disturb the peace. The two main weapons of the Common Law were seditious or criminal libel and public mischief.

The crime of sedition has existed for centuries. It was developed by the Star Chamber and survived the Restoration. It is a deliberately

be punishable as an offence of genocide, is to be regarded as an offence of a political character, and no proceedings in respect of such an offence are to be regarded as a criminal matter of a political character. Those accused of crimes of genocide overseas cannot therefore obtain sanctuary here if extradition arrangements are in force with the country concerned.

2. See generally, Longaker (1969); Dickey (1968a); Hepple (M.L.R., 1966, p. 306); Williams (1967); Brownlie (1968).

vague offence, which has sometimes been invoked to suppress the views of those who sought to alter the existing order. According to Stephen, J., it consists of the publication of oral or written words with

an intention to bring into hatred or contempt, or to excite disaffection against the person of Her Majesty, her heirs or successors, or the government and constitution of the United Kingdom, as by law established, or either House of Parliament, or the administration of justice, or to excite Her Majesty's subjects to attempt otherwise than by lawful means, the alteration of any matter in Church or State by law established, or to raise discontent or disaffection amongst Her Majesty's subjects, or to promote feelings of ill-will and hostility between different classes of such subjects.[3]

If such a broad definition were applied in practice, it would seriously threaten freedom of speech. But 'a firmly established qualification of the crime nowadays is that the words used must amount to a direct incitement to violence or public disorder' (Williams 1967, p. 198).[4] Should they be likely to stir up violence or disorder then the accused cannot prove the truth of his words so as to justify his speech or writing.

There have been several prosecutions for seditious libels which involved an incitement to racial hatred. In those which succeeded there was either violence or a likelihood of violence.

In *R*. v. *Osborne*,[5] a criminal information was granted for a libel against some Portuguese Jewish immigrants who were living in London. A scurrilous paper had been published stating that they had burnt a woman and her child because the child's father was a Christian. As a result several Jews named in the paper had been 'attacked by multitudes in several parts of the city, barbarously treated and threatened with death, in case they were found abroad any more'. The Court held that the accused should be prosecuted because the publication tended 'to raise tumults and disorders among the people, and inflame them with a spirit of universal barbarity against a whole

3. Sir J. F. Stephen, Digest of the Criminal Law (1883) art. 93; approved in *R*. v. *Burns* (1886) 16 Cox C.C. at p. 359–60, *per* Cave J.

4. See also Archbold's *Criminal Pleading and Practice* (36th edn), Sections 3147 *et seq*.

5. (1732) 2 Swanst. 503n.

body of men, as if guilty of crimes scarce practicable, and totally incredible'.

R. v. Aldred[6] was not directly concerned with racial incitement, but its facts are relevant even today. The defendant was indicted for seditiously printing in a periodical called the *Indian Sociologist* a seditious libel of 'the Government of our Lord the King of and in the Indian Empire and of the administration of the laws in force' there. The periodical which advocated the independence of India from Britain, was published by Indian students in England. Aldred's article stated that political assassination was not murder, and glorified an Indian student who had killed Sir Curzon Wylie as a martyr for Indian independence.

At the trial, Coleridge J. directed the jury that the test to be applied

is not either the truth of the language, or the innocence of the motive with which he published it, but the test is this: was the language used calculated . . . to promote public disorder or physical force or violence in a matter of State? . . . In arriving at a decision . . . you are entitled to look at the audience addressed, because language which would be innocuous, practically speaking, if used to an assembly of professors or divines, might produce a different result if used before an excited audience of young and uneducated men. You are entitled also to take into account the state of public feeling. Of course there are times when a spark will explode a powder magazine; the effect of language may be very different at one time from what it would be at another. You are entitled also to take into account the place and mode of publication.

Not surprisingly, perhaps, in view of these directions, and the period in which the trial was held, Aldred was convicted and sentenced to one year's imprisonment.[7]

6. (1909) 22 Cox C.C.l.
7. The law was and is much more strict in India itself. By section 153A of the Indian Penal Code (added in 1898) 'Whoever by words, either spoken or written or by signs, or by visible representations, or otherwise, promotes or attempts to promote feelings of enmity or hatred between different classes of Her Majesty's subjects [now, instead, "the citizens of India"], shall be punished with imprisonment which may extend to two years, or with fine or with both.' The crime is committed, regardless of the likelihood of violence, provided that 'feelings of enmity or hatred' are the actual or probable result of the offending communication. For example, in 1906, the *Punjabee* newspaper suggested that an Indian

However, in modern times, few prosecutions for sedition have succeeded, and it was the Crown's failure in the well-known case of *R.* v. *Caunt*[8] which eventually led Parliament to create the new offence of incitement to racial hatred. At the end of July 1947, a wave of indignation and disorder swept through Britain in response to the murder of two British sergeants in Palestine by members of the Irgun gang (Leitch, 1964). In Liverpool, Manchester and elsewhere, large mobs demonstrated and smashed and looted Jewish shops. A Jewish ex-servicemen's meeting was broken up by the police at Bethnal Green, in London, after it had been threatened by a large, hostile crowd. On 6 August, when a number of people were receiving stiff sentences for what a Lancashire magistrate described as these 'un-British and un-patriotic acts' of looting, an obscure newspaper called the *Morecambe and Heysham Visitor*, owned and edited by James Caunt, with a local circulation of 17,800, published an editorial entitled 'Rejoice Greatly!' The article began:

On the morn of the announcement of 'another catalogue of pains and penalties' there is very little about which to rejoice greatly except the pleasant fact that only a handful of Jews bespoil the population of the Borough! The foregoing sentence may be regarded as an outburst of anti-Semitism. It is intended to be and we make no apology, neither do we shirk any responsibility nor repercussions. . . . If British Jewry is suffering today from the righteous wrath of British citizens, then they have only themselves to blame for their passive inactivity. Violence may be the only way to bring them to the sense of their responsibility to the country in which they live.

Caunt was prosecuted at Liverpool Assizes for writing and publishing a seditious libel concerning people of Jewish faith and race in

---

police constable had been killed some six years before not by falling from his horse, but by a kick given by a European police superintendent, and that it was not a solitary instance of a deliberate murder given out to be an accidental death. 'How many poor Indians,' the article continued, 'have been mercilessly launched into eternity in the past, for being mistaken for bears and monkeys, or for having so enlarged spleens.' The editor and publisher were held to have consciously intended to promote enmity and hatred on the part of Indians towards Europeans: see *Jaswant Rai* (1907) Punjab Record no. 10. For examples of more stringent legislation in British India, see Mittall (1970).

8. The trial is reported verbatim in 'An Editor on Trial' (Morecambe Press, 1947). See also Wade (1948).

Britain. He admitted at the trial, as was obvious from its language, that he had intended his editorial to be offensive to Jews. But he denied that he had intended any violence to result from its publication. Counsel for the prosecution conceded that he had to prove that Caunt had deliberately intended to stir up disorder, and Birkett, J. stressed this test in his summing up to the jury. The question he said was whether Caunt had 'published that libel with the intention of promoting violence by stirring up hostility and ill-will between different classes of His Majesty's subjects'.

But although both judge and prosecuting and defending counsel were agreed that this was the right test, it may well have been too narrow. The approach of Coleridge, J. in *Aldred's* case had differed in a subtle but crucial respect. Instead of insisting that the accused should be proved subjectively to have intended to promote disorder, Coleridge, J. had applied an objective test, namely, taking into account the language used, the audience addressed, the state of public feeling, and the place and mode of publication, was the publication likely to promote public disorder or violence? The test was not the innocence of the motive with which the matter had been published.

Birkett J. quoted a different passage from the summing-up in *Aldred's* case where the judge had observed that seditious libel was a weapon which was likely to be abused, 'and if it is abused there is one wholesome corrective, and that is a jury of Englishmen such as you'. The judge stressed two matters in particular: that 'nothing should be done in this court to destroy or weaken the liberty of the Press; and secondly, remember at all times that it is the duty of the prosecution to prove the case beyond all reasonable doubt.' Caunt was acquitted after the jury had retired for only thirteen minutes.

The verdict was scarcely surprising for Caunt had denied any intention to promote violence and there was no evidence that any disorder had resulted from the publication of his editorial. The jury may well have been influenced also by the fact that only six Jews lived in the borough, by the Judge's emphasis upon freedom of speech, and by the prevailing mood of popular indignation against the murder of British soldiers in Palestine (Leitch, 1964).

In any event, *Caunt's* case had a profound effect upon the leaders of British Jewry. They regarded it as a threat to their well-being –

especially since they were living in the shadow of the Nazi holocaust – that a newspaper editor could publish an avowedly antisemitic editorial and go unpunished. From the date of Caunt's acquittal they were to urge successive governments to strengthen the law to deal with those who deliberately stirred up hatred, ridicule or contempt against racial groups, whether or not there was an intention to promote violence.

The test applied in *Caunt's* case of what constitutes a seditious intent has never been considered by an appellate court. If it was an accurate statement of English law, then plainly the weapon of sedition could be used only in the most extreme cases of racial incitement. In view of the subsequent enactment of section 6 of the 1965 Act, it is now mainly a matter of historical interest, but it is interesting to observe that, if Coleridge, J.'s statement contained the right test, and if the application of that test had led to Caunt's conviction, there would have been less popular support for a change in the law.

The other available Common Law weapon against racial incitement is the offence of effecting a public mischief. This is even more vaguely defined than seditious libel and includes 'all offences of a public nature, that is, all such acts or attempts as tend to the prejudice of the community'.[9]

In 1936, Arnold Leese, the then leader of the Imperial Fascist League, was prosecuted for public mischief at the Old Bailey for publishing an article in his magazine, The *Fascist*.[10] The article had associated the Jewish ritual slaughter of cattle with a number of unsolved child murders of which it suggested that the Jewish community might be guilty. Leese was charged both with seditious libel and also with 'inciting a public mischief by rendering His Majesty's subjects of the Jewish faith liable to suspicion, affront and boycott'. He was acquitted of seditious libel but found guilty of public mischief. When he refused to pay a fine, he was sentenced to six months' imprisonment. The sentence had no deterrent effect on Leese. His followers met him outside Wandsworth Prison on his release and drove him in triumph, swastikas fluttering from their cars, to a celebration party.

9. *R. v. Higgins* (1801) 2 East 5, at p. 21, *per* Lawrence J.; approved in *R. v. Manley* [1933] 1 K.B. 529, at p. 534, *per* Lord Hewart, C.J.

10. See generally, Dickey (1968a); Cross (1961), p. 156.

Leese then elaborated his ritual murder allegations in a book, against which there was no prosecution.

The scope of public mischief is wide enough to include any actions calculated to stir up prejudice against racial minorities, regardless of whether they are likely to result in violence. But the very breadth of the offence has led to severe criticism of its use.[11] It is so vaguely defined that it gives the courts virtually unlimited power to declare that something is a crime because it is against 'the moral welfare of the state'.[12] It creates uncertainty about the extent of the criminal law and represents a menace to personal liberty. Even stronger criticisms apply to the still more amorphous offence of conspiracy to effect a public mischief.[13] For these reasons, prosecutors are as reluctant to use public mischief as sedition; both crimes could not convincingly be held out as 'anything more than cumbersome weapons against racial incitement' (Williams 1967, p. 172).

However, there is also a statute which has a sharp cutting edge. The Public Order Act was passed in 1936 as a direct response to the activities of the British Union of Fascists, which had culminated that year in the battle of Cable Street and the Mile End Road antisemitic pogrom (Benewick, 1969, chs. 10, 11). The Act banned the wearing of uniforms (except with police permission on private ceremonial occasions), forbade the use of stewards at open-air meetings, and gave the police the power to ban processions if they were likely to lead to a breach of the peace. But the important provision for present purposes was section 5, which made it an offence for any person, in any public place or at any public meeting, to use 'threatening, abusive or insulting words or behaviour, with intent to provoke a breach of the peace

11. See generally, *R.* v. *Newland* [1954] 1 Q.B. 158, at p. 168, *per* Lord Goddard C.J. (criticized on other grounds in *D.P.P.* v. *Bhagwan* [1970] 3 All E.R. 97 (H.L.) at p. 105, *per* Lord Diplock); Stallybrass (1933).

12. cf. *Shaw* v. *D.P.P.* [1962] A.C. 220 (H.L.), where Viscount Simonds, L.C. advocated the exercise of such a judicial power. But see Lord Reid's vigorous dissenting speech, which appears to have been impliedly followed in *D.P.P.* v. *Bhagwan*.

13. In *D.P.P.* v. *Bhagwan*, Lord Diplock described the current role of criminal conspiracy in the Common Law as the 'least systematic, the most irrational branch of English penal law', and indicated that it was not still open to the courts 'to enlarge the number of categories of purposes which are so contrary to public policy that those who act in concert to achieve them are guilty of a criminal offence at Common Law'.

or whereby a breach of the peace is likely to be occasioned'. The maximum punishment for breach of section 5 was three months' imprisonment or a fine of £50, and offences were triable only at the summary level.

Despite the moderate nature of the penalties, section 5 achieved its immediate object. Police shorthand writers regularly attended meetings of the British Union of Fascists in search of insults, and often found them. The first conviction for insulting words was against a speaker in London's East End who had referred at an open-air meeting to 'Dirty, mongrel Russian Jews' and declared that 'Jews are the lice of the earth and must be exterminated from the national life'. He was bound over for six months in the sum of £50 and threatened with imprisonment if he committed a further offence. Other prosecutions quickly followed. 'The result was a definite modification of Fascist propaganda with less provocation to Jews and other anti-Fascists' (Cross, 1961, p. 177).

Three aspects of section 5 have contributed to its effectiveness. First, the offence is committed either if the accused deliberately intends by his actions to provoke a breach of the peace or if there is, in any event, likely to be a breach of the peace. So, unlike the test applied in *Caunt's* case, it is no defence that the accused did not intend to provoke violence, if it was likely that violence would result. Secondly, the statutory definition of 'public meeting' and 'public place' are wide enough to apply to words or behaviour used at any public meeting, whether held in a public place or on private premises. And thirdly, the key phrase 'threatening, abusive or insulting words' (which is also used in section 6 of the Race Relations Act 1965) gives the courts a very wide discretion in applying the law.[14]

Potentially, the Public Order Act has a very extensive reach, as was

14. On occasion the discretion may well have been abused. For example, it seems that, during the Second World War, section 5 was used to suppress the public expression of views which were critical of the government. In one case, a young man was imprisoned for two months for saying 'This rotten Government is holding 390 million Indians in slavery' in the course of a speech; in another, a person was convicted for distributing leaflets advertising a Communist meeting and stating: 'Bring the guilty to account. . . . Britain needs a Government based on working people, a Government in which there is no friend of Fascism' (Williams, 1967, p. 160). No doubt these were the excesses of wartime, but they illustrate the possibilities of abuse.

illustrated by the Divisional Court's decision in *Jordan* v. *Burgoyne*.[15] The case arose out of a public meeting held in Trafalgar Square in July 1962, by the National Socialist Movement. Among the crowd of several thousands gathered in the square were many committed opponents of the Movement, determined to prevent the meeting from being held by creating disorder. A speech by John Tyndall, the national secretary of the Movement, had to be stopped on four occasions for order to be restored. When Colin Jordan, the Movement's leader, began to speak, the situation grew still more turbulent.

Jordan proclaimed that on 3 September 1939, 'the blackest day in British history', the efforts of the Jews were crowned with success 'and Jews of the world rejoiced'. And he went on to say that 'more and more people every day . . . are opening their eyes and coming to say with us: Hitler was right . . . our real enemies, the people we should have fought, were not Hitler and the National Socialists of Germany but world Jewry and its associates in this country'. These words led to complete disorder, and the meeting was stopped by the police.

Jordan was charged with using insulting words whereby a breach of the peace was likely to be occasioned. At Quarter Sessions it was held that, although his words were highly insulting, they were not likely to lead ordinary reasonable people at the meeting to commit breaches of the peace. But, on appeal, the Divisional Court decided that, in construing section 5, there was no room for any test based on consideration of whether any member of the audience was a reasonable man. Lord Parker, C.J. stated that he could not imagine any reasonable citizen,

certainly one who was a Jew, not being provoked beyond endurance, and not only a Jew but also a coloured man and quite a number of people of this country who were told that they were merely tools of the Jews and that they had fought in the war on the wrong side.

And he went on,

This is . . . a Public Order Act, and if in fact it is apparent that a body of persons are present . . . yet if words are used which threaten, abuse or insult – all very strong words – then the speaker must take his audience as he finds them, and if those words to that audience, or to that part of that

15. [1963] 2 Q.B. 744.

audience, are likely to provoke a breach of the peace, then the speaker is guilty of an offence.

A literal application of this approach in other cases might seriously impair freedom of speech, for it would seem to follow that if a speaker uses insulting words to an audience of rowdy extremists bent on disrupting the meeting, it is the speaker who risks prosecution as a result of their unreasonable violent behaviour.

During the following year, the Divisional Court decided[16] that the operation of section 5 should not be confined to disorders of the kind associated with meetings and other public gatherings. Provided that the usual elements of the offence are all present, it is sufficient that the words are spoken in public and that their effect is to provoke a private quarrel. Section 5 can therefore apply where there is drunk and disorderly behaviour or a dispute between neighbours.

And, to add to this forceful judicial interpretation, section 5 has also been further strengthened by Parliament, because of the activities of the National Socialist Movement and other extreme racialist groups in the early 1960s. The Public Order Act 1963 made it possible for the accused to be tried on indictment, and increased the maximum penalties to twelve months' imprisonment and/or a fine of up to £500. Exemplary sentences can therefore now be imposed at Quarter Sessions or Assizes.

Lastly, section 7 of the Race Relations Act 1965 (which is not concerned with race relations despite its presence in that Act) has removed the shadow of a doubt about whether section 5 applies to written words and other permanent representations. Previously, it was faintly arguable[17] that the reference to 'words' in the Public Order Act included only spoken words, and that the reference to 'behaviour' did not include the display of signs or placards. The 1965 Act clarifies the point by extending the Public Order Act specifically to include the distribution or display of any 'writing, sign or visible representation which is threatening, abusive or insulting'. The

16. *Ward* v. *Holman* [1964] 2 Q.B. 58.

17. However, a number of prosecutions were brought under the unamended Public Order Act on the basis of written material (Williams, 1967, pp. 161–2). The Home Secretary described the amendment of section 5 as a clarification of its scope 'probably not enlarging it'. Sir Frank Soskice, Q.C., M.P., 3 May 1965, *Hansard*, vol. 711, col. 916.

amendment was intended to deal, in the Home Secretary's words,[18] with 'the dissemination of objectionable pamphlets, the posting of offensive notices in public places, or ... the carrying or waving of banners with objectionable inscriptions on them'.

The Public Order Act, as amended by Parliament and applied by the courts, is therefore extensive in its scope; and it amply covers the type of conduct contemplated by the Common Law crimes of sedition and public mischief. Provided that the words of the statute are applied with care only to situations where there is, beyond any reasonable doubt, an intention to provoke violence or a likelihood of violence, the statute does not threaten civil liberties. It preserves the delicate balance between public order and personal liberty.

There are, of course, many types of racialist propaganda which are not prohibited either at Common Law or under the Public Order Act, because, although they expose groups of people to prejudice, ridicule, derision or contempt on account of their colour, race, ethnic or national origins or religion, they are not likely to stir up violence. And, as will become clear later in this chapter, propaganda of this nature is still not prohibited, despite the enactment of section 6 of the Race Relations Act 1965.

Two Common Law offences – blasphemy and obscene libel – do penalize some types of speech or writing even though they create no danger of public disorder, but neither of them is relevant to most forms of racialist propaganda of a non-violent yet scurrilous kind. At one time,[19] it was blasphemous to attack the established Christian religion (but not Judaism, Mohammedanism or any disestablished sect of Christianity) without threatening the peace. But it is now settled[20] that the courts will deal with irreligious words only 'for their tendency to endanger the peace generally, to shake the fabric of society, and to be a cause of civil strife ... the attitude of the law ... towards all religions depends fundamentally on the safety of the State

18. Sir Frank Soskice, Q.C., M.P., 3 May 1965, *Hansard*, vol. 711, col. 936.

19. *R.* v. *Gathercole* (1828) 2 Lewin C.C. 237.

20. See *Bowman* v. *Secular Society Ltd* [1917] A.C. 406 (H.L.) at pp. 466–7, *per* Lord Sumner. At p. 464, Lord Sumner dismissed the statement, in *Gathercole's* case, that Christianity was part of the law of England as being not really law but rhetoric.

and not on the doctrines or metaphysics of those who profess them'.

As the result of recent cases[21] it is arguable that racialist publications could be held to be criminally obscene, if they were couched in a form which tended to 'deprave or corrupt' those who were likely to read them; for obscenity is not confined to sexual matters. But the courts would probably refrain from developing new law in this field, and would treat racialist propaganda either as a threat to the peace, punishable under the Public Order Acts, or else as an offensive but legitimate expression of personal opinion.

As for the *civil* law of defamation, members of an ethnic or racial group have no redress in respect of defamatory writings or utterances which reflect on the group at large without being referrable to particular individuals[22]. The law protects only personal not group reputation. And, unlike the Southern States of America, where it has been held actionable to write and publish of a white man that he is Negro or coloured,[23] it would not normally be actionable to do so in England, where the courts would probably decide that to describe someone falsely as belonging to a particular racial group, would not lower his reputation in the eyes of right thinking members of the community,[24] at any rate in the absence of special circumstances.

21. See *John Calder (Publications) Ltd* v. *Powell* [1965] 1 Q.B. 509; *D.P.P.* v. *A. & B.C. Chewing Gum Ltd* [1968] 1 Q.B. 159; *R.* v. *Calder & Boyars Ltd* [1969] 1 Q.B. 151; Zellick [1970].

22. *Knupffer* v. *London Express Newspaper Ltd* [1944] A.C. 116.

23. See *King* v. *Wood* Nott. & McC.(So. Car.) 184 (1818); *Upton* v. *Times Democrat* 104 La. 141 (1900); *Hargrove* v. *Oklahoma Press Co.* 265 Pac.R. 635 (1828); *Natchez Times Pub. Co.* v. *Dunigan* 72 So. 2d 681 (1954).

24. There is no recent English decision on the point, and the older authorities are more quaint than satisfactory. In *Forbes* v. *King* (1833) 1 Dowl. 672, the plaintiff brought an action for libel because of a passage in the *Satirist* newspaper, describing him as a 'Man Friday', and attributing to him the belief that black people were intellectually equal to whites. In the course of argument, Bayley, B. said, 'A man may be black, and be a subject of the realm', to which the plaintiff's counsel replied, 'You would not call a subject of this realm a member of a black population. I submit that no one can read this paragraph without seeing that its evident object and tendency is to degrade and vilify the plaintiff.' However, the action failed on procedural grounds. And, in *Hoare* v. *Silverlock* (1848) 12 Q.B. 624, Lord Denman said of *Forbes's* case, 'The imputation there implied nothing worse than being a black; a great misfortune perhaps, but no crime. . . . The "Friday" alluded to . . . was a very respectable person; black men have not been declared to be criminal by any act of Parliament.'

If the offending matter contains something more than merely a false racial epithet, an action in defamation can, of course, succeed. For example, (Cross, 1961, pp. 156–7; Benewick 1969, pp. 269–71), in 1936, John Beckett, editor of the British Union of Fascists' periodical, *Action*, published an article in which he bitterly attacked Lord Camrose, proprietor of the *Daily Telegraph*, saying that 'the Berry family is of Jewish extraction and has intimate contacts with international Jewish interests'. The plaintiffs sued for libel, alleging that the article had conveyed that Camrose was an unscrupulous, unpatriotic Jewish financier and that he was running the *Daily Telegraph* with that interest above all. Camrose was not a Jew; but the defence denied that the words were defamatory, for there was nothing derogatory in being a Jew or to call a man a Jew.

Not surprisingly, Beckett, who argued his case in person, disagreed with this line of defence, and told the jury that 'to his mind two of the deadliest insults to address a man were to tell him that he was a Jew and that his financial interest were far greater outside this country than in it'. When he discovered that these facts about Camrose were inaccurate, he explained that he wanted to apologize. But he would not apologize for his attack on the *Daily Telegraph* and he attacked the 'Press Lord' system.

The jury awarded Camrose £12,500 damages and £7500 to the *Daily Telegraph* (which Beckett, *Action* and the printers could not and never did pay). It is impossible, of course, to know what influenced the jury in awarding these sums, but the words complained of were plainly capable of being defamatory apart from the false statement that Camrose was of Jewish extraction, and the verdict should probably be approached on that basis.[25]

What emerges from a survey of the legal background is that, with-

25. Similarly, in 1939, *Blackshirt* printed an article which imputed that Horatio Meyer & Co., a furniture firm, was controlled by alien Jews and imposed unfair working conditions. The company brought proceedings which were later settled out of Court (Benewick, 1969, pp. 271–2). Again, the libel does not appear to have consisted merely of ascribing Jewish or alien origins to those in control of the company, but also of suggesting that there was something sinister about their origins and improper about their employment practices. However, there may, of course, be circumstances in which it could be defamatory to impute alien origins to someone, e.g. enemy alien origins in wartime: cf. *Weinberger* v. *Ingliss* [1919] A.C. 606 (H.L.) discussed at pp. 50–51.

out the necessity of creating a new offence of racial incitement, English law could deal effectively with racialist speeches or publications which either threatened the peace or injured the reputation of identifiable individuals. Two overlapping areas were untouched by the law as it stood before 1965: incitement to racial hatred (rather than to violence), and the defamation of racial groups (rather than of identifiable individuals). Many other countries had extended their laws to cover them (Roth, 1965; Lerner, 1968). But such an extension raised difficult problems of principle and expediency for the legislator.[26]

The issue of principle is whether it is possible to penalize the dissemination of racialist ideas without encroaching unduly upon freedom of speech. There is no moral dilemma where words are merely missiles hurled in crude verbal attacks with the deliberate intention of causing suffering to people because of their racial origins. Few libertarians would claim that language of that kind, used in those circumstances, deserved the protection of freedom of speech.[27] Usually, such conduct would in any event contravene section 5 of the Public Order Act. The difficulty arises with the dissemination not of insults but of ideas based on racial superiority, or facts, whether true or false, which may encourage racial prejudice or discrimination. It may be scientifically unsound or morally reprehensible for an educational psychologist to publish the results of research designed to prove that some racial groups are intellectually inferior to others; but ought it to be made a criminal offence for him to do so?[28] It may be grossly unfair to blame a racial group for the wrongdoing of some of its members, but again, should it be unlawful to do so, – or to identify

26. The wider issues have been analysed more closely in the United States than in this country, usually in the context of the First Amendment to the US Constitution, see, e.g. Riesman (1942); Kallen (1968); Pemberton (1968); and the majority and dissenting opinions in *Beauharnais* v. *Illinois* 343 US 250 (1952).

27. For example, the qualification of the freedom to manifest one's beliefs is recognized by Article 9 (2) of the European Human Rights Convention, which makes it subject to such limitations as are 'necessary in a democratic society in the interest of national security, public safety or the economic well-being of the country, for the prevention of disorder or crime, for the protection of health or morals, or for the protection of the rights and freedoms of others'.

28. The framers of the International Convention on the Elimination of All Forms of Racial Discrimination, 1965, would answer in the affirmative. Article 4 (a) obliges States Parties to declare an offence punishable by law 'all dissemination of ideas based on racial superiority or hatred'.

particular wrongdoers by their colour or race?[29] Should the law prevent estate agents from making representations that property values will fall if black people move into an all-white neighbourhood?[30] Each of these statements may be ugly, misleading or against the public interest but so are the statements of many dissenters. Democracy stands (and, some would say, may fall) on the conviction that unpopular ideas should be freely expressed, and that, if they are false or evil, they will ultimately be defeated, not by censorship or prosecution, but by public education and debate.

It would be possible to reconcile legal restraint upon the communication of racialist statements, with freedom of speech, by including a series of defences in the legislation. For example, it could be a defence to establish that the statements communicated were true; or that they were relevant to any subject of public interest, the discussion of which was for the public benefit, and that the communicator on reasonable grounds believed them to be true; or that he intended, in good faith, to point out, for the purpose of removing them, matters producing or tending to produce feelings of hatred towards

29. Thus, a leading national newspaper often refers to the national or racial origins of people convicted of criminal offences. According to the newspaper's correspondence editor this is both to avoid confusion between innocent and guilty people sharing the same name, and also to enable the reader to witness events through the reporter's eyes. Granted that it would sometimes be proper to use national or racial descriptions in reports of criminal trials (e.g. where offences have been committed against immigration or race relations laws); but it is difficult to understand the propriety of a general policy of this kind. The innocent Dr Khan or John Smith is as likely to be mistaken for the guilty Dr Khan or John Smith if the latter is described as 'a Pakistani', 'a Jamaican' or 'a coloured man' as if he were described simply by name. A racial description might even increase the likelihood of confusion between two people with the same name and origins. And, since newspapers do not normally describe the physical characteristics of criminals ('red-faced', 'obese', 'round-shouldered', etc.) merely because they are visible, there is no good reason why an exception should be made for skin colour. Significantly the newspaper in question would not dream of describing someone as 'Jewish-looking'. However, although this policy is, in our view, clearly undesirable, and likely to encourage racial stereotypes, it should not be prohibited by law.

30. See, e.g. *Chicago Real Estate Board* v. *City of Chicago* 224 N.E. 2d 793 (1967), where a fair housing ordinance banning such representations was upheld not only on the ground that they tended to encourage illegal discrimination, but also on the ground that they were defamatory of Negroes.

an identifiable racial group. These are all complete defences to the charge of wilfully promoting group hatred under the Canadian criminal code.[31] But at this point the issue of principle merges with problems of expediency.

Racialist statements are frequently made by dedicated fanatics, who naturally believe in the righteousness of their cause. Such people would welcome the publicity which their opinions would inevitably receive in the course of a sensational criminal trial. They would be especially likely to invite prosecution if they were permitted to attempt to convince a jury, no doubt with the aid of dubious 'expert' evidence, that their statements were true; or were relevant to matters of public interest, the discussion of which was for the public interest; or that they were made as sincere attempts to reduce racial hatred – for example, by urging that coloured immigration should be halted so as to reduce prejudice; or that a racial minority should desist from certain types of anti-social behaviour. Whatever the outcome of the trial, their prosecution might only advance their cause. If they were acquitted, their views would receive respectability and judicial legitimacy; if they were convicted, they would still have enjoyed considerable publicity, and they could plausibly present themselves as martyrs struggling to preserve freedom of speech.

In view of these difficulties, it is scarcely surprising that successive governments remained reluctant to enter such an obvious legislative minefield,[32] but the activities of the National Socialist Movement and other extremists groups caused the National Executive Committee of the Labour Party to issue a statement in 1962 condemning racialist propaganda and incitement, and urging the government to pass appropriate legislation. During the following year, the Public Order

31. Criminal Code, section 267B, added by amending legislation in 1970.

32. In 1936, Campbell Stephen, an ILP Member, introduced an amendment to the Public Order Bill to make it an offence to use insulting words or behaviour to incite racial or religious prejudice, but it was rejected by the House of Commons (see *Hansard*, vol. 378, cols. 630–54, 26 November 1936). Between 1961 and 1964, Fenner Brockway and other Labour MPs attempted unsuccessfully to introduce several Racial Discrimination and Incitement Bills. A proposal to amend the civil law so as to make group defamation an actionable wrong was rejected by the (Porter) Committee on the Law of Defamation in their report (Cmnd 7536 (1948) at pp. 30–32). Lord Silkin failed in his effort to include such a civil wrong in the Defamation Act 1952.

Act was strengthened (see p. 353). But support still continued to grow within the Labour Party for a law to deal specifically with racial incitement, until the Party pledged itself, in its 1964 General Election Manifesto, to introduce such a measure.

The path trodden by the Home Secretary, Sir Frank Soskice, to fulfil the pledge, was skilfully chosen to avoid any unreasonable infringement of freedom of speech. However, although he succeeded in skirting that particular hazard, the new statutory offence, which must now be examined, contains several practical dangers, some avoidable and other inevitable.

Racial incitement: the new offences

A person is guilty of an offence, under section 6 of the 1965 Act, if,

with intent to stir up hatred against any section of the public in Great Britain distinguished by colour, race or ethnic or national origins:

(a) He publishes or distributes written matter which is threatening, abusive or insulting,

(b) He uses in any public place or at any public meeting words which are threatening, abusive or insulting,

being matter or words likely to stir up hatred against that section on grounds of colour, race or ethnic or national origins (s. 6 (1)).

The offence is punishable, on summary conviction, by a maximum of six months' imprisonment or a fine of £200, or both; and, on conviction on indictment, by a maximum of two years' imprisonment or a fine of £1000, or both. But no prosecution can be brought except by or with the consent of the Attorney-General (s. 6 (3)).

When introducing the measure to the House of Commons, the Home Secretary explained that section 6 was

designed to deal with more dangerous, persistent and insidious forms of propaganda campaigns – the campaign which, over a period of time, engenders the hate which begets violence. That is why the penalties are substantially greater than those in section 5 of the Public Order Act. That is why, also, no prosecution can take place except by or with the consent of the Attorney-General.[33]

33. See generally, Rt Hon. Sir Frank Soskice, Q.C., M.P., Second Reading debate, 3 May 1965, *Hansard*, vol. 711, cols. 926–43.

He was also at pains to emphasize that section 6 made only a marginal change to the existing law and that it did not entrench on freedom of speech. It involved the loss only of the liberty

by the use of outrageous language, not privately but publicly, to seek to stir up actual hatred against mostly completely harmless groups of people in this country for something they cannot possibly help, namely, their origin.

And, upon closer inspection, it is indeed clear that every ingredient of the offence has been carefully defined so as to safeguard the accused against any unreasonable interference with freedom of belief and expression.

First, section 6 applies only to written matter distributed, or words spoken, on what might loosely be called a public occasion. To offend section 6, written matter has to be published or distributed 'to the public at large or to any section of the public not consisting exclusively of members of an association of which the person publishing or distributing is a member' (s. 6 (2)). As for spoken words, they have to be used in a 'public place' or at a 'public meeting', both of which have the same meanings as in the Public Order Act (s. 6 (2)). Section 6 does not affect what is said or written to one another by members of a private body. And, whereas the Public Order Act prohibits the use of threatening, abusive or insulting words or behaviour, as well as the distribution or display or any writing, sign or visible representation which is threatening abusive or insulting, section 6 includes only spoken words or written matter, not, for example, racialist behaviour expressed by mime or gesture. This omission seems to be anomalous.[34]

Secondly, the propaganda must be expressed in terms which are 'threatening, abusive or insulting' – again following the language of the Public Order Act. No offence is committed where opinions are expressed in a restrained and rational style, however unpleasant they may be for a particular section of the community.

Thirdly, and this is an especially strong safeguard for the accused, the propaganda must be disseminated with the deliberate intention of stirring up racial hatred. It will be remembered that an offence may

34. The anomaly has been repeated and aggravated by section 5 (1) of the Theatres Act 1968: see p. 367.

be committed under the Public Order Act, regardless of the accused's intentions, if threatening, abusive, or insulting words or behaviour are used, or literature is distributed, which are intended *or* likely to cause a breach of the peace. Under section 6 of the 1965 Act, the accused must actually intend to stir up racial hatred. But if he behaves in a way which would lead one reasonably to infer that he intended to do so, he cannot escape conviction by denying that he really had any such intention. In the Home Secretary's words,

The nature, virulence and persistence of the propaganda, the methods by which and the circumstances in which it was conducted, would . . . ordinarily afford the clearest pointers to the court as to what really had been the accused person's intent.

Fourthly, not only must there be an intention to stir up racial hatred, but the language used must also be likely, in fact, to do so. Unlike the Public Order Act, which requires either an intention to provoke a breach of the peace or a likelihood that a breach of the peace will result, both elements must be present in order to constitute the offence. It is true that section 6 substitutes racial hatred for public disorder. That is, as the Home Secretary explained, 'far from a momentous change'. Racial hatred contains the seeds of violence. It is a stronger and more aggressive emotion than ridicule or contempt. Where racial hatred is deliberately and successfully stirred up, it is likely to lead to public disorder. Words may be used which are abusive or insulting, and obviously motivated by racial prejudice, but, unless they are likely to stir up more violent emotions than prejudice or contempt against a racial group, section 6 does not apply.

Fifthly, hatred must be stirred up against a section of the public in *Great Britain*. It is not unlawful to foment racial hatred against people outside this country. This qualification is of slight practical importance, because threatening, abusive or insulting propaganda against coloured, or racial, or ethnic, or national groups overseas will often also amount to an attack on a section of the British public, and a threat to public order in Britain. Colin Jordan would not, for example, have escaped conviction under the Public Order Act if he had confined his notorious speech in Trafalgar Square to a virulent diatribe against 'foreign Jewry'; his conduct would still have threatened the peace in Trafalgar Square. The same would have been true of his prosecution for racial incitement – such a speech would still have been likely to stir up hatred against British Jewry. Only racialist propaganda which is specially confined to attacks against groups outside this country, and which is not likely to promote hatred against members of those groups living here, will avoid section 5 on this ground.

Sixthly, section 6 covers only racial and not religious incitement. There is an obvious distinction between them. Membership of a religious group involves personal choice, and religious beliefs and practices are as much the subject of public controversy as political opinions; membership of a racial group involves inherited and immutable physical characteristics, and is not directly relevant to controversial beliefs, ideas or behaviour. A racial attack is therefore a more fundamental assault upon a person's humanity than an attack upon his religion. But although this distinction can be made (and was made during the Parliamentary debates) it is questionable whether it justified the exclusion of religious incitement from section 6. Granted that freedom of speech should protect passionate religious controversy, there seems no reason why, as a matter of principle, it should excuse threatening, abusive or insulting propaganda deliberately disseminated so as to whip up religious hatred. Ironically, by excluding religion from the incitement provision, as well as from the anti-discrimination provisions, of the legislation (see p. 156); Parliament has left members of the Jewish community without legal protection against religious as distinct from racial persecution – ironically, because the Jewish community have been the most persistent advocates of such legislation. Probably the Government was influenced to omit religion from the Race Relations Acts more to avoid pressure to extend the measures to Northern Ireland[35] than because of nice distinctions between race and religion.

Finally, no prosecution can be brought, either summarily or upon indictment, except by the Attorney-General or with his consent. If a

35. During the passage of both statutes, attempts to apply them to Northern Ireland were resisted because of the Ulster Government's opposition. However, local legislation has since been enacted in Northern Ireland to prevent religious incitement and discrimination. It is regrettable that uniform provisions, with national enforcement machinery, do not apply throughout the United Kingdom.

private individual, a police officer, or the Director of Public Prosecutions, considers that the offence has been committed, he may refer the matter to the Attorney-General, but, if the Attorney-General refuses to bring proceedings, no one else may do so. For example, an attempt was made[36] by a resident in Britain of German origin to mount a civil action on the basis of an alleged violation of section 6 by the BBC. The plaintiff claimed that the BBC had conducted a continuous propaganda of racial hatred against the Germans, and he sought to restrain them from disseminating racialist abuse. The Court of Appeal struck out his claim on the ground that section 6 created only a criminal offence, and that any remedy for a breach of the section was under the Attorney-General's exclusive control.[37]

It could not plausibly be argued, in the face of these defences, exceptions and restrictions, that section 6 was an unreasonable infringement of freedom of speech or personal liberty. Because of its cautious drafting, and the Home Secretary's lucid explanation of its narrow effect, it was enacted without amendment, and received only desultory criticism from the Opposition.[38] Some continued to object to the provision on libertarian grounds throughout the Parliamentary debates; others complained that it was too restricted, in particular, because it excluded religious incitement and the dissemination of racial propaganda among members of a club.[39] But there was scant

36. *Thorne* v. *British Broadcasting Corporation* [1967] 1 W.L.R. 1104 (C.A.).

37. The Court of Appeal did not rule out the possibility that the Attorney-General might be able to bring an action for an injunction restraining a breach of section 6, or that an individual might be able to do so with the Attorney-General's consent.

38. Before the Parliamentary debates, the Opposition tabled an amendment declining to give a Second Reading to the Bill 'which introduces criminal sanctions into a field more appropriate to conciliation and the encouragement of fair employment practices while also importing a new principle into the law affecting freedom of speech'. However, although their Front Bench spokesman and several Opposition backbenchers attacked section 6 on libertarian grounds, they were clearly reassured by the Home Secretary's analysis of its scope. The main thrust of their attack on the Bill concentrated upon the anti-discrimination provisions (see pp. 116–19), and, in the final stages, section 6 was strongly praised by the Shadow Home Secretary, Quintin Hogg, Q.C., M.P.

39. On 19 December 1966, the House of Lords rejected a Racial and Religious Discrimination Bill, introduced by Lord Brockway. In addition to extending the scope of unlawful discrimination and increasing the powers of the Race Relations Board, the Bill would have amended section 6 by (i) making it an offence to

reference to any practical problems which might be created by section 6.

Serious problems have arisen in practice as a result of the enactment and enforcement of section 6, which will later be weighed against the advantages claimed for the measure. Nevertheless, despite these difficulties, and widespread criticism from the supporters as well as the opponents of anti-discrimination legislation, section 6 was not altered by the Race Relations Act 1968, which amended only the anti-discrimination sections of the 1965 Act. Instead, the Theatres Act 1968 applied the offence of racial incitement to a new area: the public performance of plays.

By section 5 (1) of the Theatres Act 1968, it was made an offence for any person to present or direct a public performance of a play which involves the use of threatening, abusive or insulting words, if (a) he did so with intent to stir up hatred against any section of the public in Britain distinguished by colour, race or ethnic or national origins, and (b) the performance, taken as a whole, is likely to stir up hatred against that section of the public on those grounds. Proceedings can be brought only by or with the consent of the Attorney-General (s. 8), and the maximum penalties for incitement to racial hatred by means of the public performance of a play, are the same as under section 6 of the Race Relations Act 1965 (s. 5 (2)). 'Public performance' includes any performance in a public place within the meaning of the Public Order Act (s. 18 (1)).

Section 5 (1) has been modelled on the same pattern as section 6 of the 1965 Act, and there are the same safeguards for the accused. But, in one important respect, racial incitement is more comprehensively dealt with under the Theatres Act: there is no exception for performances to members of theatre clubs. And, although there is an exception for the obscene performance of a play given on a domestic occasion in a private dwelling (s. 7 (1)), there is no equivalent exception for the racialist performance of a play.[40]

---

promote contempt of, as well as hatred against, racial groups, (ii) extending the provision to include the dissemination of racial propaganda to members of clubs, and (iii) substituting the Director of Public Prosecutions for the Attorney-General (see *Hansard* (H.L.), vol. 278, cols. 1838–1910).

40. Similarly, there is no such exception to section 6 (1) (which deals with the provocation of a breach of the peace by means of the public performance of a

Nor is it a defence to prove (as it is in cases of obscenity: section 3 (1)) that the giving of the performance in question was justified as being for the public good on the ground that it was in the interests of drama, opera, ballet or any other art, or of literature or learning. Such a defence is necessary in cases involving the presentation of an obscene stage performance because a person can be convicted for that offence whether or not he intended that a performance would deprave or corrupt members of the audience. But since a person cannot be convicted under section 5 unless (a) the performance involved the use of threatening, abusive or insulting words, (b) he presented or directed it with the deliberate intention of stirring up racial hatred, and (c) the performance, taken as a whole, was likely to do so, freedom of speech is at least as well protected under the racial incitement provision of the Theatres Act as under section 6 of the 1965 Act. To allow the defence of the public interest would not merely be an unnecessary further additional safeguard, for it would also undermine the aims of the law. It could never be in the public interest to present or direct the public performance of a play in the extreme circumstances contemplated by section 5; and the opinion of experts as to the artistic, literary or other merits of the performance (admissible in a prosecution for obscenity under section 3 (2)) could not establish that it was in the public interest to do so in those circumstances.

In deciding whether a performance is likely to stir up racial hatred, the performance is to be 'taken as a whole' (s. 5 (1) (b)). Threatening, abusive or insulting words should not be considered in isolation, but within the context of the entire performance. And a person who merely takes part in a performance directed by someone else will not be guilty of an offence, unless without reasonable excuse, he disregards that person's directions (s. 18 (2)). These additional restrictions have been properly placed upon section 5 because of the special nature of stage plays.

However, the restrictive wording of section 5 also contains the

---

play). There is a general exemption for the performance of a play given solely or primarily for the purpose of a rehearsal, recording, filming, or broadcast, but in any proceedings under sections 2, 5 or 6, if it is proved that the performance was attended by persons other than those directly connected with the giving of the performance, recording, etc., the burden is upon the accused to prove that the performance was solely or primarily for an exempted purpose (s. 7 (1)).

same loophole as section 6 of the 1965 Act, in that it applies only to words and not behaviour. This is particularly anomalous because offensive mime or gestures are more likely to accompany the performance of a play than a public speech. Indeed, this is recognized by the definition of a play, which refers to what is done by the performers, whether by way of 'speech, singing *or action*', involving 'the playing of a role' (s. 18 (1)). And the anomaly is further aggravated by the fact that it is only for the purposes of the law of defamation, and not racial incitement, that the Theatres Act defines 'words' to include 'pictures, visual images, gestures and other methods of signifying meaning' (s. 4 (3)); whilst the offence of provoking a breach of the peace by means of the public performance of a play *does* include behaviour as well as words (s. 6 (1)).

No prosecutions have as yet been brought under section 5 of the Theatres Act. However, in view of its similarity to section 6 of the Race Relations Act 1965, much of the following discussion of the practical operation of section 6 would equally apply to section 5. Several of the cases in which the courts have interpreted the former offence would be relevant to the latter; and the two provisions have the same virtues – and drawbacks.

The enforcement of section 6 (Dickey, 1968a; 1968b)

The first prosecution under section 6 was brought almost a year after the 1965 Act had become law. Although section 6 had been presented to Parliament as a measure 'designed to deal with more dangerous, persistent and insidious forms of propaganda', it was invoked in a trivial case against Christopher Britton, a seventeen-year-old labourer, because he had attached a racialist tract ('Blacks Not Wanted Here') to the front door of Sydney Bidwell's house, the MP for Southall, and had left several others outside the door, wrapping one of them round a beer bottle which he had thrown through the door glass.

The Court of Appeal quashed the conviction[41] of the 'wretched little youth' on the ground that Britton's actions did not constitute publication or distribution 'to the public at large or to any section of the public' within the meaning of section 6 (2). The occupiers of Mr

41. *R.* v. *Britton* [1967] 2 Q.B. 51.

Bidwell's house – he and his family – were clearly not 'the public at large'; but were they 'a section of the public'? The Court held that they were not, and although their reasoning was somewhat obscure (Dickey, 1968a, p. 319; Partington, 1967, p. 497), the decision itself was justifiable. The distribution of pamphlets, on a single occasion, to a family at their home, was distribution to a small, domestic group which would not normally be described as having been to a section of the public.

It was unfortunate that the Attorney-General had chosen such a weak case in which to apply section 6. The court observed disapprovingly that it seemed

difficult to believe that Parliament ever intended that there should be distribution within the meaning of this section by leaving a pamphlet of this sort with a Member of Parliament with the object of persuading him to change his policy, and fight against allowing immigrants to come into the country.

There was a hint in that observation that the court believed that Britton might not have intended deliberately to stir up racial hatred, but only to influence policy.

The next two prosecutions were better chosen to deal with the extreme type of racialist propaganda that Parliament had intended to prohibit. The first was brought against Colin Jordan, leader of the National Socialist Movement, and one of his accomplices. They had published and distributed a pamphlet entitled 'The Coloured Invasion' proclaiming that 'The presence of this Coloured million in our midst is a menace to our nation', and had also distributed anti-semitic stickers. At his trial, on a charge of inciting others to distribute insulting racialist literature, Jordan claimed that he had intended only to inform people truthfully of grave national problems, as he saw them, and to encourage a patriotic desire to solve these problems by lawful means. But Phillimore J. instructed the jury to look for Jordan's real intention, taking into account not only his own words, and the disclaimer of any intention to promote racial hatred, which was printed on the literature, but also the policy and purposes of the National Socialist Movement. Jordan was convicted in January 1967, and received a sentence of eighteen months' imprisonment. His accomplice was placed on probation for three months. In May 1967,

Vincent Carl Morris, another member of Jordan's organization, was found guilty at Leek Magistrates' Court of inciting two youths to distribute racialist leaflets, and was sentenced to six months' imprisonment.

The prosecutions under section 6 had so far been concerned only with racialist literature rather than speeches, and with incitement to racial hatred of Jews or coloured immigrants. In late 1967, against a background of growing anti-white invective by members of the Black Power movement, proceedings were brought against the leader of the Racial Adjustment Action Society (RAAS), Michael Abdul Malik, who was charged with using insulting words to stir up racial hatred at a Black Power meeting in Reading. Malik was convicted at Quarter Sessions in November 1967, and sentenced to twelve months' imprisonment.[42] In the same month, four members of the Universal Coloured People's Association were also prosecuted for using words to stir up hatred against white people at Speakers' Corner, Hyde Park, and were fined a total of £270.

These cases demonstrated that section 6 applied to the incitement of racial hatred against white as well as coloured people; that may indeed have been the Attorney-General's main objective in bringing the prosecutions. But the consequences may not have been foreseen. Racialist utterances to small audiences in Reading and at Speakers' Corner were prominently reported in the national Press during the trials, because the speakers represented 'Black Power'. That had not been true of the prosecutions against members of the National Socialist Movement, whose opinions had received very little attention in the Press. And, it has fairly been observed that

Neither the RAAS nor the UCPA were large or active groups, or well-known until the Government jumped at shadows and the publicity attached to the trials brought them to public notice; much the same can be said for the self-styled leaders (Longaker, 1969, p. 129).

However, apart from the misguided prosecution of Britton, it could at least be claimed that the Attorney-General had so far succeeded in enforcing section 6 whenever he had considered it appropriate to do so. In March 1968, a much more significant prosecution was brought under that provision, which was doomed to be a disastrous

42. *R.* v. *Malik* [1968] 1 All E.R. 582.

failure. In *R.* v. *Hancock* (Longaker, 1969, pp. 130–42), four members of the Racial Preservation Society were tried for incitement to racial hatred in having distributed copies of the Society's *Southern News* in East Grinstead. Inexplicably, the issue of the broadsheet selected for prosecution was relatively innocuous compared with earlier issues. It expressly disavowed any intention of preaching 'racial hatred or contempt of any other race or minority group', declaring instead that its purpose was the return of people of other races from this 'overcrowded island' to 'their own countries'. It referred to the dangers of 'race mixing', attacked politicians as 'race levellers', unwilling to face the facts of excessive immigration, and contained speculation about genetic differences between races and the dangers of racial contact. White Britain was viewed as being threatened by Liberals, Communists, scientific assimilationists and the increasing coloured population.

The authors had obviously taken care to avoid the operation of section 6 by expressing their views without overt threats, abuse or insults, and the defendants asserted that their broadsheet sought a humane solution to the problem of anti-white immigration, and that theirs was essentially an educational enterprise attacking politicians for their inaction; they denied any intention to attack coloured immigrants.

In the course of the trial at Sussex Assizes, counsel for the defence described *Southern News* as merely somewhat more hard-hitting than other public comment. He argued strongly against the application of section 6 as an unwarranted infringement of freedom of speech, and ranged broadly over matters of public policy arising from post-war immigration. Unlike the prosecution, which relied solely upon the evidence of the police officers involved in arresting the accused, and a representative from Scotland Yard, the defence witnesses included a controversial scientific expert witness, whose opinions about physical anthropology and racial characteristics were not effectively challenged. The court

became a forum for speculation about the effects of miscegenation, the purity of the races, the impact of immigration in the schools, the crime rate and the genetic inequality of the races. Possibly because the issue was one of proving intent, the prosecution offered no objection to this speculation and the judge did not question its relevance (Longaker, 1969, p. 132).

The defendants were all acquitted. And the Racial Preservation Society has since reprinted *Southern News* no. 5 with the overprint 'Souvenir Edition' and 'The Paper the Government Tried to Suppress'. Because of their acquittal, the defendants had turned section 6 to their advantage. They could now represent themselves as defenders of free speech, while claiming that their trial had given respectability, and even legitimacy, to their views.

The effects of section 6

There have been no prosecutions since *R.* v. *Hancock*. The very failure of the prosecution in that case ironically vindicated those who have argued that section 6 does not unreasonably restrict freedom of speech and expression, for the defendants would probably not have been convicted, even if the prosecution had adopted a more effective strategy. Future prosecutions are likely to be brought only against a speaker or distributor of written matter who is

outside the mainstream of British political life and so exceptionally odious or coarsely offensive in the virulence of his racialist statements that a jury will be willing, if not eager, to overlook the free speech counter-arguments and the ambiguous technicalities of the tests in the law itself. . . . Furthermore, the history of the section indicates that where there is an aura of violence, including a sense of its immediacy, a jury will be encouraged to arrive at the same conclusion. The irony is that a successful prosecution under section 6 will bear a remarkable resemblance to a prosecution under the Public Order Act (Longaker, 1969, p. 148).

Since the enactment of section 6 there has been a decided shift in the style of racialist publications. They tend to be more cautiously worded. Their contents are less antisemitic and more directed to pseudo-national discussion of the adverse impact of coloured immigration upon British society. They disclaim any intention to stir up racial hatred and purport to be contributions to public education. This change is not an unmixed blessing, for the apparent moderation of recent examples of racialist propaganda is likely to widen their potential audience and to deepen their effect upon public opinion.

One immediate consequence of section 6 was the creation of a network of book clubs, deliberately designed to evade the operation of the law. The cost of membership of such clubs is nominal, and membership is granted automatically to anyone wishing to obtain their publications. However, the risk that the courts might refuse to recognize them as bona fide clubs exempted from section 6, the difficulty in recruiting members, and the advantages of 'respectable' racialist propaganda, are likely to prevent such bogus book clubs from becoming a widespread phenomenon.

The libertarian dangers of section 6, foreseen during the Parliamentary debates, have not been realized in practice. But that has not prevented the common if mistaken belief that freedom of speech has been curtailed. For example, when some London dockers marched in support of Enoch Powell, one of their placards stated: 'Race Relations Act is a Gag on Free Speech'. The fact that Powell and others have repeated their views more and more vehemently, without being prosecuted, has not dispelled their aura of martyrdom in the cause of truth and public well-being.

A series of false expectations and misunderstandings have developed about the scope and operation of section 6. For example, speeches, television programmes and newspaper reports about race relations have often led to demands for prosecution, even though they could not possibly have been intended or likely to stir up racial hatred. Each such demand reinforces mistaken hopes or anxieties (according to a person's particular standpoint) that criminal proceedings will indeed be brought. Public attention is diverted from considering whether racialist propaganda is morally wrong or factually inaccurate to whether it is illegal. In such a climate, the demagogue's cowardly attack upon a defenceless minority can all-too-readily be interpreted as courageous conduct, carrying a real risk of prosecution and imprisonment, while members of the minority are regarded not as victims but as a privileged group, immune to criticism.

On the other hand, it is tempting for members of the coloured community to conclude that section 6 is unevenly applied against them. They observe that prominent white politicians are able to voice highly prejudiced and influential opinions to a national audience, without any action being taken against them, whereas Black Power spokesmen are prosecuted for making crude and flamboyant speeches at local meetings. They see a profound difference between the offensive actions of the former and the defensive responses of the latter, but the difference is not reflected in the policy underlying the enforcement of section 6. Because the trial of Black Power spokesmen has received much greater publicity than the trial of Colin Jordan and his supporters, there is a widespread and erroneous impression that most of the prosecutions have been brought against black people. And distrust is aggravated because it is the Attorney-General, rather than the Director of Public Prosecutions, who decides whether a prosecution should be brought. It may be wrong to suspect that the Attorney-General might be influenced by political considerations in refraining from prosecuting a powerful fellow politician, but it is understandable that some should harbour such suspicions.

On both sides of the colour-line there are therefore firmly held and mistaken beliefs that people are unfairly affected by section 6. There is also considerable uncertainty among the public about the relationship of section 6 to the other provisions of the Race Relations Acts. The origins of the confusion are to be found within the structure of the legislation, because the anti-discrimination provisions are in juxtaposition with the prohibition of incitement to racial hatred. As a result, complaints about racialist propaganda are continually being made to the Race Relations Board instead of to the Attorney-General, and there is a persistent impression that racial discrimination is punishable by a fine or even imprisonment, instead of being tackled by informal conciliation and civil proceedings. Such confusion is likely to encourage public sympathy for the alleged discriminator, believed to be in danger of being harshly punished, and to be the source of misplaced resentment against the Race Relations Board.

Misunderstanding about the state of the law has been taken to absurdity by section 7 of the Race Relations Act 1965, which, it will be recalled, widened the scope of the Public Order Act so that it applied to written matter as well as words or behaviour. Section 7 has no direct connection with race relations; it is exclusively concerned with public order. However, because section 7 is part of the 1965 Act, a prosecution for breach of its terms can easily become muddled with racial issues. For example, a woman was prosecuted for distributing a leaflet outside an American servicemen's club urging Americans to consider objecting to the Vietnam war by participating in demonstrations or by other non-violent acts, including desertion. No racial issue was involved, but she was charged and convicted under the Public Order Act 'as amended by section 7 of the Race Relations

Act'. The description of her offence was technically accurate but misleading.

Apart from the doubtful advantage that racialist propaganda has become more sophisticated, the effect of section 6 has probably been adverse to race relations in Britain. Certainly it has been at best marginal in its impact; it has also impaired the enforcement of the anti-discrimination provisions of the Race Relations Acts, and has therefore been strongly criticized by supporters of those provisions (Rose *et al.*, 1969, pp. 687–8; Longaker, 1969).

But it would not be desirable to repeal section 6 altogether, because such a step would encourage a spate of scurrilous racialist literature purporting to be circulated with Parliamentary approval. The wiser course would be to extend section 6 to include incitement to group hatred (rather than racial hatred) and incorporate it in a separate statute where it cannot be confused – and in conflict with – the use of law to combat racial discrimination.

Chapter 11
Conclusion

In our account of the Race Relations Acts we have drawn attention to some unnecessary exceptions to the scope of the legislation, and to more serious deficiencies in its enforcement provisions. We began by expressing the hope that Parliament would not regard the present statutes as the end of wisdom in the use of law to combat racial discrimination. At the time of writing (October 1971) there is no indication that the Government is considering any measures to remove the worst defects from the Race Relations Acts, or indeed to enforce the present statutes more vigorously. But in our view, reforms are needed if the legislation is to be saved from falling into disrepute with those whom it was designed to benefit. It would be tragic if Britain's new ethnic minorities were to lose confidence in the willingness of the community to ensure that there are effective legal remedies against racial discrimination in employment, housing and elsewhere. Recent events in the United States and Northern Ireland provide a grim warning of the consequences of acting too timidly and too late to guarantee genuine equality before the law.

It may be helpful to summarize the main recommendations to improve the race relations legislation which arise out of the earlier discussion. But, before doing so, it should be emphasized that not even the best-drafted statute will work in an unfavourable economic and social environment. Equality of opportunity will remain a pious declaration of hope so long as there is high unemployment, widespread scarcity in the housing market, gross deprivation in primary and secondary education, and inadequate social welfare benefits.

Similarly, we believe that the effectiveness of the Race Relations Acts is and will continue to be undermined by discriminatory immigration laws.

The use of such laws to prevent immigration to Britain from the coloured Commonwealth inevitably impairs the Race Relations Board's endeavours to persuade employers, trade unions, local authorities and commercial undertakings to treat people regardless of colour or race, and encourages profound insecurity among Commonwealth immigrants in Britain. The absence of a coherent code of civil rights for all United Kingdom citizens, and the existence of a pseudo-citizenship for 'non-patrial' citizens, reinforce the harmful effect of these laws.

Immigration legislation is outside the scope of this book, but vitally affects its subject matter. So too, of course, does the action or inaction of Government. The Administration which was responsible for enacting the Race Relations Acts is no longer in office. Its successors have been strikingly reticent in acknowledging the problems of racial inequality. The best token of their readiness to tackle them would be the introduction of a comprehensive Bill to strengthen the Race Relations Acts. The following recommendations are intended to provide an agenda for such reforms.

The Scope of the Race Relations Acts[1]

1. The meaning of 'unlawful discrimination' should be clarified so as to prevent racial discrimination from being practised in the guise of religious discrimination. There is also a powerful case for extending its scope to include other forms of unfair discrimination (e.g. sex, religion, age or class) and for applying the legislation, undiluted, to Northern Ireland.

2. Section 2 should prohibit discrimination not only by persons concerned with providing goods, facilities and services to the public, but also by those (e.g. professional firms, educational institutions and working men's clubs) who provide facilities and services to their own members.

3. It should be made unlawful for a police officer to discriminate on racial grounds in the exercise of his powers or the performance of his duties.

4. Section 3 should be extended to include discrimination against

1. Except where otherwise stated, references to sections in the following summary relate to the 1968 Act.

resident aliens in employment in the public service. This change will assume particular importance if Britain joins the European Economic Community and is obliged to ensure equal employment opportunities for workers from EEC countries. The present blanket exceptions, in sections 3(2) and 27(9), should be replaced by a narrow exception for employment in the public service on work involving national security.

5. The 'racial balance' exception (section 8(2)) is incompatible with the spirit of the legislation and is not justifiable. It is unnecessary to wait for amending legislation, since the Secretary of State has a special statutory power to repeal the provision by order. This power should be exercised forthwith.

6. A 'racial imbalance' provision should be added, so as to permit positive discrimination programmes to be implemented, where appropriate, in employment, housing and education in order to overcome the effects of past discrimination.

7. The exception for the employment of any person 'for the purposes of a private household' (section 8(6)) should be limited to the employment of any person 'in a private household', so that occupations such as domestic electrical repairs and window-cleaning are brought unequivocally within the scope of the law.

8. The exceptions for advertising for employment overseas (section 6(2)) and for recruitment for employment overseas (section 8(7) (a)) are an unnecessary concession to racially discriminatory practices outside Britain. Since there is no justification for exempting such acts of discrimination committed in this country, they should be repealed.

9. The various exceptions for racial discrimination in employment on British and foreign ships and aircraft, both within and outside British territory (section 8(7) (8), (9) and (10)) should be repealed.

10. The exception for acts of racial discrimination done on British ships and aircraft in foreign waters or airspace for the purpose of complying with the laws of foreign countries (section 11(2)) should be repealed.

11. The exception for racial discrimination in the allocation of

sleeping cabins for passengers on a ship (section 7(6)) should be repealed.

12. The exception for the selection of a person of a particular nationality or descent for employment requiring 'attributes especially possessed by persons of that nationality or descent' (section 8(11)) is unnecessarily broad and should either be narrowed or repealed.

13. The exception for acts of racial discrimination done 'for the purpose of safeguarding national security' (section 10) should be repealed or restricted to discrimination on the ground of national origins in employment in the public service on work involving national security.

14. Section 23, which enables racially discriminatory contractual terms to be revised by the courts, should be replaced by a provision that any contract or term of a contract which is racially discriminatory shall be completely void and unenforceable.

15. Section 5 of the Race Relations Act 1965 is inconsistent with the 1968 Act in dealing with racial restrictions imposed on the disposal of tenancies. It should be replaced by a provision that any covenant, agreement or stipulation purporting to restrict the sale or letting of property on racial grounds shall be completely void and unenforceable.

16. In order to prevent people from mistakenly assuming that racially discriminatory terms in contracts, leases, etc. are valid and enforceable, it should be made a criminal offence to include them in such documents.

The enforcement of the Race Relations Acts

17. The Race Relations Board's power to investigate suspected instances of unlawful discrimination in the absence of any specific complaint (section 17) should be widened, so that the Board is able to investigate any situation which it regards as important, without the need for the Board to suspect that a particular person may have been discriminated against. This would free the Board from its excessive dependence upon individual complaints.

18. The Board should be empowered to investigate employment

discrimination where no complaint has been made without the need to refer the investigation, in the first instance, to voluntary industrial machinery (sch. 3, pt II). The work of such machinery should be confined to specific complaints, leaving the Board free to conduct general investigations in employment as elsewhere.

19. The procedures for the investigation of employment complaints by voluntary industrial machinery are cumbersome, and should be more strictly regulated.

20. The normal time within which a complaint should be made to the Board or its conciliation committees should be increased from two months (section 15(2)) to six months from the act of which complaint is made.

21. The Board should be enabled to refuse to investigate any complaint which, in its opinion, has been made frivolously or vexatiously.

22. The Board should be empowered to compel the attendance of witnesses, the disclosure of documents, and the keeping and production of relevant records. This reform is especially important because the Board may be seriously hampered in its work by its dependence on winning the cooperation of the respondent in order to obtain the necessary information with which to evaluate the complaint against him.

23. The Board's power to bring legal proceedings (section 19) should be extended so as to enable the Board to apply to the court, if an emergency arises at any stage in its investigations, for an interim order restraining any further violations of the law until the complaint has been dealt with. The Board should be able, in an appropriate case, to give an undertaking to compensate the respondent for any loss or damage suffered by him as a result of such an order, if he is later exonerated by the Board or by the court.

24. If the court is satisfied that a defendant has acted unlawfully, and that he is likely, unless restrained by order of the court, to engage in the future in such conduct, the court should be empowered to grant an injunction. The present additional requirement that the defendant should have engaged in such conduct before the particular act complained of (section 21(1)(b)) should be repealed.

25. Where appropriate, the court should be empowered not only to grant an injunction restraining future unlawful conduct, but also to order the defendant to put right the wrong done to the complainant (e.g. by offering him employment or reinstatement, or by granting him a tenancy). The court should be able to make other forms of positive order to ensure future compliance with the law (e.g. the keeping and production of relevant records).

26. The court should be empowered to award damages for humiliation and distress suffered as a result of unlawful discrimination. Such damages should be at large but should be limited to a reasonable maximum (e.g. the normal county court limit of £750).

27. Where the Board forms an opinion that there has been no unlawful discrimination, or decides not to bring legal proceedings, or fails to make any determination within a specified period of time (e.g. six months from the date of a complaint), the complainant should be entitled to bring legal proceedings on his own behalf in the county court. Alternatively, the complainant should be entitled to appeal to the court against the Board's determination that there has been no unlawful discrimination and its refusal to bring proceedings on his behalf. This reform is urgently needed to overcome the apparently widespread sense of alienation among victims of racial discrimination, and to give them the same opportunity as the victims of any other civil wrong to seek a remedy from the courts.

28. Under section 24, evidence of any communication made to the Board or its conciliation committees, in the course of the process of investigation and conciliation, may not be given in legal proceedings without the consent of the person by whom it was made. The Board should be empowered, with leave of the court, to give evidence of any voluntary admission of guilt or of any previous communication which casts doubt upon the credit of any witness. Alternatively, it should be a criminal offence for any person to make a false statement to the Board or its conciliation committees, knowing that it is false, or not caring whether it be true or false.

29. It should be a criminal offence to intimidate, harass or discriminate against, any person in order to prevent or discourage him from exercising his rights under the Race Relations Acts.

30. Special measures should be taken to promote equal employment

opportunities among government contractors. It is not sufficient, as at present, merely to require contractors to give an assurance that they are complying with their obligations under the 1968 Act. Contractors should be obliged to disclose relevant information about their employment policies annually to the Board. Where necessary, they should be required to take affirmative steps to improve their policies before Government contracts are granted or renewed. If they act in breach of the non-discrimination clause, it should be possible for the government department or other public body concerned to cancel the contract.

31. Special measures are also needed to secure the enforcement of the law in the field of local authority housing. The detailed recommendations of the Select Committee on Race Relations and Immigration, in their report on Housing (HMSO, July 1971) should be implemented as a matter of urgency.

Incitement to racial hatred

32. Section 6 of the 1965 Act, and section 5 of the Theatres Act 1968, which create the criminal offence of incitement to racial hatred, should be extended to include incitement to religious and other forms of hatred against particular sections of the community. The new offence, together with section 7 of the 1965 Act (extending the Public Order Act 1936 to written matter) should be included in the legislation on public order rather than on race relations. If this recommendation, and the change proposed in paragraph (15) above, were implemented, the whole of the 1965 Act could be repealed, and the race relations legislation would be contained in a single comprehensive statute.

Appendix 1
The First British
Anti-Discrimination Law:
A Cautionary Tale

The conquest of the earth, which mostly means the taking it away from those who have a different complexion or slightly flatter noses than ourselves, is not a pretty thing when you look into it too much. What redeems it is the idea only. An idea at the back of it; not a sentimental pretence but an idea; and an unselfish belief in the idea – something you can set up, and bow down before, and offer a sacrifice to.
Joseph Conrad, *Heart of Darkness* (1902)

No one was aware, during the passage of the Race Relations Acts in the 1960s, that Parliament had long before legislated against racial discrimination in employment. That measure and its subsequent fate are a forgotten chapter of British Imperial history. It is relevant to the theme of this book to recall those events. They are a reminder that Britain acquired a deep experience of race relations, as an Imperial power, and that the present manifestations of racial prejudice and discrimination in Britain reflect that experience. They reveal the existence of similar conflicts to those which have arisen in modern times, about the use of legislation in promoting racial equality; and they provide a cautionary tale about the dangers of using law as a mere totem to be worshipped self-righteously in the name of liberal morality, without any marked effect on the conduct of either the worshippers or of those in whose name they seek to govern.

The mood of Britain in the 1820s, influenced by the writings of Jeremy Bentham and his disciples, was increasingly receptive to a period of reform, both at home and abroad. In the late 1920s, 'Liberals, Evangelicals and humanitarians were the most influential groups in determining British attitudes towards India' (Bearce, 1961, p. 153). In 1827, Lord William Bentinck, who was a representative of Liberal and Evangelical attitudes, was made Governor-General of India. And, by 1830, 'inspired by another French Revolution, the

British public dispensed with Wellington's Conservative Government and entrusted political power to men sympathetic to Liberal and humanitarian reforms. The way was open for Liberal and humanitarian attitudes to attempt a decisive transformation of India.'

At that time, the East India Company still ruled India indirectly on behalf of the British Government, under a charter which had to be renewed by Parliament every twenty years. And, in 1833, the charter came before Parliament for renewal. Earl Gray's Government was at the height of its reforming activities. In the previous year, the enactment of the Reform Bill had marked the first major advance towards universal suffrage. Early in 1833 a vigorous (but unsuccessful) attack had been mounted in the Commons on the civil disabilities suffered by Jews. Later in that year, Parliament was at last to abolish slavery in the colonies.

One of the main targets of the reformers was the policy which had been carried through by Cornwallis, and consolidated by Wellesley, as Governors-General of India at the end of the nineteenth century, of 'a sweeping anglicization of the British power, removing all Indians from all but the petty offices' (Stokes, 1959, p. 6). The principal motive for this policy had been Cornwallis's conviction that Indians could not be 'honest or efficient as public officials' (Bearce, 1961, p. 46). The issue was especially important in India, where 'Government had always been the largest employer, and service under it the main avenue of employment for the literate and professional classes of the country' (Seal, 1968, pp. 115–16).

A Select Committee had recently scrutinized the affairs of the East India Company, and had reported[1] that Indians were only employed in subordinate situations, and were 'alive to the grievance of being excluded from a larger share in the executive government'. The Committee had concluded from the evidence that their exclusion was 'not warranted on the score of incapacity for business, or the want of application or trustworthiness'. The Government responded by including clause 87 in the new Government of India Bill 1833, prohibiting racial and religious discrimination in the public service.

Clause 87 seems to have been framed at Bentinck's own suggestion[2]

1. Report from the Select Committee on the Affairs of the East India Company (1832), Parliamentary Papers (1831–2), vol. 9, p. 21.
2. According to Lord Monteagle, 5 August 1853, *Hansard*, vol. 128, col. 1366.

and it was strongly supported by Macaulay, the Secretary of the Board of Control for India, who 'voiced the trenchant, generous, empirical liberalism' of the time (Stokes, 1959, p. xiv). It was probably also accepted readily enough by the hard-pressed East India Company, anxious to demonstrate their own liberalism and fitness to continue to govern. The clause was clear and concise. It stated that no native of India nor any natural born subject of His Majesty resident in India 'shall, by reason only of his religion, place of birth, descent, colour, or any of them, be disabled from holding any place, office or employment' in the East India Company.

And the strongest praise for it came in the Second Reading debate from Macaulay in one of his most famous speeches. He referred to clause 87[3] as 'that benevolent, that noble clause' and went on:

To the last day of my life, I shall be proud of having been one of those who assisted in the framing of the Bill which contains that clause. We are told that the time can never come when the native of India can be admitted to high civil and military office. We are told that this is the condition on which we hold our power. We are told that we are bound to confer on our subjects every benefit . . . which we can confer on them without hazard to our own domination. Against that proposition I solemnly protest as inconsistent alike with sound policy and sound morality. I am far, very far, from wishing to proceed hastily in this most delicate matter. I feel that, for the good of India itself, the admission of natives to high office must be effected by slow degrees. But that, when the fulness of time is come, when the interest of India requires the change, we ought to refuse to make that change lest we should endanger our own power: this is a doctrine which I cannot think of without indignation. Governments, like men, may buy existence too dear.

In view of Macaulay's subsequent role, it is interesting to find that he developed this approach further in his Minute on Education (Trevelyan, 1864, pp. 410–24) written in 1835, where he urged that the first object of British policy in India should be to raise up an English-educated middle class 'who may be interpreters between us and the millions whom we govern – a class of persons Indian in colour and blood, but English in tastes, in opinions, in morals and in intellect'. The most ardent advocate of Macaulay's view was his young brother-in-law, Charles Trevelyan, 'in whose person the fusion

3. 10 July 1833, *Hansard*, vol. 19, col. 534.

of the Evangelical and Radical outlook was most completely realized' (Stokes, 1959, p. 46).

Clause 87 was not opposed during the Commons debate, but, in the Lords, Ellenborough, the former President of the Board of Control in Wellington's Government and a future Governor-General of India, exclaimed that he never 'looked forward to a period when all offices in India would be placed in the hands of natives . . . We had won the Empire of India by the sword, and we must preserve it by the same means.'[4] The Duke of Wellington added that he 'certainly thought that it was advisable to admit the natives to certain inferior civil and other offices, but the higher ones must as yet be closed against them, if our Empire in India was to be maintained'.[5] In spite of this Conservative opposition, clause 87 was duly enacted without amendment.

It is doubtful whether the government believed that clause 87 would have much practical significance, even at that stage. Within a few months, Charles Grant, the President of the Board of Control, described it, in a message to Bentinck,[6] as a rather 'barren assertion of principle', because, with all the desire 'to advance and employ' Indians in the public services, the Government doubted if Indians were ready for such posts. In the following year, a public dispatch to the Government of India[7] set out the directors' view of the effect of clause 87. The dispatch began unequivocally:

It is fitting that this important enactment should be understood in order that its full spirit and intention may be transfused through our whole system of administration . . . its object is not to ascertain qualification, but to remove disqualification. . . . The meaning of the enactment we take to be that there shall be no governing caste in British India: that whatever other tests of qualification may be adopted, distinctions of race or religion shall

4. 5 July 1833, *Hansard*, vol. 19, col. 191.

5. 5 August 1833, *Hansard*, vol. 20, col. 323.

6. 25 December 1833; cited by Bearce (1961, p. 174).

7. Extracts from the Dispatch from the Court of Directors of the East India Company to the Government of India (no. 44, dated 10 December 1834) are reprinted in Mukherji (1915, p. 59). The authorship of the Dispatch is traditionally ascribed to James Mill. Its stress on the test of 'fitness' rather than race had certainly been reflected in Mill's powerful evidence to the Select Committee on the Affairs of the East India Company (see Minutes of Evidence (Public), vol. 1 (1832) para. 400).

not be of their number: that no subject of the King, whether of Indian or British or mixed descent, shall be excluded either from the posts usually conferred on our uncovenanted servants in India, or from the covenanted service itself, provided that he be otherwise eligible consistently with the rules and agreeable to the conditions observed in the one case and in the other. . . . Fitness is henceforth to be the criterion of eligibility. To this altered rule it will be necessary that you should both in your acts and your language conform.

But it went on significantly

Practically, perhaps, no very marked difference of results will be occasioned. The distinction between situations allotted to the covenanted service and all other situations of an official or public nature will remain generally as at present.

The sting was in the tail, for covenanted servants filled all the best paid and most responsible positions in the Indian civil service. The covenanted service was an administrative elite, which had been created in 1765 to counter the notorious corruption of many of the Company's employees. Its name derived from the covenants which were entered into by newly appointed servants by which they promised not to engage in trade nor to accept 'valuable presents' from natives. Ever since 1793, all positions in the Company's service with an annual salary of more than £500 had been required by statute to be filled by covenanted men nominated by the Company's directors. So, in their Dispatch, one year after the passage of the 'noble clause', the Company's Court of Directors were in effect reassuring the Government of India that, although the new law required equal opportunities for Indians and Europeans alike to enter all branches of the administration, in practice Englishmen would continue to monopolize the covenanted service, which wielded the real power in India.

During the next seven years, two incidents[8] showed how the Government of India intended to interpret the law. In November 1836, the Lieutenant-Governor of the North-West Provinces sought permission from the Government of India to appoint uncovenanted servants, and, in particular, certain classes of native officer, to act as

8. We are indebted to Miss Vasudha Dhagamwar who brought these incidents to our attention. The records are in the India Office Library, London.

assistants to European magistrates.[9] He explained that this change would benefit the administration of justice, while at the same time encouraging the Indian population to 'interest themselves in the formation and presentation of a good police and zealously to aid the Government and its officers'.

Shakespear, a member of the Indian Legislative Council, questioned the necessity and expediency of the proposal. He thought that native officers had sufficient power already, and did not believe that those who worked 'at a distance from European control' were 'to be trusted with the power of fine or imprisonment'. Macaulay, who had arrived in India in 1834 as law member to the new Legislative Council, wrote that he fully agreed with Shakespear 'in thinking that criminal powers cannot be safely entrusted to the moonsiffs', but hoped that 'in no long time' it would be possible to employ some of the principal native officers in the administration of criminal justice. Acting on this advice, the Government informed the Lieutenant-Governor that his request had been refused.

Meanwhile, the seeds of a more protracted controversy were being sown in another part of India.[10] In April 1836, the Madras Board of Revenue recommended to the Government that it should be allowed to experiment with the practice which had succeeded in Bengal of appointing uncovenanted or native assistant collectors. The proposed experiment was authorized by the Court of Directors and the Government of India; and in due course two native assistants were appointed. It was an important step, for the collector was the key official on whom the whole administrative machine depended. He ran everything within his district; not only the revenue, but the police, petty justice, health and roads.

In 1837, the Board of Revenue was asked to indicate in which districts 'the aid of natives' was urgently required so as to enable the Madras Government to afford the experiment 'a full and fair trial' by appointing several native assistants. The Board in turn asked its local officials for their reactions to the proposal. Their replies showed that they were divided in their views. A minority reported that the aid of native assistants was uncalled for and that no advantage would result; of the remainder, some believed that their duties should be

9. See generally, Indian Legislative Consultations 1836, 206/84.
10. See generally, Indian Legislative Consultations 1836, 207/6.

confined to revenue matters, while others considered that their functions should be exactly the same as those of the Europeans' assistants.

However, although a majority of the replies were more or less favourable, in April 1839, the Revenue Board informed the Madras Government that 'on a mature consideration of the several communications from the revenue officers' it was not satisfied that the appointment of native officers was required. The main objections which were now put forward by the Board to its own earlier proposal were that it would be expensive to implement, and that it would compromise or conflict with the authority of the head sheristedars and talukdars, the senior native officers under the existing regime. It was only several months later that the Board was driven by criticism from the Madras Government to admit that the real reason for its volte-face was 'the general disinclination' shown by the local European officers in the districts where the experiment was to be tried, for it was 'obvious that the success of the system would in great measure depend upon the cordial cooperation of local officers, and the support they would afford to its practical development'.

The Revenue Board made an alternative suggestion. Instead of appointing natives as assistants to collectors – a post which the Board insisted should continue to be reserved exclusively for Europeans – there should be some increase in the pay and status of the existing establishment of native officers.

The Governor of Madras, Lord (John) Elphinstone, reacted swiftly. In a sharply ironical Minute he brushed aside the Board's objections to an experiment which, he observed, had not been given a fair trial. Only two uncovenanted assistants had been appointed; one had been moved from one district to another three times in less than that number of years: the other had been appointed for less than three months.

A week after Elphinstone's Minute had been circulated, the Revenue Board responded with another Minute written by one of its members, John Bird. 'I should be sorry,' wrote Bird, 'to see native assistant collectors substituted for European assistants for reasons which I need not state on the present occasion, since it does not appear likely that the experiment will be tried to any great extent.' After repeating the Board's objections, Bird added a new twist. It would be illegal under the Madras Regulations, he thought, to vest the police powers and powers of punishment in native assistant collectors.

On 7 August 1839, the Governor in Council discussed and rejected all the Revenue Board's arguments and found the Board's alternative proposal to increase the salaries and powers of native officers totally inadequate. It was decided to call upon the Judges of the Sudder and Foujdany Adawlut (the High Court of Madras) to report whether it was illegal for the newly appointed native assistant collectors to exercise criminal powers, which had been vested by the Regulations in some existing native officers. If so, the Judges were to draft an appropriate statute to legalize the position, and to empower the Madras Government to vest police and punitive powers in any class of public servants it might deem expedient.

The Judges duly reported that, in their view, enabling legislation was required, and they submitted an appropriate draft Act. But the Judges went on to express their opinion on the much wider issue (about which they had not been consulted) as to the legality of appointing uncovenanted servants as assistants to collectors. They referred to several old Madras Regulations which, in their view, prevented a native of India from being appointed to this office, and confined it to Europeans.

But what of clause 87 of the Charter Act, which stated that no one should, by reason only of his religion, place of birth, descent or colour, be disabled from holding any place, office or employment in the Company? The Judges considered that the word 'only' in clause 87 was 'very significant'. They reasoned that where there was a restriction against the appointment of a native to a particular office, the native could not be said to be excluded *only* by his descent.

The Legislature has by express provision or implication, and by long established practice, limited certain offices to European covenanted servants. It cannot be said that it was 'only' on account of descent, colour, etc. that the distinction was established. These the Act declares shall be no bar, but it leaves every other bar untouched.

Ten days after this extraordinary opinion had been conveyed, the Governor in Council requested the Judges 'without delay' to prepare and submit a further draft Act to legalize the experiment, which would be forwarded to the Government of India for approval. His Lordship in Council, it was acidly added, regretted 'that the circumstances now noticed by the Judges were not sooner brought to the knowledge of the Government'.

On 16 October 1839, the Madras Government asked the Government of India to enact the Judges' new draft, which would make it competent for the Governor in Council to appoint persons not covenanted servants of the East India Company to be assistant collectors, validate all such existing appointments, and enable the Governor in Council to vest in any class of public servants, all police powers and criminal judicial powers enjoyed by talukdars.

The Government of India promptly rejected the request. It did not accept the Judges' view that racially discriminatory regulations remained in force despite the Charter Act. Parliament had repealed all such restrictions. But the Government of India did accept the Judges' formalistic argument that the Madras Regulations, under which the powers of an assistant collector were possessed, contemplated only covenanted servants being appointed to that office. 'This restriction, which has no reference to birth-place, is not affected by the Charter Act and on this point His Honour in Council conceives that the opinion of the Sudder [Court] must be considered as conclusive.' In other words a man could not be barred only because of his religion, place of birth, descent or colour, but he could be barred because he was a native.

Nor was the Supreme Government willing to repeal the Madras Regulations. Its letter observed that the proposed measure was 'desired not for the sake of any object of immediate importance but in order to legalize a measure sanctioned ... merely as an experiment ... this experiment has been very sparingly tried by the government and still more sparingly put into practical operation by the local authorities.' As for the argument that large numbers of uncovenanted deputy collectors had been employed in Bengal, this, it was said, had been caused by the temporary shortage of Europeans there. The vast majority of these officers would be abolished when the temporary shortage had ceased. For these reasons the Government concluded that 'the discontinuance of the experiment for the present will be preferable to passing a general law for the specific purpose of legalizing it'.

Elphinstone and the Madras Government must have been furious. But they made one last attempt to save the experiment. In April 1840, a further letter was sent[11] to the Government of India pointing out that the Court's interpretation of Madras Regulations, as sanctioned by the Government of India, would mean that individuals already holding office as native assistants would have to be removed unless some means could be found of reconciling their appointment with existing law. The Madras Government commended the suggestion of John Sullivan, a member of its Legislative Council that the office of native assistant should be renamed to comply with the titles of offices described in the Regulations, so that native assistants, under their new title, might exercise the same police powers as were vested in taluk-dars and whatever revenue duties the collectors might choose to give them.

Enclosed with this letter was a remarkable Minute by Sullivan in which he analysed the Madras Regulations in detail and found nothing in them which could be 'an obstacle to the making a native of India assistant to a collector'. Sullivan went on, acutely,

As before the passing of the Charter Act the want of an appointment to the covenanted service was the only bar to the holding of an office by a native it may be asked, if that bar continues, for what purpose was the enactment passed. Although it was invariable usage to name Europeans and Europeans only to that service yet there was nothing in law that could have prevented the Court of Directors from appointing any British subject to their covenanted service on account of his religion, place of birth, descent or colour. If therefore the only bar that ever opposed the entrance of natives into office exists now, in as much force as ever, the passing of the enactment was positively mischievous in as much as it tends to create expectations which never can be realized.

'When I hear the investiture of a native with those duties which are entrusted to every young European officer in the service spoken of as an *experiment*, by some as an hazardous experiment,' Sullivan reflected, 'I naturally ask myself how this country was governed before we got possession of it. There are evident marks that it was at one time in a much higher state of prosperity than it is now.' And he concluded

Whether natives will make as good or better administrators than Europeans can never be known until a fair trial has been made, and there is no other way of making a fair trial but by putting both classes of persons into the same classes of offices, by having native judges and collectors as well as

11. See generally, Indian Legislative Consultations, 1841, 207/15.

Europeans. . . . Shall we *begin* to give them fair play and allow certain numbers of native assistants (no matter what name they may have) to compete with the Europeans' assistants?

Sullivan's sad, rhetorical question went to the heart of the controversy. The reply of the Government of India was blunt and final. In May 1841, it merely informed the authorities in Madras that 'the Minute of Mr Sullivan . . . has made no change in the manner in which the Supreme Government views the matter'.[12]

However, although the Government of India could kill its hazardous experiment when it had scarcely begun, it could not prevent the subject from being debated at Westminster. Twelve years later, in 1852, the British Government decided to appoint a Select Committee to inquire into the operation of the 1833 Act, in preparation for the renewal of the Company's Charter in the following year. The President of the Board of Control told the Commons[13] that he had ascertained

What progress had been made in introducing natives into offices of administration. He had found a persevering determination on the part of the Indian government to promote by all means the employment of natives in posts of considerable importance.

The President then gave statistics to the House, showing the number of Indians employed by the Government of India and the range of

12. Sullivan's scathing evidence, nine years earlier, to the Select Committee on the Affairs of the East India Company, could not have endeared him to the Government of India. In reply to a circular letter from the Secretary to the Commission, requesting information, Sullivan had written: 'The general disadvantages under which the natives labour, are, their exclusion from all offices of trust and emolument; their degradation from the station which they hold in society under the native governments; the appropriation by Europeans of the merit due to public service, although in fact such service may have been rendered by the natives; the precarious tenure upon which they hold their offices, and the incomes of those offices; the inconsiderate treatment which they too frequently meet with from Europeans, and our heavy system of taxation, imposed for maintaining expensive European establishments. To this list of grievances may be added, this crowning one, that we never think it worth our while to consult them upon any of those measures of government, which have the interests of the natives for their preferred object' (see Minutes of Evidence (Public), vol. 1, Appendix (A); for Sullivan's oral evidence, see para. 503).

13. 19 April 1852, *Hansard*, vol. 120, cols. 814–15.

their salaries. One member, Chisholm Anstey, argued in vain for the appointment of a Royal Commission which would visit India in order to obtain first-hand knowledge of conditions there. He pointed out that racial discrimination had continued to be practised in the public service, regardless of the 1833 Act, and that Indians were not being recruited for responsible posts. The Governor-General, Lord Dalhousie, 'had indeed appointed one native to an office of trust and power; but the income was reduced from 1500 rupees to 800, to be raised again probably if a European should succeed him.'

It was scarcely surprising that, when Parliament came to consider the renewal of the Company's Charter in 1853, 'there was a general feeling that the work of the 1833 Charter Act had been left unfinished. [Before the Select Committee] . . . Charles Trevelyan appeared as the unswerving champion of the liberalism of the earlier reforming period' (Stokes 1959, p. 253). And no doubt partly because of Trevelyan's influence, in the very year in which the Northcote–Trevelyan report on the British civil service was published, the new Bill provided for recruitment to the covenanted service on the basis of competitive examinations, following a period of compulsory instruction in England, at Haileybury College.

But the stress in the 1853 debates, unlike those of twenty years earlier, was put upon education and gradualism, rather than upon legal equality. Macaulay's tepid, defensive speech during the Second Reading debate, was strikingly different from his earlier encomium of the 'noble clause'. He declared that the proposal for competitive examinations would provide

the best means that can be imagined for effecting an object . . . which I admit to be desirable – the gradual admission of natives to a share in the higher offices of the government. Legally, they are now admissible; practically, none have been admitted. I do not blame those who do not admit them, for it is my belief that there is not in India a young native whom it would be a kindness to the native population to place, at the present moment, in your civil service.[14]

The transition from the rhetorical idealism of Macaulay's earlier speech to his apology for non-performance, justified by reference to the greater good of those whom the provision was intended to benefit,

14. 24 June 1853, *Hansard*, vol. 128, col. 757.

is not a unique one in the history of legislation of this kind. After a series of lofty speeches, designed to raise aspirations, it is usually discovered first that no-one is qualified to be employed according to his aspirations; then, that it would do more harm than good to force the pace; and the entire process is accompanied by repeated assurances that no-one need fear the effects of the legislation, because they will not be very substantial.

During the debate in the Lords, Earl Granville, speaking for the Government, stressed this last point. While asserting that the new Bill made an opening for the entry of Indians into the covenanted service, he observed sanguinely that 'The most timorous persons cannot be alarmed at this, when they consider that the natives who have to compete for this service, will have to come to this country for their education.'[15]

However, a stinging attack was made on the Government by a Liberal, Lord Monteagle. He had previously complained[16] that not one native had, during the twenty years, been appointed to any office to which he would not have been eligible before the 1833 Act, and during the Second Reading debate on the new Bill he was more explicit. Clause 87, he said,

was distinct; it was unlimited, and without any reservation whatever – there was no power of evading it, except by bad faith. But what had been the practice? Why, the clause had been evaded; and in what way? . . . It was argued that, although Parliament had passed a Bill declaring in absolute terms that all persons should be eligible, the East India Company should be at liberty to interpret the clause as meaning that although all natives should be eligible to the uncovenanted service, yet none but British-born subjects should be eligible to the covenanted service – an interpretation whether right or wrong, which was totally at variance with the rights and interests claimed for the natives of India on the introduction of the Bill of 1833, and with the letter and spirit of the Act itself. . . . Native appointments were made for the most part to offices of the most subordinate rank, and the salaries paid, in most cases were of insignificant value. . . . These Indian appointments . . . ought to be weighed, not numbered.[17]

Monteagle moved an amendment to make it clear that clause 87

15. 5 August 1853, *Hansard*, vol. 129, col. 1335.
16. 13 June 1853, *Hansard*, vol. 129, col. 49.
17. 5 August 1853, *Hansard*, vol. 129, vol. 1366.

was 'not to be construed or controlled by any reference to or by any distinction drawn between the covenanted and the uncovenanted service'. If it was 'intended that the spirit of the 87th clause . . . should be carried out, they must insert a statutable provision to carry out and enforce their own intentions', which would otherwise be treated by the Company as 'mere moonshine'.

The Government opposed the amendment, because in Earl Granville's words it was 'directed against an imaginary evil'.[18] Granville had no doubt that Indians would be found fully qualified to fill senior posts in the civil service.

The reason why natives had not been employed in the civil service was this: the clause in the existing Act was merely permissive, and the civil service being entirely dependent on nomination, it had happened that no director had nominated a native. Had a native been nominated, he must have been employed. The present Bill abolished the system of nomination, and any native who exhibited . . . equal talent with Englishmen at the examination would obtain employment.

The amendment was defeated; but clause 87 remained on the statute book, and henceforth the principle of equality of opportunity was to be combined with the principle of selection by open competition. In reality, however, the latter was used to nullify the former.

Three months after these debates, Sir Charles Wood, President of the Board of Control, wrote confidentially to the Governor-General, Lord Dalhousie,[19] that the right of Indians to compete with Englishmen for posts in the covenanted service

seems to be a point of honour, and we have arranged our matters so that they *may* come here and be admitted. But I cannot say that I either expect or wish them to do this to any extent. I am for keeping the covenanted service as the means of maintaining the European Indian servants on a high footing of acquirement and character. I hope that we may govern India

18. 8 August 1853, *Hansard*, col. 1449. Professor Cornford once commended to those seeking to prevent reform the argument that the machinery for effecting the proposed objects already exists. 'This should be urged in cases where the existing machinery has never worked, and is now so rusty that there is no chance of its being set in motion. When this is ascertained it is safe to add that "it is far better that all reform should come from within" ' (Cornford, 1964, p. 25).

19. Wood to Dalhousie, 24 November 1853, quoted in Compton (1967, pp. 99–100).

for many years but it is clear to my mind that we shall always govern it as aliens.

Once more there was a striking contrast between ministerial speeches in Parliament and private communications between the British Government and their officials in India.

In 1857, four years after the East India Company's Charter had been renewed, its rule in India was abruptly ended by the Indian Mutiny, which

was the rising of the old order against the new, the last unsuccessful struggle of feudal and conservative forces of India against the progressive forces that had been released by British administration in the last hundred years. The British suppressed the mutiny and at the same time entered into an alliance with the forces that had caused it (Pandey, 1969, pp. 17–18).

In the following year, the Government of India was transferred from the Company to the Crown.

Although the Mutiny had a traumatic effect on British policies and attitudes in India, clause 87 survived the transfer of power and was deliberately reaffirmed. On 1 November 1858, Queen Victoria issued a Proclamation on future British policy in India, in which she expressed her will that, 'so far as may be, our subjects, of whatever race or creed, be freely admitted to office in our service, the duties of which they may be qualified by their education, ability and integrity duly to discharge'.

Under the Indian Civil Service Act 1861, almost all higher appointments were reserved for members of the covenanted service who were to be recruited by open competitive examinations held annually in London under the supervision of the civil service commissioners. In 1860 the maximum age for candidates to take these examinations had been lowered to twenty-two, and in 1866 it was further lowered to twenty-one. The effect of these changes was that all higher civil appointments were effectively denied to Indians, for under the prevailing social and educational conditions, it was impossible for Indians to compete in London at such an early age (Singh, 1933, p. 123).[20] A committee appointed by the Indian Council, in 1860, had recommended that the only way of implementing clause 87 was by

20. The following account draws heavily on Professor Singh's work.

holding simultaneous examinations in England and India for recruitment to the covenanted service, but the Government rejected this recommendation, even though the Civil Service Commission had stated that they did 'not anticipate much difficulty in arranging for this'.

In 1863, while Charles Trevelyan was serving as Financial Member on the Indian Legislative Council, his son George Otto, acted as his private secretary for twelve months, and wrote a series of pseudonymous letters to Macmillan's Magazine, which were later collected in a celebrated book, *The Competition Wallah* (1864). While the young Trevelyan found it painful 'to observe the deep pride and insolence of race which is engrained in our nature and which yields only to the highest degree of education and enlightenment,' he reserved his strictures for the 'Damned Nigger Party' which had become so popular among the European settlers in India. His praise for the Government of India was without limit. 'It is a rare phenomenon this,' he wrote.

of a race of statesmen and judges scattered throughout a conquered land, ruling it, not with an eye to private profit, not even in the selfish interests of the mother country, but in single-minded solicitude for the happiness and improvement of the children of the soil.

As for the prizes enjoyed by members of the Indian Civil Service, they

are open to every subject of the Queen, though his father be as poor as Job subsequently to the crash in that patriarch's affairs, and though he does not number so much as the butler of a member of Parliament among his patrons and connection.

Yet, impressive though the integrity and impartiality of the Queen's servants may have seemed, it did not occur to their youthful hagiographer to add that the prizes of high office were open only to Her Majesty's European subjects.

In 1868, Henry Fawcett introduced a resolution in the Commons calling for simultaneous examinations for the Indian civil service in Britain and India. It was opposed by Sir Stafford Northcote, joint author with Charles Trevelyan of the 1853 report on the organization of the civil service, in which he had advocated the principle of competitive recruitment. Northcote explained that, without casting 'any reflection upon the native character as a whole, he doubted whether an average native was able to stand alone and to control the Englishman under his jurisdiction. Therefore the competitive system, applied in an unfettered way, was not suitable for providing the class of men wanted.'[21]

Sir George Otto Trevelyan, now Liberal member for Tynemouth, put the matter less delicately,[22] revealing the 'deep pride and insolence of race' ingrained in his own nature. He said

The natives of Bengal are remarkable for extreme quickness and cleverness, but, as compared with Europeans, are singularly deficient in the bolder and hardier virtues – in pluck, self-reliance and veracity – the three great national attributes by which we gained, and by which we retain our hold upon British India. In such a competition as is proposed . . . they would be eminently successful; for remarkable as is their capacity, it is not so peculiar as the premature ripeness of their intellect . . . if you open these doors at Calcutta, Madras and Bombay, the natives would come in by shoals, and just reflect a moment on what you are doing. The Hindoos are strong in intellect, and confessedly weak in moral. You submit them to an intellectual test, which the great number are pretty sure to pass. You dispense with the moral test, by which the great number are sure to fail . . . where you find one young English civil servant unequal to the duties of his career, you will find ten or twenty natives; for the very plain fact that we, as a race, are far superior to them in force of character. . . . We are there because nine Englishmen out of ten are born to rule, and ninety-nine out of a hundred Hindoos are born to be governed; because we are manly, and they are effeminate . . . the secret of our power in India is not so much our valour, not so much our enterprise, as that we, as a nation, speak the truth and never take bribes.

At the end of the debate, Fawcett, who was nicknamed the Member for India, withdrew his resolution, accepting a straw offered by Northcote, who had indicated that he would insert into his impending India Bill a clause giving the Government power to introduce natives into appointments in the covenanted service, if they proved fit for them. After hearing the speeches from the Front Bench, Fawcett cannot have had much confidence in Northcote's proposal. The objective, intellectual test on which the principle of open competition

21. 5 May 1868, *Hansard*, vol. 191, col. 1856.
22. Cols. 1845–6. Yet, according to his son, in the later 1860s, a 'strong wave of reforming liberalism' caught hold of him (see G. M. Trevelyan, 1932, p. 62).

for the civil service depended, had, when applied to India, been transformed into a moral test, based upon the superiority of the English 'as a race'.

In the same year as this ugly debate, Surendranath Banerjea and two other Bengalis went to England to study, and the next year the three were successful in the Indian civil service examinations. Woodruff describes what happened to them:

There were four Indians that year, these three from Bengal and another man from Bombay. Once before and once only, in 1863, an Indian had overcome the immense obstacles he had to encounter and been successful. Now there were four, and all over India, and particularly in Bengal, there were loud rejoicings. It transpired however, after the results had been announced, that three of the four candidates had given an age for a school examination four years before which did not agree with the age they had given for the ICS examination. Two of them, including Banerjea, were over age for the ICS if the age they had given before was correct. The Civil Service Commission rejected their explanation that, according to their own way of reckoning, the three candidates were nine months old when they were born. They refused to hear evidence on this point. They refused to consider horoscopes, which for another seventy years at least were usually the best evidence of age in India. They declared Banerjea and the other man disqualified and their seats vacant (1954, pp. 169–70).[23]

With characteristic moderation (and a curious idea of the judicial process), Woodruff comments:

This no doubt was due to nothing more sinister than an obstinate pedantry; the Commission was perhaps too judicial in its outlook and too much divorced from executive functions. But the India Office took no step to put things right. Banerjea sued the Secretary of State in the court of Queen's Bench and won his case. He and his companions were re-instated. There could hardly have been a worse start to a career.

Banerjea was later dismissed from the service, probably unfairly, for sending a false return to his superior. Like many others who were denied employment in the Indian Civil Service, he was later to make his mark in the politics of Indian nationalism.

One concrete result of Northcote's work was the establishment in

23. See also Compton (1967, pp. 104–5). Compare the later case of Amanda Mohan Bose, the first Indian wrangler at Cambridge, who 'successfully took all the intellectual hurdles, only to be unseated in the riding test' (Seal, 1968, p. 117).

1868 of nine Government-sponsored scholarships (Compton, 1967, pp. 103–4). Three were to be open to competition and six were for nominees. They were intended to enable the holders to come to England to qualify themselves for the professions, the civil service, or other branches of the public service. And, apart from two privately-financed scholarships a year, these state scholarships provided the only alternative to private means of support in England.

The scholarship scheme had hardly been in operation for long enough for the first scholars to leave India, when in 1869, the new Secretary of State, the Duke of Argyll, suspended it. Argyll 'explained to a justifiably baffled Government of India that a Bill he had laid before Parliament would obviate any necessity for the scholarships by providing for the admission of Indians to high office by means other than competitive entry. This was nothing more than a pretext to exclude Indians whose only claim to office was their educational attainment' (Compton, 1967, pp. 103–4).

The clause in the Bill to which Argyll referred was intended to give effect to Northcote's proposal, by empowering the Governor-General to appoint Indians to posts previously reserved for the covenanted service, although they had not passed the competitive examination. It became law in 1870, but rules and regulations were needed to work the Act. It was the covenanted service itself which was to draft them; and it was reluctant to do so.

In 1872, in a Public Dispatch to the Governor in Council, Argyll enunciated three principles for guidance in making the new rules: 'a high proportion of the top posts must remain in British hands; Indians could be considered for senior judicial but not for executive appointments; and they should be paid less than Englishmen' (Seal, 1968, p. 138). The Government of India was formally instructed to frame rules to give effect to these principles. At the end of the year, the Governor-General, Northbrook, whose policy was one of masterly inactivity, wrote privately to Argyll, reluctantly informing him that his Government would do its best to frame the rules. Argyll's answer revealed what he really thought about his own official policy. Argyll wrote:[24]

I should not be disappointed if you reply that no RULES can be laid down. I entirely agree with you that to test natives by competitive examinations in

24. Argyll to Northbrook, 7 January 1873, cited in Compton (1967, p. 106).

learning would be the height of absurdity. . . . Do not, therefore, think yourself under any necessity of formulating such rules, if you think that none can prudently be drawn up, unless the terms of the Act of Parliament (which at this moment I have not before me) compel us to have something laid down which can be considered and treated as 'Rules'.

In view of Argyll's attitude, it is scarcely surprising that when Northbrook's draft regulations were received in England, they were found by the Law Officers of the Crown 'to be clearly opposed to the spirit and intention of the Act' and 'to place too narrow a construction upon the statute' (Singh, 1933, p. 133). Fresh rules were made and at last approved in 1875, but, except for one or two appointments to the judicial branch of the service, they remained inoperative. In the following year, another Secretary of State, Lord Salisbury, reduced the maximum age at which the entrance examinations could be taken for the covenanted service from twenty-one to nineteen, making it impossible for all but a handful of Indian candidates to compete for entrance into the service.

In 1877, four decades after the enactment of the 'noble clause', the Government's representatives in India proposed that the covenanted service should be *officially* closed to Indians, because a policy of blatant discrimination would be honest and realistic. In a confidential despatch, the Viceroy, Lord Lytton, confessed that 'both the Government of England and of India appear . . . unable to answer satisfactorily the charge of having taken every means in their power of breaking to the heart the words of the promise they had uttered to the ear'. He went on:

Under the terms of the Act, which are studied and laid to heart by that increasing class of educated natives, whose development the Government encourages without being able to satisfy the aspirations of its existing members, every such native if once admitted to government employment in posts previously reserved to the covenanted service, is entitled to expect and claim appointment in the fair course of promotion to the higher posts in that service. We all know that these claims and expectations never can and will be fulfilled. We have to choose between prohibiting them and cheating them, and we have chosen the least straightforward course. The application to natives of the competitive examination system as conducted in England and the recent reduction in age at which candidates can compete, are all so many deliberate and transparent subterfuges for stultifying the Act and reducing it to a dead letter.

In view of this confession, one wonders what Lytton would have made of George Otto Trevelyan's boast that, unlike the Indians, the British 'as a nation, speak the truth'. The 'straightforward course' which Lytton proposed instead was to bar Indians from the covenanted service altogether, while admitting them to a new 'closed native service' to satisfy the provisions of the 1870 Act. Lytton's own values are more clearly revealed elsewhere. 'It is one thing' he wrote to one of his officials,

to admit the public into your park, and quite another thing to admit it into your drawing room. . . . Already great mischief has been done by the deplorable tendency of second-rate Indian officials, and superficial English philanthropists to ignore the essential and insurmountable distinctions of race qualities, which are fundamental to our position in India; and thus, unintentionally, to pamper the conceit and vanity of half-educated natives, to the serious detriment of commonsense, and of the wholesome recognition of realities (Seal, 1968, p. 140).[25]

The inspiration for this brand of 'realism' seems to have been Sir John Strachey, who was the Indian civil service's 'political philosopher and gave to its prejudices and emotions a reasoned and logical support' (Stokes, 1959, p. 305).[26]

However, if the British Government had to choose between prohibiting Indians altogether, as a 'wholesome recognition of realities', and cheating them with 'deliberate and transparent subterfuges', it preferred to continue with the latter course. Since Lytton's proposal 'would mean amending the Queen's Proclamation, revising several Acts of Parliament and breaking a good many pledges, it would require legislation. Cranbrook, who was Secretary of State in 1878, saw the political impossibility of going to Parliament with such a bill . . . Cranbrook refused point blank to introduce the measure' (Seal 1968, pp. 141–2).

25. Seal also quotes Lytton (at p. 141) as writing of the educated Indian that 'For most forms of administrative employment he appears to me quite unfit. The educated, and educable, natives of Bengal, Madras and Bombay are probably unfit for employment out of their own presidencies, and the hardier and more energetic races of the north will not submit to any educational process imposed by us as qualification for Government employment.'

26. In a Minute written in 1869, Strachey wrote that 'Physical peculiarities of races render the political opinions of Bengalees of comparatively little importance' (Seal, 1968, p. 141, note 1).

Instead the Secretary of State proposed that the Indian authorities should 'stick to the code as it stood; each year a few Indians should enter the covenanted service under the 1870 Act, but they should be kept out of the top offices. . . . On this basis new rules were formulated, and the statutory civil service was created in 1879' (Seal, 1968, p. 142). The Governor in Council was empowered to make appointments to the statutory service from nominated Indians 'of good family and social standing'. The total number of appointments in any year was limited to one-fifth of the appointments to the covenanted service.

But Lytton should have been well satisfied with the outcome of his negotiations with London, for, although the Indian civil service was not to be as blatantly racially segregated as he would have wished, what followed came close to his ideal. By reducing the maximum age for examinations to nineteen years, the British Government had virtually excluded all Indians from competing for the covenanted service. As for the new statutory service, 'since it was recruited by nomination and lacked the rewards or the standing of the covenanted service, it satisfied no one, not even the men of good family and social position whom it aimed to patronize. By 1886 twenty-seven Hindus, fifteen Muslims, two Parsis and two Sikhs had been appointed under the statutory rules of 1879.[27] This left the uncovenanted service as the

27. The record was even worse in Ceylon. The first Ceylonese member of the civil service was Simon Casie Chitty, who was nominated by the Governor in about 1840. The second was Sir Ponnambalam Arunchalam, who passed the competitive examination in 1870; but, when he was sufficiently senior to be a Government Agent, he was instead appointed to the comparatively powerless post of Registrar-General; and, when sufficiently senior to act as Colonial Secretary, although he was promoted to the first class with the highest salary possible to a Civil Servant and given a place in the Legislative and Executive Councils, an Englishman who was his junior was appointed to act as Colonial Secretary in his stead. After 1880, the examination was held only in London, and Ceylonese had to study in an English University to sit for it – an expense which very few could afford. The first Ceylonese to be appointed as Assistant Government Agent was C. L. Wickremasinghe, was was given the smallest and most unimportant assistant agency, Hannar, as late as 1923. The selection examination was not held locally in Ceylon, as well as in England, until 1924. Until almost the end of British rule, no non-European was given any post of importance in the central administration in Colombo, the solitary exception being Sir Oliver Goonetilleke's appointment as Financial Secretary in 1944 (see the introduction

best opening for Indians. But here promotion and pay went so far and no further' (Seal, 1968, p. 118).[28]

In 1880, the second Gladstone Government was formed, and Lytton was immediately replaced as Viceroy by Lord Ripon, a liberal who believed that only by the infusion of earlier Victorian ideals could modern India be reconciled to British rule. As part of Ripon's re-appraisal of British policy, he attempted to re-open the civil service question, and proposed to raise the age-limit for the covenanted service, but the British Government would not allow him to do so.

Then, in 1883, with Ripon's support, Lord Ilbert introduced a Bill in Parliament to give Indian district magistrates and sessions judges the same powers as their European counterparts to try Europeans. There was immediate uproar among the European community in India which expressed itself in the crudest racial terms. As Ripon recognized, the opposition was not confined to the Ilbert Bill, but to 'the whole policy of Parliament by which natives have been admitted to the covenanted service'. The real issue was 'whether natives are, or are not to continue, in accordance with the repeatedly declared policy of Parliament, to be admitted in considerable numbers [*sic*] to the covenanted civil service. If they are, the existing law about the trial of Europeans *must* be altered, if not now, at all events in a few years.' After a year of ferocious European opposition to the Ilbert Bill, both in India and in Britain, Ripon was forced to accept defeat; 'when it came to the crisis, Ripon's protestations of liberal virtue had not been able to conceal his weakness.'

The lesson was not lost on his successor as Viceroy, Lord Dufferin, another Liberal, who went to India in 1885. 'Others might have dreamt of throwing back the forces of unrest; Dufferin's ambition was to lull them to sleep' (Seal, 1968, p. 180). But the impotence of Ripon's liberalism had released a powerful wave of Indian demands for genuine equality of opportunity in the public service, through a reduced age-limit and simultaneous examinations in India. In 1886, Dufferin, optimistically believed that he could thereby solve the problem, set up a Public Service Commission which was instructed to produce a scheme 'which may reasonably be hoped to possess the

by 'S.D.S.' to Leonard Woolf, *Diaries in Ceylon 1908–11*, *Ceylon Historical Journal* (1959–60), vol. 9, at p. xviii).

28. The account in the next two paragraphs is taken from Seal's work.

necessary elements of finality, and to do full justice to the claims of natives of India to higher and more extensive employment in the public service'.

The Commission reported at the end of the following year. It recommended (Singh, 1933, pp. 135–6) against the holding of simultaneous examinations in India and England, since it doubted whether successful Indian candidates 'would possess in a sufficient degree the qualities essential for high administrative office'. With hypocrisy which would have upset Lord Lytton, the report feared that 'competition in India . . . would operate with inequality excluding altogether some important classes of the community while giving undue advantage to others'. And the Commission expressed concern that, owing to the inevitable failure of the vast majority to obtain the very small number of posts falling vacant each year, there would be created 'a large disappointed and thereby probably discontented class which would cause embarrassment to the Government'. Finally, it stressed 'the importance of recruiting that service . . . with reference to the maintenance of English principles and methods of government'.

The Commission proposed the creation of two distinct services, both open to Indians (Seal, 1968, pp. 181–2). One was to be the covenanted service, recruited exclusively by open competition in England, with the age limit raised to twenty-three years; the other, a provincial service, recruited in India. The statutory service was to be abolished and its members were to be absorbed into the new provincial service. Certain posts formerly in the covenanted service would be listed as part of the provincial service. 'But ninety-two of these posts were in any case scheduled for Indians under the statutory service programme. So a mere sixteen posts were to be the sum of the benefit. In the event only ninety-three posts were listed. The total gain was thus one post' (Seal, 1968, p. 182).[29] Even these proposals were regarded as too radical for some of the Government's advisers, and, when they were eventually put into effect some four years later, they had become more moderate (p. 184).[30]

29. Writing in 1933, Singh added (p. 136) that men holding these 'listed posts' still 'do not enter the superior service, and are paid only two-thirds of the salaries paid to Europeans holding the same posts'.

30. With a sublime unawareness of its irony P. E. Roberts's comment was that 'Henceforward . . . the Imperial Indian civil service [was] recruited in England,

However, the campaign to abolish discrimination in the public service continued. In 1893, Dadabhai Naoroji, who had been elected in the previous year[31] as the first Indian Member of the House of Commons, asked[32] the Under Secretary of State for India whether, in order to afford greater facilities to Indian candidates, he would arrange for the holding of competitive examinations simultaneously in England and India. He was told that there were 'various practical objections to that scheme'. Later, he supported another Member, Herbert Paul, who moved a resolution to the same effect. Paul estimated[33] that the expense of coming from India to live in England and take the examinations was £1000. He said that there were two main arguments against his proposition, one dishonest and the other honest. The dishonest argument was 'that it was a positive stimulus to the natives of India ... if they were compelled ... to expatriate themselves for several years, and subject themselves to considerable expense in the hope of obtaining ultimate success'. The honest argument was 'that we did not want the natives of India in the civil service at all'.

That argument could not be reasonably maintained, as it was contrary to the law of the land, and the Queen's Proclamation; contrary to the promises given to the natives, to the policy that had always been laid down by every Governor-General and every Secretary of State. It might be said

---

but open to Indians *who cared to make the journey* and were successful to the competition' (1910, p. 480 (emphasis added)).

31. Naoroji's electoral prospects had initially been poor, but he was encouraged to stand by his many British friends, and the Conservative Prime Minister, Lord Salisbury, ironically, ensured his success. While explaining why the Conservative majority in Dadabhai's constituency had dwindled in a previous election, Salisbury observed that 'However great the progress of mankind has been and however far we have advanced in overcoming prejudices, I doubt if we have yet got to that point of view where a British constituency would elect a black man.' Those two last words, 'wide of applicability to Dadabhai, whose skin was little darker than that of Salisbury himself, simply kicked Dadabhai into fame. The first to fall on Salisbury for his blazing indiscretion was John Morley. . . . Then came Gladstone's turn. He demanded an apology from the Prime Minister for giving deep offence to "many millions of their fellow-countrymen in India". From that date the chance of election of the "Black Man" greatly improved and the contest ended in his favour' (Mansani, 1960, pp. 73–4).

32. 13 April 1893, *Hansard*, vol. 11, col. 202.

33. 2 June 1893, *Hansard*, vol. 13, col. 104.

that they had no objection to a few men being admitted under certain conditions, but they objected to the civil service being flooded. He did not think it showed a very great reliance upon the vigour and powers of our own countrymen to assume that they would be defeated in this wholesale way by the natives of India.

Naoroji sadly recalled the history.

Sixty years ago it was distinctly laid down by Act of Parliament . . . that in India there should be no distinction of race, class or creed, but that all should be admitted equally, according to their qualifications, to the service of the Crown. The pledge had been repeated on the renewal of the Company's Charter, on the transference of India to the Crown, on the assumption by the Queen of the title of Empress, and again, on the celebration of the Queen's Jubilee. These pledges and promises had been intentionally broken over and over again . . . he could not admit that the Parliament of England passed Acts with hypocrisy and did not mean what they said. But it was an unfortunate fact that no sooner were Acts passed favouring the Indian population than means were devised to prevent them from deriving benefit from them.[34]

Another Member, William Wedderburn, supported the critics from personal experience. 'The Indian bureaucracy,' he said, 'waited nine years [after 1870] before making any rules at all, and then they made rules which perverted the purposes of the Act, and which enabled them to give away to their favourites and *protégés* the good things of the covenanted service. It was the re-establishment of jobbery; he had seen it with his own eyes.'[35]

The debate took place on a Friday, when many members of the Government were probably absent from the Commons. But the House must have been fairly well attended, because 160 members voted on a procedural Division. Paul and Naoroji managed to carry their Resolution against Government opposition. But their victory was short-lived. After angry protests from both Front Benches during the following week, Gladstone announced[36] that the Government had decided to refer the Resolution to the Government of India for local reactions. In due course, it was sent to both the Central and Provincial Governments by the Secretary of State. With the notable

34. Cols. 111–13. cf. Commonwealth Immigrations Act 1968, section 1.
35. Col. 134.
36. 8 June 1893, cols. 535–6.

exception of the Madras Government, all of them reported against the proposal, and the Secretary of State, 'fortified with the strong opposition of the Indian bureaucracy, consigned the resolution to the musty files of the India Office' (Singh, 1933, p. 240–41).

However, in spite of the odds against them, some Indians managed to compete for the examinations in England, and in 1900, the new Viceroy, Lord Curzon, complained to Lord Hamilton, the Secretary of State:

Some day I must address you about the extreme danger of the system under which every year an increasing number of the 900 and odd higher posts that were meant, and ought to have been exclusively and specially reserved, for Europeans, are being filched away by the superior wits of the native in the English examinations. I believe it to be the greatest peril with which our administration is confronted (Pandey, 1969, pp. 9–10).

Curzon thought that a racial qualification should have been insisted upon in the very beginning and lamented that it was now too late to exclude Indians from the civil service on that ground 'for there would probably be a storm'. In the last year of the nineteenth century, the 'peril' which so alarmed Curzon was represented by thirty-three Indians, as against 988 Europeans, in the civil service.

The continual failure of British Governments, throughout the nineteenth century, to honour either their pledges or their law, did not inhibit them from repeating their commitment to both, early in the twentieth century. Edward VII's Proclamation of 2 November 1908, solemnly reaffirmed the principle of equality of opportunity which had been enshrined in Queen Victoria's Proclamation of 1858. And, in February 1909, Lord Morley, the Secretary of State for India, declared in the Lords that there was 'nothing so important' as clause 87 of the 1833 Act.[37] 'It lays down in the broadest way possible the desire of Parliament of that day that there was to be no difference in appointing to office in India between one race and another.' It was not, however, so important that the Government altered their previous policy after these pronouncements.

On 17 March 1911, the Indian Legislative Council passed a resolution recommending the appointment of a Royal Commission 'to consider claims of Indians to higher and more extensive employment in the Public Service connected with the civil administration of the

37. 23 February 1909, *Hansard* (H.L.), vol. 1, col. 127.

country'. In the following year, Lord Hardinge's Government responded to this request by appointing a Royal Commission with Lord Islington, the Governor General of New Zealand, as chairman, and Ramsay MacDonald as a member of the Commission.

In 1915, before the Commission had reported, an incident occurred which illustrates the scant importance which was given to clause 87. The Coalition Government introduced a new Government of India Bill to consolidate previous legislation. The Government spokesman recognized, during the Second Reading debate[38] that Parliament would 'want to be assured that, under cover of a Consolidation Bill, we are not smuggling in Amendments which are not proper to insert in a Consolidation Bill'. But the Government had overlooked the fact that the Fourth Schedule of the new Bill would repeal clause 87 of the 1833 Act, although that provision was described[39] during the Committee Stage on the following day, as 'the Indian Magna Carta'. In the result, the Government had to amend its own Bill so as to restore clause 87, which duly became clause 96 of the 1915 Act. The 'noble clause' was saved by a hair's breadth from extinction by accidental repeal.

In January 1917, the Islington Report was at last published. Its contents had not been disclosed previously in the hope of avoiding controversy during the war. It is easy to understand why it was controversial. Statistics were included showing the extent of employment of Indians in the public service for the year 1913. Almost all appointments carrying a salary of less than 200 rupees a month were held by non-Europeans; 42 per cent out of 11,064 appointments at between 200 and 500 rupees a month were held by Indians; but they were employed in only 19 per cent of 4984 posts at between 500 and 800 rupees a month. Indians occupied a bare 10 per cent of the posts at 800 rupees per month and above. And, 'as the salary rose higher and higher the number of Indians occupying posts became less and less until such posts were reached to which no Indian had ever been appointed. The small number of Indians in the higher posts was due not to the paucity of well qualified Indian candidates but to a deliberate policy of exclusion adopted by the Government' (Singh, 1933, pp. 448–9).

38. 19 July 1915, *Hansard*, vol. 73, col. 127.9.
39. Sir J. D. Rees, 20 July 1915, col. 1462.

Undaunted by this situation, the Islington Commission, like its predecessors, rejected the proposal for holding competitive examinations in India. It concluded that 'whilst competitive examinations should ordinarily be continued where they are now held, the time is not yet ripe[40] for the general adoption of any such system'. This was because educational facilities were neither sufficiently developed in all provinces and communities in India, and because 'Indian schools and colleges did not give the same guarantee of the moulding and development of character as is afforded by the English schools and colleges'. Once more, George Otto Trevelyan's 'moral test' was added to the 'intellectual test'. The Commission also rejected a proposal to fix a definite proportion of places in each service which would be reserved for Indians. They adopted a quota in a few cases 'as a temporary palliative', but opposed it 'as a universal measure, partly because of the general undesirability of proportions based on race, but mainly because we recognise the tendency of a minimum to become a maximum'.

The Islington Commission made two main proposals to extend the employment of Indians: they added a few more services to the list of those for which recruitment was normally made in India; and they divided the remaining services into three main groups. 'In the first,' they wrote, 'should be placed the Indian Civil Service and the Police Department, in which it should be recognized that a preponderating proportion of the officers should be recruited in Europe.' In the case of the Indian Civil Service, threequarters of the posts were to be recruited through open competition in England, and the maximum age for competition was again to be lowered to nineteen. In the case of the Police Service, only 10 per cent of recruitment was initially to be made in India, to be increased gradually to 20 per cent 'as occasion offers'. In the second group, the Commission placed 'services like education, medical, public works and so on, in which there are grounds of policy for continuing to have . . . an admixture of both western and eastern elements.' In the third group, the Commission proposed to place 'certain scientific and technical services, such as the agricultural and civil veterinary departments, etc., for the normal

40. 'The Principle of Unripe Time is that people should not do at the present moment what they think right at that moment, because the moment at which they think it right has not yet arrived' (Cornford, 1964, p. 24).

requirements of which it should be the aim to recruit eventually in India'.

In Professor Singh's words:

These proposals were not only inadequate, but they were insulting . . . as well. They implied the racial superiority of the British and were based on the assumption that as long a British rule lasts in India certain services at least must retain a preponderating proportion of the British element. No wonder they were universally condemned in India as soon as they were published (1933, pp. 451–2).

In 1916, Lord Chelmsford became Governor-General of India, and he, together with Edwin Montagu, Secretary of State for India, initiated a period of genuine reform. On 20 August 1917, Montagu made a declaration of British policy in Parliament which promised 'the association of Indians in every branch of the administration'. And, in 1919, the Mountford Report was published, against the background of the Russian Revolution, a massive influenza epidemic which had killed some fourteen million Indians in 1918, a succession of mutinous incidents in the Indian Army and the growing strength of the Nationalist Movement.

The Report recommended a wide range of reforms, including the removal from the regulations of 'the few remaining distinctions that are based on race', and appointments to the public service 'without racial discrimination'. For those services that were still recruited in England, the Report proposed a system of appointment in India 'by fixing a definite percentage of recruitment to be made in India'. In the case of the Indian civil service, it suggested that 33 per cent of superior posts should be recruited in India and that this percentage should be increased by $1\frac{1}{2}$ per cent annually until a commission was appointed to re-examine the whole question. In the same year, a new Government of India Act was passed; under rules made by the Secretary of State under the 1919 Act, a system of simultaneous competitive examinations was partially adopted, and provision was made to secure the representation in the public service of the various Indian communities and Provinces. However, the whole question of the Indian civil service was referred to yet another Royal Commission, under the chairmanship of Lord Lee.

It is ironical that 1919, which was the beginning of the period of real reform, was also the year of the death-blow to the morality of the British Raj. At Amritsar, in April 1919, General Dyer opened fire on an unarmed crowd and killed 379 of them. 'This was the worst bloodshed since the Mutiny, and the decisive moment when Indians were completely alienated from British Rule.' The Amritsar massacre gave a bitter impetus to the implementation of the Mountford Report, but 'the heart had gone from the Raj. Ghandi held the moral lead. The British had only power. The Indian empire was kept going largely from habit. The British sensed the notice to quit' (Taylor, 1965, pp. 153–5).

In 1924, the Lee Commission recommended that recruitment should be so adjusted as to ensure that one-half of the Indian civil service would be Indian after fifteen years, and one-half of the Indian police service after twenty-five years. It also proposed that the other services should be transferred from the control of the Secretary of State to that of the Provincial Governments, which meant in effect that no more British officials would be recruited for them. These recommendations were accepted by the new Ramsay MacDonald Government. But they were not fully implemented, even though between 1919 and 1929 the number of Indians employed in the Indian civil service trebled, from seventy-eight to 241.[41]

(Woodruff, 1954, p. 363, Appendix B). Woodruff, notes that these figures do not include the 'Listed Posts', 'i.e. posts filled by Indians or Anglo-Indians who did not start their careers in the ICS but were selected after approved service in the provincial services and then taken into the ICS. There were eighty-five posts so filled in 1939'.

In 1930, a Statutory Commission recommended that, by 1939, instead of the Lee Commission's proposal that one-half of the service

41. The following figures indicate the rate of change in the strength and composition of the Indian civil service between 1859–1939:

Year	Europeans	Indians	Total
1859	846		846
1869	882	1	883
1879	907	7	914
1889	884	12	896
1899	988	33	1021
1909	1082	60	1142
1919	1177	78	1255
1929	881	241	1122
1939	759	540	1299

should be Indian, there should in fact be 643 Indians and 715 Europeans, and the senior posts should thereafter continue to be manned by Europeans (Mittal, 1970, p. 62). The actual figures for 1939 proved to be well below even the Statutory Commission's downward estimate: only 540 Indians as against 759 Europeans.

And the proportion of Indians would have been smaller still, if the British Government had been able to obtain more British recruits to the service. But after 1919 it was never able to do so.

Between 1924 and 1935 the India Office wanted 339 British recruits. It got only 256 and this was after standards had been allowed to fall. By the 1930s the weakened Indian civil service was under severe pressure from the locally-recruited Indians in the government departments. At the actual technical work of government the British officials on occasion found themselves inferior to the Indians, who had themselves been selected by severe competitive examination. The balance of power changed. The Indian officials were no longer the subservient clerks of the past . . . in the main it was an unplanned process. As late as 1939 the India Office was still recruiting British Civilians with the expectation that they would be essential to the working of the Indian Government for at least a further generation (Cross, 1968, p. 43).

In 1935, the last Government of India Act was passed by a British Government. There were widespread demands in India for an enforceable Bill of Rights to be included in the Act, but they were resisted by English constitutional lawyers on the ground that a Bill of Rights 'would either be a string of empty platitudes or a handicap to effective legislation' (Gledhill, 1964a, p. 7).[42] However, the 1935 Act did considerably widen the prohibition of racial discrimination so as to include the field of private as well as public employment, together

42. The Indian National Congress had pressed for a declaration of rights ever since 1918. But, in 1930, the Statutory Commission rejected their demand for such a declaration to be enshrined in a written constitution. The Commission considered that it would be of no great practical value, for abstract declarations were useless unless there existed the will and the means to make them effective. Despite protests from the Congress, this view was endorsed by the Joint Parliamentary Select Committee on Indian Constitutional Reform (1933–4). The Select Committee concluded that either the declaration of rights, being of abstract nature, would have no legal effect, or else it would impose an embarrassing restriction on legislative power and create a grave risk that many laws would be declared unconstitutional (Mittal, 1970, pp. 45–6).

with the acquisition of property.[43] No reference was made in the debates on the Bill to the history of clause 87, though the Solicitor-General stated[44] that the language of clause 111 was derived from the 1833 Act.

In view of the implacable opposition of British constitutional lawyers to Indian demands for a Bill of Rights, it is strange that these provisions were included in the 1935 Act, for they closely resemble that part of a normal Bill of Rights which guarantees the right to equal treatment without discrimination. It is also ironical that the 1935 Act suffered from the very disadvantage which had been assumed by British lawyers to be inherent in a Bill of Rights, namely that it would be a string of platitudes, unable to be enforced in the courts. That had, of course, always been the obvious weakness of the 1833 Act. No attempt seems ever to have been made to invoke clause 87 in the courts and it is extremely unlikely that any British government ever intended that it should be capable of being legally enforced. Yet in spite of this history, it did not occur to the framers of the 1935 Act then to provide an effective legal remedy against unfair discrimination.

Between 1939 and 1946, the number of Europeans employed in the Indian civil service fell from 759 to 560, and the number of Indians rose from 540 to 629. In March 1946, when preparations for independence were well under way, Arthur Henderson, the Under-Secretary of State for India, was asked in the Commons why British recruitment for the Indian civil service was still taking place and being advertised. Henderson replied that vacancies which had accrued during the war were 'being filled on the basis of the pre-war ratios as between British and Indian recruits (1) in order to implement undertakings given in respect of such vacancies for candidates with

43. Section 298 (1) provided that 'No subject of His Majesty domiciled in India shall on grounds only of religion, place of birth, descent, colour or any of them be ineligible for office under the Crown in India, or be prohibited on any such grounds from acquiring, holding or disposing of property or carrying on any occupation, trade, business, or profession in British India.' Section 298 (3) enabled the Governor-General to safeguard the 'legitimate interests of minorities'. Section 111 protected British subjects domiciled in the United Kingdom from any Federal or Provincial law which would otherwise discriminate against them.

44. 9 April 1835, *Hansard*, vol. 300, col. 1045.

'war service', and (2) in order to maintain the administrative machine pending the transfer of responsibility'. The reference to 'pre-war ratios' and the justification put forward for this method of recruitment suggest that, even at this late stage, the British Government was not pursuing a policy of non-discrimination wholly in accordance with the 1935 Act.

When India eventually attained independence in 1947, she continued to be governed by the 1935 Act, with appropriate modifications, until a new Constitution had been drawn up by a special Constitutent Assembly, and brought into force in 1950. Part III of the Constitution sets out certain 'fundamental rights', and it is obvious that the language of some of its provisions was borrowed from the 1935 Act.[45] But a crucial departure from the English legal tradition was made in article 32 (1) of the Indian Constitution, which guarantees the right to seek the Supreme Court's protection for these fundamental rights. At last India had obtained a Bill of Rights which was directly enforceable in the courts.

Soon after the adoption of these provisions, Sir Ivor Jennings, the distinguished architect of several Commonwealth Constitutions, observed that 'Generally speaking ... fundamental liberties are protected not by law but by public opinion ... it may reasonably be asked whether India will not lose more than it gains from this complex Bill of Rights' (1953, p. 53). It may as reasonably be wondered whether Jennings was aware of the history which had led the Indian people to demand a Bill of Rights.

The events which have been described are not, of course, simply about racial prejudice and discrimination; they reflect Britain's determination to retain control of executive power in India, so as to preserve her Imperial rule. But equally the episode should not be dismissed as a mere power struggle.

45. Article 16 (2) provides that 'No citizen shall on grounds only of religion, race, caste, sex, descent, place of birth, residence or any of them, be ineligible for, or discriminated against in respect of any employment under the State.' Apart from the inclusion of sex, and the exclusion of colour, this article is similar to the first limb of section 298 (1) of the 1935 Act. Article 19 (1) guarantees the right of all citizens 'to acquire, hold and dispose of property, and to practise any profession, or to carry on any occupation, trade or business'. This provision is similar to the second limb of section 298 (1). See generally, Gledhill (1964b, p. 73); Austin (1966, pp. 50–115); Ghosh (1966, ch. 4).

The Benthamites genuinely believed in a doctrine of equality of opportunity. The law which they drafted in 1833 was simple and un-ambiguous, and gave effect to that belief. But, during the decades which followed, the closer that conditions approached in India to those in which equality might become a reality, the more alarmed British liberals became at the consequences of what they had pro-posed. Unable to acquiesce in a transfer of power to Indians, yet un-willing to abandon the rhetoric of their old ideals, they searched for arguments which would justify their disregard for their own law, and invented devices to ensure that the law would continue to be frus-trated.

At first they reasoned that it would take time to educate Indians for high office. Then they discovered that intellectual qualities were not enough; Indians might pass examinations, indeed they would pass them only too well; but they lacked the moral fibre of the British as a race, prepared at Haileybury to rule as guardians across the world. They persuaded themselves that it was in the interests of the Indian population that they should be ruled by the British; by a fortunate coincidence, what was good for Britian was also good for India. Later, a new school of realists exposed the hypocrisy of the liberal position, not in order to press for the implementation of the 1833 Act, but to urge that it be repealed and replaced by a blatant racial barrier.

When the precarious nature of Britain's hold over her Empire eventually forced her to allow Indians to be employed in positions of responsibility, it became necessary, because of the past decades of discrimination, to discriminate positively in favour of those who had been unjustly excluded. And finally, after the transfer of power to those whose moral qualities had been derided, a stronger law than that which had been framed by the British was passed, containing legally enforceable guarantees.

Others must decide whether the new guardians in India, less Platonic than their British predecessors, now genuinely practise what Macaulay once so eloquently preached in Parliament. Certainly, prejudice and discrimination have not been removed from India merely by the winning of independence, even if they are now ex-pressed in terms of caste, language and religion, rather than colour or race.

It should come as no surprise that, throughout most of the period of the British Raj, the men who ruled India believed as fervently in their racial superiority over their brown-skinned subjects as they rejoiced in their own moral rectitude in carrying the white man's burden. Nor is it surprising that in India, as elsewhere in the Empire successive British governments maintained rigid racial barriers in the public service and in private life, for the sake of efficient administration and the good of their supposed inferiors. It is more unexpected to discover that, for more than a hundred years, there were some English politicians and administrators who protested at these attitudes and practices in strikingly modern terms.

Race relations cannot be properly understood in contemporary Britain without an awareness of the inheritance of racial attitudes from the Imperial age. But these historical events are also more directly relevant to the theme of this book. They are an extreme instance of the use of law as a declaratory gesture rather than as an effective instrument of individual justice and social change; and they teach a lesson in the evasion and abuse of the law.

Appendix 2
Race Relations Act 1965
Chapter 73

Arrangement of Sections

[*Note: the sections and words printed in square brackets have been repealed by the Race Relations Act 1968, section 28 (8). They are printed in full for comparison with the provisions of the 1968 Act.*]

An Act to prohibit discrimination on racial grounds in places of public resort; to prevent the enforcement or imposition on racial grounds of restrictions on the transfer of tenancies; to penalize incitement to racial hatred; and to amend section 5 of the Public Order Act 1936.
8 November 1965

Discrimination

[1. (1) It shall be unlawful for any person, being the proprietor or manager of or employed for the purposes of any place of public resort to which this section applies, to practise discrimination on the ground of colour, race or ethnic or national origins against persons seeking access to or facilities or services at that place.

(2) This section applies to the following places of public resort, that is to say—

(a) any hotel, and any restaurant, café, public house or other place where food or drink is supplied for consumption by the public therein;

(b) any theatre, cinema, dance hall, sports ground, swimming pool or other place of public entertainment or recreation;

(c) any premises, vehicle, vessel or aircraft used for the purposes of a regular service of public transport;

(d) any place of public resort maintained by a local authority or other public authority.

(3) For the purposes of this section a person discriminates against another person if he refuses or neglects to afford him access to the place in question, or any facilities or services available there, in the like manner and on the like terms in and on which such access, facilities or services are available to other members of the public resorting thereto.

(4) Except as provided by sections 3 and 4 of this Act, no proceedings, whether civil or criminal, shall lie against any person in respect of an act or omission which is unlawful by virtue only of this section.

(5) In this section 'hotel' means an hotel within the meaning of the Hotel Proprietors Act 1956 (that is to say an establishment held out by the proprietor as offering food, drink and, if so required, sleeping accommodation, without special contract, to any traveller presenting himself who appears able and willing to pay a reasonable sum for the services and facilities provided and who is in a fit state to be received) and any establishment which would be an hotel within the meaning of that Act apart from any discrimination on grounds mentioned in this section.]

[2. (1) For the purposes of securing compliance with the provisions of section 1 of this Act and the resolution of difficulties arising out of those provisions, there shall be constituted a Board to be known as the Race Relations Board, consisting of a chairman and two other members appointed by the Secretary of State.

(2) The Board shall constitute committees, to be known as local conciliation committees, for such areas as the Board consider necessary for the purposes of this section; and it shall be the duty of every such committee—

(a) to receive and consider any complaint of discrimination in contravention of section 1 of this Act which may be made to them (or made to the Board and referred by the Board to them), being a complaint made by or with the authority in writing of the person against whom the discrimination is alleged to have been practised;

(b) to make such inquiries as they think necessary with respect to the facts alleged in any such complaint; and

(c) where appropriate, to use their best endeavours by communication with the parties concerned or otherwise to secure a settlement of any difference between them and a satisfactory assurance against further discrimination contrary to the said section 1 by the party against whom the complaint is made.

(3) In any case where the local conciliation committee are unable to secure such a settlement, or such a settlement and assurance, as aforesaid, or it appears to the committee that any such assurance is not being complied with, the committee shall make a report to that effect to the Board; and if it appears to the Board, in consequence of such reports —

(a) that there has taken place in any place of public resort to which the said section 1 applies a course of conduct in contravention of that section; and

(b) that that conduct is likely to continue,

the Board shall report the matter to the Attorney-General or the Lord Advocate, as the case may be.

(4) The local conciliation committees shall make to the Board such periodical reports with respect to the exercise of their functions as the Board may require, and the Board, shall, at such times as the Secretary of State may direct, make annual reports to the Secretary of State with respect to the exercise of their functions; and the Secretary of State shall lay before Parliament any report made to him under this subsection.

(5) The supplementary provisions contained in the Schedule to this Act shall have effect with respect to the Race Relations Board and local conciliation committees.

(6) In Part II of Schedule 1 to the House of Commons Disqualification Act 1957 (bodies of which all members are disqualified under that Act) there shall be inserted (at the appropriate point in alphabetical order) the entry 'The Race Relations Board and any local conciliation committee constituted by the Board under section 2 of the Race Relations Act 1965'; and the like amendment shall be made in the Part substituted for the said Part II by Schedule 3 to that Act in its application to the Senate and House of Commons of Northern Ireland.]

[**3.** (1) Civil proceedings for the enforcement of section 1 of this Act by injunction may be brought in England and Wales by the Attorney-General; and if in proceedings under this section the court is satisfied—

(a) that the defendant has (by himself or by his servants or agents) engaged in connection with a place of public resort to which section 1 of this Act applies in a course of conduct in contravention of that section; and

(b) that he is likely, unless restrained by order of the court, to persist in such conduct,

the court may grant such injunction as appears to the court to be proper in all the circumstances, and in particular an injunction to restrain the defendant from committing or causing or permitting acts of discrimination in contravention of the said section 1 of such kinds, against such persons or against persons of such descriptions, as may be specified in the order of the court.

(2) In proceedings under this section, evidence of any communication made to the Race Relations Board, a local conciliation committee, or any officer or servant of the Board or of such a committee, for the purpose of or in connection with the exercise of their functions under section 2 of this Act shall not be admitted except with the consent of the party by whom it was made.

(3) Notwithstanding anything to the contrary in any enactment or rule of law relating to the jurisdiction of county courts, proceedings under this section may be brought in a county court; and any proceedings so brought shall be included among the proceedings mentioned in subsection (2) of section 109 of the County Courts Act 1959 (appeals on questions of fact).]

[**4.** (1) If it appears to the sheriff, on an application made by or on behalf of the Lord Advocate, that any person—

(a) has (by himself or by his servants or agents) engaged in connection with a place of public resort to which section 1 of this Act applies in a course of conduct in contravention of that section, and

(b) is likely, unless prohibited by an order of the court, to persist in such conduct,

the sheriff may make an order prohibiting that person from committing or causing or permitting acts of discrimination in contravention of the said section 1 of such kinds, against such persons or against persons of such descriptions, as may be specified in the order.

(2) An appeal shall lie to the Court of Session against any order of the sheriff—

(a) made under the last preceding subsection, or

(b) imposing on any person any punishment in respect of a breach of an order made under that subsection;
and on any such appeal the decision of the Court of Session shall be final.

(3) Subsection (2) of section 3 of this Act shall apply in the case of proceedings under this section as it applies in the case of proceedings under that section.]

5. (1) In any case where the licence or consent of the landlord or of any other person is required for the disposal to any person of premises comprised in a tenancy, that licence or consent shall be treated as unreasonably withheld if and so far as it is withheld on the ground of colour, race or ethnic or national origins:

Provided that this subsection does not apply to a tenancy of premises forming part of a dwelling-house of which the remainder or part of the remainder is occupied by the person whose licence or consent is required as his own residence if the tenant is entitled in common with that person to the use of any accommodation other than accommodation required for the purposes of access to the premises.

(2) Any covenant, agreement or stipulation which purports to prohibit the disposal of premises comprised in a tenancy to any persons by reference to colour, race or ethnic or national origins shall be construed as prohibiting such disposal except with the consent of the landlord, such consent not to be unreasonably withheld.

(3) In this section 'tenancy' means a tenancy created by a lease or sublease, by an agreement for a lease or sublease or by a tenancy agreement or in pursuance of any enactment; and 'disposal', in relation to premises comprised in a tenancy, includes assignment or assignation of the tenancy and subletting or parting with possession of the premises or any part of the premises.

(4) This section applies to tenancies created before as well as after the passing of this Act.

Public order

6. (1) A person shall be guilty of an offence under this section if, with intent to stir up hatred against any section of the public in Great Britain distinguished by colour, race or ethnic or national origins—
(a) he publishes or distributes written matter which is threatening, abusive or insulting; or
(b) he uses in any public place or at any public meeting words which are threatening, abusive or insulting,

being matter or words likely to stir up hatred against that section on grounds of colour, race or ethnic or national origins.

(2) In this section the following expressions have the meanings hereby assigned to them, that is to say:—

'public meeting' and 'public place' have the same meanings as in the Public Order Act 1936'

'publish' and 'distribute' mean publish or distribute to the public at large or to any section of the public not consisting exclusively of members of an association of which the person publishing or distributing is a member;

'written matter' includes any writing, sign or visible representation.

(3) A person guilty of an offence under this section shall be liable—

(a) on summary conviction, to imprisonment for a term not exceeding six months or to a fine not exceeding two hundred pounds, or both;

(b) on conviction on indictment, to imprisonment for a term not exceeding two years or to a fine not exceeding one thousand pounds, or both;

but no prosecution for such an offence shall be instituted in England and Wales except by or with the consent of the Attorney-General.

7. For section 5 of the Public Order Act 1936 there shall be substituted the following section:—

'**5.** Any person who in any public place or at any public meeting—

(a) uses threatening, abusive or insulting words or behaviour, or

(b) distributes or displays any writing, sign or visible representation which is threatening, abusive or insulting,

with intent to provoke a breach of the peace or whereby a breach of the peace is likely to be occasioned, shall be guilty of an offence.'

Supplemental

8. (1) This Act may be cited as the Race Relations Act 1965.

[(2) This Act shall come into operation at the expiration of one month from the date of its passing.]

(3) This Act, [except so much of section 2 as amends the House of Commons Disqualification Act 1957,] does not extend to Northern Ireland.

Schedule

Provisions as to Race Relations Board and Local Conciliation Committees

The Race Relations Board

[1. A person appointed to be a member of the Race Relations Board shall hold and vacate office under the terms of the instrument by which he is appointed, but may at any time resign his office; and a person who ceases to hold office as a member of the Board shall be eligible for reappointment.]

[2. The Board may appoint such officers and servants as they may, after consultation with the Secretary of State and with the consent of the Treasury, determine; and the Board shall be included among the bodies specified in the Table comprised in paragraph 25 of Schedule 2 to the Superannuation (Amendment) Act 1965.]

[3. (1) The Secretary of State shall pay to the members of the Board such remuneration and allowances as he may, with the consent of the Treasury, determine.

(2) The Board shall pay to their officers and servants such remuneration and allowances as they may, with the consent of the Treasury and after consultation with the Secretary of State, determine.]

[4. There shall be defrayed out of moneys provided by Parliament the expenses of the Secretary of State under paragraph 3 (1) of this Schedule, together with the expenses of the Board under paragraph 3 (2) thereof and, to such amount as the Secretary of State may with the consent of the Treasury approve, any other expenses of the Board.]

Local conciliation committees

[5. The Chairman and other members of a local conciliation committee shall be appointed by the Board.]

[6. Paragraph 1 of this Schedule shall apply in relation to a local conciliation committee as it applies in relation to the Board.]

[7. The Board may pay to members of a local conciliation committee, and to persons assisting in or concerned with the carrying out of the functions of any such committee, travelling or other allowances in accordance with such scales as may be approved by the Secretary of State with the consent of the Treasury, and may defray any other expenses of such committees to such amount as may be so approved.]

Appendix 3
Race Relations Act 1968
Chapter 71

Arrangement of Sections

Elizabeth II 1968 Chapter 71

An Act to make fresh provision with respect to discrimination on racial grounds, and to make provision with respect to relations between people of different racial origins.
[25 October 1968]

Part I Discrimination

General

1. (1) For the purposes of this Act a person discriminates against another if on the ground of colour, race or ethnic or national origins he treats that other, in any situation to which section 2, 3, 4 or 5 below applies, less favourably than he treats or would treat other persons, and in this Act references to discrimination are references to discrimination on any of those grounds.

(2) It is hereby declared that for those purposes segregating a person from other persons on any of those grounds is treating him less favourably than they are treated.

Unlawful discrimination

2. (1) It shall be unlawful for any person concerned with the provision to the public or a section of the public (whether on payment or otherwise) of any goods, facilities or services to discriminate against any person seeking to obtain or use those goods, facilities or services by refusing or deliberately omitting to provide him with any of them or to provide him with goods, services or facilities of the like quality, in the like manner and on the like terms in and on which the former normally makes them available to other members of the public.

(2) The following are examples of the facilities and services mentioned in subsection (1) above, that is to say—

access to and use of any place which members of the public are permitted to enter;

accommodation in a hotel, boarding house or other similar establishment;

facilities by way of banking or insurance or for grants, loans, credit or finance;

facilities for education, instruction or training;

facilities for entertainment, recreation or refreshment;

facilities for transport or travel;

the services of any business, profession or trade or local or other public authority.

3. (1) It shall be unlawful for an employer or any person concerned with the employment of others to discriminate against any other person—

(a) if that other person is seeking employment, by refusing or deliberately omitting to employ him on work of any description which is available and for which he is qualified;

(b) if that other person is employed or seeking employment on work of any description, by refusing or deliberately omitting to afford or offer him the like terms of employment, the like conditions of work and the like opportunities for training and promotion as the employer makes available for persons of the like qualifications employed in like circumstances on work of that description; or

(c) if that other person is employed on work of any description, by dismissing him in circumstances in which other persons employed on work of that description by the employer are not, or would not be, dismissed.

(2) The provisions of this section shall not affect the provisions of any enactment relating to the employment or qualification for employment of persons or of any instrument so relating made under any enactment, or any

condition or requirement so relating imposed by virtue of any enactment, or render unlawful anything done in pursuance of any such provision, condition or requirement.

4. (1) It shall be unlawful for an organization to which this section applies or any person concerned with the affairs of such an organization—

(a) to discriminate against a person who is not a member of the organization by refusing or deliberately omitting to admit him to membership of the organization on the like terms as other persons applying for membership;

(b) to discriminate against a member of the organization by refusing or deliberately omitting to accord him the same benefits as are accorded to other members thereof, or to take the like action on his behalf as is taken on behalf of other members, or by expelling him from the organization.

(2) This section applies to organizations of employers or workers or other organizations concerned with the carrying on of trades, businesses, professions or occupations.

5. It shall be unlawful for any person having power to dispose, or being otherwise concerned with the disposal, of housing accommodation, business premises or other land to discriminate—

(a) against any person seeking to acquire any such accommodation, premises or other land by refusing or deliberately omitting to dispose of it to him, or to dispose of it to him on the like terms and in the like circumstances as in the case of other persons;

(b) against any person occupying any such accommodation, premises or other land, by deliberately treating him differently from other such occupiers in the like circumstances; or

(c) against any person in need of any such accommodation, premises or other land by deliberately treating that other person differently from others in respect of any list of persons in need of it.

6. (1) It shall be unlawful for any person to publish or display, or to cause to be published or displayed, any advertisement or notice which indicates, or which could reasonably be understood as indicating, an intention to do an act of discrimination, whether or not it would be unlawful by virtue of any other provision of this Act.

(2) Subsection (1) above shall not render unlawful the publication or display, or causing the publication or display, of an advertisement or notice which indicates that Commonwealth citizens or any class of such citizens are required for employment outside Great Britain or that persons other than such citizens are required for employment in Great Britain.

Race Relations Act 1968 429

Acts which are not unlawful

7. (1) It shall not be unlawful by virtue of section 2 or 5 of this Act to discriminate against any person with respect to the provision or disposal of any residential accommodation in any premises if at the time of the disposal—

(a) the premises are treated for the purposes of this subsection as small premises; and

(b) the person having power to provide or dispose of the accommodation (in this subsection and subsection (2) below referred to as 'the landlord') resides and intends to continue to reside on the premises; and

(c) there is on the premises, in addition to the accommodation occupied by the landlord, relevant accommodation shared by him with other persons residing on the premises who are not members of his household.

(2) Premises shall be treated for the purposes of subsection (1) above as small premises if—

(a) in the case of premises comprising residential accommodation for one or more households (under separate letting or similar agreements) in addition to the accommodation occupied by the landlord, there is not normally residential accommodation for more than two such households and only the landlord and any member of his household reside in the accommodation occupied by him;

(b) in the case of premises not falling within paragraph (a) above, there is not normally residential accommodation on the premises for more than six persons in addition to the landlord and any members of his household.

(3) During the two years beginning with the commencement of this Act, subsection (2) (b) above shall have effect as if for the reference to six persons there were substituted a reference to twelve persons.

(4) In the foregoing provisions of this section any reference to a person having power to provide or dispose of any accommodation or to the landlord shall be construed as including a reference to any member of his family; and for the purposes of this subsection a person is a member of another's family if that person is—

(a) the other's wife or husband; or

(b) a son or daughter or a son-in-law or daughter-in-law of the other, or of the other's wife or husband; or

(c) the father or mother of the other, or of the other's wife or husband.

In paragraph (b) above any reference to a person's son or daughter includes a reference to any step-son or step-daughter, any illegitimate son or daughter, and any adopted son or daughter, of that person, and 'son-in-law' and 'daughter-in-law' shall be construed accordingly.

(5) In the foregoing provisions of this section 'residential accommodation' includes accommodation in a hotel, boarding house or other similar establishment and 'relevant accommodation' means any accommodation other than storage accommodation and means of access.

(6) It shall not be unlawful by virtue of section 2 above to discriminate against any person in respect of the provision of sleeping cabins for passengers on a ship if compliance with that section in that respect would result in persons of different colour, race or ethnic or national origins being compelled to share any such cabin.

(7) It shall not be unlawful by virtue of section 5 above for any person to discriminate against another with respect to the disposal by the former of his interest in any premises owned and wholly occupied by him unless he uses the services of an estate agent for the purposes of the disposal, or publishes or displays, or causes the publication or display, of an advertisement or notice in connection with the disposal.

(8) For the purposes of subsection (7) above a person shall be taken to own premises if the fee simple or a lease of the premises is vested in him, and in that subsection 'estate agent' means a person who in connection with the disposal of an interest in land does any of the following acts in the course of a trade, business or profession, that is to say, he brings together or takes steps to bring together the person proposing to dispose of the interest and the prospective purchaser thereof, or acts as an auctioneer.

In the application of this subsection to Scotland 'fee simple' means the estate or interest of the proprietor of the dominium utile.

8. (1) Sections 2 and 3 above shall not apply—
(a) during the two years beginning with the commencement of this Act, to employment with an employer who employs not more than twenty-five persons in addition to any employed for the purposes of his private household;
(b) during the two years following those two years, to employment with an employer who employs not more than ten persons in addition to any employed for the purposes of his private household.

(2) It shall not be unlawful by virtue of either of those sections to discriminate against any person with respect to the engagement for employment in, or the selection for work within, an undertaking or part of an undertaking if the act is done in good faith for the purpose of securing or preserving a reasonable balance of persons of different racial groups employed

in the undertaking or that part of the undertaking, as the case may be.

(3) In determining for the purposes of subsection (2) above whether a balance is reasonable regard shall be had to all the circumstances and, in particular, to the proportion of persons employed in those groups in the undertaking or part of the undertaking, as the case may be, and to the extent, if any, to which the employer engages, with respect to employment in the undertaking or part of the undertaking, as the case may be, in discrimination of any kind which is unlawful by virtue of this Part of this Act.

(4) In subsection (2) above 'racial group' means a group of persons defined by reference to colour, race or ethnic or national origins and for the purposes of that subsection persons wholly or mainly educated in Great Britain shall be treated as members of the same racial group.

(5) The Secretary of State may, if it appears to him expedient to do so, by order repeal subsections (2) to (4) above, but no such order shall be made unless a draft of the order has been laid before Parliament and approved by each House of Parliament.

(6) Those sections shall not apply to the employment of any person for the purposes of a private household.

(7) Those sections shall not apply to any employment which is, or an application for any employment which is to be,—
    (a) wholly or mainly in a country outside Great Britain;
    (b) wholly on a British ship or aircraft outside Great Britain; or
    (c) wholly or mainly on a ship or aircraft outside Great Britain other than a British ship or aircraft;
notwithstanding that the person employed or seeking employment was engaged or applied for it in Great Britain.

(8) Without prejudice to subsection (7) above, sections 2 and 3 above shall not apply to the employment or an application for the employment of a person on a ship or aircraft if the person employed or seeking employment was engaged or applied for it outside Great Britain.

(9) For the purposes of subsection (8) above a person brought to Great Britain with a view to his entering into an agreement in Great Britain to be employed on any ship or aircraft shall be treated as engaged for or seeking the employment outside Great Britain.

(10) It shall not be unlawful by virtue of section 2 or 3 above to discriminate against any person in respect of employment on a ship, if compliance with either of those sections in that respect would result in persons of different colour, race or ethnic or national origins being compelled to share sleeping rooms, mess rooms or sanitary accommodation.

(11) Section 3 above shall not render unlawful the selection of a person of a particular nationality or particular descent for employment requiring attributes especially possessed by persons of that nationality or descent.

9. (1) Nothing in this Part of this Act shall—

(a) be construed as affecting a provision which is contained in a future charitable instrument and confers benefits on persons of a particular race, particular descent or particular ethnic or national origins; or

(b) render unlawful an act which is done in order to comply with any such provision or with the provisions of any existing charitable instrument of any description.

(2) In this section 'charitable instrument' means as enactment passed or instrument made for purposes which are exclusively charitable according to the law of England and Wales and 'future instrument' and 'existing instrument' mean respectively an instrument taking effect after, and an instrument taking effect before, the commencement of this Act.

10. (1) Nothing in this Part of this Act shall render unlawful an act which is done for the purpose of safeguarding national security.

(2) A certificate purporting to be signed by or on behalf of a Minister of the Crown and certifying that an act specified in the certificate was done for the purpose aforesaid shall be conclusive evidence that it was done for that purpose.

11. (1) This Part of this Act shall not render unlawful—

(a) any refusal or omission—

(i) to provide goods, services or facilities, other than travel facilities, outside Great Britain elsewhere than on a British ship or aircraft;

(ii) to provide any banking, financial or insurance facilities for a purpose to be carried out, or in connection with risks wholly or mainly arising, outside Great Britain; or

(iii) to dispose of land outside Great Britain;

(b) any contract or term therein the main object of which is to do any act mentioned in paragraph (a) (i), (ii) or (iii) above;

notwithstanding that the refusal or omission occurred or the contract was made in Great Britain or on a British ship or aircraft.

(2) This Part of this Act shall not render unlawful an act done on a British ship while in the national waters or territorial waters of a country outside Great Britain, or on a British aircraft while in, or in flight over, such a country (or its territorial waters) if the act was done for the purpose of complying with the laws of that country.

Supplemental

12. Any person who deliberately aids, induces or incites another person to do an act which is unlawful by virtue of any provision of this Part of this Act shall be treated for the purposes of this Act as doing that act.

13. (1) Anything done by a person in the course of his employment shall be treated for the purposes of this Act as done by his employer as well as by him, whether or not it was done with the employer's knowledge or approval.

(2) Anything done by a person as agent for another person with the authority (whether express or implied and whether precedent or subsequent) of that other person shall be treated for the purposes of this Act as done by that other person as well as by him.

(3) In proceedings brought under section 19 or 20 of this Act against any person in respect of an act alleged to have been done by an employee of his it shall be a defence for that person to prove that he took such steps as were reasonably practicable to prevent the employee from doing in the course of his employment acts of the same description as that act.

Part II Concilation and Enforcement
Consideration of complaints

14. (1) There shall continue to be a Board known as the Race Relations Board constituted in accordance with this section instead of section 2 (1) of the Race Relations Act 1965 and having the function of securing compliance with the provisions of Part I of this Act and the resolution of differences arising out of any of those provisions.

(2) The Race Relations Board shall consist of a chairman and not more than eleven other members appointed by the Secretary of State.

(3) The Board shall discharge their functions in accordance with arrangements made by the Board and approved by the Secretary of State.

(4) The said arrangements may provide for the discharge under the general direction of the Board of the Board's functions in relation to any complaint or other matter falling to be dealt with by them, or in relation to any class of such matters, by a group of members of the Board selected by the chairman of the Board; and where any such functions are in accordance with such arrangements to be discharged by a group of members of the Board, anything done by or in relation to the group in or in connection with the discharge of those functions shall have the same effect as if done by or in relation to the Board.

(5) The Board shall constitute committees, to be known as conciliation committees, for such areas as the Board consider necessary for the purpose of assisting the Board in the discharge of their functions.

(6) The provisions of Schedule 1 to this Act shall have effect with respect to the Board and the conciliation committees.

(7) A conciliation committee shall make to the Board such periodical reports with respect to the exercise of their functions as the Board may require, and the Board shall, at such times as the Secretary of State may direct, make annual reports to the Secretary of State with respect to the exercise of their functions; and the Secretary of State shall lay before Parliament any report made to him under this subsection.

15. (1) This section applies to any complaint made to the Race Relations Board or a conciliation committee that an act has been done which is unlawful by virtue of any provision of Part I of this Act, except an act mentioned in section 16 below, and any reference in the following provisions of this section to a complaint shall be construed accordingly.

(2) It shall be the duty of the Board or a conciliation committee to receive any complaint which is made to them within two months of the act complained of and also, if the Board think that special circumstances warrant its reception, any complaint made to them or a conciliation committee after the expiration of that period, if in either case the complaint is accompanied by the name and address of the person by whom it is made and, in the case of an act of discrimination against any person, it is made by him or with his written authority, and—

(a) the Board may refer any complaint received by them to a conciliation committee or may direct such a committee to refer to the Board a particular complaint received by the committee or a complaint of any class so received; and

(b) the Board and any conciliation committee shall respectively investigate any complaint received by them and not referred to the other and any complaint referred to them.

(3) In investigating any complaint the Board or a conciliation committee—

(a) shall make such inquiries as they think necessary with regard to the facts alleged in the complaint and form an opinion whether any person has done any act which is unlawful by virtue of any provision of Part I of this Act; and

(b) in the case of a complaint that the act was one of discrimination against a particular person, shall use their best endeavours by communication with the parties concerned or otherwise to secure a settlement of any difference between them and, where appropriate, a satisfactory written assurance against any repetition of the act considered to be unlawful or the doing of further acts of a similar kind by the party against whom the complaint is made; and,

(c) in the case of any other complaint, shall, where appropriate, use their best endeavours to secure such an assurance as aforesaid.

(4) If on investigating a complaint the Board form the opinion that an act has been done which is unlawful by virtue of any provision of Part I of this Act and either they are unable to secure such a settlement and assurance, or, as the case may be, such an assurance, as aforesaid, or it appears to them that the act was done in breach of a relevant assurance, they shall determine whether or not to bring proceedings under section 19 or 20 of this Act.

(5) If on investigating a complaint a conciliation committee form the opinion that any such act as aforesaid has been done and either they are unable to secure such a settlement and assurance, or, as the case may be, such an assurance, as aforesaid, or it appears to them that the act was done in breach of a relevant assurance, they shall make a report to that effect to the Race Relations Board and the Board shall consider the report and shall either investigate the complaint themselves or, without investigating it, determine whether or not to bring proceedings under section 19 or 20 of this Act.

(6) Where the Board or a conciliation committee investigate a complaint under subsection (2) or (5) above they shall on completing the investigation give a written notification to the parties stating—

(a) whether or not they have been able to form an opinion with respect to the complaint and, if they have, what opinion;

(b) whether or not they have secured such a settlement and assurance or, as the case may be, such an assurance as are mentioned in subsection (3) above; and

(c) what action, if any, they propose to take in the matter.

(7) Where the Board come to a determination under subsection (5) above without investigating a complaint, they shall give the parties a written notification of their determination stating what action, if any, they propose to take in the matter.

16. (1) The provisions of Schedule 2 to this Act shall have effect with respect to any complaint made to the Secretary of State for Employment and Productivity, the Race Relations Board or a conciliation committee that an act has been done which is unlawful by virtue of any provision of Part I of this Act and is an act of discrimination with respect to employment or to membership of, or services or facilities provided by, an organization of employers or workers or an act of aiding, inducing or inciting the doing of such an act of discrimination.

(2) A Secretary of State may make regulations amending or repealing any provision of the said Schedule 2, but no regulations shall be made under this subsection unless a draft of the regulations has been laid before Parliament and approved by each House of Parliament.

17. (1) If the Race Relations Board have reason to suspect, in consequence of an allegation made by any person that he has been discriminated against in contravention of any provision of Part I of this Act or for any other cause, that during the two months preceding the day on which the matter first comes to their notice, or such longer period as the Board may in special circumstances allow, an act has been done which is unlawful by virtue of any such provision, but no complaint has been made to them, to the Secretary of State for Employment and Productivity or to a conciliation committee or any complaint so made has been withdrawn, the Board may investigate the matter or refer it for investigation,—

(a) in the case of an investigation not relating to an act mentioned in section 16 above, in accordance with Part I of Schedule 3 to this Act; and

(b) in the case of an investigation relating to such an act, in accordance with Part II of that Schedule.

(2) A Secretary of State may make regulations amending or repealing any provision of Part II of that Schedule, but no regulations shall be made under this subsection unless a draft of the regulations has been laid before Parliament and approved by each House of Parliament.

18. The Race Relations Board may appoint as assessors to assist the Board or any conciliation committee in their investigation of any complaint or other matter persons appearing to the Board to have special knowledge and experience of the circumstances in which the act to which the investigation relates is alleged to have occurred and of any other circumstances appearing to the Board to be relevant.

Legal proceedings

19. (1) Civil proceedings may be brought in England and Wales by the Race Relations Board, in pursuance of a determination of theirs under section 15 of, or Schedule 2 or 3 to, this Act and not otherwise, in respect of any act alleged to be unlawful by virtue of any provision of Part I of this Act, and in those proceedings a claim—

(a) may be made for such an injunction as is mentioned in section 21 below;

(b) may be made, on behalf of a person alleged to have suffered loss as a result of that act, for such damages as are mentioned in section 22 below;

(c) may be made for such an injunction and such damages; or

(d) may be made for a declaration that that act is unlawful by virtue of that provision or any other provision of the said Part I;

and in those proceedings, whether or not such a claim is made, an application may be made in accordance with section 23 below for revision of any contract or term in a contract alleged to contravene any such provision.

(2) Notwithstanding anything to the contrary in any enactment or rule of law relating to the jurisdiction of county courts, proceedings under this section in England and Wales may be brought in a county court for the time being appointed to have jurisdiction to entertain such proceedings by an order made by the Lord Chancellor and shall not be brought in any other court.

(3) An order under subsection (2) above appointing any court to have jurisdiction under this section shall assign to that court as its district for the purposes of this section any county court district or two or more county court districts.

(4) An order under subsection (2) above may be varied or revoked by a subsequent order made thereunder.

(5) An order for the discontinuance of the jurisdiction of any county court, whether wholly or within a part of the district assigned to it for the purposes of this section, may include provision with respect to any proceedings under this section commenced in that court before the order comes into operation.

(6) A county court appointed to have jurisdiction under this section shall have jurisdiction to entertain proceedings under this section with respect to things done on ships or aircraft outside the district assigned to the court for the purposes of this section, including things done on British ships or aircraft outside Great Britain.

(7) In any proceedings under this section in England and Wales the judge shall be assisted by two assessors appointed from a list of persons prepared and maintained by the Lord Chancellor, being persons appearing to the Lord Chancellor to have special knowledge and experience of problems connected with race and community relations.

(8) The remuneration of any assessors appointed under subsection (7) above shall be at such rate as may be determined by the Lord Chancellor

with the approval of the Treasury and shall be defrayed out of moneys provided by Parliament.

(9) Any proceedings brought under this section in England and Wales shall be included among the proceedings mentioned in section 109 (2) of the County Courts Act 1959 (appeals on questions of fact).

(10) Nothing in this Act shall affect the right to bring any proceedings in England and Wales, whether civil or criminal, which might have been brought if this Act had not been passed, but except as provided by subsection (1) above and this subsection no proceedings, whether civil or criminal, shall lie against any person in respect of any act which is unlawful by virtue only of a provision of Part I of this Act.

20. (1) Civil proceedings may be brought in Scotland by the Race Relations Board, in pursuance of a determination of theirs under section 15 of, or Schedule 2 or 3 to, this Act and not otherwise, in respect of any act alleged to be unlawful by virtue of any provision of Part I of this Act, and in those proceedings an application or claim—

(a) may be made for such an order as is mentioned in section 21 below;
(b) may be made, on behalf of a person alleged to have suffered loss as a result of that act, for such damages as are mentioned in section 22 below;
(c) may be made for such an order and such damages; or
(d) may be made for declarator that that act is unlawful by virtue of that provision or any other provision of the said Part I;

and in those proceedings, whether or not such an application or claim is made, an application may be made in accordance with section 23 below for revision of any contract or term in a contract alleged to contravene any such provision.

(2) Notwithstanding anything to the contrary in any enactment or rule of law relating to the jurisdiction of sheriff courts, proceedings under this section may be brought in a sheriff court for the time being appointed to have jurisdiction to entertain such proceedings by an order made by the Secretary of State and, subject to subsection (9) below, shall not be brought in any other court.

(3) An order under subsection (2) above appointing any court to have jurisdiction under this section shall assign to that court as its district for the purposes of this section any part or parts of any sheriffdom or two or more sheriffdoms.

(4) An order under subsection (2) above may be varied or revoked by a subsequent order made thereunder.

(5) An order for the discontinuance of the jurisdiction of any sheriff court,

whether wholly or within a part of the district assigned to it for the purposes of this section, may include provision with respect to any proceedings under this section commenced in that court before the order comes into operation.

(6) A sheriff court appointed to have jurisdiction under this section shall have jurisdiction to entertain proceedings under this section with respect to things done on ships or aircraft outside the district assigned to the court for the purposes of this section, including things done on British ships or aircraft outside Great Britain.

(7) In any proceedings under this section the sheriff shall be assisted by two assessors appointed from a list of persons prepared and maintained by the Secretary of State, being persons appearing to the Secretary of State to have special knowledge and experience of problems connected with race and community relations.

(8) The remuneration of any assessors appointed under subsection (7) above shall be at such rate as may be determined by the Secretary of State with the approval of the Treasury and shall be defrayed out of moneys provided by Parliament.

(9) An appeal shall lie to the Court of Session against any decision of the sheriff in proceedings under this section, or imposing on any person any punishment in respect of a breach of such an order as is mentioned in section 21 below, and on any such appeal the decision of the Court of Session shall be final.

(10) Nothing in this Act shall affect the right to bring any proceedings in Scotland, whether civil or criminal, which might have been brought if this Act had not been passed, but except as provided by subsection (1) above and this subsection no proceedings, whether civil or criminal, shall lie against any person in respect of any act which is unlawful by virtue only of a provision of Part I of this Act.

21. (1) In proceedings brought under section 19 above in which an injunction is claimed in respect of an act alleged to be unlawful by virtue of any provision of Part I of this Act the court, if satisfied—

(a) that the act was done by the defendant and was unlawful as aforesaid;

(b) that the defendant had previously engaged in conduct which was of the same kind as, or a similar kind to, that act and was unlawful as aforesaid; and

(c) that he is likely, unless restrained by order of the court, to engage in the future in such conduct;

may grant such injunction as appears to the court to be proper in all the circumstances, being an injunction restraining the defendant from engaging in, or causing or permitting others to engage in, conduct of the same kind as that act, or conduct of any similar kind specified in an order of the court.

(2) In proceedings brought under section 20 above in which an order is applied for in respect of an act alleged to be unlawful by virtue of any provision of Part I of this Act, the sheriff, if satisfied—

(a) that the act was done by any person and was unlawful as aforesaid;

(b) that that person had previously engaged in conduct which was of the same kind as, or a similar kind to, that act and was unlawful as aforesaid; and

(c) that he is likely, unless prohibited by an order of the court, to engage in the future in such conduct;

may make such order as appears to the court to be proper in all the circumstances, being an order prohibiting that person from engaging in, or causing or permitting others to engage in, conduct of the same kind as that act, or conduct of any similar kind specified in the order.

(3) The court may, in determining for the purposes of any such proceedings as are mentioned in subsection (1) or (2) above whether or not a person has engaged in a course of conduct, take into account not only the act or acts to which the proceedings relate, but also any other act, whether or not the subject of an investigation under section 15 of, or Schedule 2 or 3 to, this Act.

22. (1) In proceedings brought under section 19 or 20 above in which damages are claimed on behalf of any person in respect of an act alleged to be unlawful by virtue of any provision of Part I of this Act the court, if satisfied that the act was done and was unlawful, may award—

(a) special damages or, in Scotland, damages for any expenses reasonably incurred by him for the purpose of the transaction or activity out of which that act arose; and

(b) such damages as the court thinks just in all the circumstances for loss of opportunity, that is to say, loss of any benefit which that person might reasonably be expected to have had but for that act;

subject, however, to the application of the same rule concerning the duty of a person to mitigate his loss as applies in relation to damages recoverable under the common law of England and Wales or of Scotland, as the case may be.

(2) A court shall not award damages under this section for loss of opportunity in respect of any person unless the court is satisfied that at the time of

the unlawful act he was in a position to acquire the goods, services, facilities or land constituting or giving rise to the benefit or, as the case may be, had the qualifications necessary for him to obtain or retain the benefit.

(3) Damages recovered under this section by the Race Relations Board in respect of any person shall be accounted for to him by the Board.

23. (1) A contract or term in a contract which contravenes any provision of Part I of this Act shall not be void or unenforceable by reason only of the contravention, but may be revised in accordance with the following provisions of this section.

(2) Any such contract or term in a contract may be revised by the court in proceedings under section 19 or 20 above on an application made by the Race Relations Board on behalf of any party to the contract or by any such party who is the defendant or, in Scotland, the defender, in the proceedings.

(3) On an application under this section to revise a contract or term in a contract the court may, if it appears to the court feasible to do so without affecting the rights of persons who are not parties to the contract, make such order as it thinks just in all the circumstances revising the contract or term so as to secure that, as from the date of the order, it does not contravene any provision of Part I of this Act, and any party to the contract, whether or not a party to the application, shall be bound by the order accordingly.

(4) Any reference in this section to a party to a contract shall, where the rights of that party are for the time being vested in any other person, be construed as a reference to that other person.

24. In proceedings under section 19 or 20 above evidence of any communication made, other than an assurance given, to the Secretary of State for Employment and Productivity, the Race Relations Board, a conciliation committee or a body of persons to whom a complaint or other matter is referred under Schedule 2 or 3 to this Act, or any officer or servant of the Secretary of State, the Board or such a committee or body, for the purpose of or in connection with the exercise of their functions under this Part of this Act shall not be admitted except with the consent of the person by whom it was made.

Part III Miscellaneous and General

25. (1) There shall be constituted a Commission to be known as the Community Relations Commission consisting of a chairman and not more than eleven other members appointed by the Secretary of State.

(2) The provisions of Schedule 4 to this Act shall have effect with respect to the Commission.

(3) It shall be the duty of the Commission—

(a) to encourage the establishment of, and assist others to take steps to secure the establishment of, harmonious community relations and to coordinate on a national basis the measures adopted for that purpose by others; and

(b) to advise the Secretary of State on any matter referred to the Commission by him and to make recommendations to him on any matter which the Commission consider should be brought to his attention.

(4) For the purpose of discharging their functions under subsection (3) (a) above the Commission may—

(a) establish services for giving advice on community relations to local authorities and other local organizations concerned therewith and for collecting information with respect to community relations;

(b) provide courses of training in connection with community relations; and

(c) arrange or promote the holding of conferences on matters connected with community relations.

(5) Without prejudice to subsection (3) above, the Commission may—

(a) subject to subsection (6) below, give financial assistance to any local organizations appearing to the Commission to be concerned with community relations;

(b) with the approval of the Secretary of State, appoint advisory committees for the purpose of such of their functions as the Commission think fit.

(6) The Commission shall not give any financial assistance under subsection (5) (a) above out of moneys provided by Parliament except with the approval of the Secretary of State and the consent of the Treasury.

(7) The Commission shall, at such times as the Secretary of State may direct, make annual reports to him with respect to the exercising of their functions; and the Secretary of State shall lay any such report before Parliament.

26. (1) The Secretary of State may conduct or assist in conducting research into any matter connected with relations between people of different colour, race or ethnic or national origins.

(2) Any expenses incurred by the Secretary of State with the consent of the Treasury for the purposes of his functions under this section shall be defrayed out of moneys provided by Parliament.

27. (1) This Act binds the Crown.

(2) The provisions of Parts II to IV of the Crown Proceedings Act 1947 shall apply to proceedings against the Crown under section 19 above as they apply to proceedings in England and Wales which by virtue of section 23 of that Act are treated for the purposes of Part II of that Act as civil proceedings by or against the Crown, except that in their application to proceedings under the said section 19—

(a) section 20 of that Act (removal of proceedings from county court to High Court) shall not apply; and

(b) section 28 of that Act (discovery) shall have effect subject to section 24 of this Act;

and any restriction in the said provisions on the bringing of proceedings in tort shall apply to proceedings against the Crown under the said section 19.

(3) The provisions of Parts II to V of the Crown Proceedings Act 1947 shall apply to proceedings against the Crown under section 20 above as they apply to proceedings in Scotland by or against the Crown under that Act, except that in their application to proceedings under the said section 20—

(a) the proviso to section 44 of that Act (remission of proceedings from sheriff court to Court of Session) shall not apply; and

(b) section 47 of that Act (recovery of documents) shall have effect subject to section 24 of this Act;

and any restriction in the said provisions on the bringing of any proceedings in respect of any such act or omission as is described in section 43 (b) of that Act shall apply to proceedings against the Crown under the said section 20.

(4) For the purposes of this Act the office of constable shall be treated as if it were employment and a constable shall be treated as if he were employed by the authority by whom he is appointed, except that a constable appointed by justices of the peace on the nomination or application of any authority shall be treated as if he were employed by the authority on whose nomination or application he is appointed, and accordingly the authority by whom or, as the case may be, on whose nomination or application a constable is appointed shall be treated for those purposes as if he or they were an employer or employers.

(5) A police cadet shall be treated for those purposes as if he were employed by the authority by whom he is appointed and accordingly—

(a) any such authority shall be treated for those purposes as if he were an employer; and

(b) section 17 (3) of the Police Act 1964 and section 8 (3) of the Police (Scotland) Act 1967 (police authority to be treated as the employer of a police cadet for certain purposes) shall not apply for the purposes of this Act.

(6) Where by virtue of subsection (4) or (5) above a chief officer of police is treated as if he were the employer of any constable or police cadet, there shall be paid out of the police fund or, in Scotland, by the police authority—

(a) any damages, costs or expenses awarded against the chief officer of police in any proceedings brought against him under Part II of this Act and any costs or expenses incurred by him in any such proceedings so far as not recovered by him in the proceedings; and

(b) any sum required by him in connection with the settlement of any claim made against him by virtue of this section, including any settlement made under Part II of this Act, if the settlement is approved by the police authority.

(7) Any proceedings under Part II of this Act which by virtue of subsection (4) or (5) above and apart from this subsection would lie against a chief officer of police shall be brought against the chief officer of police for the time being or, in the case of a vacancy in that office, against the person for the time being performing the functions of the chief officer of police; and references in subsection (6) above to the chief officer of police shall be construed accordingly.

(8) Section 8 (2) and (3) of this Act shall have effect as if any reference to employment, work or persons employed in an undertaking or part of an undertaking included a reference to employment, work or persons employed in the service of the Crown or in any government department or any police force, or part thereof.

(9) Nothing in this Act shall—

(a) invalidate any rules (whether made before or after the passing of this Act) restricting employment in the service of the Crown or by any public body prescribed for the purposes of this subsection by regulations made by the Treasury to persons of particular birth, citizenship, nationality, descent or residence; or

(b) render unlawful the publication, display or implementation of any such rules or the publication or display of advertisements stating the gist of any such rules.

(10) Any statutory instrument containing regulations under this section shall be subject to annulment in pursuance of a resolution of either House of Parliament.

(11) References in this section to the Crown include references to Her Majesty in right of the Duchy of Lancaster or the Duke of Cornwall.

(12) In this section 'public body' means a body of persons, whether corporate or unincorporate, carrying on a service or undertaking of a public nature and expressions used in subsections (6) and (7) above and in the Police Act 1964 have the same meaning in those subsections as they have in that Act.

In the application of this subsection to Scotland, for the reference to the Police Act 1964 there shall be substituted a reference to the Police (Scotland) Act 1967.

28. (1) In this Act, except so far as the context otherwise requires—

'act' includes omission, and any reference to an act or other thing done shall be construed accordingly;

'British ship or aircraft' means a ship or aircraft registered in the United Kingdom or belonging to the Crown or to a Government Department or for the time being in possession of such a Department;

'community relations' means relations within the community between people of different colour, race or ethnic or national origins;

'disposal', in relation to land, includes granting a right to occupy land and any reference to acquiring land shall be construed accordingly;

'relevant assurance' means an assurance given for the purposes of section 15(3) of this Act or paragraph 3 of Schedule 2 or paragraph 2 or 8 of Schedule 3 thereto.

(2) Any reference in sections 1 to 6 of this Act to the doing of anything by any person is a reference to the doing of that thing by him as employer or employee or as principal or agent.

(3) For the purposes of this Act the territorial waters of Great Britain shall be treated as forming part of Great Britain.

(4) Any reference in this Act to the territorial waters of a country is a reference to such part of the sea adjacent to the coast of that country as is recognized by international law as forming the territorial waters of that country.

(5) Any reference in this Act to a body of persons shall, in relation to any description of employment, disputes about which are normally considered by an organization of such bodies, be construed as a reference to that organization.

(6) Any power conferred by this Act on a Minister of the Crown or the Treasury to make regulations or orders shall be exercisable by statutory instrument.

(7) Any reference in this Act to any other enactment is a reference thereto as amended, and includes a reference thereto as extended or applied, by or under any other enactment, including this Act.

(8) The following provisions of the Race Relations Act 1965, that is to say, sections 1 to 4 and 8(2), the words of exception in section 8(3) and the Schedule, are hereby repealed except as respect things done before the commencement of this Act.

(9) Anything which was done before the commencement of this Act in contravention of section 1 of the said Act of 1965 and would, if done after the commencement of this Act, have contravened section 2 of this Act shall be taken into account in determining under section 21(1) or (2) of this Act whether an injunction should be granted or an order made in respect of an act of discrimination in contravention of the said section 2.

(10) Any local conciliation committee constituted under the said Act of 1965 before the commencement of this Act shall be treated for the purposes of this Act or any enactment thereby amended as a conciliation committee constituted under this Act, and any person appointed to be a member, officer or servant of the Race Relations Board or a local conciliation committee and holding office as such immediately before the commencement of this Act shall be so treated as having been appointed to the Board or the conciliation committee, as the case may be, under this Act.

29. (1) This Act may be cited as the Race Relations Act 1968.

(2) The Race Relations Act 1965 and this Act may be cited together as the Race Relations Acts 1965 and 1968.

(3) This Act shall come into operation at the expiration of one month from the date of its passing.

(4) This Act, except so much thereof as amends the House of Commons Disqualification Act 1957, does not extend to Northern Ireland.

Schedules

Schedule 1

Provisions as to the Race Relations Board and Conciliation Committees

The Race Relations Board

1. The Race Relations Board shall be a body corporate having perpetual succession and a common seal.

2. A person appointed to be a member of the Board shall hold and vacate office under the terms of the instrument by which he is appointed, but may at any time resign his office; and a person who ceases to hold office as a member of the Board shall be eligible for reappointment.

3. The Board may appoint such officers and servants as they may, after

consultation with the Secretary of State and with the consent of the Treasury, determine; and the Board shall be included among the bodies listed in Schedule 8 to the Superannuation Act 1965.

4. (1) The Secretary of State shall pay to the members of the Board such remuneration and allowances as he may, with the consent of the Treasury, determine.

(2) The Board shall pay to any assessors appointed by them under section 18 of this Act and to the officers and servants of the Board such remuneration and allowances as they may, with the consent of the Treasury and after consultation with the Secretary of State, determine.

5. There shall be defrayed out of moneys provided by Parliament the expenses of the Secretary of State under paragraph 4(1) of this Schedule, together with the expenses of the Board under paragraph 4(2) thereof and, to such amount as the Secretary of State may with the consent of the Treasury approve, any other expenses of the Board.

Conciliation committees

6. The Chairman and other members of a conciliation committee shall be appointed by the Board.

7. Paragraph 2 of this Schedule shall apply in relation to a conciliation committee as it applies in relation to the Board.

8. The Board may pay to members of a conciliation committee, and to persons assisting in or concerned with the carrying out of the functions of any such committee, travelling or other allowances in accordance with such scales as may be approved by the Secretary of State with the consent of the Treasury, and may defray any other expenses of such committees to such amount as may be so approved.

Proceedings of the Board and committees

9. The validity of any proceedings of the Board, a group of members of the Board or a concilication committee shall not be affected by any vacancy among the members or by any defect in the appointment of any member.

10. The quorum of the Board or a group of members of the Board and the arrangements relating to meetings of the Board or any such group shall be such as the Board may determine.

11. The quorum of a concilation committee and the arrangements relating to meetings of such a committee shall be such as the committee may determine.

Disqualification for Membership of Parliament

12. In Part II of Schedule 1 to the House of Commons Disqualification Act 1957 (bodies of which all members are disqualified under this Act), both in its application to the House of Commons of the Parliament of the United Kingdom and in its application to the Senate and House of Commons of Northern Ireland, for the entry relating to the Race Relations Board there shall be substituted the entry 'The Race Relations Board and any conciliation committee constituted by the Board under section 14 of the Race Relations Act 1968'.

Schedule 2
Complaints relating to Employment, Trade Unions and Organizations of Employers

1. It shall be the duty of any authority mentioned in section 16 of this Act to receive any complaint to which that section applies and which is made to them within two months of the act complained of and also, if the Race Relations Board think that special circumstances warrant its reception, any complaint made to the authority after the expiration of that period, if in either case the complaint is accompanied by the name and address of the person by whom it is made and, in the case of an act of discrimination against any person, it is made by him or with his written authorisation and, subject to paragraphs 13 and 16 below, the authority shall, if not the Secretary of State for Employment and Productivity, refer any complaint received by them under this paragraph to him.

2. Where any such complaint is referred or made to the Secretary of State for Employment and Productivity then, subject to those paragraphs, the Secretary of State shall—

(a) if satisfied that there is a body of persons suitable to consider that complaint, refer it to that body for investigation by them;

(b) if not, refer it to the Board for investigation by them or a conciliation committee.

3. A body of persons investigating a complaint referred to them under this Schedule—

(a) shall make such inquiries as they think necessary with respect to the facts alleged in the complaint and form an opinion whether any person has done any act which is unlawful by virtue of any provision of Part I of this Act; and

(b) in the case of a complaint that the act was one of discrimination against a particular person, shall use their best endeavours by communication with the parties concerned or otherwise to secure a settlement of any difference between them and, where appropriate, a satisfactory assurance against any repetition of the act considered to be unlawful or the doing of further acts of a similar kind by the party against whom the complaint was made; and

(c) in the case of any other complaint, shall, where appropriate, use their best endeavours to secure such an assurance as aforesaid.

4. A body of persons to whom a complaint is referred under this Schedule shall, on the expiration of the period of four weeks from the reference of the complaint to them or on completion of their investigation, whichever occurs first, report to the Secretary of State for Employment and Productivity whether in their opinion an act has been done which is unlawful by virtue of any provision of Part I of this Act and, if so, whether they have been able to secure such a settlement and assurance or, as the case may be, such an assurance as are mentioned in paragraph 3 above.

5. Where the Secretary of State—

(a) receives a report from a body of persons under paragraph 4 above that they have failed within the said period of four weeks to secure such a settlement and assurance, or, as the case may be, such an assurance, or

(b) receives no report under that paragraph from such a body;

he may after consultation with the Race Relations Board request that body to continue to investigate the matter for a specified period or to cease investigating it.

6. Where the Secretary of State requests a body of persons to continue as aforesaid, paragraphs 3 to 5 above shall apply to the complaint as they apply to a complaint on its original reference under this Schedule with the substitution of references to the specified period for references to the said period of four weeks.

7. A body of persons to whom a complaint is referred under this Schedule shall, on completion of their investigation, give a written notification to the parties stating—

(a) whether or not they have been able to form an opinion with respect to the complaint and, if they have, what opinion;

(b) whether or not they have secured such a settlement and assurance or, as the case may be, such an assurance as are mentioned in paragraph 3 above; and

(c) that they will report to the Secretary of State for Employment and Productivity on their investigation;

and stating the rights of any party aggrieved by the conclusion or any other decision of that body.

8. Where in pursuance of paragraph 5 above the Secretary of State requests a body of persons to whom a complaint has been referred under this Schedule to cease investigating the complaint, he shall refer the complaint to the Race Relations Board and it shall be the duty of the Board to investigate it.

9. Where the Race Relations Board are notified by any of the parties that he is aggrieved by a decision of any body of persons to whom a complaint has been referred under this Schedule, then, subject to the following provisions of this Schedule, the Board may determine that the complaint be not further entertained or may refer the complaint back to that body for further investigation or may investigate it themselves, and where the Board refer the complaint back to that body, paragraphs 3, 4, 7 and 8 above shall apply to the complaint as they apply to a complaint referred to such a body by the Secretary of State for Employment and Productivity—

(a) with the substitution for references to the Secretary of State of references to the Board; and

(b) with the omission in paragraphs 4 and 8 of any reference to any period or to dealing with a complaint within or after the end of a period.

10. Where the Race Relations Board are notified by any of the parties that he is aggrieved by any such decision and it appears to the Board that that decision was not disputed by him within a week of his being given a written notification of the decision in accordance with paragraph 7 above, or within such further period as the Board may in special circumstances allow, the Board shall disregard the notification under paragraph 9 above.

11. Where a complaint originally referred to a body of persons by the Secretary of State for Employment and Productivity under this Schedule is again referred to them by the Race Relations Board for further consideration and that body reports to the Board that they have been unable to secure such a settlement and assurance or, as the case may be, such an assurance as are mentioned in paragraph 3 above or where it appears to the Board that that body have been unable to secure such a settlement and assurance, or, as the case may be, such an assurance, the Board may investigate the complaint themselves or determine that it be not further entertained.

12. Subject to paragraphs 13 to 15 below, where a complaint is referred to the Board under this Schedule, section 15(2) to (6) of this Act shall apply to the complaint as those subsections apply to a complaint to which the said section 15 applies and which is received by the Board, except that section 15(2)(a) and (5) of this Act shall not apply to a complaint referred to the Board under paragraph 8 above.

13. Where it appears to the Secretary of State for Employment and Productivity or the Race Relations Board on receiving a complaint to which section 16 of this Act applies or on the reference to the Secretary of State of such a complaint by a conciliation committee, that the complaint may relate to an act done in breach of a relevant assurance, then, notwithstanding anything in the foregoing provisions of this Schedule, the Secretary of State shall refer the complaint to the Board, or, as the case may be, the Board shall retain the complaint, for investigation in accordance with paragraph 14 below.

14. Where a complaint falls to be investigated in accordance with this paragraph, the Race Relations Board shall either investigate it themselves or—

(a) if there is a body of persons notified to them by the Secretary of State for Employment and Productivity as being a body suitable to consider the complaint, refer it to them for investigation;

(b) if there is not, refer it to a conciliation committee for investigation.

15. Where on investigating a complaint under this Schedule the Board or any such body or committee form the opinion that an act has been done which is unlawful by virtue of any provision of Part I of this Act, they shall also form an opinion whether it was done in breach of a relevant assurance; and—

(a) where any such committee form the opinion that it was done in breach of such an assurance, they may, without more, report that fact to the Board;

(b) where any such body of persons form that opinion, they may, without more, report that fact to the Secretary of State for Employment and Productivity and the Board; and

(c) where the Board form that opinion or where they receive a report made by any such committee or body under this paragraph, they may, without more, determine to bring proceedings under section 19 or 20 of this Act.

16. Where it appears to the authority to whom a complaint to which section 16 of this Act applies is made that an act which is the subject of the complaint relates to employment and that it was done by a person acting as agent for another person but without the authorization of that other person, the authority shall—

(a) if the Secretary of State for Employment and Productivity, refer it to the Race Relations Board; and

(b) if not, deal with it as if it were a complaint to which section 15 of this Act applies;

and in either event the provisions of the said section 15 shall, notwithstanding anything in section 16(1) of this Act, apply to the complaint accordingly and if the complaint was originally made to the Secretary of State or a conciliation committee shall so apply as if it had been made to the Board.

Schedule 3
Investigation of Unlawful Conduct where no Complaint Made
Part I Normal Provisions as to Investigations

1. The Race Relations Board may themselves investigate or may refer to a conciliation committee a matter which falls to be investigated under this Part of this Schedule, and it shall be the duty of a committee to whom a matter is referred under this paragraph to investigate the matter.

2. In investigating any matter under this Part of this Schedule the Board or a conciliation committee—

(a) shall make such inquiries as they think necessary with regard thereto and form an opinion whether any person has done any act which is unlawful by virtue of any provision of Part I of this Act; and

(b) where the investigation relates to an act suspected of amounting to discrimination against a particular person, shall use their best endeavours by communication with the persons concerned or otherwise to secure a settlement of any difference between them and, where appropriate, a satisfactory written assurance against any repetition of the act considered to be unlawful or the doing of further acts of a similar kind by the person by whom it was done; and

(c) where the investigation does not so relate, where appropriate, use their best endeavours to secure such an assurance as aforesaid.

3. If on investigating any matter the Board form the opinion that an act has been done which is unlawful by virtue of any provision of Part I of this Act and either they are unable to secure such a settlement and assurance, or, as the case may be, such an assurance, as aforesaid, or it appears to them that the act was done in breach of a relevant assurance, they shall determine whether or not to bring proceedings under section 19 or 20 of this Act.

4. If on investigating any matter a conciliation committee form the opinion that any such act as aforesaid has been done and either they are unable to secure such a settlement and assurance, or, as the case may be, such an assurance as aforesaid, or it appears to them that the act was done in breach of a relevant assurance, they shall make a report to that effect to the Race Relations Board and the Board shall consider the report and shall either investigate the matter themselves or, without investigating it,

determine whether or not to bring proceedings under section 19 or 20 of this Act.

5. Where the Board or a conciliation committee investigate any matter under this Part of this Schedule they shall on completing the investigation give a written notification to the persons appearing to them to be concerned stating—

(a) whether or not they have been able to form an opinion with respect to the matter and, if they have, what opinion;

(b) whether or not they have secured such a settlement and assurance or, as the case may be, such an assurance as are mentioned in paragraph 2 above; and

(c) what action if any they propose to take with respect to the matter.

6. Where the Board come to a determination under paragraph 4 above without investigating a matter, they shall give a written notification to the persons appearing to them to be concerned of their determination.

Part II Investigation of Matters Relating to Employment,
Trade Unions and Organizations of Employers

7. Subject to paragraphs 18 and 21 below, the Race Relations Board shall not in the first instance investigate any matter falling to be investigated under this Part of this Schedule, but shall refer it to the Secretary of State for Employment and Productivity, and (subject as aforesaid) the Secretary of State shall—

(a) if satisfied that there is a body of persons suitable to consider any matter referred to him under this paragraph, refer it to that body for investigation by them;

(b) if not, refer it to the Board for investigation by them or by a conciliation committee.

8. A body of persons investigating any matter referred to them under this Part of this Schedule—

(a) shall make such inquiries as they think necessary with respect thereto and form an opinion whether any person has done any act which is unlawful by virtue of any provision of Part I of this Act; and

(b) where the investigation relates to an act suspected of amounting to discrimination against a particular person, shall use their best endeavours by communication with the persons concerned or otherwise to secure a settlement of any difference between them and, where appropriate, a satisfactory assurance against any repetition of the act considered to be unlawful or the doing of further acts of a similar kind by the person by whom it was done; and

(c) where the investigation does not so relate, shall, where appropriate, use their best endeavours to secure such an assurance as aforesaid.

9. A body of persons to whom a matter is referred under this Schedule shall, on the expiration of the period of four weeks from the reference of the matter to them or on completion of their investigation, whichever occurs first, report to the Secretary of State for Employment and Productivity whether in their opinion an act has been done which is unlawful by virtue of any provision of Part I of this Act and, if so, whether they have been able to secure such a settlement and assurance or, as the case may be, such an assurance as are mentioned in paragraph 8 above.

10. Where the Secretary of State—
    (a) receives a report from a body of persons under paragraph 9 above that they have failed within the said period of four weeks to secure such a settlement and assurance or, as the case may be, such an assurance; or
    (b) receives no report under that paragraph from such a body;
he may after consultation with the Race Relations Board request that body to continue to investigate the matter for a specified period or to cease investigating it.

11. Where the Secretary of State requests a body of persons to continue as aforesaid, paragraphs 8 to 10 above shall apply to the investigation as they apply to an investigation on its original reference under this Part of this Schedule with the substitution of references to the specified period for references to the said period of four weeks.

12. A body of persons to whom a matter is referred under this Part of this Schedule shall, on completion of their investigation, give a written notification to the persons appearing to them to be concerned stating—
    (a) whether or not they have been able to form an opinion with respect to the matter and, if they have, what opinion;
    (b) whether or not they have secured such a settlement and assurance or, as the case may be, such an assurance as are mentioned in paragraph 8 above; and
    (c) that they will report to the Secretary of State for Employment and Productivity on their investigation;
and stating the rights of any such person who is aggrieved by the conclusion or any other decision of that body.

13. Where in pursuance of paragraph 10 above the Secretary of State requests a body of persons to whom a matter has been referred under this Part of this Schedule to cease investigating the matter, he shall refer the matter to the Race Relations Board and it shall be the duty of the Board to investigate it.

14. Where the Race Relations Board are notified by any person appearing to them to be concerned that he is aggrieved by a decision of any body of persons to whom a matter has been referred under this Schedule, then, subject to the following provisions of this Schedule, the Board may determine that the matter be not further investigated or may refer it back to that body for further investigation or may investigate it themselves, and where the Board refer the matter back to that body, paragraphs 8, 9, 12 and 13 above shall apply to the matter as they apply to a matter referred to such a body by the Secretary of State for Employment and Productivity—

    (a) with the substitution for references to the Secretary of State of references to the Board; and

    (b) with the omission in paragraphs 9 and 13 of any reference to any period or to dealing with a matter within or after the end of a period.

15. Where the Race Relations Board are notified by any such person that he is aggrieved by any such decision and it appears to the Board that that decision was not disputed by him within a week of his being given a written notification of the decision in accordance with paragraph 12 above, or within such further period as the Board may in special circumstances allow, the Board shall disregard the notification under paragraph 14 above.

16. Where a matter originally referred to a body of persons by the Secretary of State for Employment and Productivity under this Schedule is again referred to them by the Race Relations Board for further consideration and that body reports to the Board that they have been unable to secure such a settlement and assurance or, as the case may be, such an assurance as are mentioned in paragraph 8 above or where it appears to the Board that that body have been unable to secure such a settlement and assurance, or, as the case may, such an assurance, the Board may investigate the matter themselves or determine that it be not further investigated.

17. Subject to paragraphs 18 to 20 below, where a matter falling to be investigated under this Part of this Schedule is referred to the Board thereunder, Part I of this Schedule shall apply to the matter as it applies to a matter falling to be investigated under that Part of this Schedule, except that so much of paragraph 1 as provides for the reference of a matter to a conciliation committee and paragraphs 4 and 6 of this Schedule shall not apply to a matter referred to the Board under paragraph 13 above.

18. Where it appears to the Race Relations Board on first considering a matter falling to be investigated under this Part of this Schedule that it may relate to an act done in breach of a relevant assurance, then, notwith-

standing anything in paragraph 7 above, the Board shall retain the complaint for investigation in accordance with paragraph 19 below.

19. Where a matter falls to be investigated in accordance with this paragraph, the Race Relations Board shall either investigate it themselves or—
    (a) if there is a body of persons notified to them by the Secretary of State for Employment and Productivity as being a body suitable to consider the matter, refer it to them for investigation;
    (b) if there is not, refer it to a conciliation committee for investigation.

20. Where on investigating a matter under this Part of this Schedule the Board or any such body or committee form the opinion that an act has been done which is unlawful by virtue of any provision of Part I of this Act, they shall also form an opinion whether the act was done in breach of a relevant assurance; and—
    (a) where any such committee form the opinion that it was done in breach of such an assurance they may, without more, report that fact to the Board;
    (b) where any such body form that opinion, they may, without more, report that fact to the Secretary of State for Employment and Productivity and the Board; and
    (c) where the Board form that opinion or where they receive a report made by any such committee or body under this paragraph, they may, without more, determine to bring proceedings under section 19 or 20 of this Act.

21. Where it appears to the Race Relations Board that an act suspected of being unlawful by virtue of any provision of Part I of this Act relates to employment and that it was done by a person acting as agent for another person, but without the authority of that other person, the Board shall deal with it as a matter falling to be investigated under Part I of this Schedule, and that Part of this Schedule shall, notwithstanding anything in section 17 of this Act, apply to the investigation of the matter accordingly.

Schedule 4
Provisions as to the Community Relations Commission

1. A person appointed to be a member of the Community Relations Commission shall hold and vacate office under the terms of the instrument by which he is appointed, but may at any time resign his office; and a person who ceases to hold office as a member of the Commission shall be eligible for reappointment.

2. The Commission may appoint such officers and servants as they may, after consultation with the Secretary of State and with the consent of the Treasury, determine.

3. The Secretary of State shall pay to the members of the Commission such remuneration and allowances as he may, with the consent of the Treasury, determine.

4. The Commission shall pay to their officers and servants such remuneration as they may, with the consent of the Treasury and after consultation with the Secretary of State, determine.

5. The Commission may, in the case of such of its members, officers and servants as the Secretary of State may with the approval of the Treasury determine, pay to or in respect of them such pensions or gratuities, or make such payments towards the provision of pensions or gratuities, as may be so determined.

6. There shall be defrayed out of moneys provided by Parliament the expenses of the Secretary of State under paragraph 3 above, together with the expenses of the Commission under paragraph 4 or 5 above and, to such amount as the Secretary of State may with the consent of the Treasury approve, any other expenses of the Commission.

7. Notwithstanding anything in paragraph 6 above, the Commission may accept financial assistance otherwise than out of moneys provided by Parliament towards the defraying of their expenses.

8. In Part II of Schedule 1 to the House of Commons Disqualification Act 1957 (bodies of which all members are disqualified under that Act), in its application to the House of Commons of the Parliament of the United Kingdom, there shall be inserted (at the appropriate point in alphabetical order) the entry 'The Community Relations Commission'.

References

Allport, G. W. (1958), *The Nature of Prejudice* (abridged), Doubleday.
Austin, G. (1966), *The Indian Constitution: Cornerstone of a Nation*, Oxford University Press.

Banton, M. (1967), *Race Relations*, Social Science Paperbacks.
Bearce, G. D. (1961), *British Attitudes Towards India, 1784–1858*, Oxford University Press.
Benewick, R (1969), *Political Violence and Public Order*, Allen Lane, The Penguin Press.
Berger, M. (1968), *Equality by Statute*, Doubleday.
Bindman, G. (1969), ' The Race Relations Act 1968', 66 *Law Society's Gazette*, 100.
Bonfield, A. E. (1964), 'State civil rights statutes: some proposals', *Iowa L.R.*, vol. 49.
Bonham Carter, M. (1967), 'Measures against discrimination: the North American scene', *Race*, vol. 9, no. 1.
Bostead, W. (1968), *Agency*, Sweet & Maxwell.
Boyle, Lord (1968), 'Race relations: the limits of voluntary action', *Race*, vol. 9, no. 3, pp. 289–302.
Brockway, F. (1967), *This Shrinking, Explosive World: A Study of Race Relations*, Epworth Press.
Brownlie, I. (1968), *The Law Relating to Public Order*, Butterworth.
Burney, E. (1967), *Housing on Trial: A Study of Immigrants and Local Government*, Oxford University Press.

Cable, V. (1969), 'Whither Kenyan emigrants?', The Fabian Society, *Young Fabian Pamphlet*, no. 18.
Clark, K. (1965), *Dark Ghetto*, Gollancz.
Cohen, D. K. (1968), 'Children and their primary schools, vol. 2', *Harvard Educ. Rev.*, vol. 38, pp. 329–40.
Coleman Report (1966), *Equality of Educational Opportunity*, US Government Printing Office.
Compton, J. M. (1967), 'Indians and the Indian civil service, 1853–79: a study in national agitation and imperial embarrassment', *J. Royal Asiatic Soc.*

Cooper, G., and **Sobol, R. B.** (1969), 'Seniority and testing under fair employment laws: a general approach to objective criteria of hiring and promotion', *Harvard L.R.*, vol. 82, pp. 1598–1679.

Cornford, F. M. (1964), *Microcosmographia Academica*, Bowes, 6th edn.

Cretney, S. (1968), 'Racial discrimination', *New L.J.* vol. 118, p. 1094.

Cross, C. (1961), *The Fascists in Britain*, Pall Mall.

Cross, C. (1968), *The Fall of the British Empire*, Hodder & Stoughton.

Cullingworth Report (1969), *Council Housing Purposes, Procedures and Priorities*, HMSO.

Daniel, W. W. (1968), *Racial Discrimination in England*, Penguin.

Davis, D. B. (1966), *The Problem of Slavery in Western Culture*, Cornell University Press; Penguin, 1970.

Deakin, N. (1965), *Colour and the British Electorate, 1964*, Pall Mall.

Department of Employment and Productivity (1970a), 'Employment and the Race Relations Act', *Employment and Productivity Gazette*, vol. 78, no. 2, p. 100.

Department of Employment and Productivity (1970b), 'Race Relations in Employment', *Employment and Productivity Gazette*, vol. 78, no. 2, p. 968.

Devlin, Lord (1968), *The Enforcement of Morals*, Oxford University Press.

Dicey, A. V. (1961), *Introduction to the Study of Law and of Constitution*, Macmillan, 10th edn.

Dicey, A. V. (1967), *The Conflict of Laws*, Stevens, 8th edn.

Dickey, A. F. (1968a), 'English law and incitement to racial hatred', *Race*, vol. 9, no. 3, pp. 311–29.

Dickey, A. F. (1968b), 'Prosecutions under the Race Relations Act 1965, section 6 (incitement to racial hatred)', *Crim. L.R.*, pp. 489–96.

Dorsen, N. (1967), 'The Model Anti-Discrimination Act', 4 *Harvard J. Legislation*, 212.

Fiddes, E. (1934), 'Lord Mansfield and the Sommersett Case', *L.Q.R.*, vol. 50.

Foot, P. (1965), *Immigration and Race in British Politics*, Penguin.

Gartner, L. P. (1960), *The Jewish Immigrant in England 1870–1914*, Allen & Unwin.

Ghosh, P. K. (1966), *The Constitution of India: How It Has Been Formed*, Calcutta.

Gledhill, A. (1964a), 'The expansion of judicial process in Republican India' in *Some Aspects of Indian Law Today*, International and Comparative Law Q., supp. 8.

Gledhill, A. (1964b), *The Republic of India: The Development of Its Laws and Constitution*, Stevens.

Gould, W. B. (1967), 'Employment, seniority and race: the role of Title VII of the Civil Rights Act of 1964', *Hansard L.J.*, vol. 13, p. 1.

Gould, W. B. (1969), 'Job discrimination on account of race: collective bargaining and the burger court', *Michigan L.R.*, vol. 68, no. 2, pp. 237–58.

Gould, W. B. (1969), 'Seniority and the black worker: reflections on Quarles and its implications', *Texas L.R.*, vol. 47, pp. 1039–74.
Griswold, E. N. (1964), *Law and Lawyers in the United States*, Stevens.

Hailsham, Lord (1970), 'Race relations and Parliament', *Race*, vol. 12, no. 1, pp. 1–13.
Hart, H. L. A. (1968), *Law, Liberty and Morality*, Oxford University Press.
Harvard Law Review (1969), 'Developments in the law: equal protection', vol. 82, pp. 1067–1192.
Harvard Law Review (1971), 'Developments in the Law: Employment Discrimination and Title VII of the Civil Rights Act 1964', vol. 84, pp. 1109–1316.
Hasson, R. A. (1969), 'The doctrine of *uberrima fides* in insurance law: a critical evaluation', *Mod.L.R.*, vol. 32.
Hattersley, R. (1965), 'Dealing with race prejudice', *Socialist Commentary*, July, pp.14–16.
Henriques, H. S. Q. (1908), *The Jews and the English Law*, Oxford University Press.
Hepple, B. (1966), 'The Race Relations Act 1965', *Mod.L.R.*, vol. 29, no. 3, p. 306.
Hepple, B. (1968), *Race, Jobs and the Law in Britain*, Allen Lane The Penguin Press.
Hepple, B. (1969), 'The British Race Relations Acts 1965 and 1968', *University of Toronto L.J.*, vol. 19.
Hepple, B. (1970), *Race Jobs and the Law in Britain*, Penguin, 2nd edn.
Higbee, J. A. (1966), *Development and Administration of the New York State Law against Discrimination*, University of Alabama Press.
Hindell, K. (1965), 'The genesis of the race relations bill', *Polit. Q.*, vol.36, no. 4, pp. 390–405.

Jaffe, L. L. (1969), *English and American Judges as Lawmakers*, Oxford University Press.
Jenkins, R. (1967), *Essays and Speeches*, Collins.
Jennings, I. (1953), *Some Characteristics of the Indian Constitution*, Oxford University Press.
Josling, J. F., and **Alexander, L.** (1964), *The Law of Clubs*, Oyez.
Jowell, J. (1965), 'The administrative enforcement of laws against discrimination', *Public Law*, p. 119.
Jowell, R., and **Prescott-Clarke, P.** (1970), 'Racial discrimination and white-collar workers in Britain', *Race*, vol. 11, pp. 397–417.

Kahn-Freund, O. (1959), 'Attacking the colour-bar: a lawful purpose', *Mod.L.R.*, vol. 22.
Kallan, H. M. (1968), '"Group libel" and equal liberty', *New York Law Forum*, vol. 14, no. 1, pp. 1–8.

Kiernan, V. G. (1969), *The Lords of Human Kind*, Weidenfeld & Nicolson.
Kirp, D. L. (1968), 'The poor, the schools and equal protection', *Harvard L.R.*, vol. 38, pp. 635–68.

Leitch, D. (1964), 'Explosion at the King David Hotel', in M. Sissons and P. French (eds.), *Age of Austerity 1945–51*, Penguin.
Lerner, N. (1968), 'International definitions of incitement to racial hatred', *New York Law Forum*, vol. 14, no. 1, pp. 49–59.
Lester, A., and **Deakin, N.** (1967), *Policies for Racial Equality*, Fabian Research series 262.
Lockard, D. (1968), *Toward Equal Opportunity*, Macmillan Co.
Locke, J. (1965), Two Treatises of Government, Cambridge University Press.
Longaker, R. P. (1969), 'The Race Relations Act of 1965: an evaluation of the incitement provision', *Race*, vol. 11, no. 2, pp. 125–56

MacDonald, I. A. (1969), *Race Relations and Immigration Law*, Butterworth.
McPherson, K., and **Gaitskell, J.** (1969), *Immigrants and Employment: Two Case Studies in East London and Croydon*, Institute of Race Relations.
Mansani, R. P. (1960), *Britain in India*, Oxford University Press.
Mittall, J. K. (1970), 'Right to equality in the Indian constitution', *Public Law*, vol. 36, pp. 38–50.
Montagu, A. (ed.) (1964), *The Concept of Race*, Free Press.
Morse, A. E. (1968), *While Six Million Died*, Secker & Warburg.
Mukherji, P. (1915), *Indian Constitutional Documents, 1773–1915*, Calcutta.

Norgen, P. H., and **Hill, S. E.** (1964a), *Towards Fair Employment*, Columbia University Press.
Norgen, P. H., and **Hill, S. E.** (1964b), 'Towards equal opportunity in employment', *Buffalo L.R.*, vol. 14, no. 1.

Oldham, J. H. (1924), *Christianity and the Race Problem*, Student Christian Movement.

Pandey, B. N. (1969), *The Break-up of British India*, Macmillan.
Partington, M. (1967), 'Race Relations Act 1965: a too restricted view?', *Crim. L.R.*, p. 497.
Passmore, J. H. (1965), 'The malleability of man in eighteenth-century thought', in E. Wasserman (ed.), *Aspects of the Eighteenth Century*, Johns Hopkins Press.
Patterson, S. (1969), *Immigration and Race Relations in Britain 1960–1967*, Oxford University Press.
Pemberton, A. (1968), 'Can the law provide a remedy for race defamation in the United States?', *New York Law Forum*, vol. 14, no. 1, p. 33.
Plowden Report (1966), *Children and their Primary Schools*, HMSO.
Political and Economic Planning (1967), *Report on Racial Discrimination*, PEP.

Race Relations Board (1967), *Report for 1966–7*, HMSO.
Race Relations Board (1968), *Report for 1967–8*, HMSO.
Race Relations Board (1969), *Report for 1968–9*, HMSO.
Race Relations Board (1970), *Report for 1969–70*, HMSO.
Race Relations Board (1971), *Report for 1970–71*, HMSO.
Radcliffe, Lord (1960), *The Law and Its Compass*, Faber.
Radcliffe, Lord (1969), 'Immigration and settlement: some general considerations', *Race*, vol. 11, no. 1, pp. 35–51.
Rex, J., and Moore, R. (1967), *Race, Community and Conflict*, Oxford University Press.
Riesman, D. (1942), 'Democracy and defamation: control of group libel', *Columbia L.R.*, vol. 42.
Roberts, P. E. (1910), *Cambridge Modern History, vol. 12*, Cambridge University Press.
Rose, E. J. B., Deakin, N., Abrams, M., Jackson, V., Peston, M., Vanags, A. H., Cohen, B., Gaitskell, J., and Ward, P. (1969), *Colour and Citizenship*, Oxford University Press.
Roth, C. (1964), *A History of the Jews in England*, Oxford University Press.
Roth, S. J. (ed.) (1965), *Legal Curbs on Racial Incitement: A Survey of International Measures and Domestic Legislation*, World Jewish Congress.

Schmeiser, D. A. (1964), *Civil Liberties in Canada*, Oxford University Press.
Seal, A. (1968), *The Emergence of Indian Nationalism: Competition and Collaboration in the late Nineteenth Century*, Cambridge University Press.
Select Committee on Race Relations and Immigration (1969), *The Problems of Coloured School Leavers*, HMSO.
Select Committee on Race Relations and Immigration (1971), *Housing*, HMSO.
Singh, G. N. (1933), *Landmarks in Indian Constitutional and National Development, 1660–1919*, Benares.
Smith, S. A. de (1964), *The New Commonwealth and Its Constitutions*, Stevens.
Smithies, B., and Fiddick, P. (1969), *Enoch Powell on Immigration*, Sphere.
Sorrenson, M. P. K. (1968), *Origins of European Settlement in Kenya*, Oxford University Press.
Sovern, M. I. (1966), *Legal Restraints on Racial Discrimination in Employment*, Twentieth-Century Fund.
Stallybrass, W. H. R. (1933), 'Public mischief', *L.Q.R.*, vol. 49.
Steel, D. (1969), *No Entry*, Hurst.
Stokes, E. (1959), *The English Utilitarians and India*, Oxford University Press.
Street, H. (1962), *Principles of the Law of Damages*, Sweet & Maxwell.
Street, H., Howe, G., and Bindman, G. (1967), *Street Report on Anti-Discrimination Legislation*, Political and Economic Planning.

Tajfel, H. (1966), 'Cooperation between human groups', *Eugenics Rev.*, vol. 58, no. 2.
Taylor, A. J. P. (1965), *English History 1914–45*, Oxford University Press.

Trevelyan, G. M. (1932), *Sir George Otto Trevelyan: A Memoir*, Longman.
Trevelyan, G. O. (1864), *The Competition Wallah*, Macmillan.

United Nations (1949), *The Main Types and Causes of Discrimination*, vol. 14, New York.

Wade, E. C. S. (1948), 'Seditious libel and the press', *L.Q.R.*, vol. 68, p. 203.
Wedderburn, K. W. (1971), *The Worker and the Law*, Penguin, 2nd edn.
Weisbord, R. (1969), 'The case of the slave ship *Zong*, 1783', *History Today*, vol. 6, pp. 561–7.
Williams, B. (1962), 'The idea of equality', in P. Laslett and W. G. Runciman (eds.), *Philosophy, Politics and Society*, Blackwell.
Williams, D. (1967), *Keeping the Peace: The Police and Public Order*, Hutchinson.
Woodruff, P. (1954), *The Men who Ruled India, vol. 2: The Guardians*, Cape.
Woolf, L. (1959), Introduction by SDS to 'Diaries in Ceylon, 1908–11', *Ceylon Historical J.*, vol. 9.

Zamir, I. (1962), *The Declaratory Judgment*, Stevers.
Zellick, G. (1970), 'Violence as pornography', *Crim. L.R.*, pp. 188–92.

Select Bibliography

This bibliography lists a number of works which have *not* been specifically referred to in the text. Its intention is to collect together, when added to the references in the text, the main sources on the law and racial discrimination. The emphasis is on Britain. Only a small selection from the massive amount of United States material and from the less extensive literature of other countries is given.

Racial prejudice and discrimination
General works

T. W. Adorno *et al*, *The Authoritarian Personality*, Harper & Row, 1950.
Philip Mason, *Race Relations*, Oxford University Press, 1970.
Philip Mason, *Patterns of Dominance*, Oxford University Press, 1970.
M. Mead (ed.), *Science and the Concept of Race*, Columbia University Press, 1968.
G. Myrdal *et al*, *An American Dilemma*, Harper & Row, 1944.
Ronald Segal, *The Race War*, Cape, 1966.
C. E. Silberman, *Crisis in Black and White*, Random House, 1964.
UNESCO Secretariat, *Race and Science*, Columbia University Press, 1970.

Race relations in Britain
Reports

Alien Immigration, Cmnd 1741, 1903.
Housing in London (Milner-Holland), HMSO, 1965.
Immigration from the Commonwealth, Cmnd 2739, 1965.
Report of the Committee on the Rent Acts (Francis), HMSO, 1971.

Books, articles, etc.

R. B. Davison, *Black British*, Institute of Race Relations/Oxford University Press, 1966.
Nicholas Deakin, *Colour Citizenship and British Society*, Panther, 1970.
W. Deedes, *Race Without Rancour*, Conservative Research Department, 1968.
Paul Foot, *The Rise of Enoch Powell: An Examination of Enoch Powell's Attitude to Immigrants*, Penguin, 1969.

John A. Garrard, *The English and Immigration: A Comparative Study of the English Influx 1880–1910*, Institute of Race Relations/Oxford University Press, 1971.

J. A. G. Griffith, *et al.*, *Coloured Immigrants in Britain*, Oxford University Press/Institute of Race Relations, 1960.

Mary Grigg, *The White Question*, Secker & Warburg, 1967.

Derek Humphry and Gus John, *Because They're Black*, Penguin, 1971.

K. Jones, *Immigrants and the Social Services*, National Institute for Economic and Social Research, 14 *Economic Review*, 1967.

Lewis Donnelly (ed.), *Justice First*, Sheed & Ward, 1969.

A. Lester, 'The Act and the British constitution' *Venture*, March, 1968.

V. D. Lipman, *Social History of the Jews in England 1850–1950*, Watts, 1954.

M. Meth, *Here to Stay: A Study of Good Employment Practices in the Employment of Coloured Workers*, Runnymede Trust, 1969.

Dipak Nandy, *Race and Community*, University of Kent, 1968.

S. Patterson, *Immigrants in Industry*, Institute of Race Relations/Oxford University Press, 1968.

A. H. Richmond, *The Colour Problem* (revised), Penguin, 1961.

T. W. E. Roche, *The Key in the Lock: Immigration Control in England from 1000 to the Present Day*, Murray, 1969.

A. Sivanandan, *Coloured Immigrants in Britain: A Select Bibliography* (3rd edn.) Institute of Race Relations, 1969.

David Stephen, *Immigration and Race Relations*, Fabian Society, 1970.

Peter L. Wright, *The Coloured Worker in British Industry*, Institute of Race Relations/Oxford University Press, 1968.

Racial discrimination and law in Britain

G. Bindman, 'Racial discrimination and the law', 32 *Law Guardian* 9, 1967.

A. E. Bonfield, 'The role of legislation in eliminating racial discrimination', *Race*, vol. 7, no. 2, p. 107, October 1965.

M. Bonham Carter, *Legislation and the Race Relations Board*, Institute of Race Relations, Newsletter, p. 176, April 1967.

M. Bonham Carter, 'The Race Relations Board', *Race Today*, vol. 1, 1969.

C. Brocklebank-Fowler, *Race Relations: Legislation and Conciliation*, Bow Publications, 1967.

P. Calvocoressi, 'The structure of conciliation', 39 *Political Q*. p. 54, 1968.

P. Davis, *A Sledgehammer to Crack a Nut: An Examination of the Race Relations Bill 1965*, Bow Publications, 1965.

J. S. Hall, 'Racial discrimination', 115 *Law J.* 706, 1965.

S. J. Hartz, 'Race relations and the law in Britain', 41 *Temple Law Q.*, 429, 1968.

B. A. Hepple, 'The Street Report on anti-discrimination legislation and the report of the Wilson Committee on immigration appeals', 31 *Mod. L. R.* 310, 1968.

B. A. Hepple, 'Race Relations Act 1968', 32 *Mod. L. R.* 181, 1969.

Institute of Personnel Management, Edinburgh Group, *How the Race Relations Act Affects Personnel*, Runnymede Trust, 1969.

D. Lasok, 'Some legal aspects of race relations in the United Kingdom and the United States', 16 *J. Public L.* 326, 1967.

A. Lester, 'Laws against discrimination', *New Society*, 3 December 1964.

A. Lester, *Racial Discrimination and the Law*, Institute of Race Relations Newsletter (supplement), June 1965.

A. Lester, 'The broken compass', *New L. J.*, vol. 119, pp. 443–5, 8 May 1969.

A. Lester, 'Is there equality before the law?' in M. Zander (ed.) *What's Wrong With the Law*, BBC, 1970.

A. Lester, 'Legislation against discrimination', 117 *New L. J.*, 1223, 1967.

O. R. Marshall, 'The law and race relations', 39 *Polit. Q.* 70, 1968.

O. R. Marshall, 'Legislation and racial equality', *Current Legal Problems*, p. 46, 1969.

S. J. Roth, 'British race legislation and international law', 2 *Patterns of Prejudice* 14, May 1968.

Cedric Thornberry, 'Commitment or withdrawal? The place of law in race relations in Britain', *Race*, vol. 7, no. 1, p. 73, July 1965.

Cedric Thornberry, 'Law, opinion and the immigrant', 25 *Mod. L. R.* 654, 1962.

D. G. T. Williams, 'Legal aspects of positive discrimination', *Soc. Econ. Admin.*, vol. 2, no. 4, 1968.

I. M. Yeats, 'The Race Relations Act 1968', 112 *Solicitor's J.* 893, 1968.

G. Zellick, 'The meaning of "national origins"', 121 *New L. J.* 341, 1971.

'*Mills* v. *Cooper* [1967] 2 All E.R. 100', 31 *Mod L. R.* 567, 1968.

Race and law in the United States

R. I. Bloch, 'Race discrimination in industry and the grievance process', 21 *Lab. L. J.* 627, 1970.

Alfred W. Blumrosen, 'Anti-discrimination laws in action in New Jersey: a law–sociology study', *Rutgers L. R.*, vol. 19, no. 2, 1965.

Alfred W. Blumrosen, 'Administrative creativity: the first year of the Equal Employment Opportunity Council', 38 *Geo. Washington L. R.*, May 1970.

Alfred W. Blumrosen, *Black Employment and the Law*, Rutgers University Press.

Paul Bullock, *Equal Opportunity in Employment*, Institute of Industrial Relations, University of California, Los Angeles, 1966.

Vern Countryman (ed.), *Discrimination and the Law*, University of Chicago Press, 1965.

J. H. Denton, 'The effectiveness of state anti-discrimination laws in the US', *Race*, vol. 9, no. 1, p. 85, 1967.

N. Dorsen, 'The American law on racial discrimination', *Public L.* 304, 1968.

N. Dorsen, 'Discrimination in employment and in housing: private enforcement provisions of the Civil Rights Acts of 1964 and 1968', 82 *Harvard L. R.* 834, 1669.

T. I. Emerson, D. Haber and **N. Dorsen,** *Political and Civil Rights in the United States*, Little Brown, 1967, 3rd edn.

W. B. Gould, 'The emerging law against racial discrimination in employment', 64 *Northwestern U. L. R.* 359, 1969.

Jack Greenberg, *Race Relations and American Law*, Columbia University Press, 1959.

P. Hartman, 'Law on housing discrimination in the United States', 2 *J. Int. & Comp. L.* 459, 1969.

Rose Halper, *Racial Policies and Practices of Real Estate Brokers*, Minnesota University Press, 1969.

A. Larson, 'New law of race relations', *Wisconsin L. R.* 470, 1969.

A. Lester, *Justice in the American South*, Amnesty International, 1964.

H. M. Levy, 'Role of the law in the United States and England in protecting the worker from discharge and discrimination', 18 *Int. & Comp. L. Q.* 558, 1969.

Leon H. Mayhew, *Law and Equal Opportunity: A Study of the Massachusetts Commission against Discrimination*, Harvard University Press, 1968.

John E. Means, 'Fair employment practices legislation and enforcement in the United States', *Int. L. R.* vol. 93, no. 3, 1966.

Loren Miller, *The Petitioners: The Story of the Supreme Court of the United States and the Negro*, Meridian Books, 1967.

Race and law in other countries

T. M. Eberlee and **D. G. Hill,** 'Ontario Human Rights Code', *University of Toronto L. J.*, vol. 15, p. 448, 1964.

J. E. S. Fawcett, *The Application of the European Convention on Human Rights*, Oxford University Press, 1969.

T. C. Hartley, 'Race relations law in Ontario', 20 *Public L.*, 175, 1970.

D. G. Hill, 'Role of a human rights commission: the Ontario experience', 19 *University of Toronto L. J.* 390, 1969.

N. Lerner, *The UN Convention on the Elimination of All Forms of Racial Discrimination*, Sijthoff, Leyden, 1970.

R. A. Metall and others, 'Equality of opportunity in a multi-racial society: Brazil', *Int. Lab. R.*, vol. 93, no. 5, 1966.

D. A. Schmeiser, *Civil Liberties in Canada*, Oxford University Press, 1964.

A. N. Sherwin-White, *Racial Prejudice in Imperial Rome*, Cambridge University Press, 1967.

A. H. Smith, 'Prevention of discrimination under Kenya law', 20 *Int. & Comp. Law Q.* 136, 1971.

A. H. Smith, 'Legislation against racialism: Belgium, Britain, Canada', 1 *Patterns of Prejudice* 23, January 1967.

Table of Cases

Table of Statutes and Regulations

Race Relations Act (c. 71) – *continued*

Index

Two Law and Society titles to be published simultaneously with *Race and Law*

Law in a Changing Society
Second edition

Wolfgang Friedmann

Law in a Changing Society is a classic work of contemporary thought. Professor Friedmann writes of the law's great theses – its complex interaction with social change, its intervention into economics and the environment, its balance of public power and private rights, its place in the growth of international order, its own changing role in the interdependent society – these themes are carried to the reader with insight, imagination and an exciting breadth of scholarship.

For this second edition, Professor Friedmann has largely rewritten his text and added two new chapters. The author sums up in his Preface the developments to which he has responded: 'In some areas, such as family law, the last decade has brought fundamental changes in many countries, with respect to divorce, abortion, the status of illegitimate children, matrimonial property, and other matters. The very function and ambit of criminal law and criminal sanction has been put in question by recent developments in social psychology and genetic engineering. The substitution of insurance for tort liability, particularly in the field of motor-car accidents, has become a problem of increasing urgency. The growing mechanization, and the centralization of power, both at the government and the corporate level, has made a re-examination of the relation between public power and the individual a matter of urgent necessity. The role of international law and organization in international society has more and more become a question on which the ordered survival of mankind will depend. And any student of the relation of law and society must reflect on the changing function of law in the increasingly interdependent society of the 1970s, as one of a number of interacting components in a complex web of systems analysis, social planning and decision-making.'

Some comments on the first edition: 'The scope of this survey is immense. . . . The research involved must have been prodigious, and the result is an important book.' *Law Society's Gazette*

'No one can fail to be grateful to him for his vivid presentation of matters that are of importance to all of us.'
Law Quarterly Review

Government Contracts
Colin Turpin

In a world of sophisticated 'public sector' – 'private enterprise' interaction, the British government alone places contracts to an annual value of over £1000 million, and whole industries depend for their prosperity upon the flow of government work. Much government procurement is carried out in great uncertainty with unpredictable costs and frequent change in project development as technology advances. Government procurement raises central issues of public accountability for expenditure and the welfare of industry. Is the government's expenditure on procurement under effective public control? Does government buying contribute to efficiency in industry? These are among the questions considered in this book, the first in Britain to deal with the law and practice of government contracting in the context of procurement of goods and services by central government departments.

Many of the leading principles of government contracting were established in a political and economic environment vastly different from that of today. The author examines the genesis and status of government-contracting principles and shows how these are being modified to reflect a new kind of relationship between government and its suppliers in industry. Aspects of this relationship – equitable treatment for contractors, 'equality of information' for the government, joint planning of projects by government and industry – constitute an important theme of the book.

The essential element in the relationship between government and suppliers is the individual contract, a flexible instrument for getting value for public money and also a weapon, if the government chooses so to use it, for advancing particular social or economic policies. The author considers the various types of contract used in procurement and standard conditions which, for the parties to these contracts, take effect as law.

Also in the Law and Society series

Race Jobs and the Law in Britain
Second edition

Bob Hepple

The first edition of this book was widely acclaimed as a unique and authoritative study of the role of the law in the field of industrial race relations. Since that edition the Race Relations Act of 1968 has been passed. It is a unique piece of legislation, in which the law is used consciously and deliberately, to raise not the standard of the nation's technical equipment, not the standard of its wealth or of its welfare, but the standard of its very civilization.

In the light of this central Act, Bob Hepple has written, in effect, an entirely new book which, like the first edition, is an illuminating and important piece of work. By making industrial relations the focal point of his study he has been able to show how the legacy of past discrimination, managerial decisions about qualifications for the job, seniority rules, and other non-racial barriers operate alongside colour discrimination to condemn Britain's minorities to permanent inferiority. He provides a detailed analysis of the shift from the *laissez-faire* attitudes of the common law to positive legislation. Emphasizing the supreme importance of effective procedures, he examines the enforcement provisions of the Race Relations Act in the light of British and American experience.

This book contains many important proposals for improving the law and shows how the practical actions of managers, unions, minorities and government could lead towards the achievement of the present avowed policy: 'Equal Employment Opportunity for All'.

This new edition is essential reading for all – students, practitioners and laymen – who want real insight into the aims and limits of the law in changing economic and social patterns and, at the same time, redressing individual wrongs.

Some comments on the first edition: 'A thorough and scholarly work. It deserves to be read by all those in industry and outside who will have to tackle the mounting problems of colour discrimination in Britain.' *New Statesman*

'A thorough guide . . . to the basic principles underlying legislation on race relations and employment. . . . His contribution is in almost every way a model of its kind.' *New Society*